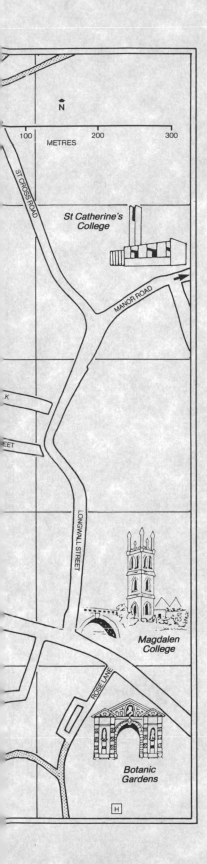

N

100   200   300
METRES

ST CROSS ROAD

St Catherine's College

MANOR ROAD

LONGWALL STREET

Magdalen College

ROSE LANE

Botanic Gardens

H

D0875473

Oxford in English Literature

Oxford
in English Literature

THE MAKING, AND UNDOING, OF
'THE ENGLISH ATHENS'

John Dougill

Ann Arbor

THE UNIVERSITY OF MICHIGAN PRESS

Copyright © by the University of Michigan 1998
All rights reserved
Published in the United States of America by
The University of Michigan Press
Manufactured in the United States of America
⊗ Printed on acid-free paper

2001   2000   1999   1998   4   3   2   1

A CIP catalog record for this book is available from the British Library.

Library of Congress Cataloging-in-Publication Data

Dougill, John.
    Oxford in English literature : the making, and undoing, of the 'English Athens' / John Dougill.
        p.   cm.
    Includes bibliographical references (p.   ) and index.
    ISBN 0-472-10784-4 (acid-free paper)
    1. English literature—England—Oxford—History and criticism. 2. Oxford (England)—Intellectual life.   3. University of Oxford—In literature.   4. Oxford (England)—In literature.   I. Title.
PR8489.O93   D68   1998
820.9'3242574—dc21   98-8954
                                                                    CIP

Endsheet map of Oxford courtesy of *Daily Information*, Oxford.

Books are the city's and the island's insulators, writers
the terminal gods who cordon off and defend our idiosyncratic
national reality.
　　　—Peter Conrad, *The Everyman History of English Literature*

Acknowledgments

A WORK OF THIS nature could not have been accomplished without help from a number of different sources, and I would like to acknowledge those to whom I am most grateful. Dr. Bernard Richards and Dr. Norman Whitney provided invaluable input when the manuscript was in its formative stage, and their encouragement and guiding influence were greatly appreciated. T.V. Buttery of the Pevensey Press helped to secure publication, and I should also like to acknowledge the cooperation of I.P. Fooke, Philip Pullman, and Graham Chainey. During the writing of the book I was fortunate in being able to test out ideas on a number of people, amongst whom the following were particularly helpful: Dr. Albrecht Decke-Cornill, Mark Ford, Rob Cross, Professor John Honey, Roli and Ewa Huggins, Mark Baumfield, Paul Hays, Catriona Mundle, Susie Medley, Trevor Williams, and Reginald Cave. My thanks to all of them. Peter Edwards, Julie Cox, and Amanda Jeffries looked over the manuscript, contributed a number of valuable suggestions, and were a constant source of encouragement for which I am grateful. David Jay deserves a special mention for providing feedback and research information during the final stages of the book. His depth of knowledge and overview of the subject matter were of enormous benefit, and without his archival burrowings in the Bodleian the final version would never have been completed.

Much of the work on the book was carried out in Japan, and I am grateful to the institutions to which I have been attached for the past ten years for providing me with the use of their resources and also for the consideration with which I have been treated. These include the two universities where I was a visiting lecturer, Kanazawa University and Kyoto Women's University, as well as Ryukoku University, where I am presently employed as an associate professor. At Kanazawa University Professors Mitsui and Fujita were particularly helpful, as was the departmental secretary, Mrs. Hashimoto, without whom I could not have managed at all. At Kyoto Women's University I was fortunate in having an extremely kind set of colleagues, amongst whom I should like to thank Professor Kato for a number of suggestions and Risa Kotera for offering intellectual and moral support in the endless matter of rewriting and revising. At my present university, Dr. Michael Lazarin, Professor Kodani, and Professor

Higashinaka have been most supportive, and the pleasant working environment facilitated the completion of the book.

As regards the acquisition of illustrations, I am indebted to Linda Proud for her hard work and perseverance in chasing after the requisite pictures. Without her efforts the book would not have had such visual appeal. Matthew Kneale kindly gave up a day to walk round Oxford with me photographing various features, and I am grateful to him for the following pictures: Merton College Mob Quad, the entrance of Queen's College, the passage in Worcester College, the Martyrs' Cross set in Broad Street, the bust of Robert Burton, Samuel Johnson's rooms above Pembroke entrance, Shelley's Memorial, the view of central Oxford from the Parks to the east, Binsey Poplars viewed from Port Meadow, Christ Church Meadows Building, and the front entrance of Christ Church. As for the other illustrations, acknowledgment is gratefully made as follows for permission to reproduce copyright material.

The National Portrait Gallery, London, for the pictures of Geoffrey Chaucer and Evelyn Waugh.

Unichrome (Bath) Ltd. for the aerial view of Christ Church.

The Earl of Dartmouth (picture on loan to the Museum of Oxford) for the painting of Oxford during the Civil War.

The Bodleian library for the cover photograph of early nineteenth-century Oxford taken from an aquatint in Ackerman's *A History of the University* (1814), and also for the bust of Anthony Wood.

The Ashmolean Museum for the painting of John Aubrey by William Fairthorne.

The President and Fellows of Trinity College, London, for the portrait of Thomas Warton by Sir Joshua Reynolds.

Thomas Photos (Merton College) for the self-portrait by Max Beerbohm, and Thomas Photos for the Reynolds window in New College chapel and the Christ Church fireplace.

Lincoln College/John Gibbons Studios for the portrait of Mark Pattison.

Keble College/Woodmansterne for the portrait of John Newman.

Hulton Getty for the pictures of the gowned undergraduates in the dining-hall and in front of Queen's College, also for the portraits of Matthew Arnold, Compton Mackenzie, Dorothy Sayers, C.S. Lewis, and J.I.M. Stewart in conversation with C. Day-Lewis.

Oxfordshire Photographic Archive, OCC/Brasenose College, for the portrait of Walter Pater by A.A. McEvoy.

Oxfordshire Photographic Archive, OCC, for the pictures of Benjamin Jowett, Matthew Arnold's tree, the view from Matthew Arnold's tree, and the Eights Week races.

Balliol College for the portrait of F.F. Urquhart (Sligger).

The governing Body of Christ Church, Oxford, for the photograph of J.I.M. Stewart and the Christ Church courtesy of M.J. St. Clair for the photographs of Charles Dodgson and Alice Liddell.

Paul Popper Limited for the picture of Oscar Wilde.

Chris Donaghue Photography/The Oxford Photo Library for the aerial view of Oxford.

De Agostini Editions for the overview of nineteenth- and twentieth-century Oxford writers.

Dorset Museum for the picture of Thomas Hardy.

Polygram Filmed Entertainment/Pictorial Press Ltd. for the still photograph from the film *Jude the Obscure.*

Hutchinson/Random for the cover of *Masterstroke.*

Carlton Television for the picture of Morse and Lewis from the series *Inspector Morse.*

Daily Information for the map of Oxford.

In addition to the above, permission was granted to reproduce written copyright material as follows:

John Murray (Publishers) Ltd. for the extract from *Summoned by Bells,* by John Betjeman.

Simon & Schuster and Curtis Brown Group Ltd. for the extract from *A Middle Class Education,* by Wilfrid Sheed. Copyright © 1961 by Wilfrid Sheed.

Curtis Brown Group Ltd. for the extract from *That Hideous Strength,* by C.S. Lewis. Copyright © 1945 by C.S. Lewis Pte. Ltd.

Contents

Introduction

. . . what I have to tell is an Oxford story—or, at least, is a collegiate story.
—J.I.M. Stewart, *The Aylwins* (1966)

'OXFORD! THE VERY SIGHT of the word printed, or sound of it spoken, is fraught for me with most actual magic', wrote Max Beerbohm in *Zuleika Dobson* (1911). While others might not share the thrill, the associative resonance of the word attests not only to the legendary and world-wide renown of the university but to its use as a cachet synonymous with distinction, applied to an accent, to 'bags', to shoes, to a philosophy, to a colour, to a marmalade, to a movement, to a group and—most potently—to a myth. The magic derives from the myth, and the myth derives from the literature. For over six hundred years the portrayal of Oxford in poetry and prose has made the city as much a fiction as an actuality, a representation as well as a reality. Indeed, the topographical fiction called Oxford exudes a far greater presence than its real-life counterpart. To the postwar generation Oxford is overlaid with the image of *Brideshead Revisited* (1945), to the interwar generation it was *Sinister Street* (1914), to the Victorians *Verdant Green* (1853–57). Towering over all stand the 'dreaming spires' of Matthew Arnold. For some the whole notion of 'Oxford literature' derives from Arnold, for by envisaging the university as a 'home of lost causes' he launched a cult of sentimental affection which gave birth to the 'Oxford myth' of modern times—a university peopled by Bright Young Things of wealth, wit and leisure, devoted to the pursuit of pleasure and heir to glittering prizes. It is the purpose of this book to place that myth in a wider historical context and to show how it derived from an older tradition, that of the 'English Athens'. This concept of Oxford, which owes its origins to the celebratory instincts of Elizabethans, served for almost four hundred years as the dominant model for writings about the university and played a vital role in underpinning the glorification of the university following Arnold. Though no longer in favour, the notion has proved so powerful that its legacy is still apparent even in contemporary depictions of Oxford.

'No City or landscape', writes V.S. Naipaul, 'is truly rich unless it has been given the quality of myth by writer, painter or by association with great events.' Oxford in this respect can count itself rich indeed, for no other town except London can rival its place in the culture of the country. Not only has it been home to many of the great figures of the past, but for over six hundred years it has been lauded, slighted, analysed, and celebrated in poems, essays, memoirs, histories, anthologies, commentaries, and guides. It has been the setting for over five hundred novels that range from romance to intrigue, from the biographical to the fantastic. 'The literature devoted to Oxford and its Colleges', claims the anthologist William Knight, 'is probably greater than that relating to any other University in the world', an assertion supported by three heavy folio volumes in the Bodleian Library which detail the writings. It is the nature of that literature, in as far as it has impinged on the public consciousness, that is the concern of this book. It does not purport to be an account of Oxford graduates or even of writers associated with the city—a study of such authors would constitute work of quite a different nature. Consequently writers who were not concerned to portray Oxford lie beyond the terms of reference; these include former students such as Philip Sidney and Walter Raleigh, college fellows such as Andrew Lang and Charles Reade, and residents of the city such as Ronald Firbank, Joyce Cary, Elizabeth Bowen and Charles Williams, who are only mentioned in passing if at all. Moreover, the book makes no claim to offer a record of Oxford's historical development, which has been told often enough, for the relationship of representation to reality is complex and tentative, as literary theorists have been at pains to point out. The physical city of Oxford and its literary re-creation exist in altogether different dimensions, for the word-city only comes to life in the mind of the reader, and the imaging of Oxford has led to many fanciful portrayals, amongst which the most striking is undoubtedly *Alice in Wonderland*. The tenuous link between life and literature can be seen in the demise of the 'English Athens' as a viable concept in recent times, for the desire to strip the university of glamour has had little to do with the academic standing of an institution which is much praised for its vitality and recognised internationally as one of the top three or four of its kind in the world.

For all the centrality of Oxford to the life of the nation, the story of its representation has only been told once before. In *The Clerk of Oxford in Fiction* (1909) S.F. Hulton claimed with the unabashed pride of an Edwardian that at the heart of the literature stood the virtuous and dedicated scholar of Chaucer's Prologue. It is the purpose of this book to argue that it is not so much a character as an institution that informs the literature, and that just as the college lies at the core of the university, so it shapes and determines the literary response. 'What I have to tell is an Oxford story—or, at least, is a collegiate story', states the cultured narrator of Stewart's *The Aylwins,* and the conflation tells all. Historically speaking, there is a move inward from the college-less portrayal of Chaucer's 'The Miller's Tale' to the restricted boundaries of collegiate literature. The distinction made here between college and university may be puzzling to some and requires clarification. 'For an Oxford man, Oxford is primarily his college,' claimed the classicist Dacre Balsdon, and he illustrated the point in *Oxford Now and Then* (1970) through an imaginary conversation on an Oxford street.

> 'Please, sir, can you tell me where is the University?'
> 'L'Université, où est-ce qu'on le trouve?'
> 'Prego, signore, dov'è l'Università?'
> 'Sorry, madam, I've lived here sixty years and never seen it.'
> 'Mon dieu, qu'est-ce que vous dites? Que l'Université d'Oxford n'existe pas?'
> 'There are the Colleges, lady.'

Balsdon was indulging in playful exaggeration, but his dialogue nonetheless serves to make the point that the university as such plays second fiddle to the colleges whose buildings dominate the city centre. The relationship between these autonomous colleges and the central institution is one that has evolved over centuries and is of such complexity in its finer points that it is claimed to be beyond the grasp of any single individual. In 1831 when university reform was a matter of national concern, Sir William Hamilton in the *Edinburgh Review* provided an overview of the collegiate system which remains an admirably concise explication of this tangled web.

> Oxford and Cambridge, as establishments for education, consist of two parts, of the *Universities proper,* and of the *Colleges.* The former, original and essential, is founded, controlled, and privileged by public authority, for the advantage of the state. The latter, accessory and contingent, are created, regulated, and endowed by private munificence, for the interest of certain favoured individuals. Time was when the Colleges did not exist, and the University was there; and were the Colleges again abolished, the University would remain entire. The former, founded solely for education, exists only as it accomplishes the end of its institution; the latter, founded principally for aliment and habitation, would still exist, were all education abandoned within their walls. The University, as a national establishment, is necessarily open to the lieges in general; the Colleges, as private institutions, might universally do as some have actually done—close their gates upon all, except their foundation members.

The colleges, then, are independent, self-governing, property-owning corporations which distinguish Oxford and Cambridge from other universities. They have been much envied but never emulated. Other universities (such as Durham) are collegiate in nature, Yale and Harvard have equivalents, but the originals retain a distinctive quality having to do with their age, tradition, splendour and historical associations. It is indeed these very attributes, much acclaimed by poets, which are held to constitute the essence of Oxford.

Just as 'Oxford' refers ambiguously to both town and university, so the word 'college' has a dual reference, denoting both the academic community as well as the buildings in which they are housed. Oxford colleges vary considerably, and it is this very diversity that has been hailed as the strength of the university. Some colleges boast architecture of grace and beauty, some occupy drab and dismal buildings; some date back to the thirteenth century, some are twentieth-century foundations. Magdalen has a deer park, Worcester an ornamental lake, New College contains part of the medieval city wall, Christ Church a cathedral. Some colleges were tied by their founders to particular geographical regions, some to particular schools. Student numbers range from zero at All Souls to nearly six hundred at New College. The wealthiest, such as St. John's, Christ Church and Magdalen, are said to be worth up to a hundred times as much as the poorest. These differences make themselves felt in the college character, for as Peter Snow has noted in *Oxford Observed* (1991), 'A college is not simply a place or organization where certain kinds of teaching and research take place. Like a tribe its identity is intimately interwoven with its surroundings—its pictures and its ornaments, its buildings and its gardens.'

The role of the college in literary terms has been vital not simply as setting but in providing the tone. 'We all react, consciously and unconsciously, to the places where we live and work, in ways we scarcely notice or that are only now becoming known to us', writes Tony Hiss in *The Experience of Place* (1991): 'In short, the places where we spend our time affect the people we are and can become.' Few places can compare in this respect to the overpowering presence of an Oxford college. The structure of the college is of such imposing self-sufficiency that earlier generations spent most of their academic career shielded within the shelter of its walls. To enter within its guarded portals is to step out of the busy whirl of the everyday world and into an enclosed space of timeless tranquillity framed by ancient walls of such imposing solidity that visitors are sometimes moved to talk in a reverential whisper. Minuscule beside the vastness of the wooden gate, the individual cannot but feel humbled before a spectacle that speaks of the passage of centuries, and it becomes all too apparent how the buildings intend and command insularity by forcing inhabitants in on themselves. Within the college walls lie hall and chapel, bathroom and dining-room, cloister, garden, bars and common rooms designed to cater for a compact and regulated community: kitchen and maintenance staff, scout, porter, undergraduate, postgraduate, junior research fellow, fellow, senior fellow, dean and master. When the door in the formidable gates closes, the 'ivory tower' is sealed and the outside world excluded. 'Inside the gates of such a community', writes Jan Morris in her much admired *Oxford* (1965), 'you can feel most comfortably insulated.'

It is this sense of insulation, deepened by immersion in speculative thought, that forms the keynote of the literature. Oxford is depicted as a city of dream and a world of its own—enclosed, secluded, conservative and eccentric, a closed community with its own customs, its own rituals, and its own concerns. Idealised, it becomes a cloistered utopia, a student paradise, or an Athenian city-state. Here again the college architecture shapes the response, for the grandeur of the 'lordly buildings' is as essential an element in fashioning the English Athens as the intellectual distinction of the university. The college gardens play a particularly vital part in this, for by their secluded and private setting they speak at one and the same time of the academic grove and of Englishness. 'Most of all, perhaps,' claims Jan Morris, 'it is the gardens that keep the heart of Oxford, for all the ravages of time and progress, still a place of breathtaking allure.' From the 'gorgeous bowers' of Drayton to the Arcadia of Waugh, the enclosed and enchanted garden is the secret within the walls which fuels the utopian tendency in the literature. The atmosphere of the college gardens particularly struck the transatlantic visitors of the nineteenth century, perhaps because they were unused to restricted boundaries and antique settings. For Melville the gardens were 'Lands for centuries never molested by labor. Sacred to beauty and tranquillity.' For Hawthorne the colleges derived their character from the 'grassy quadrangles, where cloistered walks have echoed to the quiet footsteps of twenty generations.' And for Henry James in *English Hours* (1905) the gardens speak of a paradisical existence: the fellows of All Souls, for example, are presumed to be the happiest people in the world, for 'having no dreary instruction to administer, no noisy hobbledehoys to govern, no obligations but toward their own culture, no care save for learning as learning and truth as truth', they were free to 'stroll about together in the grassy courts, in learned comradeship, discussing'. In an earlier story, 'A Passionate Pilgrim' (1875), the narrator accompanies an ailing acquaintance to his old college, where the pair look enviously at the combination of youth and surroundings: 'When to the exhibition of so much of the clearest joy of wind and limb we added the great sense of perfumed protection shed by all the enclosed lawns and groves and bowers, we felt that to be young in such scholastic shades must be a double, an infinite blessing.'

Just as the college garden reflects the theme of paradise lost in English literature, so the story of Oxford itself mirrors the history of England. The first charter of the university came in 1214, Magna Carta in 1215—the two stories run parallel, are indeed mutually inseparable, for the identification of university with state has been one of the salient features of Oxford's development. Love of learning has gone hand in glove with love of patronage, and if Oxford has been hailed as the embodiment of excellence, beauty and truth on the one hand, it has also been vilified as the epitome of privilege, élitism and exclusivity. By its very nature Oxford produces extreme reactions, for the stance of the university as a purveyor of excellence is provocative and contentious, while its role as nursery of the ruling classes makes it a target for those seeking a different social order. In any one age adoration is offset by antipathy, and the delight and pleasure of one writer is countered by the animosity of another. Ambivalence is widespread. Vested interests and personal agenda determine the nature of the response, and the writing can be broken down in this way into a number of different categories. Firstly, there are those among the senior community who seek to explain, justify or celebrate the institution to which they belong. Secondly, there are former students who write retrospectively of 'a golden age' which took place in their fondly remembered youth. These rose-tinted accounts of a mythic Oxford are characterised by nostalgia for a younger self and an elegiac sense of loss. Thirdly, there are former members of the university whose critical accounts are either aimed at promoting reform or fuelled by grudges and the desire for revenge. Fourthly, there are 'outsiders' who write in praise of the university and whose accounts are typically underwritten by a 'longing for the cloister' and the attractions of a life of the mind. And finally, there are outsiders who resent or deplore the standing of the university and its social impact. Laid out in this way, the oversimplification is top-heavy in that most of the writing belongs to the first three categories, which is to say that the vast bulk of Oxford writing is by Oxford writers. Both the Elizabethan construct of an English Athens and the Oxford myth of Victorian-Edwardian times were championed by university men, and self-congratulation forms a common thread from Camden to the twentieth century. The spell cast by the literature has had important social consequences, for the rhetorical skills of the academic community helped foster the cultural hegemony and social preeminence of the university. To state that Oxford writing serves Oxford ends might seem tautological, but it should be borne in mind that fiction is an important myth-making mechanism which promotes a particular view of reality. According to cultural psychology, stories are the primary means by which young children make sense of the world and derive their values. The primacy of the narrative art is also reflected in the inner world of dreams and in the biographical 'story' individuals construct to bind together the different selves and invest their life with meaning. Viewed in the light of this, the constant rewriting of Oxford can be seen as part of an ongoing discourse about the national identity, for in its guise as the English Athens the city has served as a paradigm within which to define the cultural purpose. The view of Englishness that emerges has proved widely influential though it has not necessarily been to the delight of all, as can be seen by reference to the Irish militant of John Wain's *Hungry Generations* (1994) for whom Oxford is not a university as such, or even a town, but rather 'a symbol of everything he hates about England'. The dialogue that takes place between his sister Mairead and her husband, Peter Leonard, illustrates the potency of images in the public domain:

> 'Does he actually know anything about Oxford? Has he set eyes on the place?'
> 'Never. He'd take good care not to. He only knows the things about Oxford that everybody knows.'
> 'The things that everybody knows about Oxford are mostly myths and illusions, as you'll find out when you come to live here.'
> 'I'm expecting to find that. All the same, Leonard, you don't need me to tell you that myths and illusions are very powerful forces. People who are the victims of injustice console themselves by creating them and disseminating them. And people who inflict injustice get consolation from them in their own way. They simply view the same myths and illusions from the other side.'

For some commentators cultural history is little more than the struggle to shape the myths and illusions by which society maintains its sense of identity. In this respect the story of Oxford literature offers a rich and valuable insight into the national psyche. Its salient traits have been highlighted by the contrast in cultures afforded by the Japanese background against which work on this book has been carried out, for it has taken its final form in Kyoto, a city whose myths and illusions are, if anything, even more remarkable than those of Oxford. This has provided a fresh and stimulating perspective, not only because of the distance involved but because everyday life in the city bears little resemblance to the construction of 'Kyoto' which draws tourists in their thousands from around the world. Were the term not such a cultural contradiction, the city could lay claim to being the 'Japanese Athens', and indeed according to Jan Morris it is the only place in the world that bears comparison to Oxford.

> Oxford is at heart an intensely English city. The only foreign place she reminds me of is Kyoto. Like Kyoto, she is old, and private, and embeds her beauties in gardens behind high walls. . . . The English tradition she embodies is, like the Japanese tradition, peculiar to the island—and as in Kyoto, it is only heightened by the fact that this is a provincial city, removed from the pressures of the capital. In both cities you feel that a manner of thought is stubbornly defying all that the world can do to humiliate it. . . . In both cities an ancient religion infuses every wall and every custom. In Kyoto the students burn prayer-sticks at a Shinto shrine before taking their examinations: in Oxford the students used to pray in the hexagonal chapel of St. Catherine's, on the corner of New College Lane, before they crossed Catte Street for their disputations in the Schools.

The distancing effect and cultural contrast of work in the two cities, so alike yet so alien, has been both challenging and rewarding, yet as the book nears completion I am all too well aware that a publication of this nature is a hostage to fortune to an even greater extent than is usually the case. Those who are familiar with Oxford are many and learned, and the faults of the book will no doubt be ruthlessly exposed. In the end I can but take heart from the maxim of Benjamin Jowett, one of the greatest of all Oxford figures, who gave the following piece of advice to a contemporary who hovered nervously on the same threshold—'Publish, and let them howl.'

CHAPTER 1

From Mists to Myths:
Enchantments of the Middle Ages

A clerk hadde litherly biset his whyle,
But if he koude a carpenter bigyle.
— Geoffrey Chaucer, 'The Miller's Tale' (c. 1381)

THE TUTELARY SPIRIT that presides over Oxford literature is formed from the peculiarity of the terrain that it inhabits. 'Different places on the face of the earth have different vital effluence, different vibration, different chemical exhalation, different polarity with different stars: call it what you like. But the spirit of place is a great reality', wrote D.H. Lawrence. That reality pervades the literature. Oxford has a setting that has won the praise of poets and in the past, when its crenellated skyline stood unimpaired by gas-works and high-rises, it was possible to look down from the surrounding hills on the settlement and delight in the cluster of buildings nestled in the plain. There below stood the array of pinnacles, domes, turrets and 'dreaming spires' which so impressed distant onlookers, both fictional and historical. It was from some ten to twenty miles away to the south-west, perched precariously on a ladder, that Jude the Obscure first caught a glimpse of his 'heavenly Jerusalem', and from Cumnor ridge to the west Matthew Arnold's scholar-gipsy gazed down upon 'The line of festal light in Christ Church hall'. To the south-east Queen Elizabeth I looked back from Shotover Hill after being royally entertained in the city and uttered her famous valedictory, 'Farewell, farewell, dear Oxford, God bless thee, and increase thy sons in number, holiness and virtue.'

The hills around Oxford have played an integral part in fashioning the city's character. 'No one can understand Oxford unless he knows the Oxford countryside', wrote John Buchan, intimate of both the city and its environs.

> Half her beauty lies in her setting. Cambridge, which has many special lovelinesses, is a city of the plains, and over what she calls her hills one is apt to walk without noticing them. But Oxford has a cincture of green uplands and a multitude of little valleys. It is only from her adjacent heights that her charms can be comprised into one picture and the true background found to her towers.

Within the cradle of these low-lying hills lies a plexus of rivers, rivulets and streams, to which for good measure a canal was added in the late eighteenth century. Just ten minutes' walk from the crowds at Carfax, the city's central crossroads, lies the semi-rural confluence of the Cherwell and Thames (or Isis as the latter's passage through Oxford is known) and the watery aspect of the city has been much commented on. In *The Faerie Queene* (1590–96) Edmund Spenser portrays the Isis as weak and crooked, in need of the support of her tributary streams. Drayton's imagery in *Polyolbion* (1612–22) is happier, with Oxford and her Muses attending at the marriage of 'lovely Isis' with 'lusty Cherwell'.

> So lovely Isis comming on,
> At Oxford all the Muses meet her,
> And with a Prothalamion greet her.
> The nymphs are in the bridall bowres,
> Some strowing sweets, some sorting flowers;
> Where lustie Charwell himselfe raises,
> And sings of Rivers, and their praises.
> Then Tames his way tow'rd Windsor tends.
> Thus, with the song, the mariage ends.

Since the serpentine path of the Thames links Oxford with the national capital, the river has won particular attention from writers. The sixteenth-century archivist John Leland wrote a poem in Latin in which a swan sets out from Oxford to London, and the journey is undertaken in reverse direction by the *Three Men in a Boat* (1889) of Jerome K. Jerome, who arrive with their dog Montmorency at Folly Bridge. This in turn is the starting-point in 1862 for an outing of more momentous nature when the mathematics don Charles Dodgson embarks with his 'dream-child' to row upstream to Godstow. The story he made up that day has become known to the world at large as *Alice's Adventures in Wonderland* (1865). Further along the same river Matthew Arnold's scholar-gipsy crosses by ferry at Bablockhythe, where he is pictured trailing his hands in the cool waters. By contrast Oxford's other river has been neglected, though for the French novelist Jean Fayard the Cherwell was *the* Oxford river, 'doomed as the Thames is to forget in the smoke of London the clear fancies of Oxford'.

The literary significance of the rivers extends beyond boating and punting idylls, however, for their tendency to flood has helped to preserve the slices of countryside that still enter deep into the city centre and to prevent the overcrowding that mars less fortunate cities. For writers of an earlier age the rural setting and riverside meadows lent the city a strong sense of *rus in urbe,* though later literature tells of a steady diminution of that charm. The seventeenth-century Thomas Baskerville observed that Oxford was 'sweetly hugged in the pleasant arms of those two pure rivers, the Thames and Cherwell whose timely floods enrich the meadows with excellent herbage', but by the time of G.M. Hopkins in the mid–nineteenth century the 'neighbour-nature' of Oxford was under threat from the expanding suburbs. With the coming of the motor industry in the twentieth century, the city's pastoral quality was badly affected, though significant vestiges remain along the Thames at Port Meadow, by the sides of the Cherwell in the University Parks, and above all in Christ Church Meadow, where in the interspace of Thames and Cherwell cows graze in apparent indifference to the surrounding bustle of urban activity. For modern authors such as John Wain, here writing in *Comedies* (1990), the rivers are the sole guardians of the green spaces, the front line as it were in the war with industrialisation.

> For the millionth time I found reason to bless the semi-rural character of Oxford—the way, in spite of its growth in population, there was always a finger of countryside that reached to you wherever you were—the result of course of the rivers and their tendency to flood the low-lying flat fields. . . . Billy Morris, dumping a vast load of industry and commerce on Oxford, had gone a long way towards wrecking the lovely balance, but even he couldn't destroy it altogether; the rivers and reed-beds and the marshy fields had beaten him.

Yet though the rivers have been hailed as Oxford's saving grace in this respect, they have also been blamed for their contribution to Oxford's damp climate. Misty, moist, muggy and enervating, the heavy-hanging air has been held responsible for the torpor of Oxford life and condemned for causing a variety of illnesses: 'Le rheumatisme vert' was Alphonse Daudet's summary dismissal of Christ Church Meadows. In his concern to laud his native city, the archivist Anthony Wood (1632–95) declared surprisingly that Oxford is blessed with a 'sweet wholsome and well-tempered aire, such an air that hath bin publickly admired and applauded by persons far and neare.' In his diary, however, he allowed himself greater frankness: 'Certainly Oxford's no good air.'

It is to the stultifying dampness that is attributed the general quirkiness of the Oxford character, as if the lack of fresh, invigorating air encourages eccentricities to moulder and multiply. 'River valleys', noted the Cambridge scholar J.A.W. Bennett, 'have their own distinctive intellectual "climate".' The most celebrated description of that character came from the pen of Max Beerbohm, who saw in the city's mirky mists the nebulous form of the *genius loci* itself. When the narrator of his novel *Zuleika Dobson* takes imaginative flight over Oxford, the city below him lies bathed in moonlight, suggestive of dream and enchantment, while from off the Isis vapours swirl about the meadows to add further mystification. So admired is the passage, so delicately worded, and so central to an understanding of the literature as a whole, that it warrants quoting at length.

> Yes, certainly, it is this mild, miasmal air, not less than the grey beauty and gravity of the buildings, that has helped Oxford to produce, and foster eternally, her peculiar race of artist-scholars, scholar-artists. The undergraduate, in his brief periods of residence, is too buoyant to be mastered by the spirit of the place. He does not salute it, and catch the manner. It is on him who stays to spend his maturity here that the spirit will in its fullness gradually descend. The buildings and their traditions keep astir in his mind whatsoever is gracious; the climate, enfolding and enfeebling him, lulling him, keeps him careless of the sharp, harsh exigent realities of the outer world. . . . Oxford, that lotus-land, saps the will-power, the power of action. But, in doing so, it clarifies the mind, makes larger the vision, gives, above all, that playful and caressing suavity of manner which comes of a conviction that nothing matters, except ideas, and that not even ideas are worth dying for, inasmuch as the ghosts of them slain seem worthy of yet more piously elaborate homage than can be given to them in their heyday. If the colleges could be transferred to the dry and bracing top of some hill, doubtless they would be more evidently useful to the nation. But let us be glad there is no engineer or enchanter to compass that task. *Egomet*, I would liefer have the rest of England subside into the sea than have Oxford set on a salubrious level. For there is nothing in England to be matched with what lurks in the vapours of these meadows, and in the shadows of these spires—that mysterious, inenubilable spirit, spirit of Oxford.

('Inenubilable' is an instance of Beerbohm's penchant for neologisms and would seem to mean 'incapable of being made uncloudy'.)

Beneath Beerbohm's superciliousness lies a glorification of his *alma mater* (Beerbohm studied at Merton), which places him firmly in the tradition of Oxford writing. The distinction between insider and outsider, between the cloistered utopia and the rigours of the world at large, is a theme that runs throughout the literature. The passage is marked too by an imaginative leap that sets the bone-chilling damp of the city as background to a lotus-land peopled, not by mere academics, but a race of scholar-artists. This too is in keeping with the tendency of Oxford authors to rewrite the physical city in glorified terms, for to writers like Beerbohm the name of Oxford was invested with a significancy that derived from the championing of artistic over analytical truth. For such figures the fictional city represented more than just a city of the mind; it was the capital of the imagination. By leading straight from mist to myth,

Beerbohm's passage thus provides an example of the precarious link that exists between the geographical and fictional Oxfords—two cities which approximate but do not coincide.

FRIDESWIDE AND THE LEARNED IMPS

Etymologically speaking, in the beginning was the ford and the ford was for oxen, though the exact location of that ox-ford has been the subject of much fanciful speculation. Some have opted for an eastern approach, placing the ford on the river Cherwell near the present Magdalen Bridge. Others have looked to the Thames at the points where it runs below Botley Road in the west, or further north where it intersects Binsey Green and Port Meadow. That dedicated chronicler of Oxford, Anthony Wood, championed Hinksey Ferry on the western side of the town, a site endorsed by a leading modern medievalist, H.E. Salter. Edward Thomas, however, in *Oxford* (1922) staked a claim for Folly Bridge in the south of the city, and recent excavations have unearthed evidence which strongly supports the contention.

The fiction of Oxford could be said to begin with its very foundation, for in a bid to shed glory on their city, imaginative historians have claimed at various times that Oxford was founded by Trojans, or by Druids, or by Alfred the Great. The commonly accepted story, however, concerns an eighth-century Saxon princess named Frideswide. The earliest surviving account is by William of Malmesbury in around 1125, but there are at least two other surviving medieval versions which differ substantially, and to add to the confusion Anthony Wood also provided one of his own. The story is commemorated too in a stained-glass window by Edward Burne-Jones (1859) in the Latin Chapel of Christ Church Cathedral (regarded by many as the artist's best early work). In some accounts it is assumed that Oxford already existed, while in others the princess herself is celebrated as the founder. The following anonymous account, which used to adorn the door of Binsey Church, provides a brief and attractive outline.

> The legendary story of the foundation of the church of St. Margaret at the Well near Binsey is on this wise. When the most Reverend Princess ffrediswyde, Abbess of Oxford, disdaining the attentions of the enamoured prince of Mercia, Algar, had fled to Thornbury, or Binsey, she was pursued there by the Prince, who had the temerity to attempt to take hold of her hand and was forthwith smitten blind by a great clap of lightning which flashed forth from a justly wrathful Heaven. A sentiment of sorrow then pierced the heart of the Maiden Princess when she saw her lover's plight and immediately there appeared before her St Margaret of Antioch with

her little dragon and St Catherine of Alexandria with her wheel. Little St Margaret told the saint to strike her Abbatial staff in the ground which when it was done there gushed forth a fount of water. The Princess's Lady Maidens then laved the eyes of luckless Algar with this healing tide and forthwith his sight was given back and seeing the error of his ways he stooped to the ground and kissed the hem of the Princess's robe thereafter returning to lead a better and a wiser life.

For medieval Oxford citizens the legend had a powerful and mystical fascination. There was a mythic resonance to many of its elements, such as the attack on a virtuous god-fearing virgin, which spoke powerfully of the sinfulness of mankind, and the story also carried pagan overtones of earth magic in the healing quality of spring water. The mythic element was heightened in some versions of the legend, for Frideswide escapes from Algar (or Ulfgar) to found a convent on the site where Christ Church cathedral now stands, around which the early town developed. The miraculous 'virgin birth' of the city thus took on some of the drama and mystery of other foundation myths. Yet curiously the story may not be altogether fanciful, for modern historians are inclined to believe that it may contain a grain of truth—'Legend usually crystallizes round a nucleus of genuine tradition,' writes Falconer Madan, 'and we may accept as very probable that a small religious house, founded perhaps 720–30, and occupying the position of the present Cathedral, was the first important fact of early Oxford.' Archaeological excavations carried out at the site lend weight to the supposition.

Frideswide was a very real presence in the life of medieval Oxford, both as founder and patron saint, and in the twelfth century her grave was located, her bones enshrined, and the memorial turned into a place of pilgrimage. Given the flair for self-publicity of medieval monks, this warrants a degree of scepticism. Nonetheless, the evoking of Frideswide's name by the carpenter of Chaucer's 'Miller's Tale' indicates the strength of the imaginative hold that the princess had on Oxford citizenry. The story has left its mark on later literature too, for in *Alice in Wonderland* there is a reference to the well at Binsey from which Frideswide drew the water to bathe her aggressor's eyes. This became an important place of pilgrimage in the Middle Ages, famed for its curative powers, and even Henry VIII is said to have visited the well to pray for a son and heir. It was known locally as the 'treacle well', as treacle was used in medicinal compounds and suggested a healing property. Carroll was drawn to use it in his story because Alice Liddell and her sisters, for whom he made up the story, were sometimes taken to Binsey by their governess, who had relatives there. With his keen sense of the absurd, Carroll could not resist making a play on words.

'Once upon a time there were three little sisters,' the Dormouse began in a great hurry; 'and their names were Elsie, Lacie and Tillie; and they lived at the bottom of a well —'

'What did they live on?' said Alice, who always took a great interest in questions of eating and drinking.

'They lived on treacle,' said the Dormouse after thinking a minute or two. . . .

'Why did they live at the bottom of a well?'

The Dormouse again took a minute or two to think about it, and then said, 'It was a treacle-well.'

After the time of Frideswide, Oxford rose rapidly to become one of the leading towns in the realm. The earliest surviving written record dates from the Anglo-Saxon Chronicle of 912: 'Edward cyng feng to Lunden-byrig and to Oxnaforda, and to thaem landum eallum the thaier to heridon'—Edward took possession of London and Oxford, and of all the lands which owed allegiance. Thereafter the fortunes of the town prospered, and because of its strategic significance between the Saxon and Danish parts of the country, Oxford had by the early eleventh century become the most important town outside of London. The development of hunting grounds at nearby Woodstock brought royal residence to the town; Beaumont Palace, founded by Henry I, was a favourite place of residence for Henry II and supposedly the birthplace of both Richard the Lionheart and King John (a small plaque marks the spot where the palace was sited at the western end of the present Beaumont St.).

The town's royal connections spurred the establishment of a number of religious communities, and these in time led to the development of the university, for it was out of the nucleus of scholarly monks that there first arose an informal centre of study in the town. One such figure was Geoffrey of Monmouth, who belonged to the college of canons attached to the chapel of Oxford castle, and it was there that he wrote the seminal *History of the Kings of Britain* (c. 1136), which inspired the Arthurian romances of later writers such as Malory and Tennyson. (Not far from the spot where Geoffrey worked on his imaginative history, the present-day Oxford Union boasts murals, newly restored, depicting scenes from Arthurian legends painted by Pre-Raphaelites including Rossetti, Burne-Jones and William Morris.)

The early days of the university are portrayed in an historical romance, *A Clerk of Oxford* (1897) by Evelyn Everett-Green. Intrusive authorial commentary and stilted medieval dialogue full of 'methinks' mar what might have been an entertaining account, for Everett-Green's Oxford is a strange, rowdy, bustling town where friars, Jews, continentals and Celts intermingle with the local townspeople. Students are fun-lov-

ing and riotous fighters who owe allegiance to differing 'nations': the
Scots and Northerners are allied against the Welsh, Irish and Southern-
ers. 'I had thought,' says the newcomer Leofric, 'that Oxford would be
full of grave and reverend doctors, whose presence would impose order
and gravity upon all. But methinks it is full of wantonness and revelling
and fighting.' Brawls are endemic, books scarce, and distractions many
in this medieval fiction.

In historical terms this was the age of the great medieval schoolmen,
those doctors of high acclaim who, as Spenser puts it in *The Faerie Queene*,
were like 'so many learned imps that shoot abroad / And with their
branches spread all Britainy'. Three of the most illustrious came from
the ranks of Franciscan friars: the *Doctor mirabilis*, Roger Bacon (c.
1214–94); the *Doctor subtilis*, Duns Scotus (1266–1308); and the *Doctor
invincibilis*, William of Ockham (d. 1349). Ockham's name remains
familiar through 'Ockham's razor'—a philosophical tenet that needless
complexities be omitted in the pursuit of truth—while the two other
doctors have been celebrated in works of literature. In the melodrama
Frier Bacon, and Frier Bongay (1594), Robert Greene depicts Roger Bacon
as 'a braue scholler, sirra; they say he is a braue Nigromancer, that he can
make women of deuils, and hee can iuggle cats into Costermongers.'
One of the play's central scenes depicts a contest of magicians in which
Bongay and Bacon vie with each other to outdo a German rival, Vandermast, whose ability to summon up the spirit of Hercules is overshadowed
by Bacon's riposte—making both spirit and Vandermast disappear. Following in the tradition of the morality play, Greene has Bacon renounce
his use of necromancy to indicate his conversion to goodness. In Oxford
terms the chief interest of the play is to indicate the strength of suspicion
which surrounded the scholarly genius in medieval times. Theologian,
philologist, astrologer, alchemist, and, supposedly, the inventor of gunpowder and spectacles—Bacon was so far ahead of his time that he
aroused the suspicions of the church and the envy of his contemporaries. Even after his death his name continued to attract attention as a
source of Faustian romance, and the house on Folly Bridge (known as
Friar Bacon's Study) where he was said to have carried out experiments
remained for centuries one of the city's main tourist sites: when Samuel
Pepys made a visit to Oxford in 1668, he paid a shilling to be shown the
rooms of this remarkable figure. (The building was demolished in
1779.)

The air of black arts that hung over Bacon was symptomatic of the suspicion that surrounded academe as a whole, for the investigations and
experiments appeared to ordinary folk to be interference with the nat-

ural order. In Chaucer's 'Miller's Tale', John the carpenter contrasts the intellectual's speculations with the plain man's simple belief.

> Men sholde nat knowe of Goddes pryvetee.
> Ye, blessed be alwey a lewed man
> That noght but oonly his bileve kan!

The medieval misgiving about academics was so deeply felt that traces linger in the literature of later ages, even into that of the nineteenth century. When the titular character of James Hogg's *Justified Sinner* (1824), for example, assumes a false identity as an Oxford scholar, the reaction of the 'poor and ignorant' villagers of Nacrum is unexpected.

> I said I was a poor scholar of theology, on my way to Oxford. They stared at one another with expressions of wonder, disappointment, and fear. I afterwards came to learn, that the term *theology* was by them quite misunderstood, and that they had some crude conceptions that nothing was taught at Oxford but the *black arts,* which ridiculous idea prevailed over all the south of Scotland.

In recent times attitudes have changed to such an extent that far from being seen as suspect, figures like Bacon and the sixteenth-century Dr. John Dee of Cambridge have been 'reinvented' as magical seers with insights that lie beyond the scope of conventional science. In James Blish's *Doctor Mirabilis* (1964), Bacon is portrayed as an alchemical seeker of truth who is unjustly persecuted by a reactionary clerical establishment and held in a dank dungeon for over ten years for daring to challenge the church orthodoxy. The novel is based on the few known facts about the historical character (which are summarised at the back), and the fictionalised biography makes compelling reading by an author whose main claim to fame was his work with the Star Trek series. (Blish [1921–75] was an American science fiction writer drawn to England by the teachings of C.S. Lewis and lies buried in Oxford's Holywell cemetery.)

For all the allure of the *Doctor mirabilis,* the literary star of the *Doctor subtilis* shines yet brighter, and that on the strength of a single sonnet. Scotus excelled in the type of sophisticated metaphysics barely intelligible to ordinary minds, and it is from Duns by a linguistic irony that the word 'dunce' derives, for Renaissance humanists had little time for his intricate arguments and coined the term to disparage those who clung to his old-fashioned way of thinking. One of the few modern figures to find Scotus sympathetic was the poet-priest Gerard Manley Hopkins (1844–89), for whom the medieval theologian held a special appeal. Like Scotus, Hopkins viewed the world as an expression of the universal in and through the individual, and he invented the notion of 'inscape' to express the unique individuality of each natural phenomenon. When he discovered in his readings that this was similar in concept to Scotus's 'haeccitas' (thisness), his delight was such that he came to look on his medieval predecessor as a kind of mentor.

Hopkins returned to Oxford when he was appointed in late 1878 to work at the church of St. Aloysius on the Woodstock Road, and the association of place with predecessor moved him to write a poem, 'Duns Scotus's Oxford'. The octet with its dense and melodic interplay contains in its opening lines one of the most quoted of all Oxford descriptions, though ironically their celebratory tone is but a precursor to condemnation of nineteenth-century Oxford and its 'graceless growth' in the east. With 'Yet ah!' at the start of the sestet, the poet's thought turns to Scotus himself. The phrase 'the rarest-veined unraveller' refers to the subtleties of Scotus's form of realism, but by also calling to mind Hopkins's acute botanical interests it serves to reinforce the bond between poet and subject which stands at the heart of the poem.

> Towery city and branchy between towers;
> Cuckoo-echoing, bell-swarmèd, lark-charmèd, rook-racked,
>   river-rounded;
> The dapple-eared lily below thee; that country and town did
> Once encounter in, here coped and poisèd powers;
>
> Thou hast a base and brickish skirt there, sours
> That neighbour-nature thy grey beauty is grounded
> Best in; graceless growth, thou hast confounded
> Rural rural keeping—folk, flocks, and flowers.
>
> Yet ah! this air I gather and I release
> He lived on; these weeds and waters, these walls are what
> He haunted who of all men most sways my spirits to peace;
>
> Of realty the rarest-veinèd unraveller; a not
> Rivalled insight, be rival Italy or Greece;
> Who fired France for Mary without spot.

The abrupt and enigmatic ending of the poem, far removed from the towery city with which it opens, presumes familiarity with Scotus's life and suggests the centrality of the metaphysician to the thought of the poet (the lack of a name in the body of the poem—only the reverential 'He' is used—emphasises the point). According to legend, Scotus was summoned by the Church to France to account for his religious views, where he successfully defended his unorthodox view that the virgin Mary had been born free of original sin ('Mary without spot'). Hopkins could identify with the theological isolation of Scotus, for he himself felt estranged as a Jesuit in the anti-Catholic atmosphere of post-Tractarian Oxford. The identification of poet with the medieval scholar thus permeates the whole poem, from the towers of Oxford at the start to the trials of France at the end.

The sonnet touches on a central theme of later literature, namely the human associations evoked by the city's physical aspect. The retrospective and elegiac tone of Hopkins's poem is a hallmark of the writing as a whole—it might indeed be considered the salient characteristic. For Thomas Warton, here writing in 1758 in an article for Samuel Johnson's *Idler*, the two ancient universities were inherently edifying, for they possessed

> a sort of inspiring deity, which every youth of quick sensibility and ingenious disposition creates to himself, by reflecting that he is placed under those venerable walls, where a Hooker and a Hammond, a Bacon and a Newton, once pursued the same course of science, and from whence they soared to the most elevated heights of literary fame.

(The theologian Richard Hooker was educated at Corpus Christi, Oxford; Henry Hammond, whose writings were admired by Johnson, studied at Magdalen College, Oxford; Francis Bacon, the Elizabethan statesman and writer, was at Trinity College, Cambridge, as was Isaac Newton, discoverer of the law of gravity.) Nineteenth-century writers with their sense of historical unfolding were particularly appreciative of the city's richness of association, and Thomas Hardy in prose and Lionel Johnson in poetry captured the inspirational appeal of a city 'Where at each coign of every antique street, / A memory hath taken root in stone'. Compared with such historical vistas, the concerns of the moment appeared, in Matthew Arnold's words, to be merely 'petty aspirations'. The lofty vantage-point of later literature, sustained as it is by notions of continuity and heritage, thus owes itself to the foundations laid in early times by the medieval friars who first established Oxford's reputation for excellence. The genius of the *genius loci* is in a sense theirs.

CHAUCER'S CLERKS OF OXENFORD

Amongst the multitude of characters featured in *The Canterbury Tales* are five university clerks, three of whom are from Oxford and two, both in 'The Reeve's Tale', from Cambridge. The title of 'clerk' provides in itself an important indicator of the nature of the medieval university, for it denotes a person in clerical orders which was a *sine qua non* for academics of the time. Learning took place solely within the parameters set by the church; teachers were all drawn from the ranks of the clergy, and students were essentially seminarists who wore the clerical tonsure and enjoyed the right to be tried by church courts. This led to friction with townspeople, who resented the outsiders with their special privileges, foreign ways, and youthful high spirits. University members had cause for complaint too, for they were subject to overcharging, taunts, and discrimination.

The antagonism between gown and town sometimes erupted into violence when the two factions would summon followers by ringing the bells of their respective churches: St. Martin's at Carfax for town, and St. Mary's on the High for gown. Between them lay but a short distance, and it was here that battle was joined. According to Hastings Rashdall, 'there is probably not a single yard of ground in any part of the classic High Street that lies between St. Martin's and St. Mary's which has not, at one time or another, been stained with blood. There are historic battlefields on which less has been spilt.' Cambridge University owes its origins to one such confrontation for in 1209, following the hanging of scholars in revenge for the death of a townswoman, part of the academic community abandoned Oxford altogether and set up in East Anglia.

In 1355, when young Geoffrey Chaucer (c. 1343–1400) was nearing student age (students entered the medieval university at twelve or thirteen), Oxford witnessed the St. Scholastica Day's riot, the bloodiest of all the fights between town and gown. It was an event of momentous importance, for it determined the balance of power within the city for the subsequent five hundred years. Anthony Wood described the occasion in terms which betray his bias towards the university at which he studied— an early example of how gown's literary skills have served the cause of propaganda. In his *Annals* for 1354 (the discrepancy in date is due to the later change of calendar), the city's chronicler describes the initial cause of the riot.

> On Tuesday 10 Feb. (being the Feast of S. Scholastic the Virgin) came Walter de Springheuse, Roger de Chesterfield, and other Clerks, to the Tavern called Swyndlestock . . . and there calling for wine, John de Croydon the Vintner brought them some, but they disliking it, as it should seem, and he avouching it to be good, several snappish words passed between them. At length the Vintner giving them stubborn and saucy language, they threw the wine and vessel at his head.

Such were the volatile relations between the two communities that out of this unremarkable incident ensued three days of bloody fighting. Unconcerned to mask his sympathy for the university faction, Wood describes the events of Thursday, February 12, on which day the rioting reached its ferocious climax when the said Townsmen about sun rising, having rung out their bell, assembled themselves together in a numberless multitude, desiring to heap mischief upon mischief, and to perfect by a more terrible conclusion that wicked enterprise which they had begun. This being done they with hideous noises and clamours came and invaded the Scholars' houses in a wretchless sort, which they forced open with iron bars and other engines; and entring into them, those that resisted and stood upon their defence (particularly some Chaplains) they killed or else in a grievous sort maimed. Some innocent wretches, after they had killed, they scornfully cast into houses of easment, others they buried in dunghills, and some they let lie above ground. The crowns of some Chaplains, viz. all the skin so far as the tonsure went, these diabolical imps flayed off in scorn of their Clergy. Divers others whom they had mortally wounded, they hailed to prison, carrying the entrails in their hands in a most lamentable manner.

Wood's depiction of the 'confounded sons of Satan' battling against innocent clergy-scholars makes for good copy, though it finds little support among modern scholars: the university archivist, W.A. Pantin, noted soberly in 1972, 'It was generally the chronic indiscipline of the scholars that caused the town-and-gown battles'. Royal and ecclesiastical intervention nonetheless favoured the university, which was granted greater powers, while the townsfolk were penalised with a heavy fine and their representatives ordered to attend the university church each St. Scholastica's Day in atonement (a custom maintained, remarkably, for almost five hundred years).

It was not long after these events that Chaucer wrote 'The Miller's Tale', in which a student by the name of Nicholas lodges with a carpenter and sets out to bed his attractive young wife. Having won her affections, he makes arrangements to ensure the absence of her husband so as to spend the night with her. The convoluted plan of deception involves getting the gullible carpenter to sleep in a tub suspended from the roof in the belief that there is to be a major flood. The two young lovers are thus able to occupy the bedroom, only to be interrupted by the dandy Absolon, who has come to court the wife. When from outside the window he asks her for a kiss, she sticks out 'her nether eye', much to the couple's amusement, and he makes off with offended feelings. When he appears later and again asks for a kiss, Nicholas sticks out his bottom, but this time instead of his lips Absolon applies a red-hot ploughshare. 'Water!' hollers Nicholas in distress, thereby waking the carpenter and prompting the story's frenetic ending. Imagining the flood to have arrived, the carpenter cuts the ropes suspending his tub and plunges to the ground, breaking his arm in the process. When the neighbours hear the commotion, Nicholas is caught in an awkward predicament, not only with his trousers down, as it were, but also with his bottom burnt, yet he manages to extricate himself even from this situation by convincing the crowd that the carpenter is mad.

Like Wood, Chaucer takes a partisan view of Oxford and weights his story firmly in favour of the university. The handsome young hero is given the epithet 'hende Nicholas' (pleasant or courteous) and referred to as 'this sweete clerk'; the carpenter by contrast is a 'senex amans', too old for his wife and too stupid to deserve sympathy. Rather than a duplicitous adulterer Nicholas emerges as a lovable rogue, for the lightness, fragrance, springtime song-and-dance which characterise the tale make it plain that it is to be taken as an enjoyable prank. This it certainly is, but it is also much more for the tale offers a revealing insight into the nature of medieval Oxford. For all its bawdiness the story accurately reflects developments within the city. In the guise of the bright young Nicholas gown takes lodgings with town and makes use of superior wits to win dominion. The humiliation of the carpenter in his own house parallels the humbling of the citizens of Oxford in their home city after the St. Scholastica's Day riot; that Chaucer intended this is suggested by his choice of seducer, for in the sources for the story the husband is cuckolded either by a friar or a priest or a miller. It does not seem too fanciful, therefore, to suppose that the sexual conquest reflects the mastery won by the cuckoo gown in the nest of town.

Onto this broad canvas of medieval Oxford Chaucer inserts a wealth of details which taken altogether add up to a remarkably vivid picture. Nicholas himself is a case in point. Though he is referred to as a 'poure scoler', a common enough description of students down the ages, he is able to rent a room of his own with a landlord who has a stable and servants at a time when many students bedded down in spartan cells or on dormitory floors. Moreover, the description of his room suggests comparative luxury, for he has herbs to sweeten the air and a number of valuable possessions—a psaltery, a collection of books and even an astrolabe, which was an object rare enough to comprise one of the perks of becoming a fellow of Merton. While mention is made of a clothes chest, there is no reference to a desk, reinforcing the impression that this is not the room of a serious student. The label of 'poure scoler' hung on Nicholas would seem therefore to be ironical, acting as counterpart to the 'rich gnof' of a landlord. By the end of the story it is plainly the carpenter who deserves the epithet 'poure'.

Chaucer's mastery of form is evident in the way that the naughty Nicholas stands as counterpoise to the saintly Clerk of Oxford, the academic standard-bearer amongst the parade of pilgrims in the General Prologue. The Clerk exudes a dignified and scholarly presence: he is a man of few words and high moral virtue who sacrifices worldly gain for the pursuit of knowledge. Here is the idealised view of the man of learning. By depicting Nicholas as a lusty rascal Chaucer deliberately undermines the rosy image of scholarship he has established, as if the poet were first presenting the impersonalised ideal (the Clerk has no name) and then fleshing out the human failings.

If the Clerk represents the genuine 'poure scoler' as opposed to Nicholas, there would appear to be serious anomalies in the account of his background. In an age when books were considered so valuable that they were chained to library walls, the Clerk possesses 'Twenty bookes, clad in blak or reed, / Of Aristotle and his philosophie'. (According to one assessment the books in the Clerk's possession may have equalled the value of two or three houses.) In the lines below there is an indication as to how the Clerk might have acquired such a collection.

> Yet hadde he but litel gold in cofre;
> But al that he myghte of his freendes hente,
> On bookes and on lernynge he it spente,
> And bisily gan for the soules preye
> Of hem that yaf hym wherwith to scoleye.

The practice of making charitable donations in return for prayer and intercession on behalf of the donor's soul was common practice in the Middle Ages. Because of his devotion and dedication, the Clerk would presumably have attracted rich sponsors, and the money that he might have spent on himself—his clothes are threadbare and his body 'hollow'—he chooses instead to spend on his studies. Rather than conflicting with the Clerk's standing as a 'poure scoler', then, the books actually serve to emphasise his self-sacrifice.

Consideration of the Clerk's foreign travels proves no less revealing about the nature of the university. In the prologue to his tale about Griselda, he mentions having been to Padua, where he learnt the story from the poet Francis Petrarch. That a poor scholar could afford the journey to Italy might seem incongruous, though the medieval university as a whole was characterised by its mobility and multiculturalism. Scholars such as the Clerk frequently undertook long journeys to learn at the feet of renowned figures, for they had few needs and were able to support themselves by begging. Bound by the universal brotherhood of the church and sharing a common tongue in Latin, they could rely on members of the same clerical order to provide food and lodging wherever they wandered.

The tale the Clerk claims to have learnt from Petrarch portrays the long-suffering Griselda as the embodiment of virtuous self-sacrifice. The story is told by way of response to the taunt of the formidable Wife of

Bath, who claimed that clerics never speak well of women. When he finishes his story, the Clerk appears to back down, for he acknowledges that no such woman as Griselda could really exist and that women like the Wife of Bath who are merciless with their husbands provide more realistic role models. He thereby delivers a double refutation of the charge against clerics, not only speaking well of Griselda but of the obtuse Wife too, who misses the ironic tone of his epilogue. Once again Chaucer displays the benefits of a university education, for the suggestion is that the Clerk's subtlety, like Nicholas's shrewdness, owes itself to his academic training.

The third of Chaucer's university figures is the 'joly clerk, Jankyn'— jolly despite having been manoeuvred into marriage by the Wife of Bath, who at forty to his twenty was embarking on her fifth marriage. Jankyn is a minor character, overshadowed by his forceful wife, though the reader learns that he 'som tyme was a clerk of Oxenford, / And hadde left scole, and wente at hom to bord'. His young age and relatively lowly work as parish assistant suggest that he may have dropped out of the university. If this were the case, it would not have been unusual, for the seven years needed to graduate as a fully fledged master in medieval times proved for many too much of a financial hardship. Like the other clerks, Jankyn is portrayed in positive terms, and he shares with Nicholas the adjectival description of 'hende'. Even the male-bashing Wife of Bath is moved to say that of her five husbands she loves him the best, despite the fact that he once lost his temper and hit her. This happened after she had torn out pages from his book—a provocative act to a man of learning.

The three Oxford clerks are thus all portrayed sympathetically by Chaucer, and this is perhaps not surprising given that he was a man of letters and personally acquainted with Oxford scholars. Such indeed is the familiarity that he shows with the city — 'not a detail . . . can be faulted', according to the medievalist J.A.W. Bennet—that some commentators suspect that he was once attached to the university himself. Anthony Wood claimed improbably that the poet studied under John Wyclif, precursor of the Reformation, and at least one imaginative biography has given him an Oxford education. The suggestion has even been made that the Clerk might be an idealised self-portrait. Such speculation has been fuelled by knowledge of Chaucer's links with the fellows of Merton, the library of which claims to this day to house the poet's astrolabe (interestingly, the tables in Chaucer's *A Treatise on the Astrolabe* are 'compownded after the latitude of Oxenforde').

Given his ties with the men of Merton, it seems strange that Chaucer does not make reference to a college in his *Tales*. The three thirteenth-century colleges—Merton, University, and Balliol—had been joined by a further three during the early fourteenth century: Exeter, Oriel, and Queen's. In 1379 the foundation of New College virtually doubled the number of Oxford fellows at a stroke, and in 1386, just when it is thought Chaucer was planning the *Canterbury Tales,* the college members moved into the first set of buildings. With his familiarity with the town Chaucer could hardly have been ignorant of such developments, yet the only institution referred to in the 'The Miller's Tale' is Oseney Abbey, the huge religious establishment on the western outskirts of the city (which at one time ranked as the third largest in the country). Nonetheless, the author's emphasis would seem to bear testimony to his prescience. At the time that Chaucer was writing, the university population amounted to some fifteen hundred members, of whom fewer than a hundred lived in college. These were graduates, proceeding to higher degrees in theology for the most part and with little influence in the university at large. More important were the licensed halls and lodgings where the majority of university members lived. Even with the addition of New College the proportion of college members remained small: 'If all the colleges had been dissolved in 1400', commented the historian H.E. Salter, 'it would not have been a crushing blow to the University.' Chaucer's Oxford thus reflects the essentially pre-collegiate nature of the medieval university. Moreover, it was precisely because of the antics of miscreants like Nicholas that the collegiate system came into its own. In 1410, not long after the writing of 'The Miller's Tale', the university authorities introduced legislation to control indiscipline in terms which suggest that Nicholas was indeed 'hende' by comparison with students who spent their time, in the words of the statute, 'sleeping by day and haunting taverns and brothels by night, intent on robbery and homicide'. The need for tighter supervision of students led the university to look increasingly to college accommodation, and the statistics tell of a rapid transformation in the nature of the university. In 1450 there were seventy halls and nine colleges; by 1550 there were just eight halls compared with thirteen colleges.

Chaucer's achievements are no less remarkable in imaginative as in narrative terms, for medieval Oxford and its characters are brought vividly to life by the poet's gift for descriptive detail. Nowhere is this clearer than in the account of Nicholas and his room. The good-looking, effeminate student with his astrological obsession might be a figure of the late twentieth century, so familiar does he seem. The model Clerk likewise with his solemn manner and threadbare clothes comes fresh to the mind's eye: 'And gladly would he learne and gladly teache', runs the summary description. Not only is his moral rectitude convincingly portrayed (goodness is famously difficult to convey), but the contrast with

Nicholas sets up a polarity appropriated by later Oxford fiction, for the student-heroes of the nineteenth century are torn between virtue and vice and struggle with their consciences on the path to maturity. Though the morality was new, the template is Chaucer's, and in its way 'The Miller's Tale' constitutes the first Oxford novel. It is therefore not simply for his remoteness in time but in a very real sense that the 'father of English literature' can also justly be considered the father of Oxford literature. The seduction of a carpenter's wife could be said to have spawned a rich progeny.

FOXE'S MARTYRS AND A CARDINAL DEVELOPMENT

In 1484 William Caxton published an epilogue to his version of *Aesop* which tells of two masters of art from Oxford, the one eager to achieve success and the other 'good and symple' with little worldly ambition. The former rose to the position of dean in the chapel of a prince, and while travelling around the country happened to come across his former friend working in a prosperous parish. He enquired as to the value of the church living, but was astonished to find his unworldly friend had no idea. When pressed further, the parish priest answered after due consideration that the living must be worth heaven or hell, since that would be the reward for his performance. The reply shamed the dean into a true appreciation of spiritual worth.

Caxton's epilogue belongs to the same moral climate which produced *The Jests of Scogin* and *The Merie Tales of Skelton*. These flippant put-downs of university life, whose titular references to a John Scogin of Oriel and the poet John Skelton are thought to be apocryphal, propose that worldly rather than academic success matters most and contain moral lessons such as 'Here a man may see that Money is better than Learning'. With their cynical wit, these early satires foreshadow eighteenth-century verse which pricked at a similar state of indulgence and torpor, for after Chaucer's time the university underwent a period of intellectual stagnation. This mirrored the plight of the country as a whole: 'Oxford had reached the height of its prosperity in the fourteenth century', writes Headlam. 'Then the Black Death, the decadence of the Friars, the French Wars, the withdrawal of foreign students and the severance of the ties between English and foreign Universities, commenced a decay which was accelerated by the decline of the ecclesiastical monopoly of learning, by the Wycliffite movement and, later, by the Wars of the Roses.'

Worse was to come, however, for the decay in learning of the fifteenth century was followed by the disruption of studies in the sixteenth century, when religious turmoil brought intrigue, factionalism, and dismissals to the clerically dominated university. Genuine study all but ceased. The troubles reached their bloody climax during the reign of Mary (1553–58), and it was in Oxford that the most shocking events of those years took place, recorded for posterity by John Foxe (1516–87). Foxe was himself a victim of the times, for as an outspoken Protestant he was forced to resign his fellowship at Magdalen to flee abroad. He lived in penury compiling material for a work of propaganda, *Actes and Monuments* (1563) (better known as *Foxe's Book of Martyrs*), which detailed the lives and sufferings of those persecuted by Catholicism. A man of perfervid beliefs, Foxe lost little opportunity in his book to rail against 'the great Antichrist of Europe, or Pope of Rome, and his diversely disguised host of anointed hypocrites'. The vehemence of his writing proved attractive to the anti-Catholic mood in Elizabethan England, and the church ordered a copy to be placed in every cathedral and church official's home. The book proved enormously influential; not only was it the best-seller of its day, but in houses up and down the country it remained for centuries a treasured item alongside the family Bible.

Among the martyrs Foxe includes are two early Oxford figures: John Wyclif (c. 1330–84), 'the morning star of the Reformation', and William Tyndale (c. 1495–1536), who excelled 'especially in the knowledge of the Scriptures, whereunto his mind was singularly addicted'. But it is with the account of the trials of Archbishop Cranmer (1489–1556) and the two bishops Latimer (1485–1555) and Ridley (1502–55) that Oxford comes into its own. The three men had resisted Mary's coercive attempts at conversion and been ordered to engage in public disputation. As centres of theology the two universities were crucial to the religious dispute, and though the three clerics were Cambridge men, they were brought to Oxford for the debate in the belief that it was more sympathetic to the Catholic cause. The proceedings retained all the flavour of medieval sophistry; while the Renaissance was proceeding in earnest elsewhere, Oxford was preoccupied with the great religious matter of the age.

> We do object to thee, Nicholas Ridley, and to thee Hugh Latimer, jointly and severally; first that thou Nicholas Ridley, in this high university of Oxford, anno 1554, in the months of April, May, June, July, or in some one or more of them, has affirmed, and openly defended and maintained, and in many other times and places besides, that the true and naturel body of Christ, after the consecration of the priest, is not really present in the sacrament of the altar.

A partisan audience packed the Divinity School venue for what amounted to a grand theatrical occasion. The ingenuity (and ingenu-

ousness) of the arguments makes intriguing reading: Ridley, for
instance, claimed that since Christ sat on the right hand of God he could
not simultaneously be present in the sacraments. Such arguments made
little impact on the audience. Ridley complained of their hissing and
booing, but like a modern show trial the primary concern was with propaganda rather than justice. As a result Latimer and Ridley were duly
condemned as heretics (as archbishop, Cranmer constituted a special
case to be dealt with later), but since the disputation lacked proper
authorisation, the men were detained pending the arrival of a papal
commissioner.

Foxe gives only a perfunctory account of the official trial of the bishops, held in the university church of St. Mary's, for he is impatient to get
to the burning. The place of execution was in the ditch by Balliol College
(the site is marked by a cobble cross set in the road of present-day Broad
Street), and to arouse indignation Foxe emphasises the pitiable appearance of the two men, noting that the frail and aged Latimer 'stirred
men's hearts to rue'. As the bishops make their final preparations, Ridley's brother ties bags of gunpowder around the men's necks to minimise
the length of suffering and the steadfast Latimer delivers his famous
words of comfort.

> Be of good comfort, master Ridley, and play the man. We shall this day
> light such a candle, by God's grace, in England, as I trust shall never be put
> out.

A more circumspect writer might have brushed over the horror of the
burning, but for Foxe there is no blanching. Latimer has a merciful
release, receiving the flame 'as it were embracing of it' and with little
apparent pain. Ridley on the other hand, atop a compacted pile of faggots, undergoes the most horrendous of deaths as the flames consume
his lower parts but leave his senses intact. The torture is unwittingly furthered by his brother-in-law who, by piling on more faggots, only succeeds in smothering the flames. Ridley's cries of supplication are inter-
spersed with pitiful calls for mercy until at last an attendant intervenes
and enables the flames to reach the gunpowder around his neck. The
reader is spared little in these gruesome details, for Foxe is clearly determined to wrest from the episode its full propaganda value.

Meanwhile, in an attempt to wear down and confuse the church's
highest officeholder, the sixty-six-year-old Cranmer was subjected to day-
long disputing by divines and kept in the city's prison (the Bocardo next
to St. Michael at the North Gate). With their continual 'threatening,
flattering, entreating, and promising', the papal interrogators show
themselves to be well-versed in methods of breaking a man. From the

harsh regime of the Bocardo, Cranmer is allowed a few days at the Dean's house at Christ Church to remind him of worldly ease and pleasure, before being returned once more to the deprivations of the prison. Eventually the archbishop could hold out no longer, and he agreed to sign a series of recantations. It was just the propaganda victory for which the Catholics were looking, but Mary was nonetheless determined that Cranmer should die, goaded by the memory of the part he had played in her mother's divorce.

The date for the execution was set for March 21, 1556, and the preliminaries took place in the university church of St. Mary's. Foxe makes of them a literary set-piece. He begins with the 'lamentable' and 'sorrowful' appearance of the once revered archbishop, shorn of his finery and reduced to 'a bare and ragged gown, and ill favouredly clothed, with an old square cap, exposed to the contempt of all men'. To heighten the sense of immediacy Foxe adds a number of details to his account, some of which carry the air of probable exaggeration: Cranmer, for instance, is apparently so overwhelmed that 'More than twenty times the tears gushed out abundantly'. The high point of the proceedings comes as the assembled crowd prepare to depart for the place of execution but are called back for a final statement by Cranmer. The speech they heard was surely the most startling ever made in Oxford, for instead of the avowal of Catholicism that was expected, the former archbishop made a declaration which ended in the following manner:

> And now I come to the great thing, which so much troubleth my conscience, more than any thing that ever I did or said in my whole life, and that is the setting abroad of a writing contrary to the truth; which now here I renounce and refuse, as things written with my hand, contrary to the truth which I thought in my heart, and written for fear of death, and to save my life if it might be; and that is, all such bills and papers which I have written or signed with my hand since my degradation; wherein I have written many things untrue. And forasmuch as my hand offended, writing contrary to my heart, my hand shall first be punished there-for; for, may I come to the fire, it shall be first burned.
>
> And as for the Pope, I refuse him, as Christ's enemy, and antichrist, with all his false doctrine.

Foxe can barely contain his delight at the discomfort this must have caused. 'Here the standers-by were all astonied, marvelled, were amazed, did look one upon another, whose expectation he had so notably deceived', he enthuses. 'Some began to admonish him of his recantation, and to accuse him of falsehood. Briefly, it was a world to see the doctors beguiled of so great a hope'. Cranmer continued with his denunciation of papism during the uproar, before being bundled away to the stake that awaited him in the town ditch. With characteristic exactitude Foxe notes that Cranmer extended his offending hand to the flame 'steadfast and immovable (saving that once with the same hand he wiped his face)', but the author wastes little space on speculation about the reasons for Cranmer's recantation, or rather the recantation of his recantation, for this would clearly undermine the purpose of his story. Whether fear, mental breakdown, theological confusion, or a simple desire to survive led to the vacillations of the father of Anglicanism remains a source of debate, even among modern commentators.

Underlying Foxe's narrative are developments within Oxford which are of importance to the literature, chief amongst which is the dominant role that the university had by this time assumed in the life of the city. As a town Oxford had suffered a sharp decline since Chaucer's time: in 1344 it ranked eighth after London in terms of taxable wealth, but by 1523 it had slipped to twenty-ninth. This was largely caused by the migration of the town's cloth industry to rural locations, and the large mansions of the Cotswolds were built at the expense of the bankrupt of Oxford. As a result the generously endowed colleges were able to buy up the prime land in the city centre which they still own and occupy to this day. The new colleges—Magdalen (1458), Brasenose (1509), and Corpus Christi (1517)—had imposing buildings which emphasised their primacy in the town. They were not only major employers of local townsfolk, but college heads were imposing figures with important connections to church and state. The importance of the university in the life of the nation had been enhanced by the establishment of the Church of England under Henry VIII, for Oxford's theologians were called on to adjudicate in religious questions and to help spread the new religion.

The links of state and university were manifest in the foundation of mighty Cardinal College, the thirteenth and most ambitious of Oxford colleges. Its founder, Cardinal Wolsey, was 'the last great medievalist' and a man of enormous religious and temporal power. His rise from lowly origins to cardinal of York and chancellor of the exchequer owed itself in large measure to his Oxford education, and he remained forever grateful. Known as 'the boy bachelor', he graduated B.A. at the remarkably young age of fifteen and was elected a fellow of Magdalen. He taught at the college school, where he was given a living by the father of three brothers under his charge: it was the first rung of a long ladder by which he rose to rival Henry VIII himself in wealth and prestige. In 1524, at the apogee of his power, he secured space and funds for the establishment of a college named, tellingly, in his own honour. Designed on a scale that dwarfed its predecessors, the college necessitated not only the suppression of numerous Oxford buildings but twenty-two lesser monasteries around the country. With his fall from favour in 1529, the college was left uncompleted. Three sides of the great quadrangle, including the dining-hall and kitchen, stood Ozymandias-like to proclaim the cardinal's might, leading the wits of the day to comment that though he had started a college, he had finished an eating-house.

In *Henry VIII*, thought to have been co-authored by Shakespeare, Katherine learns in act IV, scene ii of the death of the cardinal from her usher, Griffith, who delivers an elegant speech designed to do the dead man justice. The sympathetic account makes reference both to the college at Oxford and to a school at Ipswich which Wolsey founded but which did not survive.

> This cardinal,
> Though from an humble stock, undoubtedly
> Was fashioned to much honour. From his cradle
> He was a scholar, and a ripe and good one,
> Exceeding wise, fair-spoken, and persuading;
> Lofty and sour to them that loved him not,
> But to those men that sought him, sweet as summer.
> And though he were unsatisfied in getting -
> Which was a sin—yet in bestowing, madam,
> He was most princely: ever witness for him
> Those twins of learning that he raised in you,
> Ipswich and Oxford—one of which fell with him,
> Unwilling to outlive the good that did it;
> The other, though unfinished, yet so famous,
> So excellent in art, and still so rising,
> That Christendom shall ever speak his virtue.

In contrast to the Ipswich foundation, Wolsey's Oxford venture was saved for posterity because after long hesitation Henry refounded the college in 1546 as Christ Church. The palatial buildings overwhelmed the small city and housed the town's cathedral in one of its capacious corners. The transference there of the great bell of Oseney Abbey (which was dissolved following the see's incorporation into the cathedral) marked a symbolic transition of power. Named Great Tom in honour of St. Thomas Becket, the bell was awesome in size, weighing nearly seven tons and measuring just over seven feet. It was housed at first in the cathedral campanile, and when it was recast in 1611 Richard Corbet, Dean of Christ Church (head of both college and cathedral), celebrated the event in a witty short poem which ends resoundingly, 'And though we grieved to see thee thumped and banged, / We'll all be glad, Great Tom, to see thee hanged.' The recasting was celebrated too in a popular round:

Great Tom is cast
And Christ Church bells ring one
Two, three, four, five, six
And Tom comes last.

The re-hung Great Tom became one of the city's chief attractions, and George Wither's verse account of his student days in *Abuses Stript and Whipt* (1622) states, 'I did (as other idle freshmen do) / Long to go see the bell of Osney too'. With Tom's removal in 1682 to Christopher Wren's tower at the entrance to Christ Church, the transfer from religious to secular domicile of the ancient bell was complete. The 101 strokes (once for every student) that Great Tom sounded—and still sounds—at five past nine every evening could be heard throughout the small city, warning errant students of the closing of the college gates and reinforcing the sense of university dominion. Academic authority even extended to the right of college heads to search town houses for student miscreants. Gown had also appropriated legacy of the town's patron-saint, for guardianship of Frideswide's tomb had passed into the hands of the canons of Christ Church. With its academic element in the ascendant, the city had become the consummate university-town, and the name of Oxford now referred equally to both components. It was a name the Elizabethans festooned with garlands.

CHAPTER 2

Our Most Noble Athens:
Renaissance and Royal Capital

By the time of Elizabeth Oxford appears to have learned the lesson of the Norman Conquest, that Englishmen need governors. It endeavoured to supply them on national lines by becoming the nursery of the rich.
—Seccombe and Scott, *In Praise of Oxford* (1910–11)

THE RIPPLES PROPELLED by the Renaissance of arts and learning in southern Europe spread slowly northwards, only reaching Oxford during the late fifteenth century. The city's first printing-press was set up in 1487, around which time humanist scholars such as John Colet, William Grocyn and Thomas Linacre were establishing reputations as authoritative interpreters of classical writings. Thomas More, who studied with Grocyn and Linacre, was another follower of the new learning associated with Oxford towards the end of the century, and when the influential Dutch scholar Desiderius Erasmus visited the city, he was deeply impressed with the learning he encountered. He had only gone to Oxford out of frustration at not getting to Italy, but in a letter of 1499 he expressed few regrets: 'I have found in Oxford so much polish and learning', he wrote, 'that now I hardly care about going to Italy at all.' He was full of admiration for the state of studies, 'not of the usual pedantic and trivial kind either, but profound and learned and truly classical'. The resurgence of learning that so impressed Erasmus did not last, however, for with the religious turmoil of the mid–sixteenth century there was a return to the orthodox medieval scholarship of just the type that he disparaged.

It was not until the reign of Elizabeth I brought more settled times to the country that the spirit of inquiry again swept through the university, furthered by the Protestant emphasis on individual thought and experience. The age was characterised by an artistic and cultural flowering whose air of optimistic expansionism was exemplified in the voyages of discovery described in *Principall Navigations* (1589) by Richard Hakluyt, teacher of geography at Christ Church. His book was just one of several contemporary examples of the rewriting of England in these years, as writers seized on the interrupted reformation of Henry VIII to fashion the imaginative superstructure of a nation-state. The transfer of allegiance from pope to crown meant a reassessment of the national identity, and it was left to a remarkable generation of men to shape the emerging consciousness—writers like Spenser, Sidney, Camden, Drayton, Shakespeare, all born within fifteen years of each other, who adapted the classical models they were schooled in to promote and glorify Englishness. And the leaky structure of the Elizabethan church, patched together as it was with compromise, was shored up by a member of the same generation, the theologian Richard Hooker, who provided in his prose classic, *Of the Laws of Ecclesiastical Politie* (1593–97), an ideological defence against the Puritans.

The university itself was also much affected by the changing times, for Renaissance notions concerning 'the complete man' had led the Tudor gentry to look beyond private tutors for the education of their sons and to turn to the country's two universities. As a result students like Philip Sidney, Walter Raleigh and John Donne, true Renaissance figures, joined the clerical seminarists hoping to work their way up through the church orders. For their part colleges made efforts to adapt to these more prestigious students and to provide for the accomplishments of a gentleman by placing more emphasis on the humanities (as opposed to 'divinities'; the distinction from science came in the nineteenth century). Scholastic reasoning was played down, and greater weight given to linguistic and literary skills based on classical precepts: the course in Greats, or Literae Humaniores, dates from this time (Literae Humaniores, meaning 'more human(e) letters', comprised the study of classics). This accorded with Renaissance notions stressing the need for eloquence in order to express and exemplify the full range of human attributes. Though the changes in teaching methods were half-hearted and resisted by the theologically minded, the narrow clerical focus of the university was altered, and the institution wavered uncertainly between seminary and finishing school. Remarkably, the compromise proved viable enough to last some three hundred years, though it was not altogether satisfactory for either party. Secular students expressed distaste for the religious and medieval nature of their studies (the requirement for fellows to be in holy orders remained in force until the late nineteenth century), and writing in the sixteenth century John Aubrey commented, 'There is ample provision made in both our universities for the education of gentlemen of quality. Instead of giving them accomplishments (as required by Juvenal, Satire 14) they return home with the learning of a Benedictine monk, with some scholastic canting. Thus in lieu of giving him the breeding of a gentleman, he is sent home with that of a deacon.'

In addition to the change in the composition of its students, the Tudor university had also undergone a transformation in character to become a tightly run and college-based organisation. By Elizabeth's time supervision was constant, and movement beyond the college limits was firmly controlled. Magdalen and Brasenose had been the first to provide for complete in-house education, and Corpus Christi sought to isolate its members from contact with the town altogether. By a decree of 1576 every undergraduate had to be registered with a college tutor, and many students even shared rooms with their teachers. Such developments were necessitated partly by a rapid expansion in numbers and partly by the young age of freshmen, for although those studying for clerical orders might have been eighteen or over, the sons of gentry were barely past puberty—John Donne, for instance, entered Hart Hall at twelve. (Matriculation at such a young age evolved into the exception rather than the rule; Edward Gibbon was unusual in the eighteenth century in matriculating from Magdalen at fourteen.) In *The Compleat Gentleman* (1622), Henry Peacham observed, 'Parents take their sons from school, as birds out of the nest, ere they be flidge, and send them so young to the university that scarce one among them proveth aught. These young things of twelve, thirteen, or fourteen, have no more care, than to expect the next carrier, and where to sup on Fridays and fasting nights; no further thought of study, than to turn up their rooms with pictures, and place the fairest books in openest view, which, poor lads, they scarce ever open, and understand not.'

Compared with its medieval counterpart, the Elizabethan university was run in much closer alliance with the nation's ruling authorities, for not only had the establishment of a national church led to greater involvement of the state in university affairs, but leading secular figures often had a university education or connection. In their concern to tighten control of academic affairs, Tudor monarchs took advantage of the hierarchical nature of the college communities: 'The university was now, from the late sixteenth century onwards,' writes Pantin, 'to be governed by a tight little body of heads of houses, senior, safe, amenable men, sometimes themselves Crown nominees.' Royal recognition of the part played by the universities in the life of the nation came with the four official visits made by Elizabeth to Oxford and Cambridge (two to each). The occasions were joyous affairs, marked by festivities, speeches, plays and pageantry, and on her second visit to Oxford the aging queen underscored the university's royal connections by staying in Christ Church, the college founded by her father. The visit was particularly emotional, for there was genuine affection between 'Gloriana' and her academic subjects, and it was described by Anthony Wood in an account that in its final valedictory contains an often-repeated quotation.

In the afternoon she left Oxford, and going through Fishstreet to Quatrevois, and thence to the East Gate, received the hearty wishes (mixt with
tears) of the people; and casting her eyes on the walls of St. Mary's Church,
All Souls, University and Magdalen Colleges, which were mostly hung with
Verses and emblematical expressions of Poetry, was often seen to give gra-
cious nods to the Scholars. When she came to Shotover Hill (the utmost
confines of the University) those Doctors and Masters that brought her in,
she graciously received a farewell oration from one of them in the name of
the whole University. Which being done, she gave them many thanks, and
her hand to kiss: and then looking wistfully towards Oxford, said to this
effect in the Latin Tongue: 'Farewell, farewell, dear Oxford, God bless
thee, and increase thy sons in number, holiness and virtue, etc.'

SEAT OF THE ENGLISH MUSES

In 1586 the antiquary and historian William Camden (1551–1623) published in his *Britannia* a myth-making passage about Oxford containing
some portentous language. The book was a huge success (six different
editions appeared in Camden's lifetime), and was indicative of the Elizabethan urge to look afresh at the temporal world. This was coupled with
patriotic pride in a small and defiant country which had bravely stood up
for truth against the might of the Roman church and its powerful war-
lord, the king of Spain. The celebratory instincts of the age can be
sensed in the lengthy subtitle of Camden's book which begins 'A choro-
graphicall description of the most flourishing Kingdomes of England,
Scotland, and Ireland . . .'. Amongst the jewels in the country's treasury
Oxford is singled out as the prize of the collection: 'Where the Cherwell
flows along with the Isis,' begins his peroration,

> and their divided streams make several little sweet and pleasant islands, is
> seated on a rising vale the most famous University of Oxford, in Saxon
> Oxenford, our most noble Athens, the seat of the English Muses, the prop
> and pillar, nay the sun, the eye, the very soul of the nation; the most cele-
> brated fountain of wisdom and learning, from whence Religion, Letters
> and Good Manners, are happily diffused thro' the whole Kingdom.

Camden's choice of vocabulary with its sense of vitality and invitation
to partake in the communal good fortune speaks of a fresh, new vision of
Oxford. An 'English Athens' was no slight appellation, for the Renaissance age viewed Athens of the fifth century B.C. with its explosion of
artistic, literary and philosophic creativity as the birthplace and bench-
mark of cultural achievement. In academic terms Aristotle reigned
supreme, and his works provided the basis of learning across the curriculum; such was his status that doctors at Padua, the most famous med-

ical school in Europe, had to swear an oath to him. The prestige of such Greek figures gave the name of Athens an aura of glamour, and the championing of an English equivalent formed part of the self-glorification of the age. The association with Oxford owed itself in large measure to the large number of Elizabethan intellectuals and writers with a university background. These included Richard Hakluyt and the poet-statesman Philip Sidney, while among the 'university wits' active in the literary world, particularly the theatre, were Oxford-educated men like Robert Greene, John Lyly, Barnabe Barnes, Richard Barnfield and Thomas Lodge. Such writers enhanced Oxford's literary renown and fostered its reputation as a seat of creativity. Yet what could be said of Oxford could also be said of Renaissance Cambridge, which made no less a contribution to the nation's stock of literary talent and in the person of Christopher Marlowe had produced a genius of the stage and master of the 'mighty line'. The appropriation by Oxford of the title of 'the English Athens' would appear, then, to owe itself to self-congratulation, for Camden was himself a Christ Church man (though it is uncertain whether he ever graduated), and his use of the term reflected pride in his *alma mater* and in fellow scholars such as Sir Philip Sidney with whom he was friendly.

London at this time was a great trading and commercial centre, and the city is estimated to have been ten times bigger than any other English town. The population had more than doubled since the time of Henry VIII to nearly two hundred thousand, and the headlong expansion had led to housing spilling out beyond the limits of the City. For the thousands of migrants fleeing rural poverty, London offered the chance for worldly success, symbolised by the great ships plying back and forth along the Thames. Significantly, the story of Dick Whittington with its streets of gold dates from the late sixteenth century and indicates the town's mercantile character. For Chaucer's contemporary John Gower, it had been a Troy without the heroes, and the opportunities for wealth made it as much a city of capital as a capital city. By contrast Oxford had a spiritual aspect as a centre of Christianity, and in the cloistral atmosphere lies the key to its idealisation in Elizabethan times, for university studies remained a holy enterprise which was believed to lead scholars closer to the divine truth. This was reflected in the organisation of learning, with theology representing the highest of the faculties, to which all others were a preliminary. The layout of the Bodleian court (1613–24) reproduces the system in physical form, for the Divinity School at the far end from the entrance-arch is only reached after passing the various schools ranged on either side. Writing in earlier times, John Wyclif had referred to Oxford as 'a vineyard of the Lord', a notion which privileged

the university as divinely appointed, and Camden added to this a cultural
dimension influenced by the classical revival and the new learning. His
English Athens thus comprised two different elements, drawing on both
the Christian tradition and the Greek inheritance. By uniting in this way
the Hebraic and the Hellenic strands of the national culture, he was able
to present Oxford as the 'soul of the nation'. The phrase may owe itself
to a rhetorical flourish, but it marks a radical shift in perception, for the
medieval and clerical centre of learning is here reimagined as the spiritual heart of England. It was some time before others realised the enor-
mity of the trope.

The defeat of the Spanish Armada in 1588 brought in the minds of
Elizabethans an even closer identification with ancient Greece, for the
country rejoiced in a mood of exaltation similar to that of Athens in the
post–Persian War period. The city-state and the nation-state had both
overcome powerful enemies and both believed themselves to have
played the part of heroic saviour—Athens of Hellas, and England of
Protestantism. Drawing inspiration from Seneca and Aristotle, Elizabethan authors found new modes of literary expression, and in 'Defence
of Poesie' (1595) Edmund Spenser expounded the neo-Platonic view
that poetry could speak to a 'golden' world of goodness and beauty. The
sunny, springtime nature of the literature with its new-found sense of
communality yielded potent new images as patriotic sentiments found
outlet in works which pictured the country in ideal terms. For their part
in furthering the nation's well-being the universities too were showered
with tributes, and in a verse by the obscure Dan Rogers Oxford was given
the ultimate sanctification.

> He that hath Oxford seen, for beauty, grace
> And healthiness ne'er saw a better place.
> If God Himself on earth abode would make
> He Oxford, sure, would for his dwelling take.

In the *Faerie Queene* Edmund Spenser took the opportunity to celebrate
the country's universities in a rousing couplet which favoured Oxford—
'Ioy to you both, ye double noursery / Of Arts, but Oxford thine doth
Thame most glorify'. In Michael Drayton's *Polyolbion* in the early seventeenth century the glorification was taken a step further. Like *Britannia*,
Polyolbion was intended to awaken readers to the glories of their country,
and Drayton invests Oxford with the grandeur and mystique of Greek
myth.

> Renowned Oxford built to Apollo's learned brood;
> And on the hallowed bank of Isis' goodly flood,
> Worthy the glorious arts, did gorgeous bowers provide.

Drayton's 'gorgeous bowers' could be set alongside Greene's 'lordly' buildings, for though he was writing of the medieval university in *Frier Bacon, and Frier Bongay*, Robert Greene undoubtedly had Elizabethan Oxford in mind when claiming 'That lordly are the buildings of the town, / Spacious the rooms and full of pleasant walks.' The pleasing look of Oxford played an important part in fostering the construct of the English Athens, for during the Tudor period the townscape had undergone a striking transformation. This was initiated by the building of Magdalen College in 1474, and the impressive new college was soon followed by two further foundations, Corpus Christi and Christ Church. John Lyly, who studied at both Oxford and Cambridge, compared the two towns in his popular *Euphues* (1578), in which he commented 'that Colledges in *Oxenford* are much more stately for the building, and *Cambridge* much more sumptuous for the houses in the towne'. The Bodleian with its elegant classical edifice was a particularly striking addition to Oxford's architecture, and the library was lionised in verse by two former students: Henry Vaughan extolled the immortality of Bodley, 'for every book is thy large epitaph', while Abraham Cowley made use of Camden's imagery to declare the Bodleian 'the Tree of Knowledge' set in the midst of 'the Muses' Paradise'.

Such was the mood of the times that Robert Burton, writing from his study in the 'royal and ample foundation' of Christ Church, was able to preface *The Anatomy of Melancholy* (1621) with the presumption that he was writing in 'the most flourishing college of Europe'. For all his inclination to melancholy Burton (1577–1640) was a sociable college man, and the preface of his book suggests that he was much taken with his insular lifestyle. Adopting the nearby meadows as his groves, he assumes citizenship of an English Athens and styles himself Democritus Junior after the Greek thinker (known as the 'laughing philosopher' because of the amusement he found in the follies of mankind).

> I am not poor, I am not rich; *nihil est, nihil deest,* I have little, I want nothing: all my treasure is in Minerva's tower. . . . I live still a collegiate student, as Democritus in his garden, and lead a monastic life, *ipse mihi theatrum,* sequestered from those tumults and troubles of the world, *Et tanquam in specula positus* (as he said), in some high place above you all, like Stoicus Sapiens, *omnia saecula, praeterita praesentiaque videns, uno velut intuitu,* I hear and see what is done abroad, how others run, ride, turmoil and macerate themselves in court and country, far from those wrangling lawsuits, *aulæ vanitatem, fori ambitionem, ridere mecum soleo.*

Though posing as one who owns little and wants nothing, the privileged Burton presents a startlingly different picture to that of Chaucer's Nicholas in his town lodgings. Buttressed behind the Christ Church walls, the philosopher pictures himself looking down from above on the common tumult, and his description exudes a strong sense of insulation. The division between an inside world of monastic calm and an outside of pointless tumult testifies to the centrality of the college in the English Athens and the concomitant exclusivity.

The making of an English Athens would have been unthinkable in a period lacking Elizabethan bravura, and the concept owes itself to the enormous self-belief of the times. The formation of myths is often associated with the inception of civilisations or cultural periods, and Elizabethan writers had a strong sense of new beginnings. For Northrop Frye 'literature is a reconstructed mythology', a phrase which seems particularly apt in terms of Camden and his concern to give imaginative expression to the nation's hunger for heroic imagery. Elizabeth Goudge's historical romance of Elizabethan Oxford, *Towers in the Mist* (1938), captures the prevailing sense of optimism, and the city her dewy-eyed book evokes is one where medieval superstition sits alongside Renaissance celebration; where sorcery holds sway and the waters of Frideswide's well are believed to remove pock-marks; where sons of the gentry study and sleep alongside servitors (poor students who work their way through university); and where amongst the students are the likes of Philip Sidney, Fulke Greville and Walter Raleigh. The plot centres around the faithful Faithful, an earnest servitor at Christ Church who, like Chaucer's Clerk, is willing to sacrifice all for the love of learning. In contrast to those around him who enjoy a life of ease and luxury, Faithful endures harsh conditions and has to work long hours at the beck and call of wealthy students. The book ends with the queen's visit to Oxford and Elizabeth taking fond leave from Shotover Hill. Under her enlightened rule Oxford had been transformed from a strife-torn town of martyrs to 'seat of the English Muses', and her reception in the city was rapturous. 'Farewell,' she declares looking back at the city, 'farewell, dear Oxford, God bless thee, and increase thy sons in number, holiness and virtue'. The next age was to disappoint her on all three counts.

A YOUNG GENTLEMAN AND OTHER CHARACTERS

In 1614 there appeared a collection of essays known as the 'Overburian Characters' after Sir Thomas Overbury (1581–1613), one-time student at Queen's and friend of Ben Jonson. The essays were first published in an appendix to the second edition of his book *A Wife* and were collectively credited to Overbury and friends. The fashion for writing characters, initiated by a translation of Theophrastus in 1592, involved short, pointed descriptions of a character-type; the skill lay in the eloquence,

wit, and choice of detail. Amongst Overbury's succinct and satirical characters there are a number of academics whose titles speak for themselves: 'A Puny Clerk'; 'A Pedant'; 'A meere Fellow of an House'; and 'A
Meere Scholler'. The latter is 'an intelligible Asse' who believes himself
always right and is so long-winded that he is 'able to speak more with
ease, then any man can endure to heare with patience'. Above all he
loves to talk of his academic standing: 'The Antiquity of his University is
his Creed, and the excellency of his Colledge (though but for a match at
Foot-ball) an Article of his faith.' He is in short 'the Index of a man, and
the Title-page of a Scholler, or a Puritane in morality, much in profes-
sion, nothing in practise.' The 'meere Fellow of an House' fares little
better, for he is socially inept, conversationally incompetent, and so intellectually arrogant that he 'laughs to thinke what a foole he could make
of *Salomon*'. Taken all in all, he is one who 'respects no man in the Universitie, and is respected by no man out of it'. Overbury's satire is
informed by a distaste for the scholastic atmosphere at Oxford, and he is
keen to emphasise the lack of gentlemanly manners. This is particularly
clear in the Fellow's inability to relate to members of the opposite sex:
'Hee is never more troubled, then when he is to maintaine talk with a
Gentle-woman: wherein hee commits more absurdities, then a clowne in
eating of an egge.'

Fourteen years after the publication of the 'Overburian Characters'
there came a retort by John Earle (1601?–65), a fellow of Merton concerned to defend the university. His *Microcosmographie* (1628) proved a
popular work, prized for its wit, veracity, and insight, and the book opens
up a whole gallery of university portraits which range from 'A Plodding
Student' to 'A Pretender to Learning' and 'An Old Colledge Butler'.
Earle even includes amongst his Oxford figures 'An Universitie Dunne',
the debt-collector for town businesses. In opposition to Overbury's 'A
Meere Scholler', Earle presents 'A Downe-Right Scholler' who is blessed
with a rich inner life despite his lack of social refinements—'His smacking of a Gentle-woman is somewhat too savory, & hee mistakes her nose
for her lippe'—but in contrast to Overbury, the wit is more affectionate
than bitter.

Amongst his collection of portraits Earle introduces a relative newcomer to Oxford literature—'A Young Gentleman of the University'.
Drawn from the ranks of the gentry, the Young Gentleman has money in
abundance and a secure career ahead of him. He is sent to Oxford not
so much to study but

> to weare a gown, and to say hereafter, he has beene at the University. His
> Father sent him thither, because he heard there were the best Fencing and

> Dancing schooles. His main loytering is at the Library, where he studies
> Armes and Bookes of Honour, and turnes a Gentleman-Critick in Pedi-
> grees. Of all things hee endures not to bee mistaken for a Scholler, and
> hates a black suit though it bee of Satin.

With his flash clothes, loud manner, and idle habits, the 'Young Gentleman' threatens to elbow aside the likes of 'A Plodding Student' and 'A
Meere Scholler', whose dull lifestyles can hardly compete with his own eye-
catching antics. His real-life counterpart proved the cause of much resentment among the studious and scholarly, and intermittent expressions of
frustration make themselves heard in the literature of the times. As early
as 1549 Bishop Latimer had lamented of Cambridge that '[the Devil] gets
him to the University. He causeth great men and esquires to send their
sons thither and put out poor scholars that should be divines.' The influx
of the rich was also held responsible for an increase in corruption and a
fall in standards, and in *The Anatomy of Abuses* (1583) Philip Stubbes, graduate of Worcester College, made a stinging attack on the colleges.

> Whereas they were given to maintaine none but the poore only, now they
> maintaine none but the rich onely. For except one be able to give the
> regent or provost of the house a piece of mony, ten pound, twentie pound,
> fortie pound, yea, a hundred pound, a yoke of fatte oxen, or a couple of
> fine geldings, or the like, though he be never so toward a youth, nor have
> never so much need of maintenance, yet he comes not there I warrant
> him.

The declamation stands in opposition to the fulsome praise by the poets
of the time, and the period as a whole is characterised by its vigorous mix
of adulation and condemnation. While Oxford is being extolled on the
one hand as 'the most celebrated fountain of wisdom', it is being
denounced on the other because 'for double fees / A Dunce may
become a Doctor'. Hidden from the light of learning in the English
Athens there apparently lay dark corners of privilege and corruption.

'A Young Gentleman' is not the only newcomer whom Earle introduces, for amongst his other Characters is that favourite figure of Oxford
literature—the scholarly eccentric. 'The Hermitage of Study' runs the
title of the essay, though it is worth noting that the hermitage in question
was generally of short duration, for college fellowship constituted a step
towards work in the wider world. The extraordinary eccentrics of later
centuries enjoyed the advantage of a much longer hermitage, and Earle
here explains the nature of their peculiarity.

> The time ha's got a veine of making him ridiculous, and men laugh at him
> by tradition, and no unlucky absurdity; but is put upon his profession, and
> done like a Scholler. But his fault is only this, that his mind is somewhat

too much taken up with his minde, and his thoughts not loaden with any carriage besides. The Hermitage of his Study, ha's made him somewhat uncouth in the world, and men make him worse by staring on him. Thus is he silly and ridiculous, and it continues with him for some quarter of a yeere, out of the Universitie. But practise him a little in men, and brush him o're with good company, an hee shall out-ballance those glisterers as farre as a solid substance do's a feather, or Gold Gold-lace.

John Aubrey (1626–97) was a man well-acquainted with scholarly eccentricity. His antiquarian studies were wide-ranging but undisciplined, his biographies gossipy and anecdotal, and his lack of worldly concern such that he went bankrupt and spent the last twenty years of his life an itinerant guest in friends' houses. The idiosyncratic *Brief Lives* was compiled centuries after his death from the mass of material he left behind. Aubrey first went to Oxford as a student at Trinity in 1642 but was soon forced to leave by the Civil War. Later he resumed his studies, and his brief autobiographical account tells of golden days.

I (for the most part) enjoyed the greatest felicity of my life (ingenious youths, as rosebuds, imbibe the morning dew) till December 1648 I was sent for from Oxford home again to my sick father, who never recovered.

Though unable to complete his degree, Aubrey retained a lifelong affection for his 'beloved Oxford' and made frequent return visits, when he would meet with Anthony Wood, for whose *Athenae Oxonienses* the bulk of his *Lives* were written. The biographical pieces provide illuminating glimpses of the seventeenth-century university. Amongst the 'frolics' of the time were drinking, wenching, gambling, and walking the fifty-eight miles to London—and back! For Sir Henry Blount the chief thing learnt at the universities was debauchery—'Drunkenness he much exclaimed against, but he allowed wenching'—while the poet John Denham, who spent his student days gambling, was so pressed for money that he even staked his father's wrought gold cups. The sonneteer of Great Tom, Richard Corbet, was apparently a cleric of practical as well as witty jokes, for he cut holes in the silk stockings of a sleeping friend in a tavern at Friar Bacon's study, while on another occasion at Abingdon cross he put on a ballad-singer's leather jacket and performed before the passing throng. And in an episode which highlights the boarding-school nature of the university, a certain Dr. Potter was so prone to beating that he even whipped a student who had come merely to take his leave!

Of all Aubrey's Oxford characters the most striking is undoubtedly Ralph Kettell (1563–1643), president of Trinity. A martinet in disciplinary matters, Kettell would peep in through keyholes to see if students were studying and referred to the lazy by a variety of colourful terms—

Turds, Tarrarags, Rascal Jacks, Blindcinques, and Scobberlotchers. He disliked long hair and carried scissors in his muff ready to snip at hirsute students, though 'like a rattlesnake' he dragged his left foot, which gave warning of his coming. He also had a generous heart, for he left money anonymously inside the windows of poorer students and supported servitors by offering them work. His sermons attracted large audiences, who came in expectation of the unexpected; a verbal lashing perhaps for the college fellows for their helpings of double-beer, or a wilful misreference to Sir Thomas Pope as 'confounder' (instead of co-founder) of the college.

Aubrey's contemporary, the diarist John Evelyn (1620–1706), studied at Balliol and also recorded his impressions of Oxford, and as with *Brief Lives,* the incidentals of his account provide an insight into the nature of the university. For those like Evelyn of antiquarian tastes the city was a veritable treasure-trove, and the young student (sixteen and a half) spent the whole of his first week inspecting archives and examining college architecture. Thereafter his *Diary* tells of declamations in chapel, public disputations in hall, and the first college member, a Greek, to be seen drinking coffee (harbinger of the coffee-house culture of eighteenth-century Oxford: Anthony Wood noted the opening of a coffee house in 1650 by 'Jacob the Jew', though the mania for coffee-drinking did not develop until after 1688). Evelyn also lends support to the jibes of Earle and Overbury concerning the preoccupation of dons with college intrigue in the account he gives of his tutor.

> I ever thought my Tutor had parts enough; but as his ambition (& I fear vices) made him very much suspected of the Colledg; so his grudg to the Governor of it Dr. Lawrence (whom he afterwards supplanted) tooke up so much of his tyme, that he seldom, or never had any opportunity to discharge his duty to his Scholars.

Like Aubrey who talks of 'serene peace', Evelyn portrays pre–Civil War Oxford in idyllic terms as if looking back wistfully to the calm before the storm. Even a figure of different persuasions, the Puritan poet George Wither (1588–1667), conjures up a halcyon time in his ditty of dalliance on Port Meadow—'In summer time to Medley, / My love and I would go'. There by the banks of the Thames the couple indulge in cream, cake and, unexpectedly, prunes. It is to Wither too that is owed a rare glimpse of the state of studies, for in *Abuses Stript and Whipt* (1613) he gives a facetious verse account of his student days which reflect none too well on the 'wholesome nursery of wit'. The teaching had reverted to explications of Duns Scotus, and Wither's tutor did little to clarify matters—'For I his meaning did no more conjecture / Than if he had been reading Hebrew Lecture.' Shamed into studying by the progress of his fellow students, the poet claims facetiously to have made up for his initial slowness by pursuing rhetoric, philosophy, metaphysics, and sophistry with such diligence that in disputations 'When I opposed the Truth, I could out-face her.'

The state of teaching had been a matter of concern for some time, and Wither was by no means the first to complain of the retrograde state of studies. Even in Elizabethan times when Oxford was first being hailed as the English Athens, John Lyly countered his laudation of the university in the *Euphues* with a passage in which he describes it as characterised by

> such playing at dice, such quaffing of drinke, such dalyaunce with woe-men, such daunsing, that in my opinion ther is no quaffer in *Flaunders* so giuen to typplynge, no courtier in *Italy* so giuen to ryotte, no creature in the world so misled as a student in *Athens*. Such a confusion of degrees, that the Scholler knoweth not his duetie to the Bachelor, nor the Bachelor to the Maister, nor the Maister to the Doctor. Such corruption of manners, contempt then Philosophy, what scholler is hee that is so zealous at his booke as *Chrisippus*, who, had not his maide Melissa thrust meate into his mouth hadde perished with famine, beeinge alwaye studying?

The uproar at this was such that Lyly was led to affix an 'Address to my good friends, the Gentlemen Scholars of Oxford' to a second edition in which he disingenuously claimed that he was not writing of Oxford at all (it has been suggested that the attack was motivated by personal spite against the dons of Magdalen). Nonetheless, the *Annals* of Anthony Wood lend credence to Lyly's complaints, for there are repeated references to complaints of drinking, gaming, smoking, irreverence, and neglect between the 1580s and 1620s. It was in the early seventeenth century too that the father of Edward Hyde (later earl of Clarendon) withdrew his son from the university because of 'the custom of drinking being too much introduced and practised'.

The official response to such misconduct came in 1636 in the form of a revision of the university statutes by Archbishop Laud, chancellor of the university. The new rules placed restrictions on every aspect of university life, including behaviour, dress, and entertainment. 'Neither rope-dancers nor players (who go on the stage for gain's sake), nor sword-matches, or sword players are to be permitted', ran the injunctions, which also banned fraternisation with townspeople: 'Scholars shall not idle and wander about the City, or its suburbs, nor in the streets, or public market, or Carfax (at Penniless Bench as they commonly call it) nor be seen standing or loitering about the townsmen or worksmen shops'. Infringement of such injunctions carried severe penalties, including public flogging, and the statutes for the first time expressed in writing what already existed in practice, for power was officially transferred to the small group of college heads. Given the indiscipline which prompted such measures, it is perhaps not surprising to learn from Aubrey that an alternative university of sorts existed at Great Tew, where the amiable Lucius Carey, Viscount Falkland (1610–43)—for Robert Graves, 'the most sympathetic character of that period'—held open house for the leading intellectuals of the day. The hospitality was generous, the company genial, the conversation wide-ranging and free-flowing. Academics went about their studies, according to Clarendon, 'as in a college situated in a purer air', and dons like John Earle mixed with men of state like Edward Hyde and poets such as Ben Jonson, Edmund Waller and John Suckling. It is a reminder of how intellectual life flourished outside the stultifying boarding-house atmosphere at Oxford during much of the seventeenth and eighteenth centuries, a point made by Gibbon in his *Memoirs*.

The liberal atmosphere at Great Tew contrasted with the bitter divisions in the rest of the country, and when the religious and political dissensions erupted into Civil War, Oxford was plummeted into the very midst of the fray, for Charles I declared it his royal capital after being forced to flee from London. The small university city with its academic intriguers and eccentric scholars, its clerical trainees and gentlemen of fashion, its theologians and debauchees, its bachelor young fellows and married heads, its obscure townsmen and obscurer women, found itself all at once a frontline garrison. The monastical college buildings in which had once ruminated retiring scholars like Robert Burton now had to serve the military purpose for which their sturdy walls and crenellated rooftops seemed only too well designed. For four long years Athena put aside the patronage of learning and donned the outfit of warrior.

REBELLION, RESTORATION, AND THE LIFE OF ANTHONY WOOD

Forced to flee London by his unruly subjects, Charles I settled on the royal foundation of Christ Church as his new residence, and within the donnish surrounds of the academic college the king held court, dined in state, and received foreign ambassadors. When the queen came to join him, she occupied nearby Merton, and to provide access for the royal couple a gateway was knocked through the wall of a Corpus Christi garden. The university city had the advantage to the king of providing a compact group of large buildings which could be relatively easily defended, and work began on transforming the scholarly surrounds into a military garrison.

College rooms were commandeered for the royal retinue, university troops paraded on Christ Church Meadow, and streets that had once accommodated the unhurried feet of leisurely academics resounded to the clatter of cavalry. Corn was stored in the law and logic schools, military clothing in the music and astronomy schools, and the royal mint set up in New Inn Hall, for which college plate was appropriated. Rocks were hauled to the top of Magdalen Tower ready to hurl at attackers, and the cloister of New College was used as a magazine. The character of the small town was completely transformed as college gown gave way to military uniform and students of theology were replaced by rough young footsoldiers. Such was the disruption that Aubrey claims it hastened the death of Ralph Kettell: 'Tis probable this venerable doctor might have lived some years longer, and finished his century, had not those civil wars come on; which much grieved him, that was wont to be absolute in the college, to be affronted and disrespected by rude soldiers.'

'Never perhaps has there existed so curious a spectacle as Oxford presented in these days', writes Cecil Headlam: 'A city unique in itself . . . became the resort of a court under unique circumstances, and of an innumerable throng of people of every rank, disposition and taste, under circumstances the most extraordinary and romantic.' Given this assessment by a historian, it is hardly surprising that the period should be a favourite for novelists. *The Scholar and the Trooper* (Heygate, 1858) and *With the King at Oxford* (Church, 1885) are two early examples, and Robert Graves also covered the period in *Wife to Mr. Milton* (1943). The long middle section of Joseph Henry Shorthouse's religious novel *John Inglesant* (1880) contains a description of Civil War Oxford, though the reader has to accompany the eponymous hero on his religious odyssey to Rome and back. To be set against such historical fiction are the contemporary accounts of chroniclers who witnessed the effects of the war at first hand. These include Edward Hyde (1609–74), more famous as the earl of Clarendon, who wrote the monumental *The True Historical Narrative of the Rebellion and Civil Wars in England* (printed posthumously 1702–4). Clarendon was one of the king's closest advisors and part of the inner circle which met every Friday in Oriel College. Between 1642 and 1645 he was resident in All Souls and raised a huge loan (ten thousand pounds) from the university in support of the king. A moderate by nature, he possessed a generosity of spirit which is reflected in the sympathetic portraits of his contemporaries, even of enemies such as Fairfax. His connection with the university was renewed after the Restoration when he became chancellor, and the proceeds from his monumental *History* helped fund the press and institute in Oxford which still bear his name.

In contrast to the measured and dignified tones of Clarendon, the writings of Anthony Wood reveal a vitriolic son of Oxford concerned with the ravages of war on his native town. Though his niche in the national pantheon may be small, over Oxford Wood casts a giant shadow. Not only did he publish the first comprehensive history of the university together with biographies of Oxford notables, but at his death he left behind a mass of writings which provide a fascinating record of the age (edited in five volumes by Andrew Clark 1891–1900). Born in Postmasters' Hall opposite Merton, Wood was at New College School when war broke out and later wrote of gazing from the college cloisters at soldiers drilling in the quadrangle. When the school was requisitioned for munitions, his mother sent him to Thame, from where he followed the king's fortunes for the rest of the war.

After the decisive battle of Naseby in June 1645, Charles withdrew to Oxford, where he was slowly encircled. Meadows were flooded, houses pulled down, and the surroundings burnt. It was all to little avail, and when nearby Woodstock fell on April 26, 1646, it was clear that the end was imminent. The next day, disguised as a servant with false hair and beard, the king escaped from the city accompanied by two companions. (Charles was not Oxford's first royal escapee: in 1142 Matilda had been besieged by her cousin Stephen in the castle and was forced to flee across the frozen moat with three of her knights dressed in white.) Without the presence of the king, the city's garrison did not hold out for long, and Oxford's time as royal capital came to an end. The royalist Wood makes little reference to the defeat, offering instead a piece of telling hearsay.

> On June 24, Oxford was surrendered by the King's command. The scholars and soldiers of the garrison were deeply grieved, and indignantly declared that 'the City would never have been given up, had not the ladies etc. of the Court required fresh butter for their early peas'.

Thanks to the magnanimity of the victors, Oxford survived its military flirtation with the minimum of damage, and Aubrey noted gratefully that the first act of Fairfax on occupying the town was to despatch soldiers to guard the Bodleian. Nonetheless, as Wood notes, after four years of neglect and occupation the colleges were dilapidated and the students 'debauch'd by bearing armes and doing the duties belonging to soldiers, as watching, warding, and sitting in tipling-houses'. In the wake of defeat came a Puritan visitation, and Wood himself was one of those summoned to attend. In his account of the affair may be seen the contrariness that makes him such an intriguing personality.

Friday (May 12 [1648]) the members of Merton college appear'd, and when A.W. was call'd in (for the members were called in one by one) he was ask'd this question by one of the visitors: 'Will you submit to the authority of parliament in this visitation?' To which he gave this answer, and wrot downe on a paper, lying on the table, as he was directed: 'I do not understand the business, and therefore I am not able to give a direct answer.'

Afterwards his mother and brother Edward, who advised him to submit in plaine termes, were exceeding angry with him, and told him, that he had ruined hmself, and must therfore go a begging. At length, by the intercession of his mother made to Sr. Nathan Brent (who usually cal'd her his little daughter, for he knew her, and us'd to set her on his knee, when shee was a girle and a sojournour in her husband's house, during the time of his first wife) he was conniv'd at and kept in his place, otherwise he had infallibly gon to the pot.

Though Wood himself was saved from the 'pot', his brother was suspended as fellow of Merton for drinking the king's health at Medley and entertaining guests with 'excessive' wine. In the face of such attitudes there was considerable Puritan hostility to the university, compounded by a distaste for the lax state of teaching. The Cambridge-educated John Milton, for example, familiar with Oxford through his marriage to Mary Powell of Forest Hill, made a virulent attack in *Of Education* (1644) on the two English universities for teaching 'pure trifling at Grammar and Sophistry' based on 'the Scholastick grossness of barbarous ages'. For the Digger Gerard Winstanley, the universities were pools of 'stinking water' with the potential to poison society at large. Even the royalist sympathiser Thomas Hobbes, a former student of Magdalen Hall, was scathing about the neglect of practical studies in *The Leviathan* (1651).

'After all this,' writes A.L. Rowse, 'surprising as it may seem, we are on the threshold of the most brilliant decade, intellectually, that Oxford has ever enjoyed, especially in the realm of science.' The city was host during the 1650s to a group of remarkable figures, and when John Evelyn made a visit in 1654 he was most impressed with the men of learning he met. These included 'that most obliging & universaly Curious' Dr. Wilkins, the warden of Wadham in whose rooms gathered the nucleus of the future Royal Society, and 'that prodigious young Scholar' Christopher Wren, an astronomer and geometrician who only practised architecture as a sideline. Also in Oxford at this time was Robert Boyle of Boyle's Law fame, who according to Aubrey constituted one of the city's main attractions for visitors. Helping him was Robert Hooke, also a scientist of exceptional talents who first identified the living cell, and the collaboration of the two men led to the devising of the first air pump. (A plaque by University College in the High Street marks the site of the laboratory where the law was first formulated. The area now houses Shelley's Memorial (1894), perhaps not inappropriately given the young poet's passion for chemistry.)

Anthony Wood with his 'insatiable desire of knowledge' was also active in the 1650s, and in his burrowings amongst the Bodleian archives he came across over sixty volumes of neglected manuscripts which excited the young scholar to formulate the most ambitious of plans—a comprehensive survey of Oxford consisting of three aspects: the city with its churches, parishes, and religious houses; the colleges and halls, with their individual histories and buildings; and the central university with its composition and development. Working from the upstairs garret of Postmasters' Hall, Wood spent the rest of his life collecting information relating to Oxford. According to Thomas Hearne (1678–1735), who inherited Wood's mantel, he was such a 'wonderful pryer, that he used to go out by himself in by-places, wore his hat over his eyes, seem'd to take notice of nothing and to know nothing, and yet he took notice of every thing and knew every thing'.

In spite of all his achievements, Wood was a prickly character who grew more quarrelsome with age. His contemporary Humphrey Prideaux considered him a 'good bowzeing blad' in his youth, but as the *Life* progresses his well-being seems to deteriorate. There are grumblings about his health, problems with his publications, and altercations with his contemporaries. He rails against the moral failings of the age, deplores the general fall in standards, and decries the increase in drinking. He finds the trend towards an upper-class university particularly distasteful.

> Poore folks' sons study hard, and with much adoe obtaine their degrees in Arts and a fellowship. But now noblemen's sons are *created* Artium Magistri for nothing; get fellowships and canonries for nothing, and deprive others more deserving of their bread.

As Wood delves ever deeper into the city's archives, he seems to lose his ability to relate to fellow human beings. He falls out with his patron Dr. Fell, the Dean of Christ Church, about the quality of the Latin translation of his book, and he even comes to blows with the translator. He notes without comment the remark of a friend that he 'never spoke well of any man', and, as if to prove the point, he writes bitter remarks about his acquaintances. William Sancroft is 'a clounish, odd fellow'. John Prideaux, respected rector of Exeter College, is 'an humble man, of plain and downright behaviour, careless of money and imprudent in worldly matters'. And John Aubrey, his close friend and collaborator, is a shiftless person, roving and magotie-headed, and somtimes little better than crased. And being exceedingly credulous, would stuff his many letters sent to A.W. with fooleries, and misinformations, which somtimes would guid him into the paths of errour.

The description was unkind even by Wood's standards. Aubrey was by all accounts a genial man, and according to his biographer, Anthony Powell, 'friendship was the essential basis of his life'. After the death of his mother Aubrey's first letter had been to Wood: 'Let me desire you to write to me by the next post to let me know how you doe', he entreated, 'Your letter will be a cordiall to me.' The expressions of friendship were unreserved: 'I long as it were with a woman's longing to see Oxford and you', Aubrey writes on one occasion. Yet in 1692, following the publication of the second volume of Wood's *Athenae Oxonienses,* there came a rift between the two men which led to Wood's venomous description and which was never resolved.

Wood's book had provoked an outcry in Oxford for its outspoken attacks on respected figures, and the author noted in his jottings that 'in New College common-chamber severall of the fellowes said that I had abused their relations and that when darke nights come they will beat me.' One person particularly outraged was the second earl of Clarendon, who objected to the passages below concerning his father (Charles II's lord chancellor):

> After the restoration of K. Charles II it was expected by all that he (Jenkyns) should be made one of the judges in Westminster hall, and so might he have been, would he have given mony to the then lord chancellor.

> After the restauration of K. Ch. II he [Glynne] was made his eldest serjeant at law by the corrupt dealing of the then lord chancellor.

Wood was taken to the vice-chancellor's court (the university retained separate jurisdiction up to the twentieth century), where he made the curious defence that there was no proof that he had written the offending passages, though his was the sole name on the cover of the book. He was found guilty, expelled from the university, and ordered to pay a fine. Wood blamed his disgrace on Aubrey, who had innocently supplied the misinformation about Clarendon, and he never forgave his former friend.

As his health worsened, Wood showed little sign of mellowing. He was incensed when he complained to a Dr. South of suppression of urine, to be told that if he could not make water, he should make earth (i.e., die). When his illness took a downturn, Wood was told to prepare for the end but refused to listen: 'He knew he was a dead man', wrote a Dr. Rawlinson, 'and that he had but a few days to live, notwithstanding which, he was then able (striking his cane with vehemence on the ground) to cane any man who should dare tell him that he was so.' The cantankerous chronicler of Oxford was buried in the north-east corner of Merton chapel, where, appropriately, his plaque looks across to that of Sir Thomas Bodley, whose benefaction he utilised to such good effect. Of the many tributes made to him, the most sympathetic came from Thomas Hearne, who matriculated in the year of Wood's death. 'Anthony', he wrote affectionately, 'aim'd to be a despiser of riches, to live independent and not to be afraid to die.' Hearne was not easily given to praise, but his portrait of Wood suggests the incarnation of Chaucer's saintly Clerk—'none was more studious, none more humble, none more virtuous'. He even finds merit in Wood's characteristic bluntness, claiming, 'He was equally regardless of envy or fame, out of his great love to truth, and therefore 'twas no wonder he tooke such a liberty of speech as most other authors, out of prudence, cunning or designe, have usually declined.' As a fellow archivist, Hearne clearly identified with his predecessor and exaggerated his merits, yet it is difficult not to share his admiration for the single-mindedness which Wood showed in his lifework. For a solitary academic working from scratch, his writings constitute an astonishing achievement, and in the words of Cecil Headlam he is a man 'to whose work every writer on Oxford owes a debt unpayable'.

Wood's *Life and Times* coincided with the most dramatic period in Oxford's history. As a child of four he saw Charles I visit Oxford; he survived the Puritan visitation and was active during that 'most brilliant decade' of the 1650s; he welcomed the Restoration and witnessed the university expansion of the late seventeenth century, when the Sheldonian, the Clarendon, and the Old Ashmolean were built. Among the events he recorded was the plague of 1665, when Charles II fled London as his father had done to go and live in Christ Church—the courtiers, Wood complained in typical fashion, were 'high, proud, insolent' and 'rude, rough, whoremongers'. In 1685 the scholar saw history repeat itself again when scholars trained once more as soldiers, ready to defend James against the Monmouth uprising. The university was less favourably disposed in 1687, however, for the fellows of Magdalen defied the king's demand that they appoint a Catholic as head of college and were promptly dismissed, though in a remarkable victory of college over king they succeeded in winning their reinstatement. Following the Bloodless Revolution the next year, Wood lived on to see the university enter a new age, though it was one which was left to the younger Hearne to record.

Despite the difficulties it had undergone, Oxford emerged from the trials of the seventeenth century with its status as the English Athens enhanced by royal association and men of brilliance. The summary verdict of Samuel Pepys after a day-tour on June 9, 1668, suggests the favourable impression the city made at this time: 'Oxford mighty fine place and well set and cheap entertainment.' The flourishing state of the university prompted the Cambridge-educated John Dryden (1631–1700) to declare 'Oxford's a place, where Wit can never sterve', and in a remarkable display of rhetorical apostasy (Dryden was a notorious trimmer) he even claimed to prefer it to his own university.

> *Oxford* to him a dearer Name shall be,
> Than his own Mother University.
> *Thebes* did his Green, unkowing Youth ingage,
> He chuses *Athens* in his Riper Age.

In a prologue, 'To the University of Oxon', the poet employed his studied eloquence and classical learning to flatter his audience by further exploiting the Athenian analogy, stating, 'Here too are Annual Rites to *Pallas* done, / And here Poetique prizes lost or won.' An epilogue Dryden wrote for an Oxford audience could well serve as epilogue to the age as a whole. It was spoken to Charles II at the opening of the Oxford playhouse (1681), and the poet describes the university as having emerged from stormy times into quieter waters.

> This Place the seat of Peace, the quiet Cell
> Where Arts remov'd from noisy business dwell,
> Shou'd calm your Wills, unite the jarring parts,
> And with a kind Contagion seize your hearts:
> Oh! may its Genius, like soft Musick move,
> And tune you all to Concord and to Love.
> Our Ark that has in Tempests long been tost,
> Cou'd never land on so secure a Coast.
> From hence you may look back on Civil Rage,
> And view the ruines of the former Age.

As rage gave way to reason, the academic community withdrew within the embrace of their college walls and settled into a more comfortable existence. Removed from the 'noisy business' of the outside world, the fellows were able to enjoy the pleasures of a civilized existence. From now on comfort ousts disruption and satisfaction replaces enthusiasm as the keynote of the writings. In place of passion, Oxford assumes an air of cosy isolationism. In contrast to the roller-coaster excitement of Wood's *Life and Times,* the next chapter in Oxford literature sees the English Athens sit back, well-fed, and rest on its laurels.

CHAPTER 3

Of Palaces and Petty Kings: Reason to Reform

*Academic seclusion has all the inconveniences of a desert island, with none of its
compensations: it breeds idleness, spite, intrigue, arrogance and strange lunacies.*
—C. Day Lewis and Charles Fenby, *Anatomy of Oxford* (1938)

IN 1710 A GERMAN rejoicing in the name of Zacharias Conrad von
Uffenbach visited Oxford but was unimpressed by the glories of which
he had read. The authorities were negligent, the fellows drunk, the
Bodleian empty, and the town unremarkable. It was an unflattering view,
but it was one shared by others, for after its brief renaissance the university lapsed into a state of lethargy. It has consequently been said that the
Middle Ages at Oxford lasted until well into the nineteenth century,
when a succession of reforming jolts culminating in those of the 1870s
gave birth to the modern university with its efficiency, specialisation, and
professionalism. In the intervening period, between the age of reason
and the age of reform, accounts of Oxford portray a narrow little world
in which leisure outweighs labour and the social round takes precedence
over study.

Pre-reform Oxford was small. 'Were it not for the important colleges,
the place would be not unlike a large village', noted Uffenbach dismis-
sively. Even in 1800 the city remained a sleepy market-town with a total
population of only twelve thousand. There were eighteen colleges at the
time of Uffenbach's visit and, like ancient monasteries, they dominated
the city architecturally and socially. Two more colleges were founded
soon afterwards; then for over a hundred years there were no further
additions, symptomatic of the general lassitude. With little central
authority colleges developed distinctive characteristics: some had a reputation for learning, some for their wit, some for politics, and some for
the quality of their dinners. The tone was set by the head of house, a
figure of authority even beyond the confines of the college. With his
cauliflower wig, cassock and gown, the head was an imposing figure to
whom townsfolk and gentlemen-commoner alike paid deference. 'A
Director or Scull of a College', wrote the mocking Nicholas Amhurst, 'is
a lordly strutting Creature, who thinks all beneath him created to gratify
his Ambition, and exalt his Glory.' Unlike fellows, heads of college were
expected to make a career of their post, and alone of the senior community they were allowed to marry and were housed separately in the

college precincts within the privacy of their own garden. Some of the heads followed distinctive policies which affected the college character; John Fell of Christ Church is a notable example, for his open-door policy towards the sons of nobles (allowing them to study for a shorter period, forego examinations, and take an honorary degree) gave the college an upper-class ambience which it maintained into the twentieth century.

In contrast to the heads, fellows were for the most part non-residential, and their interest in college affairs was confined to the annual stipend, elections, and the occasional meeting. The responsibility for college property and investments made them a kind of non-executive director whose supervisory work was rewarded with an annual dividend. Plurality, the holding of more than one position at a time, was common practice: Gilbert White (1720–93), author of *Natural History and Antiquities of Selborne* (1788), was typical in combining fellowship of Oriel with his work as curate of the Hampshire village whose flora and fauna he detailed so lovingly. Though the fellowships were numerous (in the 1830s there were 540 fellows compared with an undergraduate population of some twelve hundred), eligibility was often restricted by such factors as school, place of origin, and kinship with the founder. Even as late as 1850 there were just twenty-two open fellowships.

For fellows who chose to reside in college, life could be comfortable provided relationships were good, for the communal lifestyle necessitated daily fraternisation with the same few figures. These consisted of a number of young tutors, middle-aged fellows waiting for a clerical living, and elderly figures for whom the college was their only home. The college communities could be surprisingly small: Corpus Christi, for instance, had fewer than fifty members in all, including the students, and in the late eighteenth century Lincoln College only admitted four to nine undergraduates a year, with the resident senior community consisting of just three tutors and the head of house. Since most fellows aspired to marriage, which was incompatible with fellowship, they were not long in residence; by one estimate the average duration was a little over six years. James Woodforde (1740–1803), author of *The Diary of a Country Parson* (ed. 1924–31), typified the career pattern in taking up the rectorship of Weston Longeville in his mid-thirties after being fellow and sub-warden of New College.

The pre-reform university was remarkably homogenous by comparison with its medieval counterpart, for the student intake was drawn from a narrower base and overseas students were few and far between (those from outside England and Wales are believed to have comprised less than 3 percent). The undergraduate population was dominated socially by the sons of the well-to-do, for the gentrification of the university which had started in Tudor times quickened in pace under the Stuarts and the House of Hanover. Whereas in 1557 the percentage of poor students is estimated to have been 55 percent, by 1711 this had dropped to 27 percent and by 1800 it was down to 11 percent. Increasingly upper class in nature, the colleges had forsaken their original purpose and transformed themselves into private clubs. While students from poorer backgrounds struggled to qualify as country parsons, most undergraduates had little need to worry about money or their financial future. Samuel Johnson's brief experience at Oxford—he was mocked by Christ Church men for his worn-out shoes and left after a year for want of money—illustrates the trials of being poor in a university which catered for the rich and the well-connected. (The poet Robert Hawker [1803–75], vicar of Morwenstow, solved his financial problems as a student by marrying his godmother in order to continue his studies at Pembroke.) In keeping with the move towards a class-based university, there had been a change in the nature of college membership, for the scholarly fellowship of medieval times had evolved into a strict hierarchy. This started with the head of house and was followed in descending order by fellows, scholars, gentlemen-commoners, commoners, servitors, and servants. Though numbers were few, students were ranked and divided by class and money: 'The Oxford freshman entered a highly structured society', writes a university historian, V.H.H. Green; 'Every undergraduate's status was distinguished by the gown and cap he wore, by the fees he paid, the privileges he enjoyed, the table at which he sat in hall and by the place he occupied in chapel.'

College instruction tended to be haphazard and irregular. Tutors taught across the curriculum to small groups (the one-to-one tutorial was a nineteenth-century innovation), and those who wanted to study seriously took a private coach, of whom there were many resident in the town. Aristotle and medieval syllogisms remained the staple bill of fare. As for the state of examinations (which were still oral in form), the infamous case of Lord Eldon has been held up as an example of the general laxity. For his degree the lord was asked just two questions: the Hebrew for the place of a skull, and the name of the founder of University College. His replies, Golgotha and King Alfred, secured him his degree (the latter, though incorrect, was a college tradition). Clerical in form and classical in curriculum, the university appears in the literature of the age as a conservative and corrupt bastion of privilege whose sturdy gates are shut against the outside world while those within enjoy their leisured lifestyle. An early work, Stephen Penton's *The Guardian's Instruction* (1688), sets the tone for the period. This discursive tale by a former principal of St. Edmund Hall concerns an elderly Oxford graduate educated in the days before the Civil War who despairs of his *alma mater* because of the reports of licentiousness there following the Restoration. The narrative soon gives way to didacticism as, coming to the point, Penton advises parents that choice of college should be made according to tutor and not wealth or status if their offspring are to avoid the path to perdition. Warning of lax behaviour at the university, Penton emphasises the need for tutors willing to give moral and financial guidance in addition to their academic duties. The climate of neglect which the book hints at is one which pervades the literature of the period as a whole.

AN AGE OF DETRACTION

The most celebrated account of eighteenth-century Oxford comes from the historian Edward Gibbon (1737–94), who claimed that the fourteen months he spent at Magdalen were 'the most idle and unprofitable of my whole life'. The jibe is made in the *Memoirs* (1796) which were pieced together from papers left behind at his death. As a student Gibbon had three well-furnished rooms in the 'stately pile' of Magdalen's New Buildings next to the deer park, amongst the most attractive of Oxford locations. That he was appreciative of the beauty of the city he is at pains to make clear.

> The eyes of the traveller are attracted by the size or beauty of the public edifices; and the principal colleges appear to be so many palaces which a liberal nation has erected and endowed for the habitation of science.

But when it comes to the inhabitants of these 'palaces', Gibbon cannot contain his indignation and gives voice to the great theme of the age, namely the gulf between the architectural magnificence on the one hand and the academic negligence on the other, or put another way, between the fame of the institution and the failings of the individuals. For Adam Smith, 'The greater part of the public professors have for these many years given up altogether even the pretence of teaching', and Gibbon heartily endorses the charge. Apologists for the university claim that the anti-clerical Gibbon, not yet fifteen when he matriculated at Magdalen, was alienated by having to leave following his conversion to Catholicism (he was sent by his father to Lausanne, where he reconverted to Protestantism), but the measured tones in which the passage is written hardly suggest that the account is fuelled by rancour.

> The fellows or monks of my time were decent easy men who supinely enjoyed the gifts of the founder: their days were filled by a series of uniform employments: the Chappel and the Hall, the Coffee house, and the common room, till they retired, weary and well-satisfied, to a long slumber.

> From the toil of reading or thinking or writing they had absolved their
> conscience, and the first shoots of learning and ingenuity withered on the
> ground without yielding any fruit to the owners or the public.

There has been considerable debate in recent years about the justice
of Gibbon's charges, and the official *History of the University of Oxford*
seeks in volume 5 (1986) to redefine the image of the age by pointing
to the amount of work accomplished by individual scholars and to the
zeal of men like John Wesley and the early Methodists. Yet such figures
can be seen as the exception that proves the rule, for their enthusiasm
was mocked by contemporaries and the name 'Methodist' was only
coined as a term of ridicule. Wesley himself delivered a stinging sermon
in the university church of St. Mary's in which he denounced university
fellows for their sloth, gluttony, sensuality, and general uselessness.
Samuel Johnson, a staunch supporter of the Church of England, held
the Methodists in low regard, and when a group of them were expelled
from the university he expressed his approval, though Boswell objected
that they were 'good beings'. 'Sir,' replied Johnson, 'I believe they
might be good beings; but they were not fit to be in the University of
Oxford. A cow is a very good animal in the field; but we turn her out of
a garden.'

The historical record of Oxford in this period might be a matter of
contention, but literary representations all attest to a fall in standards,
and Gibbon's denunciation is echoed by others who might be considered more well-disposed towards the university. The diary of Thomas
Hearne, one of the greatest scholars of the Hanoverian period, provides
the private views of a man very much at the heart of university affairs. It
tells of college clubbishness and cosy sinecures; of intrigue and in-fight-
ing; and of professors who never lecture. The spiteful tone makes for
lively reading, even if it suggests a churlish personality, for the comments
on colleagues are ungenerous and unrestrained. The university chancellor, Dr. Charlett, is 'an empty, frothy Man'; Bishop Trelawny is 'an illiter-
ate, mean, silly, trifling, and impertinent fellow'; Joseph Trapp, professor
of poetry, is 'a most silly rash, hott-headed fellow'; and Thomas Hoy of St.
John's is a 'little Insect', 'a ranck, low church whigg', who is 'very good at
getting Children, but nothing else that I know of.' It almost seems at
times that Hearne is competing with Wood in variety of vilification, and
indeed the similarities between the two men are remarkable. Like Wood,
Hearne spent long hours in the Bodleian, scorned worldly success, and
was devoted to Oxford. Like his predecessor too, he was a difficult and
combative figure who refused an oath of loyalty—such was Hearne's
commitment to Jacobitism (support for the right of the exiled James II
and his descendants to be king) that his career was damaged and he was

refused Chief Librarianship of the Bodleian on political grounds. Even in death Hearne followed Wood in leaving behind a mass of academic and personal writings which were patiently edited by a later hand (*Hearne's Remarks and Collections* edited by C.E. Doble [1884–1918] fill eleven volumes). In literary terms Hearne is remembered as the model for Wormius in Alexander Pope's *Dunciad* (1728/1743), in which he is characterised as a dry-as-dust scholar who is fonder of books than people—a true bookworm. 'To future ages may thy dulness last, / As thou preserv'st the dulness of the past!' is the epigraph Pope writes him. But a kinder couplet handed down from the past commemorates the bibliophile in more sympathetic terms by acknowledging the remarkable range of his knowledge—'Plague on't, quoth Time to Thomas Hearne, / *Whatever I forget*, you learn.'

For Hearne there were but two kinds of contemporary: honest high church men like himself with contempt for the usurping 'King William and his Rascally Adherents'; and the Whigs and nonconformists who supported the king and for whom no pejorative was strong enough. Hearne's Jacobitism was shared by many of his colleagues, and it was only with the accession of 'the patriot king' George III in 1760 that the university was reconciled to the Hanoverians. Cambridge by contrast was more sympathetic to the ruling dynasty and for the most part supported the Whigs. The political differences were highlighted at the time of the Jacobite uprising of 1715 when a regiment of dragoons was sent by George I to Oxford, prompting an epigram by Joseph Trapp, who compared the action with the king's gift of books to Cambridge.

> The King observing with judicious eyes
> The state of his two Universities,
> To Oxford sent a troop of horse: for why?
> That learned body wanted loyalty:
> To Cambridge books he sent, as well discerning
> How much that loyal body wanted learning.

This elicited a reply from Sir William Brown of Peterhouse, Cambridge.

> The King to Oxford sent a troop of horse,
> For Tories own no argument but force;
> With equal skill to Cambridge books he sent,
> For Whigs admit no force but argument.

One Oxford figure to buck the trend was Nicholas Amhurst (1697–1742) who as a student was low church and Whig. He seems to have paid the price by being expelled from St. John's in 1719 for 'debauchery', though political considerations are thought to have been the real reason. The antagonism the student felt towards his *alma mater* marks his satirical verse *Strephon's Revenge* (1718), in which he paints a picture of an English Athens in sad decay.

> With gen'rous Grief I mourn our *Oxford's* Fate,
> Her fading Glories and declining State;
> Her Muses, banished by an Harlot-train,
> In other Lands renew the tuneful Strain;
> *Homer* and *Virgil* quit disgrac'd the Field,
> And to the Skillful Dancing-Master yield;
> Our *Colleges* grow elegantly dull,
> Our *Schools* are empty, and our *Taverns* full.
> The gowned Youth dissolves in am'rous Dreams,
> And *Pedantry* to him all Learning seems;
> He wastes his Bloom in Vanity and Ease,
> And his Chief Studies are to *Dress* and Please.

In a bi-weekly sheet, *Terrae Filius* (1721), Amhurst launched a series of vituperative attacks on the university, producing a total of fifty-two editions in all (a collection was published under the title *Secret History of the University of Oxford*). The title of the periodical was taken from the licensed buffoon who had enlivened university ceremonies since Reformation times. When John Evelyn saw a performance at the opening of the Sheldonian Theatre in 1669 he was not amused, describing it as

> a tedious, abusive, sarcastical rhapsodie, much unbecoming the gravity of the Universitie, & that so grossly, as that unless it be suppress'd, will be of ill consequence. . . . In my life was I never witnesse of so shamefull entertainement.

The authorities apparently shared Evelyn's feelings, for the figure was gradually phased out. Amhurst took to writing to continue the tradition, and his commitment to exposing malpractice in the corridors of power led him to indulge in satirical jibes at the expense of the university. In the Oxford of *Terrae Filius* fellows enjoy sinecures, lecturers do not lecture, and undergraduates are forced to take oaths they do not understand. Academic standards barely exist: cribbed notes are used in disputations about medieval syllogisms, and empty exercises are performed before bribed examiners. College facilities are used as dining-clubs by fellows and as changing-rooms by gentlemen-commoners. The concern for fine clothes, fine wine and fine food is, in short, nowhere matched by a concern for the pursuit of learning. Anyone who wants to study seriously is considered 'a dull plodding Wretch, a mere Clown, and a Pedant'. Despite the difference in perspective from Hearne, Amhurst paints a remarkably similar picture of the university—indolent, corrupt, and a Jacobite hothouse.

Amhurst might have been motivated by the spirit of revenge, but two of the most distinguished figures of the age, Joseph Addison (1672–1719) and Richard Steele (1672–1729), also wrote in unflattering terms about their *alma mater*. For Augustans like Steele and Addison civic responsibility was a duty (Addison left his Magdalen fellowship for diplomatic service), and Oxford scholars were seen as opting for cosy isolation rather than engaging with the world. They were 'Dull Fellows; Persons, who for want of something to do, out of a certain Vacancy of Thought, rather than Curiosity, are ever meddling with things for which they are unfit.' In an article for the *Spectator* (no. 496), Addison gave an instance of the lax fashion in which college heads conducted entrance interviews. Wearing 'half a dozen night-caps', the head in question conducted the interview at night in a darkened room where he gave the trembling applicant a religious interrogation that culminated in the unnerving enquiry as to whether he was prepared for death. The boy left a wreck, never to appear again. Writing also for the *Spectator* (no. 43), Richard Steele parodied a meeting of the governing body in which pompous academics pronounce on state affairs and reserve their gravest concern for a parliamentary act which threatened to replace their 'good Solid Edifying Port' with 'plaguy French Claret'. The chairman, mischievously named Abraham Froth, is called on by two fellow members for coffee at four in the morning, an allusion to the nocturnal lifestyle of dons. The overall picture the *Spectator* paints is that of a group of comfortably housed and ineffective academics sipping port and pontificating into all hours of the night.

Addison's name is remembered in the geography of Oxford, where a riverside walk by the Cherwell is named after him. He is said to have been an urbane and retiring figure who lived for a while in the northeast corner of Magdalen's cloisters (since rebuilt), which looked onto the tree-lined walk where he was fond of strolling. Admirers of the Augustan manner have commemorated the walk in verse, and a mid-nineteenth-century poem by Robert Montgomery sought to make it hallowed ground.

> Yet here full oft, the branches waving green,
> And heaven's blue magic smiling in between,
> The pensive rambler dream'd an hour away
> Or wove the music of his Attic lay. . . .

The walk has been celebrated too by John Heath-Stubbs in twentieth-century verse, in which the troubled poet ruminates on the 'sane cool mind' who lent his name to the riverside path. The poem reflects the attractions of an age which valued order and harmony as the mark of civilised discourse. Classical symmetry, with its poise and balance, its clearly formed lines and its air of refinement, was regarded as the artistic ideal and was championed as superior in every way to the 'barbarism' of earlier times. This was most evident in architectural taste, where classical elegance was much admired: the German visitor Uffenbach, who arrived at the start of the century with new-fashioned ideas about architectural sophistication, looked at Oxford's mix of styles with distaste and complained about the 'primitiveness' of the buildings. As if stung by such comments, the city put up some of its most graceful buildings in the years that followed—the Clarendon Building (1713), the Radcliffe Camera (1748), and the remodelled Queen's College (1716–65). This still was not enough to please more advanced Germans, however, for when Uffenbach's compatriot, a pastor named Carl Moritz, visited later in the century he was struck by the paucity of classical buildings: 'Only a few of these colleges are modern in construction and the other houses are contemptible in the extreme, with shingle roofs. Oxford bears a melancholy aspect and I cannot understand how anyone can regard it as one of the finest cities in England next to London.'

The poetry of the age likewise looked to classical models, and the technical skills of Roman writers such as Horace, Virgil, Ovid and Juvenal were particularly admired. Stress was laid on form and phrasing, so that the writing of verse came to be viewed more as a decorative art than as a means of genuine expression. Thomas Tickell's ambulatory poem 'Oxford' (1706), full of admiration for classical buildings like the Bodleian and the Sheldonian, reveals the prevailing values in his favoured words—'airy', 'art', 'lofty', 'decent', 'Grace'. Yet much of the poetry in praise of Oxford during this period is full of empty adulation, as if written to order as a rhetorical exercise. Compared with the vigour of Elizabethan verse, the personifications, deifications and classical comparisons have about them a tired air, and at their worst they even take on a comic quality—'O pleasing shades! O ever green retreats,' strains Tickell, 'Ye learned grottos and ye sacred seats!' 'Hail, sacred, ever-honoured shades', mocks the echoing Combe, 'Where oft I woo'd th' immortal maids'. Not even Thomas Warton, gilded with the honours of his age, can avoid the empty encomium: 'Hail, Oxford, hail! Of all that's good and great,' he trumpets flatly, 'Of all that's fair, the guardian and the seat'. Faced with such fare, the anthologist of Oxford verse, J.B. Firth, is moved to offer an apologetic note in the preface of his collection: 'If only verses of high poetic excellence had been admitted,' he writes, 'this book would have been considerably smaller. But its interest must have been greatly diminished, for practically all the eighteenth-century pieces would have been excluded'.

The prose of the age, by contrast, reveals in its clear, measured tones a concern for truth however unpalatable, and the picture it paints of Oxford is of an altogether hue from that of the lyrical poetry. Detraction is all-pervasive, from one end of the period to the other, and the drunkenness of the academic community arouses much comment. When an early visitor, Celia Fiennes (1662–41), passed through Oxford on horseback, she was much taken with the beauty of the buildings but noted pointedly that college fellows 'may live very Neatly and well if Sober', and in *Augusta Triumphans* (1728) Daniel Defoe claimed that men went to university not to study but to drink. The pickled protagonist of Smollett's *Peregrine Pickle* (1751) is a case in point, for he arrives in Oxford with servants, guardian, and an overabundant allowance, and it is not long before he has taken up the smoking, drinking, gambling, horse-riding and amorous escapades of the men of fashion. In Sir George Farquahar's play *Sir Harry Wildair* (1701), a bumptious Oxonian is told he is impudent, in response to which he declares himself an M.A. and pleads the privilege of his standing. In Fielding's *Tom Jones* (1749) Sir George Gresham, who keeps horse and 'whore' at Oxford, delights in inveigling the less well-off into debt, while in Smollett's *Humphrey Clinker* (1771) Mr. J. Melford, undergraduate, admits that the reason for his travels is the embarrassment of fathering a baby by an Oxford serving-girl. By contrast Jane Austen, who knew of the university from the male members of her family and from her tutor, the widow of a principal of Brasenose, treats her Oxonians with deft irony. In *Sense and Sensibility* (1811) Edward Ferrars declares, 'I was therefore entered at Oxford and have been properly idle ever since', and John Thorpe of *Northanger Abbey* (1818) claims that drinking at Oxford is negligible since 'You would hardly meet with a man who goes beyond his four pints at the utmost.' Though Dickens edited a *Dictionary of the University of Oxford* (1886), he shows a distaste for arrogant graduates in his novels, and his representative Oxonian is the unsavoury Steerforth of *David Copperfield* (1849–50), who proclaims, 'I am what they call an Oxford man. That is to say, I get bored to death down there periodically.' In Trollope too the Oxford figures are of little distinction, and *Barchester Towers* (1857) features a Lazarus College whose members are antagonistic to reform and eager for preferment.

As a former fellow of St. John's, Vicesimus Knox was personally aware of the failings of the senior community, and in his *Liberal Education* (1781) he expressed concern for the effect on the students.

> In no places of education are young men more extravagant; in none do they catch the contagion of admiring hounds and horse to so violent a degree; in none do they learn to drink sooner; in none do they more effec-

tually shake off the fine sensibilities of shame, and learn to glory in
debauchery; in none do they learn more extravagantly to dissipate their
fortunes; in none do they earlier acquire a contempt for their parents; in
none do they learn so much to ridicule all that is serious and sacred.

The magnitude of the charges may owe something to rhetorical exaggeration, but the assertiveness of the language was symptomatic of an
age which saw the writer's task as crucial to the spread of knowledge and
the dissemination of truth. If enlightenment was the aim, prose was the
means—the linguistic equivalent of the allegorical beacon of Truth in
Streeter's painting on the ceiling of the Sheldonian. The generous,
expansive sentences, some as rotund and replete as the men who wrote
them, are infused with a vigorous determination to be heard. The writing could be measured, pensive, witty or bombastic, but it was all
intended to further civilised ends, and in terms of Oxford this meant
correcting perceived wrongs. The satirical jibes and contemptuous
asides, the thunderous declamations and solemn asseverations—the gist
of the message was emphatic: the English Athens was no Athens.

THE CLUB

Thomas Warton (1728–90) was a revered Oxford figure who dominated
the literary life of the university during the latter half of the eighteenth
century. He was in a sense born to the Oxford manner, for his father
(also named Thomas Warton) had been a distinguished man of letters
and the professor of poetry. As Thomas Warton the Younger, he took
readily to university conditions, entering Trinity at sixteen and remaining there for the rest of his life—he even died in the college common
room. Following in the figurative (perhaps even the literal) footsteps of
Wood and Hearne, he spent hours rummaging amongst the mass of
unsorted papers housed in the Bodleian, and in addition to his academic
studies he wrote comic and serious verse which was much admired. He
distinguished himself also by becoming professor of poetry, professor of
history, poet laureate, and a celebrated literary historian: his *History of
English Poetry* (1774–81) is considered to be the first major survey of its
kind, tracing the development of verse from its early origins towards
'civilised' standards. He was elected to Johnson's Club in 1782, to which
many of the leading members of the age belonged (his elder brother,
Joseph Warton, was already a member). The modern university has honoured Warton by establishing, in 1973, a professorship of literature in
his name (the disparity in outlook between the first two holders, John
Bayley and Terry Eagleton, would doubtless have appealed to the poet's

satirical instincts; the former once suggested that the latter hated English literature for 'being English, as well as for being literature').

For all his distinction, Warton was a man of earthy tastes who enjoyed
puns, pranks and a sociable lifestyle. He drank with bargemen, was fond
of duck-shooting, preferred the ale-house to the salon, and in his club of
satirists held the title of 'Master Grand Roll of the Sublime and Ancient
Order of the Oxford Sausages'. It is this side of Warton which is emphasised by D.L. Murray in *Folly Bridge* (1945), a rambunctious novel of eighteenth-century Oxford in which the poet is portrayed as a roguish dissolute with an inclination for witticisms, womanising, and the penning of
verse perched on a willow-tree by the banks of the Cherwell. As a student
he had showed a flair for light verse in a poem entitled 'The Progress of
Discontent' (1746), in which the career of a representative Oxonian is
charted from youth into middle age. The discontent begins when the
undergraduate finds his scholarship money insufficient and craves a fellowship—to supplement his income from student fines! Once he
becomes a fellow, however, discontent sets in again and he yearns for a
clerical living with a large salary and the opportunity to marry.

> These Fellowships are pretty things,
> We live, indeed, like petty kings:
> But who can bear to waste his whole age
> Amid the dulness of a College,
> Debarr'd the common joys of life,
> And that prime bliss—a loving wife?

When the fellow is forty, a college living falls vacant and he moves to a
country retreat where he marries and settles down to a bucolic existence.
But as the expense of wife and children weigh upon him, the joys of
domesticity turn sour.

> 'Why did I sell my college life,'
> He cries, 'for benefice and wife?
> 'Return, ye days! when endless pleasure
> 'I found in reading or in leisure!
> 'When calm around the Common Room
> 'I puff'd my daily pipe's perfume!
> 'Rode for a stomach, and inspected
> 'At annual bottlings, corks selected:
> 'And dined untaxed, untroubled, under
> 'The portrait of our pious Founder!'

Untaxed and untroubled, as Addison and Steele had charged, the resident fellows are here depicted as cosily shielded from the cares of the
world. Just eighteen when he wrote the poem, Warton evidently knew a

good thing when he saw it, for after securing a fellowship himself he avoided the example of his father, who had abandoned his Magdalen position for marriage.

Warton first came to public attention as a twenty-one-year-old with 'The Triumph of Isis' (1749), in which the poet daringly acted as spokesman for Oxford against charges made by William Mason of Cambridge in a poem of 1746 in which the university was accused of abandoning the enlightened ways of men like Addison by reverting to Gothic licence and disloyalty to the ruling dynasty. Warton's defiant reply took pride in Oxford's soaring towers and proclaimed allegiance to a greater truth than that of a usurping dynasty and Newtonian science (with which Cambridge was associated). It was a brave stance, for the championing of medieval spires suggested an unfashionable sympathy for the backward 'superstition' of pre-Enlightenment times. In a later poem, 'On Sir Joshua Reynolds's Painted Window at New College Oxford' (1782), Warton refers to himself as 'For long, enamour'd of a barbarous age, / A faithless truant to the classic page', and in his historical writings he followed a similar line in expressing regret for the loss of chivalry and the waning of imaginative power as literature moved towards enlightened values. With his interest in primitivism and appreciation of Elizabethan literature, he has been seen as an important precursor of nineteenth-century romanticism.

Warton was a friend and admirer of Samuel Johnson (1709–84), who was nineteen years his junior, though the relationship between the two men did not always run smooth. Johnson did not share the literary tastes of his senior, nor did he care for the use of archaic language in his poetry which he characterised as

> Phrase that time hath flung away,
> Uncouth words in disarray,
> Trick'd in antique ruff and bonnet,
> Ode and elegy and sonnet.

The jibe caused friction between the two men of letters, although the friendship appears to have been patched up later. Warton had helped obtain for Johnson the title of M.A. to coincide with the publication of his *Dictionary* in 1755. The degree was a source of great pride for the lexicographer, who as a student had been forced to drop out of the university after a year through lack of money. His rooms at Pembroke were on the second floor over the gateway—'the enthusiasts of learning will ever contemplate it with veneration', urges the admiring Boswell. It had not been a happy time for the lover of learning, for 'the truth is he was depressed by poverty, and irritated by disease'. Nor was the precocious student impressed by the teaching, for he skipped tutorials and on being fined twopence for missing a lecture declared defiantly that it was not even worth a penny. Yet despite this Johnson retained a lifelong affection for Oxford, in contrast to the vengeful Gibbon, and he often returned to the city in later years. He spoke out in defence of the university, arguing for the excellency of the institution even if individuals were unmindful of their duty. He told the king that the dons were improving in their habits, and he strongly rebutted Boswell's suggestion that they were ineffective through being overpaid. He was also much in favour of tutorials, claiming that lectures were redundant in an age of print.

Johnson was a clubbable man who loved nothing better than convivial dinner discussions, and here no doubt lay his fondness for Oxford. In the college dining-clubs he could indulge in long meals and learned talk with like-minded companions—men of leisurely and literary disposition, and of Tory and Anglican sympathies. Johnson was a welcome guest in university circles, where his wit and learning were much appreciated, and the esteem in which he was held led in 1775 to the awarding of a doctorship. The visit of Johnson and Boswell to Oxford the following year illustrates the appeal of the university city for the lexicographer. The pair of friends go first to University College to discuss books with the master, and then proceed to Pembroke College, where, to Johnson's approval, they learn that students have been excluded from the college common room because they inhibit the dons from free discussion. Afterwards they walk over to Christ Church, where they are invited to dinner, and though Johnson exclaims to Boswell that it is a great thing to dine with the canons there, they have to decline because of a previous engagement at University College (the mid-day dinner was the main formal meal; at the start of the century it was held as early as 11 A.M., but in keeping with a more leisurely lifestyle this was put back, and by Johnson's time it was held well after midday, and in some colleges as late as 3 P.M.). At University College Johnson and Boswell are entertained to an 'excellent' meal, before taking tea with the ex-president of Magdalen (Johnson was an indefatigable tea-drinker whose tea-pot at Pembroke is said to hold enough for twenty cups). Later they go to visit Thomas Warton at Trinity College, with whom they discuss the art of biography, and their day is rounded off with supper back at their inn.

The day might have finished with supper for Johnson, but this was not necessarily the case for the fellows, as Carl Moritz discovered when he arrived in Oxford late one evening. A schoolmaster drawn to England by his love of Milton, Moritz describes in *Journeys of a German in England* (1783) how he was stranded without accommodation and stumbled by chance upon a late-night hostelry, the Mitre, in High Street. Here he was astonished to find a group of clerics in bibulous discussion. A donnish dispute arose about whether God himself enjoyed alcohol, centring on a quotation from the Bible, 'Should I leave my wine, which cheereth God and man?' The intoxicated banter continued in animated fashion until—and here the pastor times his climax nicely—with dawn approaching, one of the company suddenly jumped up exclaiming, 'Damme! I must read prayers in All Souls College!' whereupon he hurried off to lead the morning service.

Another visitor to Oxford at this time was Fanny Burney (1752–1840), who was acquainted with the members of Johnson's circle as a young girl through her father, who was a member of the Club. She was employed in attendance to Queen Charlotte, and shortly afterwards went to Oxford as part of George III's royal visit. She was much concerned with the etiquette of those around her, and in her *Diary and Letters* (1842–46) there is an amusing account of the visit. Aging professors kneel before the king but can hardly raise themselves up except by pulling on the royal hand. Courtiers eat surreptitiously and hastily stuff their food into their pockets when the queen walks in. And a female courtier with a sprained ankle is described performing the remarkable feat of walking backwards all the length of a college hall. 'This Oxford expedition was, altogether, highly entertaining', Burney concludes.

Thomas Warton was likewise much entertained by the idiosyncracies of his contemporaries, and it is only right that the last word here should go to a man who stands in the same relation to Oxford in this age as his friend, Samuel Johnson, to the nation as a whole. Writing in Johnson's *Idler* (no. 33), he defended the college system as shielding youth from the 'general depravity of manners and laxity of principles' that characterised the outside world, yet his academic satires, affectionate though they are, suggest that the general depravity and laxity was no less on the inside than on the outside of the college walls. In his light-hearted *Companion to the Guide* (1760), Warton provided a tongue-in-cheek introduction to the university whose declared purpose was to show that scholars were a merrier lot than the world imagined. It told of an indulgent lifestyle where 'Amorous Tales may be perused over *Arrack Punch* and *Jellies;* Insipid Odes, over *Orgeat* or *Capilaire;* Politics, over *Coffee;* Divinity, over *Port;* and Defences of bad Generals, and bad Ministers, over *Whipt Syllabubs.*' To illustrate the way in which instruction and pleasure go hand in hand, Warton shows how learning is carried out everywhere but in the classroom: geometry is studied in the skittle alleys, laws of motion on the billiard-table, horsemanship on Port Meadow, navigation on the Isis, gunnery on the surrounding hills, and the motion of fluids in private rooms. Warton himself was apparently fond of a leisured lifestyle, for he was encouraged by Johnson to spend more time writing and less in the dining, ambling, gossiping and coffee-drinking that made up his daily round. In a miscellany put together by Warton titled the *Oxford Sausage* (1772) (named after a local delicacy), there are a number of items written by 'the most Celebrated Wits of University of Oxford', amongst which is a short verse entitled 'The Lounger' which gently satirises a day in the life of a student slacker and in so doing provides a delightful miniature of eighteenth-century Oxford. There are the coffee-houses, Tom's and James's, where the latest gossip is shared, and there are the inns, the Mitre and Tuns, where the toasts (daughters of towns-men) are discussed; there are those dreaded debt-collectors, the duns, and there is the neglected learning of Law, Locke and Newton, whose works were formative to the *Zeitgeist* (Law wrote influential books on reli-gion and morality; Locke's writings shaped political and philosophical thinking; and Newton's scientific work was crucial to the belief in the virtues of reason). Here then, summed up in playful verse, is the lifestyle of an undergraduate that conjures up not so much an institute of learn-ing as a gentleman's club.

> I Rise about nine, get to Breakfast by ten,
> Blow a Tune on my Flute, or perhaps make a Pen;
> Read a Play 'till eleven, or cork my lac'd Hat;
> Then step to my Neighbours, 'till Dinner, to chat.
> Dinner over, to *Tom's,* or to *James's* I go,
> The News of the Town so impatient to know;
> While Law, Locke and Newton, and all the rum Race,
> That talk of their Modes, their Ellipses, and Space,
> The Seat of the Soul, and new Systems on high,
> In Holes, as abstruse as their Mysteries, lie.
> From the Coffee-house then I to Tennis away,
> And at five I post back to my college to pray.
> I sup before eight, and secure from all Duns,
> Undauntedly march to the *Mitre* or *Tuns;*
> Where in Punch or good Claret my Sorrows I drown,
> And toss off a Bowl 'To the best in the Town';
> At One in the Morning, I call what's to pay,
> Then Home to my College I stagger away.
> Thus I tope all the Night, as I trifle all Day.

LISTLESS LANGUOR AND NATURE'S ODDITIES

The literature of Oxford is swollen by an abundance of personal writings in the form of diaries, letters, memoirs and autobiographies, most of which are of passing interest to all but the prospecting historian though a few have won lasting admiration. These include the letters of the waspish Humphrey Prideaux (1648–1724), who was at Christ Church under Dr. Fell and who berated his colleagues as 'dunces and knaves'. Those from other colleges fared little better: he thought Pembroke the 'fittest colledge in town for brutes', considered the members of Balliol 'perfect sots', and proposed a Drone Hall for all the university's useless fellows and students. By contrast the *Diaries* of James Woodforde, fellow of New College, portray a pleasant round of cricket, bowls, billiards, musical performances, and, above all, the dining and drinking of which his record is so full. Gastronomically, if not academically, the university offered full satisfaction.

Early-nineteenth-century Oxford is blessed with four particularly fine memoirs: G.V. Cox's *Recollections of Oxford* (1868), which covers the years between 1789 and 1860; Thomas Hogg's *Shelley at Oxford* (1832–33), which describes the poet's year at University College; Mark Pattison's *Memoirs* (1885), a personal account of the period between 1830 and 1860; and Rev. W. Tuckwell's *Reminiscences of Oxford* (1901), which casts a retrospective eye over Victorian Oxford in a series of elegant essays. Collectively the memoirs reveal the extraordinary insularity of pre-reform Oxford, for there is barely a mention among them of the great developments of the age—the industrial revolution, American independence, the French Revolution—save for one significant exception: the threat posed to the cosy isolation of the city by the railway. Mobility and modernisation were anathema to the inhabitants of the ivory towers, for not only would trains lead to an invasion of Oxford by the outside world but undergraduates would be tempted to forsake their studies for the illicit pleasures of London nightlife. The university successfully put off the setting up of a depot for the Great Western Railway in Oxford, and after much opposition the railway finally arrived in 1844, though it was not allowed into the city proper, for the line ran along the route of the present-day Marlborough Road to a terminus at what is now Western Road (named after the Great Western).

Before the arrival of the railway, in the first half of the century, Oxford was by all accounts in its finest array. The imposing cluster of buildings, huddled together between the Thames and the Cherwell, was fringed with open spaces and hilly woodland. The form of the original city remained, though the town wall had all but disappeared, and there was a strong rural character; industrialisation and the pressures of a swelling population had yet to make themselves felt. This was the Oxford of Ackerman's prints, where gowned figures promenade empty and unlit streets, disturbed only by the occasional coach from London or a flock of sheep on their way to market. With its green spaces and ancient towers, the city retained a sense of the distant past and exuded a strong pastoral quality. Looking back from the close of the nineteenth century, Tuckwell noted, 'The University over which the Duke of Wellington was installed as Chancellor in 1834 owned undissolved continuity with the Oxford of Addison, Thomas Hearne, and the Wartons'.

It was into this eighteenth-century atmosphere that P.B. Shelley (1792–1822) entered in 1810, and at his first meal in hall he struck up conversation with the student who was to become his closest friend. Already in his second term, James Hogg was so impressed with the force of the freshman's conversation that he invited him back to his rooms, where the pair engaged in animated talk. All of a sudden Shelley leapt up, full of eager anticipation, to attend a lecture on mineralogy, but returned soon afterwards with disappointed mien, declaring that the lecture had been so dull that he was determined never to attend another. The incident sets the tone for Hogg's account, in which the poet's boyish enthusiasm is set against 'the listless languor, the monstrous indifference, if not the absolute antipathy to learning, that so strangely darkened the collegiate atmosphere'.

Though the two friends had little regard for the dons, they remained in admiration of the institution, if only for the leisure it afforded them amongst surroundings of inspiring beauty and historical association. Shelley was particularly delighted by the practice of 'sporting the oak' (the custom of closing the outer of the pair of doors to the college room to indicate the wish not to be disturbed), and he gave Hogg an amusing account of his introduction to the term. 'Shall I sport, sir?' asked his scout: Shelley, uncomprehending but intrigued, replied, 'By all means', but to his surprise the scout immediately left the room. Some time later, when Shelley wanted to go for a walk, he hurried out of the door and banged unsuspectingly straight into the outer door, which was firmly closed. Having learnt the meaning the hard way, the freshman became an ardent practiser of sporting the oak, and praised its virtues with a pleasing pun: 'The oak alone goes far towards making this place a paradise. It is surely the tree of knowledge.' Left to his own devices, the young Shelley bubbles with excitement, barely has time to sleep, reads up to sixteen hours a day, and conducts endless experiments. The description of his rooms that Hogg gives suggests all the paraphernalia of a latter-day alchemist.

> Books, boots, papers, shoes, philosophical instruments, clothes, pistols, linen, crockery, ammunition and phials innumerable, with money, stockings, prints, crucibles, bags and boxes were scattered on the floor and in

every place, as if the young chemist, in order to analyse the mystery of creation, had endeavoured first to re-construct the primeval chaos. The
tables, and especially the carpet, were already stained with large spots of
various hues, which frequently proclaimed the agency of fire. An electrical
machine, air-pump, the galvanic trough, a solar microscope and large glass
jars and receivers, were conspicuous amidst the mass of matter. . . . I had
not been seated many minutes before the liquor in the vessel boiled over,
adding fresh stains to the table, and rising in fumes with a most disagreeable odour. Shelley snatched the glass quickly, and dashing it in pieces
among the ashes under the grate, increased the unpleasant and penetrat-
ing effluvium.

Temperamentally Shelley was given to passionate outbursts and sudden enthusiasms, and his fascination with the writings of Plato led him
to startle a woman on Magdalen Bridge one day by snatching her baby
and demanding it tell him something of pre-existence (the Platonic
doctrine of *amanuensis* holds that souls exist before birth, memory of
which soon fades). Among the favourite occupations of the young student was rambling through the nearby countryside, book in hand and
pistols in pocket like a modern-day scholar-gipsy. He was particularly
fond of Shotover Hill, where he would practise shooting or find a pond
on which to play with paper-boats, 'the dominion of a singular and most
unaccountable passion over the mind of an enthusiast,' comments a
baffled Hogg. (Legend has it that the pond where Shelley sailed his
paper-boats was at Headington Quarry, attached to the house where
C.S. Lewis later lived.)

As a schoolboy the rebellious side of Shelley had involved him in the
production of a number of anonymous publications intended to pro-
voke and stir up debate, and while at Oxford one such pamphlet, *The
Necessity of Atheism* (1811), caused such outrage among the clerical
authorities at the university that he was called to account by the head of
college. The lover of liberty took exception to the manner of his interrogation and declared self-righteously, 'I have experienced tyranny and
injustice before, and I well know what vulgar violence is; but I never met
with such unworthy treatment.' When he refused to answer questions
about the authorship of the pamphlet, he was summarily expelled. Still
only eighteen and an eager student, the young idealist was shocked and
upset. Hogg was outraged and went to the head to complain, and when
he too refused to reveal the authorship of the pamphlet, he was likewise
expelled. The pair left in disgrace. (Ironically, the college now proudly
advertises its association with Shelley and houses in a domed room a gar-
ish memorial statue of the drowned poet.)

Hogg's account of the university, coloured no doubt by the manner of his leaving, is deeply hostile and pulls no punches in its assault on the senior community. There are examinations which schoolboys could pass; the curriculum comprises Aristotle, medieval syllogisms, and little else; and the whole ethos conspires against those who wish to study. At one point Hogg works himself into a hyperbolic frenzy which commands admiration for the sheer vigour of the vitriol.

> A total neglect of all learning, an unseemly turbulence, the most monstrous irregularities, open and habitual drunkenness, vice and violence, were tolerated or encouraged with the basest sycophancy, that the prospect of perpetual licentiousness might fill the colleges with young men of fortune; whenever the rarely exercised power of coercion was extorted, it demonstrated the utter incapacity of our unworthy rulers by coarseness, ignorance and injustice.

Though Hogg might be accused of bias, he is by no means alone in making such charges, and some of his contemporaries are equally sharp in their writings. Robert Southey (1774–1843), for instance, declared pithily, 'With respect to its superiors, Oxford only exhibits waste of wigs and want of wisdom', affirming as Gibbon before him that 'Of all the months in my life (happily they did not amount to years) those which were passed at Oxford were the most unprofitable.' Thomas De Quincey (1785–1859) went to Worcester College, and it was while on a trip to London with a college friend that he first took laudanum as a cure for toothache. He claimed that he only uttered a hundred words in his first two years in college, and he left abruptly before completing his finals, observing later that he did not care for the examination system. William Cobbett (1763–1835) who passed through Oxford in 1821 on his *Rural Rides* (1830) was also moved to a vitriolic outburst: 'the great and prevalent characteristic is *folly*', he boomed, 'emptiness of head; want of talent; and one half of the fellows who are what they call *educated* here, are unfit to be clerks in a grocer's or mercer's shop.'

Such was the state of affairs at the university that even a pillar of the Oxford establishment, G.V. Cox (1786–1875), attests to the general malaise in his genial *Reminiscences,* where the university is portrayed as small, snobbish, self-centred, and stagnant. Cox knew the university well, for he served as bedel (officer in charge of processions) for an astonishing sixty years, and his memoirs are charged with a keen awareness of the insularity and corruption with which he was surrounded. Some of the observations might come straight out of *Terrae Filius:* there is, for example, a professor of Greek who has not given a single lecture in twenty years, and a principal of hall which has had no members for thirty-seven years but who continues to draw a salary. The major concerns of the clerical community are bell-ringing and sermons, and while the outside world is in turmoil about the French Revolution, academic Oxford is concerned with the consecration of Worcester College chapel. 'The Oxford fellow of these years', writes Cox, 'made Oxford his little world, viewing everything through the medium of a college and Common-room atmosphere.' Like Wood, Cox combines observation and fact with gossip and tall tales, but what gives his *Reminiscences* their special flavour is the mischievous wit of the venerable bedel, for his chronicle of university life is marked by humorous aside, donnish jest, and a love of word-play. Even in the midst of death Cox cannot resist a pun. In 1831 there was an incident involving upper-class men at Christ Church who were running riot in Peckwater Quad shortly before midnight. When Lord Osborne came out of his rooms to complain, a scuffle ensued in which he was struck so forcibly that he died—'The *blow*', quips Cox, 'was indeed a heavy one to Lord C. Osborne's family.'

Tuckwell too in his *Reminiscences* delights in anecdotes of pre-reform Oxford, particularly of the 1830s when its appearance was at its most anachronistic. In contrast to the impish humour of Cox, Tuckwell writes in retrospective mode of a far-off age which he envelops with a rosy nostalgia. Cox is on the side of progress, glad of the reforms for the improvements they bring; Tuckwell, by contrast, laments the passing beauty and the diminished character. He particularly regrets the demise of the larger-than-life figures who once filled college common rooms, for this was the age *par excellence* of the great eccentrics, and Tuckwell clearly relished them—'Nature', he observes, 'after constructing an oddity, was wont to break the mould; and her more roguish experiments stood exceptional, numerous, distinct, and sharply defined.' The doyen of Oxford characters was Dr. Routh, the ancient president of Magdalen, who drew a crowd of onlookers to watch his shuffling procession to chapel on Sundays (Cox claims he 'glided'). Born in 1755, he had the air of a bygone age with his wig, bushy eyebrows, solemn demeanour, long gown, cassock, shorts, and buckled shoes. 'Always verify references' was his watchword. His wife too attracted attention, for she was transported around Oxford in a small chaise pulled by a donkey and escorted by a hunchback. Routh remained in office until his hundredth year with faculties unimpaired, when he died, according to Tuckwell, out of chagrin at the fall of Russian securities in which his money was invested. His life was a history in itself. As a student he had seen two undergraduates hanged for highway robbery, watched Dr. Johnson enter up the steps of University College, and claimed friendship with Thomas Warton. He was the last to continue the tradition of wig-wearing, and on his death in

1854 one of the wigs was sent to be petrified. Routh lies buried in the college chapel; his wig is in the college library.

Reader in geology at this time was the naturalist Buckland, whose rooms in Tom Quad at Christ Church not only contained fossils and minerals of all kinds but a menagerie of exotic animals which included owls, hawks, ferrets, a tortoise, a jackal, a monkey, and even a bear. He was eager to try new tastes, and dinner guests were served delicacies such as crocodile, horseflesh, and mice baked in batter. He himself balked at nothing, and once had a panther exhumed so as to try some chops. On another occasion while on a visit to a foreign cathedral, he was shown some dark spots on the ground and told they were the blood of a martyr. Down went the professor to lick at the stain, and the martyr's blood was pronounced counterfeit. It was, he declared, bat's urine. The head of Buckland's college was 'Presence of Mind' Smith, the Dean of Christ Church, whose nickname originated from a reply he gave when returning alone from a two-man rowing-trip. Asked about the whereabouts of his companion, he explained that the boat had leaked and his friend had caught hold of the side, threatening to overturn it. 'Neither of us could swim,' he explained, 'and if I had not with great presence of mind hit him on the head with the boathook both would have been drowned.'

The college comforts and sheltered existence led some of the clerics to be chary of moving elsewhere, and one such was Tom Davis, senior fellow of Jesus, who was a keen admirer of the college wine cellar. Though increasingly isolated and well past the age at which he should have moved on, he turned down several offers of livings because of the inferior quality of the parish wine stores. On the other hand college life also had its irritations, and the fondness of Davis for wine was matched by the distaste for students shown by Griffith of Merton, who was once so outraged at seeing an undergraduate in hall during vacation that he ordered the manciple to have the student screened off so he could dine free of the visual offence. The frictions of the communal lifestyle could even lead on occasion to outbreaks of violence, as is illustrated by an incident involving the diminutive Dr. Frowd of Corpus. An 'irrepressible, unwearied chatterbox', Frowd was so short that on entering the pulpit of All Saints Church one day to deliver a sermon, he disappeared from view and had to haul himself up over the side to ask for a hassock on which to stand. He liked to exercise in his room by hurdling over strategically placed chairs, which was of such annoyance to the man below, 'a more advanced Bedlamite even than himself', claims Tuckwell, that he let off a bullet through the ceiling which only narrowly missed the hurdling Frowd. The feeling in the college common room was one of regret, not that the incident had taken place but that the bullet had missed its mark, for by the decease of one and the incarceration of the other the college would have been rid of two embarrassments with one shot.

It was among men such as these that the earnest young Mark Pattison (1813–84) went to work as tutor at Lincoln College, and in his *Memoirs* he gives a personal account of developments up to the period of reform. The self-disclosure is ruthless, sometimes startlingly so, and the honesty of the confessions won the book much praise: Gladstone, for instance, considered it to be one of 'the most tragic and the most memorable books of the nineteenth century'. Pattison's language is striking in its lack of restraint: he is 'repelled' and 'disgusted' by the lack of intellectualism when he first arrives at Oriel; he is consumed with 'terrors and qualms and timidities' when asked to serve as an examiner; he is 'amazed' to find the senior examiners less knowledgeable than himself; and a college fellow, whose fault is to be opposed to Pattison, is dismissed as 'nothing better than a satyr'. As college tutor Pattison was unusually conscientious, even going so far as to curtail college meals and common room drinks to perform his duties. To his colleagues he seemed 'unsociable, ungenial, and morose', but thanks to his efforts the academic standards and reputation of the college were advanced. When it was suggested in 1851 that he should stand for election as college head, he was surprised but gratified at the recognition of his hard work.

Pattison's account of the election is a classic of its kind. The feudings among the college fellows have all the tension, plot and counter-plot of C.P. Snow's *The Masters* (1961), but whereas the fictional fellows are moved by humane considerations, those of Pattison's *Memoirs* are motivated by spite, intrigue and ambition such that the complicated wranglings are hard to follow. (V.H.H. Green's *Oxford Common Room* [1957] clarifies the complexities and draws attention to the importance of pro- or anti-reform factions at a time when the royal commission was sitting.) In the end the result went against Pattison, and the tutor was left with a strong sense of betrayal. He writes of 'a blank, dumb despair', of being 'paralysed', 'benumbed and stupefied'. Such indeed is his devastation that he enters a deep depression, claiming, 'I have nothing to which I look forward with any satisfaction; no prospects; my life seems to have come to an end, my strength gone, my energies paralysed, and all my hopes dispersed.' Hereafter the *Memoirs* tell of the sacrifice of the emotional life for the intellectual—'I am fairly entitled to say that, since the year 1851, I have lived wholly for study', he writes without remorse (during his final illness the scholar called not for his friends, but for his books).

Such emotional distress at the loss of an election might be seen as dis-

proportionate given that it was for the headship of 'a small, unfashionable and unimportant College in the Turl'—the words are those of a
modern head of college, V.H.H. Green. The reaction may indicate an
oversized *amour propre,* for the *Memoirs* reveal a man marked by intellectual pride, but there is also in Pattison's account too the suggestion of an
emotional identification with the college, as if it had become a replacement for the Wensleydale rectory of his happy childhood. In this Pattison would not have been unusual, for the protective environment provided by the college prompted for many young men the transfer of
affection from mother to *alma mater,* and much of the devotional fiction
about Oxford can be read as a form of filial attachment by sensitive sons
separated from the loving embrace of their family-home. For the self-
centred and vulnerable Pattison, the loss of the election amounted to a
painful rejection by his collegiate 'family': it was a blow from which he
never fully recovered. Though he was elected head of college ten years
later, Pattison barely gives this a mention in his *Memoirs,* despite the
opportunity for vainglory. As to his marriage the same year—'the sensation of the moment'—there is not a single word.

Pattison's wife, née Emilia Francis Strong, was twenty-seven years
younger than himself, and the difference in age was compounded by
that of temperament, with the result that for most of their marriage the
couple lived apart. This has been used to support the theory that Patti
son was the model for Edward Casaubon, the 'dried-up pedant' of
George Eliot's *Middlemarch* (1871–72), and superficially all the evidence
would seem to support the suggestion. Not only were Pattison and Eliot
friends, but the college tutor had written an academic paper about the
sixteenth-century Swiss scholar, Isaac Casaubon (a Protestant academic
who worked himself to death). Moreover, like the fictional Casaubon
who never finishes his *Key to All Mythologies,* Pattison too worked all his
life on an ambitious project which he never completed, and the
identification of her husband with Casaubon apparently led Emilia to
see herself as the model for Dorothea. Set against this, however, is the
fact that Pattison and Eliot remained friends despite the disagreeable
nature of the portrait, and that according to contemporaries such as
Mrs. Humphry Ward (1851–1920), who once dined at Lincoln College
with Eliot and the Pattisons, the Oxford don was a much more human
and likeable figure than his fictional counterpart. Pattison also had a
good command of German, ignorance of which is Casaubon's fatal weak-
ness (interestingly the *Memoirs* include a similar charge levelled against
John Newman, and it might be that Eliot heard of this from one of her
Oxford acquaintances and incorporated the idea in her composition of
Casaubon). Reference books generally cite Eliot's one-time mentor, Dr.

Brabant, as probable prototype—he was much her senior in age and had plans for a definitive work on the supernatural aspects of Christianity— and a persuasive case has also been made by Richard Ellmann that Casaubon is a composite figure which includes aspects of Eliot herself. It may be that the character owes as much to imagination as to Pattison, and the choice of name could well signify nothing more than an acknowledgement of friendship.

Whatever the standing of Pattison to Casaubon, the scholar certainly seems to have served as model for two other fictional figures, and inter- estingly both of them were also the work of women writers. In Mrs. Humphry Ward's *Robert Elsmere* (1888) there is a sympathetic portrait of Pattison in the form of a dry, sceptical, and scholarly squire named Roger Wendover. At first he is indifferent to the poverty of the cottagers living on his land and gives priority to his books, but under the influence of the idealistic young Elsmere, who has come to his parish to work as parson, he begins to realise his need for more human contact and greater participation in the world. Mrs. Ward admitted to drawing on Pattison for the outward aspects, in particular the impatience with fools, and her portrayal suggests that beneath the crusty exterior lies untapped human warmth. (Pattison has also been claimed as the model for Mr. Wenlock in Mrs. Humphry Ward's *Lady Connie* [1916].) Rhoda Broughton's *Belinda* (1883), by contrast, presents the Pattison figure in its unkindest guise as Professor Forth, who is referred to as 'petty', 'hideous', 'cantankerous', 'miserly', 'old, sickly and peevish'. He is, in short, 'an old mummy'. The scholarly work to which he devotes himself is ridiculed as being of interest to 'no less than three people', and when the titular heroine (identified with Emilia Pattison) agrees to marry the much older scholar, she makes it clear that there is little sentiment involved: 'You want a secretary, housekeeper, nurse for your mother; I want a home of my own, and a "guide, philosopher and friend"'. The marriage is inevitably doomed to failure, for in response to Belinda's need for life and love, Forth can only offer only dryness and denial. (That the real-life Pattison had at least a sense of humour can be seen in an incident following publication of the book when he made a visit to Broughton's Oxford house, striking out the name on his calling-card and announcing himself as Professor Forth.)

Representations such as the above shaped the public imagination of the Victorian don as pedantic, crusty, and emotionally sterile, and it is worth noting the difference from the dining and drinking fellows of the eighteenth century. Whereas the fictional don of those days was all mutton and port, Casaubon's blood examined under a magnifying-glass would, according to Eliot, appear 'all semi-colons and parentheses'. By contrast,

Pattison himself was politically active and vigorous in university circles. As a progressive he argued the case for reform and supported moves to reshape the university, such as the introduction of women students, and in his *Memoirs* he was at pains to emphasise the moribund state of the pre-reform university and to show how much it was in need of reinvigoration. Curiously, when the much awaited revival occurred, it turned out to be theological in content and reactionary in nature. For twelve long years, from 1833 to 1845, the life of the university, as indeed that of the nation, was riven by a religious controversy known as the Oxford Movement.

OXFORD AWAKE!

Launched in a sermon at St. Mary's by John Keble (1792–1866), author of *The Christian Year* (1827), the Oxford Movement arose in reaction to the liberal and rational tendencies of the age. Its supporters were concerned to defend the Church of England against the threats they perceived to its authority, and in a series of tracts (hence the Movement's other name of Tractarianism) they agitated for a renewal of faith based on a reinterpretation of the past. Leadership soon passed into the hands of John Newman (1801–90), author of 'Lead Kindly Light', who was able to use his position as vicar of the university church of St. Mary's to spread the debate into the wider community, and the events of these years can be followed in his spiritual autobiography, *Apologia pro Vita Sua* (1864), hailed as the movement's 'abiding literary monument' and one of the classic examples of the Victorian talent for polemicism.

The origins of the movement lay in the Oriel common room, which in Newman's words 'stank of logic' before the arrival of a younger element which included the religious enthusiast, Hurrell Froude (1803–36). In these early days Newman had yet to develop firm convictions, and he only learnt of the Apostolic Succession in the course of a walk round Christ Church Meadow. Froude engaged him in discussion concerning the roots of the Church of England, and this led in time to a championing of the Catholic inheritance of Anglicanism and the adoption of a high church position in terms of ritual, dress and belief. As the small group propagated their ideas, they found a ready response in those unsettled by the developments of the age, and before long there developed a nation-wide movement. This led to bitter opposition as the orthodox and liberal elements in the Church of England fought back: 'Soon there will be no middle ground left', ran a contemporary notice, 'and every man, and especially every clergyman will be compelled to make his choice.' The questioning of Anglican roots resulted in Newman pondering the very validity of the split with Rome, and in 1841 there appeared the infamous Tract 90, which asserted that the Thirty-nine Articles were compatible with Roman Catholicism. The outrage was such that Newman was forced to resign, for not only did the proposition undermine a cornerstone of the Church of England but it seemed to attack the very *raison d'être* of the university, which still regarded itself as an Anglican seminary. Thereafter Newman moved with a small group of followers to Littlemore just outside Oxford, where for three years he deliberated his spiritual path. Then in 1845 there came the momentous news that he had converted to Roman Catholicism. For his followers the shock was overwhelming, and Newman indicates the nature of the reaction in his autobiographical novel *Loss and Gain* (1848), where an Oxford student on hearing of a friend's conversion to Catholicism wonders 'how an Englishman, a gentleman, can so eat dirt'.

There are accounts of the Oxford Movement by several contemporaries, outstanding amongst which are Thomas Mozley's personal *Reminiscences* (1882) and the classic record, *History of the Oxford Movement* (1891) by R.W. Church (1815–90), a fellow of Oriel and later dean of St. Paul's. The latter is particularly good at placing the movement in its historical context, and the elegance of the writing lends the clerical controversy a sense of immediacy, as in the passage below.

> The scene of this new Movement was as like as it could be in our modern world to a Greek *polis,* or an Italian self-centred city of the Middle Ages. Oxford stood by itself in its meadows by the rivers, having its relations with England, but, like its sister at Cambridge, living a life of its own, unlike that of any other spot in England, with its privileged powers, and exemptions from the general law, with its special mode of government and police, its usages and tastes and traditions, and even costume, which the rest of England looked at from the outside, much interested but much puzzled, or knew only by transient visits. And Oxford was as proud and jealous of its own ways as Athens or Florence; and like them it had its quaint fashions of polity; its democratic Convocation and its oligarchy; its social ranks; its discipline, severe in theory and often lax in fact; its self-governed bodies and corporations within itself; its faculties and colleges, like the guilds and 'arts' of Florence; its internal rivalries and discords; its 'sets' and factions.

For Cox the movement had been 'a much-wanted revival' which became consumed by its own fervour. For Tuckwell it was a diversion that for 'fifteen years forced Oxford back into the barren word-war of the seventeenth century'. And for Mark Pattison it was simply a 'nightmare', curious wording given that the scholar had once been an ardent supporter. By the time he wrote his *Memoirs,* however, he had turned to liberal rationalism, and as a sceptic in holy orders he searches desperately for imagery to explain away his former attachment. He writes of being 'seduced' from his better judgement; he is caught up in a 'fever of fanaticism'; he is sucked into the 'whirlpool' of Tractarianism; he is consumed by a 'fury of zeal'. In this Pattison was not alone, for many of the country's most influential minds had been similarly affected. For the iconoclastic Lytton Strachey in *Eminent Victorians* (1918), the whole affair is a source of wry amusement, and the belittling of the religious arguments makes entertaining reading. 'The waters of the true Faith', he smirks, 'had dived underground at the Reformation, and they were waiting for the wand of Newman to strike the rock before they should burst forth once more into the light of day.'

By all accounts, it was not so much the theology as the galvanising personality of Newman which lay at the centre of the furore. Pale, thin and ascetic, he had an inspirational quality which impelled men to place their trust in him. Such was his personal appeal that there gathered around him a number of 'Newmaniacs', who emulated his manner of dress and style of speech. The attempts to describe the charisma he exuded have been so numerous that they constitute a literature in themselves, and some of the descriptive passages seem in their very style of writing to have about them an inspired quality. Even Mark Pattison, a man not given to fanciful praise, is moved to write of how 'The force of his dialectic, and the beauty of his rhetorical exposition were such that one's eye and ear were charmed', and in the religious novel *Nemesis of Faith* (1849), the apostate J.A. Froude (brother of Hurrell) claimed that Newman was a genius, 'perhaps one of three or four at present alive in this planet'. Matthew Arnold too was moved to write in fulsome praise, though as the son of a liberal champion and Tractarian opponent he was not predisposed towards Anglo-Catholicism. In *Discourses in America* (1885) he recalled listening as a student to the university vicar at one of the packed sermons at St. Mary's where Newman had the audience hanging on his every word.

> The name of Cardinal Newman is a great name to the imagination still; his genius and his style are still things of power. . . . Forty years ago he was in the very prime of life; he was close at hand to us at Oxford; he was preaching in St. Mary's pulpit every Sunday; he seemed about to transform and to renew what was for us the most national and natural institution in the world, the Church of England. Who could resist the charm of that spiritual apparition, gliding in the dim afternoon light through the aisles of St. Mary's, rising into the pulpit, and then, in the most entrancing of voices, breaking the silence with words and thoughts which were a religious music—subtle, sweet, mournful?

From such accounts it is clear that the spell cast by Newman derived at least in part from his mastery of language, both spoken and written. His religious studies involved a close reading of religious texts, including the old masters, but he was also well read in secular literature and enjoyed the writings of the Romantics. He had a musical ear too, playing the violin for relaxation, which may have helped further his sensitivity to the rhythm of language. Newman himself maintained that the development of his style owed much to the example of Gibbon, a testimony to Newman's open-mindedness, for the historian was known for his anti-clericalism. Tuckwell, a stylish writer himself, was particularly aware of Newman's way with words, and in his description of the Oriel fellow he alludes to a further influence.

> The magic of his personality, the rhetorical sweetness of his sermons—he used to say that he read through *Mansfield Park* every year, in order to perfect and preserve his style—their dialectic vigour, championship of implicit faith as against evidential reasoning, contagious radiance of intense conviction, far more than the compelling suasion of his arguments and theories, drew all men after him.

Newman's own account of the movement, *Apologia pro Vita Sua,* was written some twenty-five years after the uproar of the Oxford Movement in response to an attack by Charles Kingsley (1817–95) with the intention of proving the sincerity of the convert's path to Rome. The result was a work which combined sophistication with clarity, and passion with sensitivity. For some it was a source of comfort and inspiration, for others it represented a masterpiece of prose—James Joyce praised the 'cloistral, silver-veined' quality of the writing. The composition alone bears testimony to the powers of an exceptional mind, for the recollections were written hurriedly by a sixty-three-year-old standing at a desk for up to fifteen hours a day. Yet to the modern reader the sophistry is remote and difficult to fathom: even for Andrew Lang, writing just twenty years after publication of the *Apologia,* the theological niceties were 'as meaningless as the inscriptions of Easter Island'.

In Ian Ker's biography *John Henry Newman* (1988), the author suggests that the spiritual leader had need of followers in lieu of a family, for though he was a celibate by inclination and belief, he was disinclined to solitariness and craved the affection of companions. Within the structure of the Oxford college he was able to find the fellowship he needed, and the emotional attachment to the collegiate community permeates his writings. In the *Apologia* he describes his farewell in 1846 to a friend from his undergraduate days at Trinity: 'In him I took leave of my first College, Trinity, which was so dear to me. . . . There used to be much snapdragon growing on the walls opposite my freshman's rooms there, and I had taken it as the emblem of my perpetual residence even unto death in my University.' When he left his residence in Oriel following his resignation as vicar of St. Mary's, Newman established substitute communities in his oratories at Littlemore and Birmingham, and in *The Idea of a University* (1873) he gave them ideological underpinnning by putting forward powerful arguments in support of their humanising role. For Newman participation in community life fostered the moral development of its members, whereas larger institutions were more concerned with the transmission of information and the acquisition of knowledge. The issue at stake was the true purpose of education, and for Newman the answer was unambiguous: 'If then a practical end must be assigned to a University course, I say it is that of training good members of society. Its art is the art of social life, and its end is fitness for the world.' In response to those who called for higher education to be useful or vocational, Newman argued that a 'disciplined intellect' was in the long run the most valuable attribute the university could foster, both for the individual and for society at large. Put together from a series of lectures at the Catholic university in Dublin, the book has had a profound effect on all subsequent discussions about the nature of university education, and the force of reasoning makes it still relevant to contemporary discussions. Books such as *The Idea of the University: A Reexamination* (1992) by Jaroslav Pelikan, professor of education at Yale, show that Newman continues to direct the discourse, and his ideas have had an enormous impact too on Oxford writings, where they set the parameters for defence of the college system.

In 1834, just after the launch of the Oxford Movement, there appeared a satirical poem in six parts entitled *Black Gowns and Red Coats*. The poem was written by George Cox of New College, son of the author of *Recollections,* and the titular allusion to academic and military dress was prompted by the election of the duke of Wellington, celebrated military hero and conqueror of Napoleon, as university chancellor. Cox wanted to stir Oxford out of its lethargy just as much as Newman, but the concerns that moved him were of an altogether different nature, for he hoped that if the chancellor could defeat the French tyrant, he could also vanquish the lethargy pervading academic Oxford. The verse created a considerable stir on its appearance, and for Tuckwell it was 'a satire of unusual force'. Cox junior had inherited something of the wit of his father which was used to present an oddly familiar picture—an antiquated curriculum taught by dissipated clerics to profligate students. The poem shows just how similar are the depictions of the university in the early nineteenth century to those of a hundred years earlier.

Oxford awake! the land hath borne too long
The senseless jingling of thy drowsy song,
Seen her fond youth of empty sounds the dupe,
And truck'd their birthright for a drop of soup.
Wake! doating drone, or 'ere thy dream be done,
Reform will snatch thee, as its car flies on,
And through the miry path, with whirlwind wheels,
Drag thee along, like Hector, by the heels.
The hum of men is up—strange voices now
Rise from the loom, the anvil, and the plough —
The warning trump hath echoed long and loud,
Yet hear'st thou not, nor mark'st the gath'ring crowd.

Though Cox's call for reform was drowned in the Tractarian fanfare, 'the hum of men' outside the university was growing ever louder. Indus-trialization, rural migration, railroad expansion, the Reform Act, demands for greater democracy, the rise of utilitarianism and scientific values, the establishment of a more open university in London—the social changes were far-reaching, and the pressures on Oxford were great. Even within the city there had been significant developments, for between 1800 and 1851 the population doubled. As a result university domination came into question, and in a symbolic move the annual penance for the fourteenth-century massacre of St. Scholastica's Day was terminated in 1825. Yet still the comfortably ensconced fellows remained unwilling to consider reform, for 'The public opinion of the University . . . had come to regard a college as a club, into which you should get only clubbable men', wrote Pattison. 'There were Tory majorities in all the colleges; there was the unquestioning satisfaction in the tutorial system *i.e.* one man teaching everybody everything; the same belief that all knowledge was shut up between the covers of four Greek and four Latin books; the same humdrum questions asked in the exami-nation; and the same arts of evasive reply.'

In the light of such attitudes change had to be forced on the univer-sity from outside, and in 1850 a parliamentary commission was set up. This resulted in the University Reform Act of 1854, which revised the long outdated statutes of Archbishop Laud. The effect of this was to curb college sinecure by strengthening the central university: fellowships were thrown open, the obligation to be in holy orders was ended, and the oligarchy of college heads was replaced by a more representative council. Efforts were also made to open up the university, both in com-position and curriculum. Class-based distinctions among the students were levelled out; dissenters were allowed to sit for the B.A.; and science was included among the subjects on offer. Further reforms followed in

1877 which effectively ended the medieval nature of the university, for in a mould-shattering move college fellows were allowed to marry and religious restrictions were removed altogether. The changes amounted to a complete break with the past, and the influential Edward Pusey (1800–82), who had taken over leadership of the Oxford Movement when Newman withdrew, was moved to declare that Oxford 'was lost to the Church of England'. There was no dramatic transformation, academe being inherently conservative, but in the long term the effect of the reforms became all too apparent as unmarried, clerical fellows waiting for a living gave way to lifelong, secular and married dons more at home in North Oxford than in college. Though the university continued for some time to pander to the upper classes, the bastion of privilege had finally been breached, and the way was opened up to the new faces and fiction of the twentieth century.

CHAPTER 4

Rites and Wrongs: The Oxford Novel

He has fallen prey to the first infirmity of Oxford minds—he is writing an Oxford novel.

—Gerard Hopkins, *A City in the Foreground* (1921)

IF THE EIGHTEENTH CENTURY was marked by the elegance of its prose, then the Victorian period was distinguished by the variety and quantity of its novels. According to one estimate, over forty thousand were published, many of them lengthy triple-deckers, and they portrayed everything from birth to death and politics to pastimes. Education too proved a popular subject, with *Nicholas Nickleby* (1838–39) and *Tom Brown's Schooldays* (1857) two of the more famous examples. Though novels set in Oxford were unable to compete in terms of fame, it was not for want of trying: according to a 1989 study, Judy Batson's *Oxford in Fiction*, no fewer than 533 novels have been set, or partly set, in Oxford. Despite this voluminous number the rate of publication would appear to be quickening, for Ian Carter's account of postwar campus fiction, *Ancient Cultures of Conceit* (1990), puts the number of Oxford novels at a remarkable 119, or just under 3 a year. The surfeit has not unnaturally produced distaste in some quarters, and in the prize-winning *Flaubert's Parrot* (1984) by Julian Barnes there is a call for a moratorium.

If the appeal of the novel is a matter of curiosity, as George Saintsbury maintained, then the Oxford novel is a case in point, for its popularity is closely connected with the nineteenth-century 'silver-fork' novel which pandered to the interest taken in the aristocracy by the emergent middle class. The success of such books lay in the revelation of the lifestyle behind the embroidered curtains of the rich, and the readership was provided with the opportunity to learn of the conversation and manners of their social superiors. The Oxford novel performed a similar function, for within the grey-walled college confines lay a world which only the privileged could enter. The exclusivity fostered an air of mystery, and for those unable to study there the Oxford novel offered a vicarious form of matriculation. It is no coincidence that the heyday of the genre lay in the late nineteenth and early twentieth centuries, when colleges remained self-contained, insular, and upper-class. Though there is a crucial change in tone between the Edwardian and inter-war novels, the country house atmosphere and upper-class values remain evident. World War I proved a severe jolt to the imperial confidence, but Oxford was determined to continue as if nothing had changed, and the novelists of the 1920s tried to recapture the ebullience of pre-war times. Even Evelyn Waugh's *Brideshead Revisited* (1945), set in the 1920s of the author's student days, evokes an Oxford that has more in common with the nineteenth than with the second half of the twentieth century. Social attitudes were changing as 'the age of the common man' began to take hold, and by the late 1920s the mood in student circles had altered. The lord of the aesthetes, Harold Acton, had been succeeded at Christ Church by W.H. Auden, the cult of the aristocrat by that of the proletariat, and aestheticism by modernism. As egalitarianism seeps into the ivory towers, the insular quality of the traditional Oxford novel gives way to a greater sense of openness and accessibility. The retrospective and elegiac tone of Waugh's novel thus points to the ending of an era, and its publication signified the close of a chapter in Oxford terms.

There have been many claims as to the outstanding Oxford novel, amongst which the following have all been championed at one time or another: Edward Bradley's *The Adventures of Mr. Verdant Green* (1853–57), Tom Hughes's *Tom Brown at Oxford* (1861), Mrs. Humphry Ward's *Robert Elsmere* (1888), Max Beerbohm's *Zuleika Dobson* (1911), Compton Mackenzie's *Sinister Street* (1914), Gerard Hopkins's *A City in the Foreground* (1921), and in recent times Evelyn Waugh's *Brideshead Revisited*. Despite the eagerness to nominate claimants, there would appear to have been no attempt to define the Oxford novel, presumably because the term seems so obviously self-defining. Yet though it might be assumed to be typical of any novel set in Oxford, *Brideshead Revisited* is a work of far wider canvas while Hardy's *Jude the Obscure* (1895), considered by many to be the greatest of all novels with an Oxford background, is not normally considered part of the genre. The reason would appear to lie in the perception of 'Oxford' as gown rather than town, and a certain class of gown at that. When the Scotland Yard inspector of Cole and Cole's *Off with Her Head* (1938) goes for the first time to Oxford, he is shocked to find himself in a part of the city that 'looks like a back street of Birmingham', and it is only when he enters the High Street with its parade of churches and colleges that it accords with his preconceptions. For novelistic purposes Oxford is limited to the city centre with its grouping of ancient colleges: non-'Oxford' Oxford fails to register for the most part.

If the popularity of the Oxford novel lies in its revelationary nature, this would serve to explain the preponderance of Oxbridge settings among university novels as a whole. According to Mortimer Proctor's study of *The English University Novel* (1957), an astonishing 85 percent of such books concern Oxford, with most of the others set in Cambridge.

That non-Oxbridge universities should fare so badly may be partly attributed to their late establishment, since most were not even founded by the time the Oxford novel was well into three figures, and partly to the relative openness of non-collegiate universities which made them less appealing as a subject of interest. Added to this was the lack of glamour of such institutions in an age that looked up to its élite. In this respect it is worth noting that in modern times, with the advance of egalitarianism, the most popular campus fiction has been set in non-Oxbridge universities—Kingsley Amis's *Lucky Jim* (1954), Malcolm Bradbury's *History Man* (1975), and David Lodge's *Changing Places* (1975), *Small World* (1984), and *Nice Work* (1988). Only the Cambridge of Tom Sharpe's *Porterhouse Blue* (1974) has succeeded in defying the trend.

The imbalance between Oxford and Cambridge in terms of number of novels would appear to be puzzling, given the equal lustre of the 'double noursery of Arts'. After all, Cambridge boasts a greater eminence in certain fields, a more democratic past, and a greater produce of poets: Marlowe, Spenser, Herrick, Milton, Dryden, Gray, Wordsworth, Coleridge, Byron, and Tennyson make a literary roll-call which Oxford cannot match. For much of their history the two universities have developed in tandem and what binds them is far greater than what distinguishes them. Charles Lamb was not alone in conflating the two universities in his writings, and some university novels have been set either in an unspecified college or in a composite town named 'Camford' or 'Oxbridge'. Thackeray's influential *Pendennis* (1848–50) provides an example, for the hero attends Saint Boniface in the University of Oxbridge (the first recorded use of the word). Although this is presumed to be modelled on the Cambridge education of the author, the novel has served as an important model for writings about Oxford. The cause for the imbalance has therefore to be sought elsewhere, and it would seem to lie in a difference of literary tradition encapsulated in Thomas Hardy's view that Oxford was the romantic university and Cambridge the intellectual. Primacy of age may well have played a factor in this. Though Chaucer balances his Oxford tale with one set in Cambridge, the scholarly standard-bearer of the *Canterbury Tales* belongs to the older university, and the pride of Oxonians like Anthony Wood in the antiquity of their university fostered a tendency to self-glorification such that, as Waugh notes in *A Little Learning*, although Cambridge has the better poets, Oxford has the better poems. This was fuelled on the one hand by historical associations such as that of the Civil War, and on the other by the university's self-declared status as 'the seat of the English Muses' in Elizabethan times, as the 'home of higher truths' in the eighteenth century, and its reputation in the nineteenth century for sticking resolutely to a curriculum of humanities, bolstered by the conviction that this was more suited to the education of a gentleman. The influential Dr. Arnold of Rugby, who was himself educated at Oxford, claimed that 'rather than have science the principal thing in my son's mind, I would gladly have him think the sun went round the earth, and that the stars were so many spangles set in the bright blue firmament. Surely the one thing needed for a Christian and Englishman to study is a Christian and moral philosophy.' Attachment to the humanities also derived from the belief, as Dr. Arnold's son Matthew put it, that they came 'nearer perhaps than all the science of Tübingen' to a true understanding of the world.

Fictional Oxford thus came to represent far more than the pursuit of excellence, for in an age of rising materialism and utilitarianism the city was cast as defender of humane and classical ideals. 'Let him then who is fond of indulging in a dreamlike existence go to Oxford and stay there', Hazlitt prompted, and Matthew Arnold took up the suggestion by arraying the city with 'dreaming spires'. Thereafter Oxford was no longer a geographical entity as such, but 'an adorable dreamer' which speaks of higher truths and eternal verities. This drew on Platonic notions concerning the need for a contemplative life in order to appreciate the Ideal Form that lies beyond the surface realities of the world. University life with its long hours of freedom, its sheltered existence, its historical associations and its philosophical pursuits seemed designed to further abstract speculation, and in such an environment 'dreaming became a duty' for Mackenzie's Michael Fane and his literary kin. Novelistic Oxford owes much of its character to the nature of that vision, and as a result the fictional city has a fragile and ethereal quality. Its beauty speaks of the Ideal and its antiquity serves as a reminder of human transience and mortality. 'Surely this whole city, with its happiness and its chiming bells, was merely part of a dream which would leave him, when he woke up', writes Mackenzie in *Sinister Street*. In the transmogrified Oxford of Lewis Carroll's Wonderland the dreamlike nature of the city found its most complete representation.

Dream stands to the imagination as analysis to reason, and the connection with literary invention has been often commented on. Writers like R.L. Stevenson, Katherine Mansfield, and Graham Greene claimed to have literally dreamt up stories, and in Coleridge's case an opium dream famously took the form of a poem. The three greatest horror stories in the language—*Frankenstein, Dracula,* and *The Strange Case of Dr. Jekyll and Mr. Hyde*—were all partly derived from nightmares. Thomas de Quincey wrote of the effect of dreams in 'Suspira de Profundis' (1845) and 'The English Mail Coach' (1849), influencing such writers as Poe and Baudelaire at a time before psychoanalysts became interested in the connection between the unconscious and creativity. Freud himself wrote of the significance of day-dream for literary production, and others have taken the implication further by analysing the language of dream in terms of rhetorical devices. According to some analysts, metaphor, allegory, allusion, symbol and even punning would appear to be the very stuff of dream. In *Dreaming and Storytelling* (1994), Bert States argues that the narrative art is in essence and origin a consciously reordered dream sequence; to cope with the 'rawness' of reality the sleeping brain scrambles daytime experience, then the conscious brain reassembles it in manageable and comprehensible form. Dream would thus appear to be the raw fuel which powers the fictional search for meaning, and for Joseph Campbell dreams are private myths which promote the integrity of the individual, while myths are public dreams by which society gives voice to unconscious desires.

Viewed in this light, the epithet of 'dreaming spires' implies more than a simple reference to intellectual reverie: it is the championing of Oxford as a stronghold of the imagination and the creative muse. As a result students of literary disposition were drawn to study at Oxford, where they came under the influence of dons steeped in classical writings and sympathetic to the notion of 'dream' as a creative force. When they came to write novels themselves, the students used the city as a ready paradigm within which to explore their quest for meaning; beneath the dreaming spires lay aspiring dreamers. The novelistic bias towards Oxford rather than Cambridge would thus seem to lie in self-absorption rather than any disparity in terms of literary talent (in the twentieth century alone 'the other place' has hosted figures of the stature of E.M. Forster, Virginia Woolf, F.R. Leavis, and C.P. Snow). Since Oxford novels are as often as not the product of inexperienced first-time novelists, the result is a genre that is disproportionate in quality to quantity. The major writers of the age, most of whom were debarred by class, sex or circumstance from the university, looked elsewhere with the result that few Oxford novels can consequently be classed in the front ranks of literature, and most it must be confessed are of limited interest. This was seized on with glee by the Cambridge-educated A.A. Milne, whose *Autobiography* (1939) points to a major difference between the two ancient universities.

> What distinguishes Cambridge from Oxford, broadly speaking, is that nobody who has been to Cambridge feels impelled to write about it. If it is not quite true that everybody has at least one book inside him, it seems to be the fact that every Oxonian has at least one book about Oxford inside

him, and generally gets it out. Oxford men will say that this shows what a
much more inspiring place Oxford is, and Cambridge men will say that it
shows how much less quickly Oxford men grow up, and we can leave it at
that.

DISCOVERY AND SELF-DISCOVERY

The content of the Oxford novel is almost as restricted as the milieu in
which it takes place, for despite the huge number of books the range of
themes is surprisingly limited. 'The reader who has made his way through
the long list of English university novels', writes Mortimer Proctor, the one
person who possibly has, 'cannot fail to note the remarkable sameness
their plots, and even individual fragments of action, exhibit.' Given the
nature of the genre this is unsurprising since the novels are invariably a
form of *Bildungsroman* in collegiate setting, which is to say that the university is exploited as background to the character formation of a young
adult. For eighteenth-century novelists student life had been treated as a
colourful episode in a picaresque life, and it was not until the advent of
romanticism that authors became concerned with personality development. The focus on individualism (the word itself only dates back to the
mid–nineteenth century) led to character becoming a subject in itself,
and Goethe's *Wilhelm Meisters Lehrjahre* (1795–96; translated by Carlyle,
1824) is considered the first major work of this kind. As interest deepened
in the factors which shape personality, writings flourished about childhood, youth, and upbringing. University years too, with their 'dreamy or
problematic preparation for life', as Walter Pater put it, provided novelists
with material of obvious potential. This not only allowed for the physical
description of Oxford but also for comments on the state of the university.
As James Joyce demonstrated so clearly in his Dublin writings, the novel of
character is necessarily also the novel of place, for description of the environment which shapes an individual is essential to a proper understanding. In this way, in the fusion of the emotional growth of a young student
with the exploration of Oxford, the ground was prepared in the early
nineteenth century for the rise of the Oxford novel.

A ready plot had already been outlined in an episode of Fielding's
Tom Jones (1749) involving the unnamed Man of the Hill, son of a gen-
tleman-farmer. As a child he is fond of learning, but when he goes to
study at Exeter College he falls in with Sir George Gresham, a wealthy big
spender who delights in tempting the less well endowed into debt.
Under his influence the freshman becomes addicted to pleasure and
runs up heavy debts. Unable to cope financially, he steals from a room-

mate, has a warrant issued for his arrest, and ends his student days in ignominy by running off with a woman from Witney. Drink, debt, and degeneracy—Fielding here sets the fictional curriculum. The early Oxford novels in particular are characterised by warnings about the dangers of Oxford life, which are emphasised in the most dramatic manner. 'Oxford is a place full of temptations of all kinds, offered to young men at the most critical time of their lives', states a parson to the young Tom Brown. His advice encapsulates one of the major themes, for temptations, not tutorials, provide the real lessons of novelistic Oxford. Through the struggle with vice the hero emerges ready to face the world—or a broken and penitent failure. In this way the reader is given a double 'education'; one at the university of Oxford and one at the university of Life.

The typical Oxford novel thus comprises a variation of the Dick Whittington theme in which an innocent youth goes to university with great expectations and learns the way of the world through 'the school of hard knocks'. The archetype is the adolescent youth sent out to face danger as a rite of passage to manhood. In the terms of Joseph Campbell's 'monomyth', the Hero's Journey of the Oxford novel leads away from the familiar world of home life and into the alien world of the university. Here the student is presented with a number of tests and trials arising from the strangeness of the new environment. Among his contemporaries he encounters both allies and enemies, who either help or hinder him in adapting. He will also acquire a mentor, who offers advice and guides him in the right direction. As the student passes through the university, he is faced with a series of moral, spiritual, and academic challenges, and his success in meeting them will be threatened by the temptations and distractions to which he is exposed. At some point there will come a Supreme Ordeal, or decisive moment, when the student is faced with making a change which will entail the death of his old self and the possibility of transformation. This may simply take the form of a resolution to cut former friends, or of a major insight signalling a moral change of direction. Thereafter the mettle of the student's new self is tested by his response to further challenges, and at the end the student emerges with a prize of some kind, possibly in the form of maturity of character or the success of his university career. Even awareness of moral failure constitutes a prize of sorts, for the student gains from the benefit of experience. In this way it can be seen that the real tests of the university lie not in the academic examinations but in the trials of character, and the true passage of the student is not from matriculation to graduation, but from adolescence to adulthood.

The book that launched the Oxford novel proper was J.G. Lockhart's popular *Reginald Dalton* (1823), a work which did much to establish the conventions of the genre, for around the character growth of a raw and promising youth are hung narrative digressions in praise of Oxford's beauty and past. The skeleton plot sketched by Fielding is here fleshed out by Lockhart into a full-length novel: the innocent son of a country vicar goes to Oxford, falls in with a bad crowd, is overwhelmed by debt, disgraced, and ends up a servitor who is expelled for fighting a duel. Dalton's downfall at the hands of his false friend Frederick Chisney comes complete with all the melodrama of an eighteenth-century novel, as the protagonist realises that he will have to tell his tender-hearted father of his debts. Though the aristocratic Chisney scoffs at the paltry sum involved, the debt amounts to more than the vicar's annual living, as a result of which he is forced to sell his beloved library. Reginald breaks down in distress.

> I am ruined, undone, utterly undone—blasted in the very opening—withered on the threshold! humiliation, pain misery, lie before me, as surely as folly, madness, phrenzy, wickedness, are behind—as surely as shame, burning, intolerable shame is with me *now.*

When Dalton returns to the university as a servitor, he is snubbed by those who used to befriend him, and this occasions a savage authorial attack on the snobbishness and exclusiveness of the upper-class university. The system of easy credit, whereby students could defer payment until after graduation, is later denounced in equally strong terms as the cause of untold suffering. Yet such outbursts are only squalls of indignation amongst the general air of affection with which Lockhart writes of Oxford, for taken overall the university is portrayed in sympathetic terms as an ancient and august institution in need of modification.

A son-in-law of Walter Scott, Lockhart was a former student of Balliol and a political conservative whose book was written in response to articles in the *Edinburgh Review* calling for radical overhaul of the university. The novel was intended to speak in its defence while admitting faults, and the attachment of author to his *alma mater* occasionally makes itself felt in sentimental declarations. This is nowhere more marked than in the physical descriptions of the university, and in this first Oxford novel idealisation of the university is already apparent when the young freshman is so thrilled with his surroundings that he 'said to himself, a thousand and a thousand times over, that he had at length found the terrestrial Elysium.' Even after all his humiliations and sufferings, 'the solemn antique scenery which had at first so much pleased his imagination, still kept all its beauty, and all its majesty unsullied and undiminished for his eyes'. Lockhart here lays out the 'earthly paradise' of the

Oxford novel: youth exulting in beauty. This became in time a subject in itself, with Oxford cast in religious terms as a 'sacred city' which could lead to enlightenment. The 'pilgrim's progress' was marked by the rites of passage that make up the Oxford year: arrival and meetings with college tutor and principal; dinner in hall and first friendships; the breakfast party; the wine party; rags, pranks and drunkenness; fox-hunting, rowing, punting and walks; the university sermon; the town and gown fight; Eights Week; examinations; commemoration; leave-taking. In the classic text the end of the academic year coincides with the end of the novel as the once callow youth emerges from the college cocoon fully prepared for adult life. In this way, as Anthony Powell notes in *A Question of Upbringing* (1951), Oxford marks 'a great period of discovery—and of self-discovery, too', for in the nexus of place and character lay scope for exploration of both the outer and the inner worlds. Discovery of Oxford and discovery of self: here then are the twin themes of the Oxford novel.

IN AN ENGLISH COUNTRY HOUSE

From Lockhart's first Oxford novel in 1823 to Waugh's retrospective *Brideshead Revisited* set in the 1920s, there extends a century of literature in which fictional Oxford has all the atmosphere of an institutionalised country house. The gentlemen-commoners of Pattison's time, 'being better born, or wealthier than the commoners, kept up a style of living such as is usual in large country houses' with a round of sumptuous meals, drinks, sporting activities, and daily chapel. Almost a hundred years later the cousin of Charles Ryder tells him on his arrival in Oxford, 'Dress as you do in a country house'. The behaviour, the language, the characters, the code of values—with minor alterations the stories could be easily transposed from college to stately home. Yet the college represents more than just an upper-class domicile, for it was also the country 'house' where lived the family members to whom the nation looked for leadership. The intellectual and social élite that comprised the collegiate communities thus provided opportunity for the novelist of ambitious scope to write of the state of the nation. This was an age which assumed, in the words of Mark Girouard, 'that life in the country was inherently better than life in the town, and that the life of an English country gentleman was the best life of all', and chauvinistic writers depicted Oxford as the epitome of native values and virtues. As Britain rises in power and confidence during the Victorian age, the horizons of the Oxford novel show a widening in concern, as if paralleling the overseas expansion. From debate about university reform in the early novels, writers turn first to moral and aesthetic considerations, and then to the nature of Englishness and the national destiny.

The transformation of the college from monastic community to gentleman's residence dates back to the seventeenth century, when an influx of rich students into the Restoration university brought a distinct change of tone which was noted with distaste by the studious Wood.

> Before the warr wee had scholars who made a thorough search in scholasticall and polemicall divinity, in humane authors, and naturall philosophy. But now scholars studie these things not more than what is just necessary to carry them throug the exercises of their respective colleges and the Universitie. Their aime is not to live as students ought to do, temperat, abstemious, and plaine and grave in the apparel; but to live like gent., to keep dogs and horses, to turne their studies and coleholes into places to receive bottles, to swash it in apparell, to weare long periwigs, etc; and the theologists to ride abroad in grey coats with swords by their sides.

College rooms and facilities were adapted to cater for such students in the style to which they were accustomed. At the same time, not unnaturally, dons seized on the opportunity to upgrade their own rooms. Instead of sharing, college members were assigned a set of rooms to themselves, usually a spacious living-room and small bedroom. Grander arrangements also existed: Gibbon, for instance, had a large sitting-room, a drawing-room, and a bedroom. Wainscoting was added to the whitewashed walls, and occupants were expected to provide appropriate furnishings. The gentleman-commoner of pre-reform days also brought his own servant, for the small core of college workers were not expected to provide personal service. 'Scouts' (college servants) were assigned to individual staircases in the mid–nineteenth century, after which the custom of bringing servants fell into disuse and Byron Montgomery Jilks of *Peter Priggins* (1841), who goes up with his aunt's servant, provides one of the last fictional examples. Servitors continued to work for richer students until later in the century, when reforms levelled class distinctions, and in *Tom Brown at Oxford* it is notably the servitor who is the real hero of the novel.

For wealthy undergraduates the college provided a lifestyle of ease and leisure in which academic study took a low priority. 'I suppose your idea is to diversify games with a little rudimentary study?' asks the tutor of Montague's *Rough Justice* (1928). It was customary in the pre-reform university for well-to-do students to keep a horse, and stables were provided in Holywell Street and Blue Boar Street. Dogs were kept in college and either housed in a coal-cellar or, as in *Verdant Green*, a cupboard with 'wine above and whine below'. (In one of Conan Doyle's stories, Sherlock Holmes mentions that as a student he was bitten on the way to morning chapel.) Fox-hunting was particularly popular, not just a pastime for some but a passion—Verdant Green's friend, Charles Larkyns, has a fox's mask and brushes over his mirror, whip and spurs on the antlers above his door, and, tellingly, a list of hunting appointments pinned over his list of lectures. In *Tom Brown at Oxford* students attend morning chapel dressed in hunting gear, and in Matthew Arnold's 'Thyrsis' the Cumnor hills are disturbed by the sound of Oxford riders returning from hunting with the Berkshire hounds. Christ Church with its upper-class connections was particularly associated with country sports, and when Michael Fane of *Sinister Street* walks into Peckwater Quad he finds a tableau that perfectly captures the flavour of the collegiate country house—a lone student in the middle of that imposing quadrangle cracking a horse-whip. Even without horses the upper-class students on the rampage in Waugh's *Decline and Fall* (1928) make the college buildings resound with the noise of 'English county families baying for broken glass'—the Varsity variant of Wilde's unspeakable in pursuit of the uneatable.

For those unaccustomed to the country house lifestyle the effect could be intimidating, and students from other classes had to learn to adapt. The choice of decor could be a crucial matter. 'On the walls Michael's pictures had been collected to achieve through another medium the effect of his books', writes Mackenzie of his *Sinister Street* hero, and Waugh's Ryder looks on his freshman decorations with some embarrassment once he has learnt the true upper-class manner. Following his meeting with the aristocratic Sebastian he develops a more sophisticated taste, and the change of decor in his eighteenth-century panelled rooms signifies his entry into a new phase of life. For those like John Betjeman not 'to the manner born' there were opportunities to learn in the social occasions which university life offered.

> Oxford May mornings! When the prunus bloomed
> We'd drive to Sunday lunch at Sezincote:
> First steps in learning how to be a guest,
> First wood-smoke scented luxury of life
> In the large ambience of a country house.

Just as important as manners to the sense of belonging was the correct use of language. Over the centuries the university had developed its own terminology, much of which was hard for outsiders to understand—'scout' is an example. Acquisition of such terms was an important part of the initiation process, and the Oxford novel is full of language lessons of this kind. 'By the way, d'you go back to Oxford to-morrow?' asks a student novice in Nichols' *Patchwork* (1921). 'I go up,' comes the superior reply. 'You seem to have found out a great deal about Christ Church already,' observes Michael Fane to a fellow freshman. 'The House', he is corrected, and the chastened Fane never makes the same mistake again. Once initiated in this way, students confirm their status by correcting or mocking others. The humour of such books as *Sandford of Merton,* in which porters are miscalled 'college doorkeepers', is only amusing to those 'in the know', and one of the attractions of the Oxford novel was the opportunity for readers to acquire the insider language of a social élite.

Students' lives were tightly circumscribed by their colleges, and despite the establishment of inter-college associations such as the Union debating society in 1825, college membership dominated the student experience until well into the twentieth century. Friendships were formed almost exclusively within college, and even as late as the 1920s Charles Ryder notes that his friendship with Sebastian was unusual for being intercollegiate. Just how unusual can be seen by the aristocratic Loring of Stephen McKenna's *Sonia* (1917), who boasts of not having set foot in another college during his whole four years at Oxford. The attachment to college had been deliberately fostered during the nineteenth century by the introduction of competitive sports, following the example of public schools such as Rugby. Muscular activity was seen as a healthy antidote to the distractions of youth, with team sports favoured since they were believed to foster self-discipline, cooperation, and the spirit of gentlemanly fair play in addition to physical fitness. Cricket was introduced to Oxford in the 1820s and football, both in its rugby and association form, followed not long afterwards. The teams soon became the focus of communal allegiance, and the rivalry between colleges was intense. This was most evident in terms of rowing, which developed during the nineteenth century from a pastime into a means of displaying college pride. Competitive rowing began around 1815, and the first Oxford and Cambridge boat-race took place in 1829. By the 1840s, when *Tom Brown at Oxford* is set, rowing was an entrenched part of student life. 'All rowed fast, but none so fast as stroke', runs a famous phrase, thought to be a misquotation from *Sandford of Merton.* By the end of the century the parochialism was at a peak; college members had their own blazers and scarves, sang the college song and gloried in the communal traditions (individual college histories were first published at this time). So complete was the identification that people were associated by name with their college, as book titles indicate: *Wilton of Cuthbert's* (1878); *Hugh Heron, Ch. Ch.* (1880); *Faucit of Balliol* (1882); *Blake of Oriel* (1899); *Sandford of Merton* (1903). There was deep hostility to those who refused to 'do their bit', and unsporting types ran the risk of being beaten up or having their rooms sacked. Artistic and literary undergraduates were particularly suspect. When a group of sportsmen tackled Oscar Wilde, he proved himself no less a man of action than of words by turning the tables on his would-be assailants and throwing them all downstairs. Evelyn Waugh, on the other hand, was questioned about his contribution to the college and managed to evade punishment by cavalierly replying that he drank for it.

Eights Week, when college crews raced each other for the title of head of the river, marked one of the great highlights of the Oxford year—and the fiction too. In a celebrated scene near the end of *Zuleika Dobson* the duke of Dorset plunges into the river intent on suicide, but proves himself a loyal college man by rising to the surface to ascertain his boat's progress, whereby he so startles the cox of the leading boat that his own college is able to catch up and go head of the river (first position). Victories on the river were celebrated with bacchanalian feasts and acts of destruction which were intended, paradoxically, to show the strength of attachment to the college. In *The Adventures of Downy V. Green* (1902) a bonfire is made of doors, mats, chairs and other combustibles dragged from the rooms of unpopular and unsporty students, while in *Laurel and Straw* (1927) the crew members smash their glasses after drinking to the college in order to prevent them being profaned by any other toast. Ragging, debagging and trashing inevitably follow. The unwritten rule was that you could behave as you wished inside college, drunken cavorting and minor vandalism being overlooked, but outside college one was expected to put on a display of good behaviour. This was in keeping with the upper-class code of keeping up standards, typified by the maxim of not arguing in front of the servants.

As with country houses, college prestige was closely connected to size, age and wealth. *Primus inter pares* was Christ Church, followed by the other large and ancient colleges such as Magdalen and New College. Each had its own distinct character and traditions: some were known for their athletic prowess, some for their food, some for their earnestness, and some were barely known at all outside their own confines. Social-climbers like Betjeman and Waugh aspired to friendships with the Etonians of Christ Church and pitied their contemporaries who had to make do with friends from outlying colleges. In the fictionalised Magdalen of *Sinister Street,* Michael Fane reflects that 'Keble like Mansfield and Ruskin Hall was in Oxford, but not in the least of Oxford' and even the majestic Queen's is loftily dismissed as 'that great terra incognita', presumably because of the number of northerners there on scholarships. The socially exclusive Grid of the same novel is a club restricted in

practice if not in principle 'to those seven or eight colleges that considered themselves the best', an indication of just how exclusive the student
communities could be even towards each other. In McKenna's *Sonia* a
Christ Church student gives odds of five to three that there is no such
college as Wadham, and seven to two that even if there is his companion
cannot find it. The superiority underlying the joke was accompanied by
the snubbing of those from less well-endowed institutions. The Parisian
parents of Jean Fayard's *Oxford and Margaret* (1925) labour initially
under the misconception that colleges are for different academic subjects, but 'They learned finally that the colleges were merely a series of
social differences, that at Magdalen you had money and people
respected you, whilst at Jesus you had no money and your name was
Jones.' Such social differences, though outdated now, are important to a
proper understanding of the literature, and John Betjeman's glib gener-
alisations in *An Oxford University Chest* (1938) remain instructive. Christ
Church and Magdalen are singled out as socially preeminent in that they
cater for the upper classes, while other colleges are dealt with in more
summary fashion.

> Trinity has a very high percentage of men from the larger public schools.
> New College, by reason of its foundation statutes, is primarily Wykehami-
> cal. . . . Other colleges rise and sink, though some retain characteristics,
> sometimes connected with their foundations. Exeter is West Country and
> High Church. Wadham was West Country and Evangelical. Balliol is Scot-
> tish and intellectual. Indeed Balliol produces more distinguished men, in
> politics and literature, than any other college. Its famous run of scholars in
> the nineteenth century causes one to look at its hideous Broad Street
> façade with superstitious awe. Brasenose is tough and athletic; indeed,
> there is even said to be a scholarship for Rugby Football at this college.
> Oriel is connected with Rhodes, and therefore Colonial. Queen's has very
> good food. Pembroke has a good cellar. Worcester and St. John's have nice
> gardens. Jesus is full of Welshmen. Merton is gay and hospitable. Corpus is
> hardworking. Lincoln, University, St. Edmund Hall, Hertford and Keble
> are less definable.

Even in an age of fierce loyalties, the cult of Balliol occupies a special
place in the literature. Under the leadership of Benjamin Jowett
(1817–93) the college became a byword for excellence: its undergraduates dominated exam results and university prizes; former students
became leading administrators (three successive Governor-Generals of
India were educated at the college); and so many Balliol men were
appointed head of house at other colleges that Jowett was moved to comment, 'If we had a little more money, we could absorb the University.' He
was a dedicated teacher who took his tutoring seriously, and it was largely

through his example that the adversarial manner of the modern tutorial
came into being. He was an important personal influence on a number
of literary figures including Matthew Arnold, G.M. Hopkins, Arthur
Hugh Clough, Hilaire Belloc, and particularly the wayward Swinburne
with whom he developed a curious friendship based on a mutual passion
for classics. Yet Jowett was far more than just a devoted college head: for
some historians the whole reform period can be simply labelled 'The
Age of Jowett' because of his dominating influence in university circles.
A contemporary of Pattison, Jowett was a fellow liberal determined to
reform and improve the university, but though the two men were ranged
together in this, they differed on the nature of the changes. Whereas Pattison held that the university should be a place of research, Jowett
believed its chief role should lie in the training of the future élite. In this
he was influenced by the study of Plato, and as professor of Greek he was
an influential figure in furthering the interest in classical ideals. He saw
constitutional England as heir to the Greek tradition, and treated the
classical philosophers as if they were important commentators on Victorian society. He liked to imagine Socrates as if he were a university figure,
walking around the college grounds giving instruction, discussing ethics,
and questioning sloppy thinking. In this way Jowett hoped to show the
relevance of Greek thought to those who were born to lead, and the
manner of instruction served to foster identification among the academic community with ancient Athenians.

Known as the 'Jowler', the Balliol master was an intimidating man
who did not suffer fools gladly—he once confessed to a prejudice against
all those who do not succeed in life—and he was mocked in a popular
verse which became part of university folklore.

> First come I. My name is Jowett.
> There's no knowledge but I know it.
> I am Master of this College,
> What I don't know isn't knowledge.

Stories about Jowett pepper Oxford memoirs, and he was said to have a
knack for the *bon mot:* 'You must believe in God, my dear, despite what
the clergymen say', he once told a young girl. But by all accounts his
most striking trait, and the one for which his students remembered him,
was a capacity for long silences. In *Oxford* (1936) J.A. Spender recalled
reading essays at Jowett's tutorials: 'Sometimes he rewarded you with a
brief "Good essay" or "Fair essay", but there were other occasions when
he looked at you for an interminable minute and then slowly shifted his
gaze to your neighbour and said "Next essay, please."' Augustus Hare,
the travel writer, found conversation with Jowett heavy going on the

walks they sometimes took together, for 'he scarcely ever spoke, and if, in my shyness, I said something at one milestone, he would make no response at all till we reached the next, when he would say abruptly, "Your last observation was singularly commonplace."' Jowett had a generous side too, and he was known to help poor students from out of his own pocket. He was also the first college head to throw open the doors of the college to the outside world, attracting students from the Indian subcontinent, the Middle and the Far East, and such was his legacy that the college maintained its pre-eminence in university matters long after his death. Anthony Asquith maintained that the Balliol man was marked by 'a tranquil consciousness of effortless superiority', and when Ray Sheldon of *Patchwork* goes up as a freshman after the First World War, he is upset about his failure to get a scholarship and claims, 'I'm sure I could have got one anywhere else'. 'I'm glad to see you've got the college spirit already', comes the rejoinder.

In W.H. Mallock's *The New Republic* (1877) there is a caricature of Jowett, along with several other Victorian pundits. These include Matthew Arnold (1822–88), the popular professor of poetry; John Ruskin (1819–1900), who lectured on art; and Walter Pater (1839–94), whose thought was fundamental in the development of English aestheticism. Between them the Oxford men were instrumental in shaping the cultural and artistic sensibilities of Victorian Britain. The nephew of J.A. Froude, Mallock (1849–1923) was a conservative who had studied under Jowett at Balliol, and the former student mocks his elders by satirising their viewpoints. The discussions are set in a country house whose leisurely mode has something of the atmosphere of fictional Oxford with its set round of walks, meals, and chapel. The preponderance of dons in Mallock's pantheon says much about the rise to eminence of the Victorian university, but there is too in the book something of the incestuous nature of the academic community. It was said of Oxford in this age that it constituted a world of such narrow horizons that the sun rose over Wadham and set over Worcester, and the small cluster of colleges around the city centre comprised a tightly knit social community. Paying one's respects involved little more than crossing a street, and such was the sense of self-sufficiency that the warden of Joanna Cannan's *High Table* (1931) could claim never to have set foot north of St. Giles, all of ten minutes away from his High Street college.

The introspective nature of the university serves to explain the similarity of tone and content in many of the novels, for personal contact within the small community fostered a common view of the world. Impressionable young writers were affected by the views of their elders, and those who became teachers passed on similar ideas to a younger generation. Walter Pater provides a prime example: as an undergraduate he studied under Benjamin Jowett and attended Matthew Arnold's lectures; as a don and author he played a crucial part in the development of Gerard Manley Hopkins and Oscar Wilde; and amongst his friends in the city were the likes of Mark Pattison, Charles Dodgson, John Ruskin, and Mrs. Humphry Ward. The self-centredness of this little world is reflected in the navel-gazing of writers preoccupied with defining the special 'secret' of Oxford. Of all those who seek the special essence of the university, none was more earnest or diligent than Mackenzie's Michael Fane, significantly an ardent admirer of Pater. Though it comes too early in his undergraduate life for him to appreciate it, he is in fact offered an insight into the character of the university in the welcome speech given by the head of his college. The aristocratic nonchalance, the country house manner, the college pride, the cliquish élitism, the peripheral nature of study, the sense of Englishness—the whole flavour of the period is here captured in a few choice sentences.

> You have come to Oxford, some of you to hunt foxes, some of you to wear very large and very unusual overcoats, some of you to row for your college, and a few of you to work. But all of you have come to Oxford to remain English gentlemen. In after life when you are ambassadors and pro-consuls and members of Parliament you will never remember this little address which I have the honour of now delivering to you. That will not matter, so long as you always remember that you are St. Mary's men and the heirs of an honourable and ancient foundation.

STUDENT HEROES AND MALE BONDS

At the core of the Oxford novel stands the student hero, and in this central character lies the driving-force of the story. In the early novels the hero is typically the son of a country vicar or minor gentry; in Edwardian times an Etonian or aristocrat; and in the inter-war years a minor public schoolboy or, exceptionally, a foreigner or a female. (For present purposes the student hero is assumed to be male; female protagonists are dealt with in a later section.) Round this central figure are ranged the various 'others' whose presence is necessary to the self-definition of the hero as he passes through the university. These are seen only in terms of their relation to the hero, so that in E.M. Forster's terms they are 'flat' by comparison to his 'roundness'. Whereas the hero has a sense of depth and development, those around him remain static 'types' rather than individuals. These comprise student contemporaries, both allies and enemies; dons, who are usually avuncular or eccentric; and college servants, with local accent and working-class values. Somewhere beyond the college walls there may be a woman with whom the hero becomes intimate in an unspecified manner, and during the vacations the family may make an appearance in the form of an adoring mother and sister.

The student heroes are with few exceptions typified by two characteristics. Firstly, and unsurprisingly given the nature of the genre, the heroes are made in the image of their creators. *Pendennis* has a dandified hero that Thackeray admitted to be a self-portrait; the protagonist of J.A. Froude's *Nemesis of Faith* parallels the author's own path from Tractarianism through orthodoxy to scepticism; Michael Fane, like Mackenzie, studies at a prestigious college and is involved with a university magazine; and Beverley Nichols, 'a Post-Great-War-Super-Aesthete', wrote *Patchwork* about a post–Great War super-aesthete. Waugh's Charles Ryder lives in an unfashionable college, drinks heavily, and makes up to the aristocratic aesthetes of Christ Church—not unlike his author in fact, whose autobiography *A Little Learning* (1964) tells a similar story. Typically for the genre, the action of *Brideshead Revisited* is tinged with the nostalgia of fondly remembered student days.

The second characteristic of the student hero derives from the first in that he is invariably of literary and artistic disposition. Like author, like hero. The early novels are filled with classical allusions, reflecting the specialisation of the authors, and as the passion for classics fades after the turn of the century, English becomes the preferred subject. Other disciplines are mentioned only in passing, though some are considered more kindly than others. Science is openly derided. The antipathy stemmed not only from a difference of perception, but from a feeling that the subject represented a very real threat to the traditional nature of the university. Whereas colleges were built for liberal arts, science required laboratories and research facilities which made huge demands on the university budget. Moreover, the extra-collegiate institutes undermined the collegiate lifestyle by creating alternative centres of activity. Those who wrote in praise of Oxford were therefore inclined to view science as inherently subversive, and reactionary dons who bemoan the introduction of the subject at all are given a sympathetic narrative nod.

Nineteenth-century Oxford placed particular emphasis on the study of classics as a useful training for those born to rule, whether in Britain or overseas, and Greats was considered the most prestigious course in the university. Unlike other courses which took three years, Greats entailed five terms of classical literature (leading to an exam known as Mods) followed by seven terms of ancient history and philosophy. 'It doesn't seem to me one gains the quintessence of the university unless one reads Greats', claims *Sinister Street*'s Michael Fane, and many of those who wrote about that quintessence were themselves graduates of Greats.

Science by contrast was considered to be an inferior subject, suited to those whose jobs required mere mechanical skills. The training in analysis of matter was regarded as detrimental to consideration of the larger issues needed for development of the whole person, and reductionist methods were derided as sterile and diminishing. Both Newman in *The Idea of a University* (1873) and Arnold in 'Literature and Science' (1882) put forward the view that though a training in natural sciences might produce a useful scientist, it would not produce a well-rounded human being able to provide leadership and take difficult decisions. There was in this an element of social superiority, for scientists were seen in class terms as working at a lower order with their hands rather than their minds. Such feelings were fuelled by the rising influence of Plato in the latter part of the century, for the philosopher was viewed as a visionary exponent of poetic truth. If scientists appear at all in Oxford novels, they are dull, despicable, ridiculous or criminal. The college chemist of *Oxford and Margaret* is such an oddity that 'he was treated like a Papuan dwarf in a show', and when a drunken student in *Sinister Street* assaults a passer-by in the belief he is a Boer, the victim turns out to be a miserable science don unworthy of sympathy, the same type no doubt as the 'mouse of a man connected with the Natural Sciences' who lives above Charles Ryder.

Though the student hero is restricted in terms of specialisation, his character takes many guises. He may be a seeker of pleasure like Reginald Dalton, or a seeker of truth as in *Loss and Gain*. He can incline to sports as the upright Tom Brown, or he can scorn them altogether like the deceitful Yardly Gobion of *The Hypocrite* (1898). He might be innocent as in *Verdant Green*, sensitive as in *A City in the Foreground*, or supremely self-confident as in *Zuleika Dobson*. Crucial to all are the friendships they make, for it is from these, rather than from the dons, that they learn the important lessons of life. Jane Austen was the first to hint at the camaraderie of the all-male community when Fanny takes hold of her cousin's arm in *Mansfield Park* (1814), for it reminds him of his Oxford days walking arm-in-arm with a friend. A hundred years later, and Michael Fane strolls imperiously along the High arm-in-arm with his three *Sinister Street* friends. The championing of a laddish brotherhood pervades the genre and for Hugh Kenyon of *City in the Foreground* the very essence of Oxford lies in the classical ideal of close male friendships. C.S. Lewis (1898–1963), who taught at Magdalen, was a particularly forceful proponent of the pleasures of male company, and his close friendship with J.R.R. Tolkien (1892–1973) was a shaping influence on the works of both men. The two dons were part of the informal group known as the Inklings, who used to meet twice-weekly from the 1930s onwards, and in *The Four Loves* (1960) Lewis wrote in praise of same-sex friendships bound by what he termed Appreciative Love. In the passage below he describes the sense of contentment that comes from physical exertion undertaken in the company of fellow males:

> Those are the golden sessions; when four or five of us after a hard day's walking, have come to our inn; when our slippers are on, our feet spread out towards the blaze and our drinks at our elbows; when the whole world, and something beyond the world, opens itself to our minds as we talk; and no one has any claim on or any responsibility for another, but all are freemen and equals as if we had first met an hour ago, while at the same time an Affection mellowed by the years enfolds us. Life—natural life—has no better gift to give.

The championing of male companionship that runs through the literature was often linked with, and served to justify, the traditional exclusion of women from the university. This has its origins in medieval times when Chaucer's 'hende Nicholas' and his ilk had demonstrated to the early fathers the consequences of young men lodging out and straying from 'the straight and narrow'. As a result, the early colleges were modelled after the isolating nature of monasteries, which served not only to divide town from gown but to segregate the sexes (the original statutes of New College forebade the use of female servants by insisting on the employment of 'male laundresses'). For the monkish community women were at best a distraction and at worst an evil; Nicholas Amhurst, for example, declared in *Terrae Filius* that females seduced students from their books, that thoughts of love were an aberration, and that the mixing of sexes led to debauchery. Writing in 1782, Vicesimus Knox gloried in the college as a male sanctuary: 'Delightful retreat,' he exulted, 'where never female shewed her head since the days of the founder!'

There are consequently few women characters in the traditional Oxford novel, and those who do feature can be divided into the respectable and the barely mentionable. Respectable women belong to students' families, and appear in vacation or at university ceremonies such as Eights Week and Commemoration. Mothers and sisters serve primarily to flesh out the hero's family background, and occasionally the sister of a friend will introduce a touch of romance. The feminine interest also helps to enliven the grey stones and river banks of Oxford with a dash of colour: 'How a few flounces and bright girlish smiles can change the aspect of the sternest homes of knowledge!' enthuses Bradley in *Verdant Green*. The shadowy women of the night, by comparison, are far less visible: 'Yes, 'tis a serious-minded place. Not but there's wenches in the streets o' nights', a labourer tells the young Jude Fawley, though such wenches are carefully policed in the fiction where the temptations of the flesh are often hinted at, but rarely revealed. In Farrar's *Julian Home* (1859) the priggish Jedediah Hazlet deviates from the straight and narrow, though how and with whom is unclear, and the readers are left to surmise for themselves. In *Tom Brown at Oxford* Thomas Hughes takes up the theme of Arthur Hugh Clough's verse-story, *The Bothie of Tober-na-Vuolich* (1848), which tells of the conflict of feelings of a student who falls for a working-class girl. Though Tom Brown comes perilously close to an act of moral turpitude with an attractive barmaid, he manfully resists and returns to the steady affections of his childhood friend and class equal. For Newman's Charles Reding, involvement of any kind with the opposite sex is an unsavoury distraction from the spiritual path, and there is some startling language in *Loss and Gain* to describe relations between the sexes: falling in love is referred to as 'sickening' and the engagement of a friend 'absurd'. It is symptomatic of the prevailing antagonism.

The introduction of women students to the university in the 1880s failed to make much impact on the Oxford novel, in which they are cast in the same light as male students from the working class—hard-working, peripheral, and ridiculous. Lorna Spence of *Oxford Marmalade* (1946) is a typical example, absurdly taking thirty-seven pages of notes in small spidery handwriting at a morning lecture. Since women students were housed separately, the strategy of most novels was simply to ignore them. For the duke of Dorset in Beerbohm's *Zuleika Dobson* the appearance in college of an unmarried woman is 'sheer violation of sanctuary', and when women descend on Oxford for Eights Week in *Brideshead Revisited,* Sebastian and Charles are so horrified that they make off for the countryside. 'The great point of Oxford,' stresses Mackenzie's Fane in no uncertain manner, 'in fact the whole point of Oxford, is that there are no girls'.

The exclusive attitude towards women led to male relations within the college community assuming greater importance than might otherwise have been the case, and the literature is marked by the expression of strong and life-long bonds of friendship. This was also a consequence in part of the élitist nature of the university, for partaking in a 'club' of select members tightened the sense of belonging together. Because the college was small and hard to enter, students were moved to express their loyalty through mutual support and appreciation. For George Steiner the English sensibility has always inclined towards male intimacy, as evidenced by the traditional lore of public schools, army regiments, and male clubs, and in Oxonian terms this was given its most lyrical expression in a poem by Hilaire Belloc entitled 'To the Balliol Men Still

in Africa' (1910), which provides further evidence of the legacy of
Jowett. It belongs in spirit to the music-hall ballads of Edwardian times
which told of 'chums' and laddishness, and the muscular and military
connotations give it a grandly imperial air which speaks at the same time
of a physical closeness usually associated with the trenches. Behind the
collegiate rhapsody can be sensed the poetry of the Great War with its
comrades-in-arms and comrades in death.

> Years ago when I was at Balliol,
>   Balliol men—and I was one —
> Swam together in winter rivers,
>   Wrestled together under the sun.
> And still in the heart of us, Balliol, Balliol,
>   Loved already, but hardly known,
> Welded us each of us into the others:
>   Called a levy and chose her own.
>
> Here is a House that armours a man
>   With the eyes of a boy and the heart of a ranger
> And a laughing way in the teeth of the world
>   And a holy hunger and thirst for danger:
> Balliol made me, Balliol fed me,
>   Whatever I had she gave me again:
> And the best of Balliol loved and led me.
>   God be with you, Balliol men.

Typically, the student allegiance is here addressed not to the university as
such but to the collegiate *alma mater*. The novels tell a similar story. When
Ray Sheldon of *Patchwork* has to vacate his Balliol rooms, he is devastated:
'It was as though he were leaving behind a part of his personality, as
though he were cutting himself off from the intimate and precious
motherhood of the College itself.' Such feelings only served to further
the sense of 'brotherhood' among college members, since the students
were all siblings suckled, as it were, by the same institutional wetnurse.
This was intensified by the emotional immaturity of many of the students, whose restricted lives in public schools led to an emphasis on
intellectual development: the regulated lifestyle, constricted environment, and lack of involvement with the opposite sex all served to inhibit
emotional growth. When they arrived at university, the band of young
men were forced to rely on each other for support at a time of life when
many were undergoing psycho-sexual disturbances. The college rituals,
the team sports, the drunken escapades, the town and gown fights—the
physicality of such group events all served to strengthen the masculine
bond. Small wonder then that the friendships should be so decisive in

psychological terms, for in a sense the collegiate family represented almost as formative a factor as the real family left behind at home.

Though rarely explicit, there is an undercurrent of homoeroticism in the male-male friendships which occasionally ripples the surface of the literature, as in the suggestive sensuality of Walter Pater and Oscar Wilde. In *Hellenism and Homosexuality in Victorian Oxford* (1994), Linda Dowling ascribes the relative openness of such figures to the moral climate which followed the reform of Greek studies promoted by Jowett, for works like Plato's *Symposium* were used to justify appreciation of male beauty (Jowett himself was squeamish about the subject, and in his comprehensive introduction to the *Symposium* he omitted reference to the male orientation of the writings). Platonic love originally referred to the mystical union of two men in a single perfect friendship, which the Greek philosopher claimed was of a higher dimension than the procreative relationship of man and woman. This was exploited by Wilde in his eloquent defence speech of 1895 in which he spoke of love between men as being 'such as Plato made the very basis of his philosophy, and such as you find in the sonnets of Michelangelo and Shakespeare.' In the clampdown that followed Wilde's imprisonment expressions of homosexuality had to be muted, and alongside the friendships of the early twentieth-century novel there sits a sensuality that hints at a love that dare not speak its name. 'I love watching you tub—you've such a glorious figure', says a student in *Massacre of the Innocents* (1907) about 'the one man in the whole world whom he loved with the love that passeth the love of woman'.

Effeminacy and the use of male endearments passed into fashion in the 1920s, and though much of the campness was simply a pose, this overlapped with experimental sex, as in the case of John Betjeman, and outright homosexuality, as in the case of W.H. Auden. (Betjeman and Auden are said to have been caught in bed by a scout, whom they bribed to keep quiet. Betjeman later remarked that the experience had not been worth the money.) Writing of the 1920s hedonism, A.J.P. Taylor noted, 'The strange one-sexed system of education at public schools and universities had always run to homosexuality. In Victorian times this, though gross, had been sentimental and ostensibly innocent. At the fin de siècle it had been consciously wicked. Now it was neither innocent nor wicked. It was merely, for a brief period, normal.' The boundary between platonic and physical affection was not always clear, and this led on occasion to pain and confusion: the psychological repercussion of A.E. Housman's friendship with Moses Jackson, for instance, has caused biographical speculation. In fictional terms the classic relationship is that of *Brideshead Revisited,* in which Charles Ryder and Sebastian enjoy a honeymoon period of mutual infatuation. Acceding to the convention of the times, Waugh never spells out the physical nature of their friendship, though he does coyly refer to Sebastian's downfall as caused by 'a naughtiness high in the catalogue of grave sins'.

The differing sensibilities among the all-male community could lead to friction no less than affection, as is illustrated by the strained relationship which developed between C.S. Lewis and one of his pupils at Magdalen, John Betjeman. The solid-minded Lewis was irked by his student's giggling manner and affectations, and his distaste was exacerbated by Betjeman's preference for extra-curricular activities at the expense of his studies. For his part, the young aesthete disliked Lewis's tastes both in literature and lifestyle, for he did not share his tutor's love of myth and the medieval, and he was upset by the austere furnishings of his rooms ('arid' he calls them in *Summoned by Bells* [1960]). Even humour separated the two men, and Betjeman complained peevishly that his tutor had forever ruined Coleridge's 'Kubla Khan' by wondering whether the 'pants' in the line, 'As if this earth in fast thick pants were breathing', were made of wool or fur. When Betjeman left (without a degree) and applied for a teaching post, Lewis denied him a favourable testimonial, which led the poet to harbour a lifelong grudge. In his poetry collection *Continual Dew* (1937), he thanked Lewis for a footnote on page 256, though the book contained no such page, and made fun of him in a poem entitled 'A Hike on the Downs'.

> Objectively, our Common Room
>   Is like a small Athenian State —
> Except for Lewis: he's all right
>   But do you think he's *quite* first-rate?

The difference in temperament that led to the estrangement of the two men was also reflected in the friendships they formed. Lewis's circle was typified by a tweedy, male club atmosphere as in the 'Beowulf and Beer' evenings of which he was fond. The meetings of the Inklings were characterised by pipe-smoking and the frank exchange of opinions that were intellectually but never emotionally charged. Personal talk was avoided in favour of the literary, and the carapace that Lewis had developed to shield the inner man remained intact until middle age when the American Joy Davidson entered his life (described so movingly in William Nicholson's play *Shadowlands* [1990] and the film of the same name starring Anthony Hopkins). The friendships of the Betjeman-Waugh circle, by contrast, were typified by aesthetic posing, drunken excess, and emotional outbursts. Betjeman even carried around with him a teddy-bear named Archie (short for Archibald Ormsby-Gore) to

whom he talked in public. In place of the beer and pipe-smoking of
Lewis's circle, Betjeman's friends went in for claret and Balkan Sobranies, and in contrast to the good plain fare of the Inklings there were
the *Brideshead* feasts of lavish dishes. The friendships could hardly be
more different: forbearance marked those of the former, indulgence
those of the latter.

The fictional friendships which feature in the Oxford novel tend to be
formed early in the book, sometimes at the first meal, and play a vital
part in furthering the student-hero's sense of self by giving him someone
against whom to measure himself. The tendency of young males to form
groups—the 'sets' which characterise the genre—divides his contemporaries into groups of allies and enemies, and by identifying with one set
and distancing himself from others, the hero shapes and defines his own
tastes. The rivalry between the college sets was often uneasy, and the friction was no less a marker of social and psychological boundaries than the
punch-ups between town and gown. Class differences underscored the
differences, for the 'fast men' or 'bloods' who pick on 'reading men' and
wreck their rooms were drawn from the ranks of the wealthy who had little need to study. The dull routine of the studious helps explain the representative bias towards rowdiness in the Oxford novel, and it is a measure of Newman's skill in *Loss and Gain* that he succeeds in making the
earnest Charles Reding, a 'reading' man as his name suggests, the core
of an enjoyable book—a rare example of the bookish man as hero. By
contrast the fast man leads a life in which books play little or no part: in
the words of one such character in *Tom Brown at Oxford*, 'I'm dog-tired of
driving and doing the High Street, and playing cards and billiards all
day.' Other fast men spice their boredom with such activities as dog-
fights, rat-killing, burying college silver, making bonfires, smoking parties, screwing up tutors' doors, illicit outings, outwitting proctors, and
midnight clamberings over college walls. Nothing more typifies the fast
man than getting drunk, without which the revelry and ragging which
pervades the literature could not take place. In Joseph T.J. Hewlett's *Peter
Priggins* (1841) there was so much drunkenness, violence, and rioting
that readers complained (in defence the author claimed as a don to be
drawing on first-hand knowledge!). Little had changed sixty years later
in fictional terms, for Humphrey Dickinson's *Keddy: A Story of Oxford*
(1907) also paints a graphic picture of student rampage. The hero's first
encounter with the wicked Wilton takes place when he is with a drunken
group of cavorting students who wheel a piano into the quad, sing the
Hallelujah chorus, dance across the lawn, smash a lamp, send cascades of
water down the hall steps, toboggan down them in a hip-bath, then haul
it up a ladder and hurl it over the wall into the neighbouring college.

The evening is concluded with a cat being hurled through the chaplain's window. And as if that didn't suffice, the interwar novel too boasts its fair share of riotous behaviour, the most celebrated example coming at the beginning of Waugh's *Decline and Fall* (1928). This features a drunken group of upper-class dissolutes who return to college from a meeting of the Bollinger Club—'At the last dinner, three years ago, a fox had been brought in in a cage and stoned to death with champagne bottles. What an evening that had been!' The upper-class drunks turn on the inoffensive Paul Pennyfeather who is passing nearby and debag him, with the tragi-comic result that he is expelled for causing disorder. (The Bollinger was based on the Bullingdon Club, an exclusive undergraduate dining club of the rich and well-connected whose meetings were notoriously uproarious.)

The fiction of Waugh's time is marked by a form of cultural warfare between two opposing sets known as 'aesthetes' and 'hearties'. Aesthetes first emerged in the Wildean days of the 1870s and were characterised by their sophisticated tastes, artistic temperaments, epigrammatic conversation, and self-conscious mannerisms. 'Hearties' on the other hand were ruggedly masculine, fond of sports, patriotic, and college orientated. Compton Mackenzie claimed to have invented the latter term in 1903 to describe 'the sporting unintellectuals' who were ragging in nearby Trinity while he was discussing drama in Balliol, but they certainly existed before that in type, if not in name. In the 1840s of *Loss and Gain*, for example, Charles Reding notes with distaste the appearance of a rowing set in college. To the aesthete-writer the hearties represented the philistine enemy, and the printed page provided them with the opportunity for revenge against their more physical opponents. In the novel at least, brute force is no match for quickness of wit. When that arch aesthete Anthony Blanche of *Brideshead Revisited* is assailed by college hearties who wish to immerse him in Christ Church fountain, he unnerves them by declaring, 'Dear sweet clodhoppers, if you knew anything of sexual psychology you would know that nothing could give me keener pleasure than to be manhandled by you meaty boys. It would be an ecstasy of the very naughtiest kind.' The ambiguities of the all-male community are here encapsulated by Waugh with superb finesse, and the confused hearties back away in nervous disarray.

With the student hero assuming centre stage in the Oxford novel, the senior community is left with supporting roles and the occasional cameo. Heads of houses appear briefly as eccentric and unworldly recluses, as in *Verdant Green*. Tutors are pedantic, pompous, or ridiculous, as in *Brideshead Revisited*. Dons conform for the most part to the Casaubon type, in retreat from an involvement with life. According to a student in *Massacre of the Innocents,* 'they have lost not only time, but the elasticity of youth, and often their health and the use of their eyes'. Such figures shield themselves from life behind thick volumes in high-walled sanctuaries, and the central character of Joanna Cannan's *High Table* is a case in point. This prolonged study of the don's malaise (written by the daughter of a don) tells of the attractions of the ivory tower for one of delicate disposition—'He loved his college because it protected him: its walls were arms which enfolded his too sensitive mind'. If the fictional don is not in hiding from life, then more often than not he is a figure of authority against whom the student hero proves himself by refusing to conform. The challenge to the established order by the younger generation most often takes the form of boyish pranks, and the general feeling of the young rebels is that 'Proctors and policemen were made by an all-wise Providence to supply unspeakable thrills of excitement and joy'.

Though members of the senior community are by and large marginal to the Oxford novel, there is one twentieth-century don who has been portrayed so often that he might be considered the exception that proves the rule. This is not, as one might suppose, a celebrity like Dr. Spooner of New College, nor a literary figure such as C.S. Lewis or J.R.R. Tolkien. It is rather a man whose distinction was for befriending students of status and talent. Francis Fortescue Urquhart (1868–1934), known to one and all as Sligger (Edwardian slang for 'the sleek one'), was the first Roman Catholic ever to become a fellow of Balliol and a bachelor don of the old-fashioned kind who made the college his home and hosted in his rooms a salon for gifted, upper-class, and good-looking students. Though never serving alcohol (which enraged Evelyn Waugh), he engendered an air of informality and encouraged students to treat him as an equal. This only held good for those of a certain class and ability, however: the ungifted and unconnected soon found themselves frozen out. As a student the drunken Waugh once challenged Sligger's sexuality by standing beneath his rooms at the back gate of Balliol and singing to the tune of 'Here we go gathering nuts in May' the following words: 'The dean of Balliol sleeps with men, sleeps with men, sleeps with men.' It seems unlikely that he did in fact do so, but the suggestion of inversion typifies one of the period's fictional preoccupations.

There are representations of Sligger in numerous memoirs (he was a tutor of Compton Mackenzie), and he features too in fictionalised form in several works of literature. It has been suggested that as a student he served as model for Pater's poetic portrait of a Young Apollo in 'Emerald Uthwart', which first appeared in *New Review* (1892). Thirty years later he served as prototype for the cherubic fifty-year-old don in Beverley Nichols's *Patchwork* who socialises with the student élite and hates to be called 'Sir'. In Gerard Hopkins's *City in the Foreground* there is a similar character known as the Camel, who tries to prolong his student days of happy friendships by refusing to admit his age. Though the protagonist is at first an admirer, he comes eventually to view the Camel as lacking moral stature, and with the outbreak of war the students go off *en masse* to fight while the older man is left behind to come to terms with his isolation. (A similar notion informs Desmond Coke's *The Comedy of Age* [1906], in which a member of the senior community makes a fool of himself by trying to overcome the age difference between himself and his students.) In Betjeman's *Summoned by Bells* Sligger is pictured languishing in a deck-chair surrounded by clever and well-bred students, and the memoirs such students wrote brought further portrayals. Waugh was no fan and wrote, 'He was not a wit; nor an Oxford "character" of whom people treasure and embellish memorable sayings. . . . and there were always people outside his circle who derided what they took to be its cosiness and softness'. The slickish and snobbish Samgrass of *Brideshead Revisited* is thought to owe something to the Balliol don's character (though reference books usually cite Maurice Bowra, warden of Wadham, as the model). And in Anthony Powell's *A Question of Upbringing* there is a Sliggerite character named Sillery, 'perhaps the greatest bachelor don of fiction' according to Anthony Quinton, former president of Trinity. A master of intrigue, Sillery maintains contacts with former students when they leave Oxford for the corridors of power, and this gives him enormous influence in the outside world. From his rooms in Balliol he controls a vast network that stretches out beyond Westminster to the far-flung reaches of the empire. The identification of Sillery with Sligger was explicitly denied by Powell in his memoirs, *Infants of the Spring* (1976), in which he wrote that 'Urquhart (of some university fame, social rather than academic) has undoubtedly been portrayed in more than one novel about Oxford. Had I wished to do so, I could have offered my own projection of an unusual personality. Such was not my aim, and Urquhart, far from being (like Sillery), a talkative power-seeking Left Winger, was a devout Roman Catholic, hesitant in manner, conversationally inhibited, never pontificating about public affairs, nor addicted more than most dons to the habit of intrigue.' Nonetheless, Sillery's encouragement of a gifted and good-looking entourage inevitably calls Sligger to mind, and the remarkable similarity of name (shared initial letter, same vowels and doubling of the central consonant), suggests at the very least an unconscious association in the mind of an author who was a student at Balliol. That Sligger should have served as model for the fictional don is perhaps not inappropriate, for he embodied the chief characteristics of the Oxonian persona: a ten dency to form close male friendships; unabashed snobbism; and a winning charm which could be turned on and off as the occasion demanded.

Sligger apart, dons for the most part fare rather badly in the Oxford novel, and this contrasts with the generally favourable treatment of college servants. Dr. Johnson's experience in 1754 may provide the reason for this, for when the former student returned to Pembroke, he was received coldly by the college master but with warmth by the college servants, who remembered him more fondly. The bond between student and servant was strengthened following the introduction of the scout, for the daily contact and difference in class and age led in some instances to a father-substitute relationship not unlike that of Jeeves and Wooster. 'Quarter to nine, sir! Breakfast getting cold, sir. Any further orders, sir?': the morning ritual of *Massacre of the Innocents* exemplifies the indulgence with which the scouts coddle their pampered charges. Student outrages are treated with benevolent understanding, especially if tips are generous, and the scouts serve their class superiors with unfailing loyalty. Working-class conservatism meant that the college servants were often those most concerned about maintaining traditions and standards; in *Brideshead Revisited* it is Ryder's scout who is most upset by the intrusion in Eights Week of women into the college. What is true of the scouts is true of the other college staff, for as often as not such figures are sympathetic types, and even on occasion paragons of virtue. For *Sinister Street*'s Michael Fane it is Venner, the buttery steward, who is 'a treasure-house of wise counsel and kindly advice' and who provides 'more of the essence of social history than could be gained from a term's reading of great historians'. Yet even the venerable Venner is surpassed by the Balliol porter of *A City in the Foreground,* who not only knows the name of every member of college past and present, but 'could have taken a first class in any school with consummate ease and unruffled composure'.

Despite the restriction of place, the collegiate experience brings the student hero into daily intercourse with a surprisingly wide range of social class. His conversational partners during the course of the day might include an eccentric academic from a country vicarage, a working-class scout from East Oxford and a grammar school boy from the north of England. On men such as the upper-class Geoffrey Oakleigh of *Sonia,* the effect is revelationary—'gradually I found that something might be said even for men who had never been to a public school', he remarks. Torn from the family bosom, the hero shares his collegiate home with aesthete and rower, the religious and the degenerate, the snob and the servitor. Bound by the communal lifestyle, the assorted types in the all-male hothouse are forced to interact on a daily basis, and the relationships that are formed are crucial to the character development of the young charges. Shaped, then, in this way by the college structure, the Oxford novel constructs a fictional world in which lessons are learnt outside the classroom, friendships form the chief instruction, college servants prove the real masters, and dons are largely otiose.

The Initiation of Bradley's Freshman

Perceptions of nineteenth-century Oxford have been coloured by one novel above all others. Cuthbert Bede's *The Adventures of Mr. Verdant Green* (1853–57) proved an unexpected success when it came out, and it continued to be a popular read right up until World War II. In 1883 the print run had reached 170,000, and by 1933 sales of the novel had reached over a quarter of a million copies. *Verdant Green* stands to the latter part of the nineteenth century as *Sinister Street* to the first half of the twentieth and *Brideshead Revisited* to the second—the public image of Oxford. Its impact was considerable and long-lasting. In *Memories of Victorian Oxford* (1941), the historian Sir Charles Oman recalled going up to Oxford in 1878 with expectations formed by the fictional portrayal, and both Anthony Powell and Evelyn Waugh were similarly influenced some forty years later. 'What do you expect undergraduates to be like?' asks a character in Powell's *A Question of Upbringing;* 'Keep bull-pups and drink brandies-and-soda' comes the reply, an image straight out of *Verdant Green*. Even a hundred years after publication the novel was being held up as an example to the young Frederic Raphael (scriptwriter of the television serial *Glittering Prizes* [1976]), who was given a copy of *Verdant Green* by his father in a vain attempt to persuade him to go to Oxford rather than Cambridge. The popularity inevitably spawned imitators, and in *The Cambridge Freshman* (1871) James Rice under the pseudonym of Martin Legrand tried unsuccessfully to write a counterpart. There was even an American grandson in George Calderon's *The Adventures of Downy V. Green* (1902) in which the youngster goes as a Rhodes scholar to Oxford and tries to emulate the manner of Verdant's day to the great amusement of those around him. Written almost fifty years after *Verdant Green*, it bears testimony to the remarkable durability of the original.

Cuthbert Bede was the pseudonym of a modest clergyman named Edward Bradley who was educated at Durham University, from whose two patron saints he took his *nom de plume*. After obtaining a licentiateship in theology in 1849, he spent a year in Oxford, where his observations of student life were sharpened by the comparison with Durham. *The Adventures* originated in a series of drawings intended for *Punch*, around which Bradley added a story. The drawings, a delight in themselves, are included in the book, and that lover of humorous matters, John Betjeman, used them for his *An Oxford University Chest*. Bradley's artistic eye is apparent in the loving recreation of the physical state of Oxford, but his ear is even more remarkable, for much of the appeal of the book lies in the variety and vivacity of language. The range is astonishing: accent, dialect, pontification, mumbling, slurring, stuttering, idiolect, wordplay, slang, pun, jocularity, malapropism, spoonerism, literary allusion, classical quotation, and purple passage make the book a true linguistic feast for those who enjoy stylistic versatility.

Humorous in intent, *Verdant Green* has something of the picaresque quality of the eighteenth century, yet it is a characteristic Oxford novel in terms of plot and themes. The story is one of initiation, as the gullible Verdant Green enters into the 'mysteries' of college life. The passage through Oxford leads him from adolescence to manhood, and the story is concluded, as so often in fiction, with the young man being 'married and done for'. Along the way Green's exaggerated greenness allows Bradley to spice the details of Oxford life with much light-hearted fun. The humour is unfailingly affectionate, and Bradley, ever the vicar, takes pains to impress on the reader the general good nature of it all. 'Boys will be boys,' runs the subtext. Like all good tales of initiation, this one involves a journey, as the Birmingham to Oxford coach transports the Greens, father and son, from the realm of the familiar to that of the unknown. A footnote informs the reader that the coach ceased to run in the last week of August 1852, and the action is set in a pre-reform and pre-industrial Oxford. The coach journey is positively Pickwickian in its chaos and colour; the description not only illustrates Bradley's gift for detail, but provides the first intimations of a different reality.

> They were in good time for the coach; and the ringing notes of the guard's bugle made them aware of its approach some time before they saw it rattling merrily along it its cloud of dust. What a sight it was when it did come near! The cloud that enveloped it was discovered to be not dust only, but smoke from the cigars, meerschaums, and short clay pipes of a full complement of gentlemen passengers, scarcely one of whom seemed to have passed his twentieth year. . . . The passengers were not limited to the two-legged ones, there were four-footed ones also. Sporting dogs, fancy dogs, ugly dogs, rat-killing dogs, short-haired dogs, long-haired dogs, dogs like muffs, dogs like mops, dogs of all colours and of all breeds and sizes, appeared thrusting out their black noses from all parts of the coach. Portmanteaus were piled upon the roof; gun-boxes peeped out suspiciously here and there; bundles of sticks, canes, foils, fishing-rods, and whips, appeared strapped together in every direction,
> 'Like a swarthy Indian with his belt of beads,'

hat-boxes dangled in leathery profusion. The Oxford coach on an occasion like this was a sight to be remembered.

A student named 'Four-in-hand' Fosbrooke takes over the reins, beer and spirits do the rounds, and one of the students sounds a post-horn as the coach passes by startled villagers. The Greens are nonplussed. Verdant's journey of discovery has begun.

Like the representative types of earlier fiction, the characters of the novel conform to their names. Verdant is not only Green, but has an ancestor named Witless. His college friends comprise Charley Larkyns, good-looking, roguish, and ever ready for a lark, and little Mr. Bouncer, whose bouncy disposition more than compensates for his lack of stature. This larger-than-life character never fails to stimulate: he roars through a speaking-trumpet for his scout, keeps two dogs, Huz and Buz, in his rooms, smokes incessantly, and talks in a remarkable idiolect: 'Keep your pecker up, old feller! and put your trust in old beans', he exhorts his 'tea-cakes', as he refers to his friends. The human dynamo entertains virtually non-stop and is forever full of jest and zest: 'I can call spirits from the vasty deep', he says on opening up his drinks collection, offering his guests 'some very old port, my teacakes!—I've had it since last term!' By contrast with such vigour, the dons appear dull and lifeless: the college head has spent his life compiling a disquisition on Greek particles in eight octavo volumes, and Slowcoach the tutor gives such uninspiring lessons that students spend their time playing pranks on each other. A more warmly human figure is the sociable scout, Robert Filcher, whose concern for the young gentlemen in his charge is vital to their well-being, though he lives up to his name by ensuring himself a few private 'perquisites'. It is Filcher in his local accent who helps Verdant familiarise himself with the new environment: 'The chapel's the hopposite side, sir.—Please not to walk on the grass, sir; there's a fine agin it, unless you're a Master.' The induction includes language lessons too—'Ollidays, sir?' exclaims Mr. Filcher, 'Oh, I see, sir! Vacation, you mean, sir' is the first of many such instances.

With the departure of his father Verdant is left to fend for himself, and his first trial comes with dinner in the college hall. Intimidated by the imposing formality and the grandeur of the setting, the freshman sits nervously alone and without food until his neighbour, none other than Four-in-hand-Fosbrooke, comes to his rescue by brusquely demanding of Filcher 'What the doose he meant by not waiting on his master?' Verdant is then given his first training in the manner of a gentleman: 'Always bully them [servants] well at first and then they learn manners', he is instructed. Next morning his induction is furthered as he hurries to chapel, where Fosbrooke advises him not to waste time on 'absolutions—washing, you know', but to jump straight into a top-coat and button it to the top. Verdant is surprised to find the person next to him following the service in a book of Livy, and more surprised still to find his gown tails tied to the filial when he comes to stand up. The physical aspect of the university is introduced by a walk round the town undertaken with the mischievous Charley Larkyns. This was a regular feature of the literature, done in earlier days in the form of a poem by the likes of Wither and Tickell, and some Oxford novels are little more than a guide to the city strung round a story. In Bradley's case the topographical round is spiced with humorous misinformation designed to mislead Verdant but not the reader. While the freshman is duped into thinking that Merton has 'post-masters' because of the many letters the college receives, a footnote explains that this is the term for a college exhibitioner. In similar fashion Verdant is told that the gold tassels of Christ Church noblemen are badges of drunkenness, rather than aristocratic distinction, and that the vice-chancellor is chosen from among the tallest of those eligible as only those who 'stand high' in the university can be elected. 'You see, Verdant, you are gradually being initiated into the Oxford mysteries', says Larkyns slyly. The remark could equally be addressed to the reader.

Amongst the 'rites' that Verdant undergoes is his first 'wine', for learning to drink and smoke is vital to his training as a gentleman. In contrast to the moralising of his fellow novelists, Bradley takes a fatherly and protective attitude to his characters, and while for others getting drunk may constitute the first step on the path to perdition, for Verdant it simply constitutes a stage in his development. The party consists of thirty fast types with cigars and meerschaums in full smoke, and as Verdant gets drunk conversation gives way to song. By the time the freshman is called upon to give a speech, he is barely able to function and can only speak with slurred words.

> Genelum anladies *(cheers),*—I meangenelum. *('That's about the ticket, old feller!' from Mr. Bouncer.)* Customd syam plic speakn, I—I *(hear, hear)*—feel bliged drinkmyel. I'm fresman, genelum, and prow title *(loud cheers).* Myfren Misserboucer, fallowme callm my fren! *('In course, Giglamps, you do me proud, old feller.')*

Verdant ends abruptly in mid-sentence and is carried off to his rooms, where he is found next morning embracing the coal-scuttle. 'Time for chapel, sir!' says Filcher, and Bradley, ever the punster, has the scout add to himself, 'here is a chap ill, indeed!' Having learnt the consequence of drink, Verdant gets into debt by going on a spending spree. Running up debts was part of university life for generations of students, for the notorious credit system meant that students did not have to pay up until after finishing their studies, with the result that most students, in Bradley's words, went down with 'bill-ious fever'. For some it was simply a matter of 'the pater' settling accounts, but for others it caused real anguish. Verdant, needless to say, escapes lightly from his flirtation with danger and learns the lesson of how to manage his finances. Drink and debt: here are the twin demons of Oxford life.

The training in the accomplishments of a gentleman takes up virtually all Verdant's time in his first term and leaves him with little time for study. He goes horse-riding and is ditched for his 'vaulting ambition' but recovers sufficiently to partake in fox-hunting. He tries the river, and though he fails with rowing on the Isis, he succeeds in punting on the Cherwell. He is introduced to billiards, cards and archery, and such is his progress that by part 2 of the book, when the hero returns to Oxford for his second term, he has grown in maturity and confidence. As if to prove the point, he himself now takes part in a prank on an innocent newcomer. His initiation is not yet complete, however, for he has yet to be 'blooded' in a town and gown fight. This was a common feature of the early novels, and it forms the high point of *Verdant Green*. Though his sympathies clearly lie with the students, Bradley sounds an uncharacteristically critical note by writing, 'The lettered Gown lorded it over the unlettered Town; the plebeian Town was perpetually snubbed by the aristocratic Gown.' To cope with their more physical adversaries, the students bring in a professional boxer known as the Putney Pet and dress him in gown and cap. The fight itself is a whirligig of punches and puns, fisticuffs and fancy phrases, in which Bradley is at his best—'There's a smasher for your ivories, my fine fellow!' 'There's a crack on your snuffbox'; 'That'll take the bark from your nozzle, and distil the Dutch pink for you'; 'the Bargee fell back with a howl, and gave vent to several curseory observations'. When the senior proctor comes across the fray and tries to intervene, he has to be rescued by Pet and the gallant heroes, yet even with bloodied nose the university official remains alive to his duties and particular about his syntax.

> 'Why have you not on your gown, sir?'
>
> 'I ax your pardon, guv'nor!' replied the Pet, deferentially; 'I didn't so much care about the mortar-board, but I couldn't do nothin' nohow with the t'other thing, so I pocketted him; but some cove must have gone and prigged him, for he ain't here.'
>
> 'I am unable to comprehend the nature of your language, sir,' observed the Rev. Thomas Tozer, angrily; . . . 'I don't in the least understand you, sir; but I desire at once to know your name, and College, sir!'

The obligation to wear gowns and the authority of the proctor here give rise to a comedy of misapprehension. It is all part of the strangeness of fictional Oxford.

During the fight Verdant acquires a wound, which, like the cheek-scar of the *Schlagende Verbindung*, acts as a physical signifier of initiation. Thereafter the revelations of student life lose momentum. The focus shifts from Oxford in term-time to romance in the vacation, and Verdant's sentimental education begins when he falls in love with Miss Patty Honeywood of Honeywood Hall. College room gives way to country house, and fellows yield to females. In this Bradley is not alone, for home-life and romance provide a counterpart to the confines of college, and the respite allows for self-examination away from the maelstrom of Oxford life. The intensity of love and the complexities of emotional involvement further the development of character and lead to greater self-knowledge. Dealings with the opposite sex also provide an important marker of manliness, and Verdant himself is measured in this way during the course of the book. At the beginning his greenness is ascribed to an overprotective mother who has kept him for too long at home amongst his sisters, but when he returns at the end of his first term the feeling is that Oxford has made a man of him, which he proves by secretly kissing the family maid. By the time of his graduation he is engaged and a man of the world. He takes his fiancée to the final Commemoration, where, with the authority of an initiate, he is able to reveal to her 'some of the mysteries of College life'. Yet though the theme is well developed, Bradley is better at the amusing anecdote than romantic fiction, and there is a feeling that the author has simply run out of university material—at one point two years are passed over in a single sentence. The discovery of place which served Bradley so well in part 1 proves by part 3 to be a liability, and this may well explain why the most successful of Oxford novels are those of a wider scope, for in classics like *Sinister Street* and *Brideshead Revisited* the university years form only part of a longer story.

Topographically and chronologically, then, Bradley guides the reader through the Oxford experience. But there is more to the book than this, for like all Oxford novels it is engaged in an on-going fictional debate about the state and standing of the university. At the beginning of the book the father of Charley Larkyns speaks in favour of an Oxford education to Mr. Green senior, who is pondering whether or not to send his son to university. It is a rare but revealing comment on the purpose of university education.

> It is not so much from what Verdant would learn in Latin and Greek, and
> such things as make up a part of the education, that I advise your sending

him to a university; but more from what he would gain by mixing with a large body of young men of his own age, who represent the best classes of a mixed society, and who may justly be taken as fair samples of its feelings and talents. It is formation of character that I regard as one of the greatest of the many great ends of a university system; and if for this reason alone, I should advise you to send your future country squire to college. Where else can he learn in three years,—what other men will perhaps be striving for through life, without attaining,—that self-reliance which will enable him to mix at ease in any society, and to feel the equal of its members? And besides all this, . . . where else could he be more completely 'under tutors and governors,' and more thoroughly under *surveillance,* than in a place where college-laws are no respecters of persons, and seek to keep the wild blood of youth within its due bounds?

The emphasis here on formation of character, rather than training for a career, is similar in conception to Newman's *The Idea of a University,* and the novel is closely allied with defence of the college system. At the time Bradley was writing, Newman was putting forward his ideas on education in a series of lectures and essays (the book was written up later). They would appear to have had an important influence on Bradley's perceptions, for the assumption is that there are more important matters than the learning of classics, and students only cram briefly before examinations. Significantly, when Charley Larkyns decides he wants to study seriously, he takes time off from the university to read at home, as a result of which the man who begins the novel as a rakish socialiser ends with two university prizes and headed for the Bar. As for Verdant himself, it is clear that his exam results count for little in comparison with the lessons he has learnt at the hands of his friends, for in the making of the English gentleman lies the justification of the university. Clearly reform is not on Bradley's agenda, and underwriting his viewpoint are conservative and upper-class values, since the university of which he writes is filled with students who have little need to study for a career. When little Henry Bouncer fails his final examinations, it is laughed off as of no great consequence (he jokes that a man from Harrow should not be 'ploughed'), for his privileged background assures him a guaranteed future. Accordingly, he leaves with no degree but 'great credit' due to his unpaid bills.

Bradley's Oxford is more than a place of maturation, however, for there is a distinct sense of oddness about his city. From the moment the bemused Verdant enters the smoke-filled coach with its manic inhabitants, the reader is taken into an alien world with its own rules and its own peculiar way of doing things. 'I knew that the customs of Oxford must of course be very different from those of other places', Verdant is moved to utter at one point, and the book does its best to reinforce the notion. The city hovers indeed on the very edge of normality. Absent-minded masters in long gowns quoting Latin verse; sons of gentry lording it over timid dons; the proctors at the final ceremony in 'their apparently insane promenade'—there is in all of this a sense of underlying absurdity. There is too something curiously familiar about the elements that comprise the novel: the arrested development of a young male; a rectory upbringing amidst a brood of sisters; the displacement to college life; linguistic play and donnish humour; pet animals and a smoking hookah; a world of its own rules and logic—it is a scenario that needs but an Alice and a touch of genius to complete. Five years after *Verdant Green*'s final instalment, in 1862, a mathematics don named Charles Dodgson took a young girl and her sisters on a boating-trip along the river Thames. It was the 'golden afternoon' of July 4—'as memorable a day in the history of literature', observed W.H. Auden, 'as it is in American history'.

FROM WARNINGS TO WONDERLAND

'Oxford is a place where men have lost their souls', the young eponym of *Keddy* is warned: 'The life is so sweet, and yet so full of dangers.' The clergyman friend of Keddy who delivers the solemn warning might well have gained his impression from a reading of Oxford novels, for Lockhart's attack on debt and snobbism was followed by a string of others in similar vein. Hewlett's *Peter Priggins,* for example, is basically a series of anecdotes about student mischief which is noteworthy in a genre dominated by the view from the top in having a scout as narrator. The rowdiness of Hewlett's students was matched by those of Dickinson's *Vincent Eden* (1839), an aborted novel which appeared in instalments in *Bentley's Miscellany* and made fun of an inefficient proctor; it was stopped after six issues, allegedly at the urging of the university. Plumer Ward's *De Clifford* (1841), similar in plot to Lockhart's *Reginald Dalton,* contained an even more virulent attack on snobbism at the university and its deleterious effects. The moral dangers of Oxford life also proved a favourite theme for authors of popular romance, though some of these showed such a shaky knowledge of the university that they were accused of having gleamed their information from guidebooks. Ironically, while the novels themselves have been forgotten, a spoof of such books won considerable admiration for its mocking of the warnings about sin and degradation. Desmond Coke's *Sandford of Merton* was published under the pseudonym of Belinda Blinders and told of an innocent student led down the slippery slopes to ruin. Much is made of the traditional Oxford 'temptations': when Sandford is invited to a party, he notices with horror the presence of a bottle of alcohol—'Ah, Ralph,' runs the narrative, 'could you but have seen to what depths of depravity you were soon to sink!' The book is clearly aimed at an Oxford audience, for the insider humour assumes appreciation of such misinformation as the Sheldonian Theatre being for plays, the Randolph Hotel standing in the High, college staircases having carpets, male students drinking cocoa, and bulldogs (university policemen) being so-called because they run fast.

The finest of the tales of warning was Thomas Hughes's *Tom Brown at Oxford,* which came out in 1861, four years after its popular predecessor. The novel is set in the 1840s of Hughes's student days, and in contrast to the élitism of others the author writes with a vigorous honesty and generosity of spirit. The pre-reform university is evoked in such vivid terms that for Tuckwell the book constitutes a piece of social history: 'Every phase of College life as it exuberated sixty years ago—fast and slow, tuft and Bible clerk, reading man and lounger, profligacy and debt, summer term and Commemoration, boat races, wines, University sermons, passes easily in review.' The plot is familiar enough, though the moral dimension provides a new perspective. Fresh from his experiences at Rugby, Tom enters the college of St. Ambrose's, which has sought to enhance its prestige by attracting rich gentlemen-commoners. Because of the high level of studies at Rugby, the young hero finds himself in advance of his contemporaries, and this creates a dangerous situation in which he has time on his hands. He falls in with loose-living company, is tempted by the charms of a bar-maid, and appears headed down the path to damnation. 'How in the world are youngsters with unlimited credit, plenty of ready money, and fast tastes, to be kept from making fools and blackguards of themselves up here?' is the question the book poses, and the answer it offers is the practice of muscular Christianity. This drew inspiration from Thomas Arnold's public-school ethos of hard work, vigorous sports, and school loyalty as the antidotes to mischief. 'The devil makes work for idle hands' is the guiding maxim, and in keeping with Arnold's strong opposition to snobbery, the key role in Tom's salvation is played by a despised servitor who provides an example of self-reliance and moral endeavour which contrast with the decadent pretentions of the rich and lazy. Under his steadying influence, Tom realises the error of his ways and returns to the pursuit of good. If the book had finished there, it might have won greater recognition, but Hughes lets the novel wander on well past its natural ending, and the convoluted adventures of the second half lose themselves in a maze of moralising as Tom takes to Chartism, humanism, and Christian socialism. The novel has consequently never won the popularity of its predecessor, which enjoys a tighter structure and more cohesive content. In historical terms it is a significant marker of the rise in public-school values which followed the rapid expansion of the middle classes under Victoria. The influx of socially conscious students from such schools affected the atmosphere at Oxford, for they brought with them feelings of superiority which are reflected in the literature they wrote. Ironically, the notion of individual worth that Hughes promotes in *Tom Brown* turned out to be but a harbinger of the privileged élitism that marks Edwardian fiction.

Alongside the novels of morality there are a small but significant number of novels of faith set in Oxford. The earliest example, Plumer Ward's *Tremaine* (1825), is of interest chiefly for its portrayal of Oxford as a secluded centre of theology at a time when others were writing of student vice. It serves as a reminder that even in decadent pre-reform days there were men of the stature of Newman, Keble, and Pusey at work in the city. Newman's own *Loss and Gain* remains one of the most appealing of all Oxford novels despite the difficulty of the religious arguments, and the many light touches are unexpected in a figure associated with religious earnestness. Parodying the fear of Catholicism, Newman at one stage paints a picture of Oxford alive with rumours of Jesuits, and such is the alarm that the claim is even made that the pope has been seen walking down High Street. The spiritual journey of Charles Reding from Canterbury to Rome—he belongs appropriately to a college named St. Saviour's—forms the core of the book. In the background stands pre-reform Oxford with its fast men and feasting; even those in charge find little favour with the priggish hero—'what Heads of houses, Fellows, and all of them put before them as an end is, to enjoy the world in the first place, and to serve God in the second', he complains. There are some finely crafted vignettes, and in one of the book's celebrated set-pieces Reding's tutor hosts a breakfast party at which the surfeit of food contrasts with the stiffness of conversation.

> A tutor's breakfast is always a difficult affair both for host and guest; and Vincent piqued himself on the tact with which he managed it. The material part was easy enough; there were rolls, toast, muffins, eggs, cold lamb, strawberries, on the table; and in due season the college-servant brought in mutton-cutlets and boiled ham; and every one eat to his heart's, or rather his appetite's, content. It was a more arduous undertaking to provide the running accompaniment of thought, or at least of words, without which the breakfast would have been little better than a pig-trough. The conversation or rather mono-polylogue, as some great performer calls it, ran in somewhat of the following strain:
>
> 'Mr. Bruton,' said Vincent, 'what news from Staffordshire? Are the potteries pretty quiet now? Our potteries grow in importance. You need not

look at the cup and saucer before you, Mr. Catley; those came from Derby-
shire. But you find English crockery everywhere on the Continent. I myself
found half a willow-pattern saucer in the crater of Vesuvius. Mr. Sikes, I
think *you* have *been* in Italy?'

"No, sir,' said Sikes; 'I was near going; my family set off a fortnight ago,
but I was kept here by these confounded smalls [exams].' . . .

'Take some more tea, Mr. Reding; it won't hurt your nerves. I am rather
choice in my tea; this comes overland through Russia; the sea-air destroys
the flavour of common tea. Talking of air, Mr. Tenby, I think you are a
chemist. Have you paid attention to the recent experiments on the composition and resolution of air? Not? I am surprised at it; they are well worth
your most serious consideration.'

Loss and Gain is not the only novel to have come out of the Oxford
Movement, for Hurrell Froude's brother, J.A. Froude (1818–94), also
produced two fictional works. A follower of Newman, Froude's spiritual
path had led him into a morass of confusion, and his troubled outpour-
ings are of interest as an example of the crisis of faith which so unsettled
Victorians. In the autobiographical *Shadows of the Clouds* (1847), published under the pseudonym of Zeta, Froude writes of a student who falls
under Newman's charismatic influence but ends with an indifference to
creed and form of worship. Two years later the more powerful *Nemesis of
Faith*, which was publicly burnt in outrage at its godlessness, went even
further by describing a devotee of Tractarianism who loses faith altogether and becomes a sceptic. Doubt in an all-merciful God, disbelief in
the Old Testament, dislike of clerical worldliness, and distaste for the
notion of eternal damnation—all are described in the most agonising of
terms. The pain is almost palpable: 'I would gladly give away all I am, and
all I ever may become, all the years, every one of them, which may be
given me to live, but for one week of my old child's faith, to go back to
calm and peace again, and then to die in hope.' Yet though Froude's
scepticism has more in common with modern sensibilities than Newman's theology, the latter's crystalline prose proves much the more
enjoyable to read.

Mrs. Humphry Ward's *Robert Elsmere*, which came out in 1888, belongs
in content and setting to the same period of post-Tractarian Oxford
when, in the fall-out following Newman's conversion, varieties of doubt
seemed as plentiful as varieties of faith. Ward's novel was the most successful of its time, much praised by contemporaries such as Burne-Jones
and Henry James, and Gladstone was moved to write an article by way of
refutation, '*Robert Elsmere* and the Battle of Belief', which won almost as
much fame as the novel itself (the pair met and discussed the book's
'attack on Christianity' in the warden's lodgings at Keble). Mrs. Ward fol-

lows the example of Froude in tracing the path of an Oxford student who finds his faith shaken by the advances in biblical criticism and scientific understanding, but the denouement differs in that the hero turns to philanthropic idealism inspired by the notion of Christ as human and moral exemplar. The ideas behind the book owed much to Mrs. Ward's friendship with the Oxford professor of moral philosophy, T.H. Green (1836–82). The first fellow of Balliol not to be in clerical orders, Green had a wide following among those who could neither accept the miraculous element of Christianity nor face a world without faith. As an Hegelian Idealist, he was wedded to the notion of social progress and argued the need for personal involvement in humanitarian activities. In *Robert Elsmere* Green is transmuted to Grey, a man who despite his shyness exerts a powerful influence on those around him through his strong sense of mission, and under his guidance the young Elsmere is led to forsake his clerical vocation for charitable work with the poor in London, where he eventually dies of tuberculosis. (The author herself later followed the example of her hero by devoting herself to good works in London.)

As the niece of Matthew Arnold, Mrs. Ward (1851–1920) was familiar with Oxford through family connections, and she moved to the city at the age of sixteen, slipping into her new life 'as a fish into water'. In her memoirs, *A Writer's Recollections* (1918), she looks back fondly on her time in the city: she studied on her own in the Bodleian, moved in university circles, and took the opportunity to discuss intellectual matters with the likes of Pattison, Jowett, and Pater. When she was twenty she married a fellow of Brasenose, T. Humphry Ward, and the couple had three children before moving to live in London. She used her familiarity with Oxford types to good effect in her novel, and one of the most memorable figures of *Robert Elsmere* is the protagonist's tutor, Langham. He is 'a skeleton at the feast' whose humanity has been corroded by scepticism, and though he is intellectually acute, he is emotionally sterile as shown by his inability to relate to women. As such he belongs to a select group of desiccated dons drawn by female hands which also includes Eliot's Casaubon, Broughton's Forth, and Cannan's Fletcher. Interestingly, all four of the authors spent time in Oxford and were able to observe the effect of prolonged immersion in scholarly activity on the emotional life of the dons, though this did not prevent them from harbouring an affectionate respect for the city at large. In Mrs. Ward's case this can be sensed in the descriptive passages of her novel, as when Robert Elsmere first visits Oxford as a student accompanied by his mother.

> The dreaming city seemed to be still brooding in the autumn calm over
> the long succession of her sons. The continuity, the complexity of human
> experience; the unremitting effort of the race; the stream of purpose run-
> ning through it all; these were the kind of thoughts which, in more or less
> inchoate and fragmentary shape, pervaded the boy's sensitive mind as he
> rambled with his mother from college to college.

Oxford here speaks of effort and purpose, far removed in nature from
the den of vice described in earlier novels, and it typifies the change in
tone during the course of the century as the university underwent
reform. It remains a city where men lose their souls, but in place of
moral perdition and loss of faith, there is abandonment to the charms of
a 'dreaming city'. Behind the construct lay not only the notion of dream
as product of the artistic imagination, but also that of the illusionary
nature of existence—'Life, what is it but a dream?' asks the city's most
famous author in *Alice in Wonderland* (the title is taken here to refer both
to the *Adventures* of 1865 and *Through the Looking-Glass* [1871]). The children's story played a vital part in the move towards idealisation of
Oxford as a 'city of dream', for the Wonderland became woven into the
fabric of its mythology and changed the way in which it was viewed.
Though *Alice* is not an Oxford novel as such, the fantasy might paradoxically be considered *the* Oxford novel, full of donnish humour and playfulness, and Desmond Morris was not the first to observe that it is 'a typical Oxford book—light and fantastic but with serious bits of thought
embedded in it.' It represents too the city's most radical reshaping, for
whereas the college buildings appear to young Robert Elsmere to be
monuments to historical continuity, passed through the topsy-turvy consciousness of Lewis Carroll they emerge as phantasmagoric spaces
peopled by peculiar and idiosyncratic creatures.

For all its flights of fancy, *Alice* is firmly rooted in Oxford and in particular in the Christ Church environment of its author and the young
girl who inspired him. Lewis Carroll was the pseudonym of Charles
Dodgson (1832–98), a mathematician in holy orders who lived all his
adult life in Christ Church, first as student and then as Student (the latter, the college term for a fellow, was the sort of linguistic absurdity in
which he revelled). Alice was based on Alice Liddell, the young girl with
whom he fell in love. She was the daughter of the head of the college,
Henry Liddell (1811–98), co-author of the remarkably long-lived Liddell and Scott's *Greek Lexicon* (1843), still in use today. When Dodgson
took Alice and her two sisters on a rowing-trip to Godstow in 1862, they
pressed him to tell them one of his funny stories, and the moment is
recalled in the opening poem of *Alice's Adventures*.

All in the golden afternoon
    Full leisurely we glide;
For both our oars, with little skill,
    By little arms are plied,
While little hands make vain pretence
    Our wanderings to guide.

Ah, cruel three! In such an hour,
    Beneath such dreamy weather,
To beg a tale of breath too weak
    To stir the tiniest feather!
Yet what can one poor voice avail
    Against three tongues together?

The children so enjoyed the story Dodgson told them (inspired perhaps by the rabbit-holes they passed on the way to Godstow, where they picnicked) that he wrote it out in an illustrated booklet which he later presented to Alice. Nothing more would have been heard of it had not a visitor to the Liddells been so impressed with what he read that he urged publication. The *Adventures* were given the benefit of illustrations by *Punch*'s John Tenniel, and the book proved to be such a success that even Queen Victoria was said to be an admirer. (According to a story firmly denied by Dodgson, Victoria asked to receive a copy of his next work, in response to which he sent her an abstruse mathematical work.)

Beneath the whimsy of *Alice* there lies the familiar plot of a young person's passage through Oxford, albeit in distorted and mirrored form, for in the fall down the rabbit-hole Alice is plunged into a peculiar world of its own rules, its own logic, and its own language—the university in altered guise. The reworking makes grotesque caricature of the faces and places with which Dodgson and Alice Liddell were familiar in their daily life. Many of the 'curious creatures' were modelled after the gargoyles and emblems on Oxford buildings, and some were references to animals in the University Museum and a menagerie near Christ Church. The Gryphon and the Mock Turtle were nicknames for the author's two brothers who studied at the college, and 'twinkle, twinkle, little bat' was a joke at the expense of Carroll's colleague and former tutor, Professor Bartholomew Price (nicknamed Bat). The 'drawling master' was supposedly based on the drawing master, John Ruskin, and the Mad Hatter on a haberdasher in the High Street who was unbalanced by the fumes he inhaled while making hats. The royal motif that runs through the adventures, particularly *Through the Looking-Glass,* arose out of a visit to Oxford by the Prince and Princess of Wales in 1863 when Dodgson took Alice to see the celebrations; references in the story to the event include the crown, the royal banquet, and royal emblem of the Lion and the Unicorn. Christ Church itself forms a shadowy background to the adventures: the long hall lit by lamps recalls the college dining-hall, and the decorated heads of its fireplace with their elongated necks provided the model for the fictional telescoping of Alice's neck. The Mad Hatter's tea-party has something of the manner of the riotous meals in hall where students bombarded each other with food, and the frog-footman at the duchess's door stands by impassively as a plate is hurled, much as college servants turned a blind eye to the ragging of aristocratic students. Even the college topography has something of the geography of Wonderland about it: according to Peter Conrad, who teaches there, 'Within Christ Church there are folds of puckered space which, levered open, disclose small pockets of forgotten time, like Lewis Carroll's rabbit-holes digging into the fourth dimension.' It is against this background that is set the character formation of a young girl in what amounts to a rite of initiation. At first the newcomer is distraught in the alien world, and her development necessitates coping with a series of tests and trials. The constant changes of size which she experiences signify the effect on the body of growing up, and the implication that she is entering a new stage of life is taken up in the sequel, *Through The Looking-Glass,* in which the progress of Alice from pawn to queen signals her transformation from child to adult.

The author of this remarkable story was a shy mathematician who suffered from a stutter and was devoted to his college. He was also a conscientious scholar who produced several books on mathematical subjects. But beneath the veneer of correctness (for Tuckwell he 'was stiffly conservative'), Dodgson was a man of extraordinary habits. His files of correspondence contained some ninety-eight thousand cross-references, almost as if he feared his life might veer out of control unless kept under the strictest observation. Such was his meticulousness that he even kept a record of every dinner-party he hosted in order not to serve guests the same dish. A lover of wordplay, he was fascinated with reversal and mirror images, such as 'evil' being the reverse of 'live' (symbolic, he thought, of the 'fall' and how humans move away from childhood purity). His pseudonym too derived from a reversal, for his first names, Charles Lutwidge, were transposed into Latinate form and then switched in order. Dodgson was an inventor of some originality if little practicality, and produced nearly two hundred pamphlets that range in content from how not to catch a cold to how to play billiards on a circular table. In addition, he was a gifted photographer whose portraits include celebrated poets and girls in fancy dress. He could be awkward—he once invited a lady to dinner but stipulated she should come without her husband. He could be pedantic—he calculated that the 'millions of hugs and kisses' two girls sent him at the end of a letter would take twenty-three weeks of twelve hours kissing a day. And he could be quirky—he refused letters addressed to Carroll and claimed not to know who he was. His whimsy and peculiarities make him for many the quintessential don: to A.L. Rowse he was the 'complete Oxonian' and the 'most donnish of dons', while Virginia Woolf claimed, 'If Oxford dons in the nineteenth century had an essence, he was that essence.'

The most striking of Dodgson's oddities was his series of friendships with pre-pubescent girls, whose company he found more amenable than the adults by whom he was surrounded. Though he is thought to have had over a hundred such child-friends during his life, there was one particular favourite to whom he was so attached that memory of her continued to haunt him even after she had passed beyond puberty into a world to which he could no longer relate. This was Alice, Dodgson's 'dream-child', and *Alice* is sometimes seen in terms of the post-Romantic idealisation of the child when it seemed that the innocence of childhood provided spiritual insight into heavenly purity and love. Yet at the core of *Alice* there also lies a tale of *angst,* and the darker aspects of the story have been often commented on. Though Dodgson could be stiff and awkward with adults, his stutter would disappear when in the company of his child-friends, and this may have reflected a deep-seated yearning for the happy childhood days of his parents' rectory, where he was brought up amidst a bevy of sisters. There are even grounds for thinking that he may have suffered from some form of gender confusion, and psychiatrists have suggested that he was subject to a peculiar kind of arrested development which led to his identifying himself with young girls. 'That Dodgson was fascinated by little girls and that he fantasised playfully turning into one is written often in his letters and Diaries and demonstrated in his life itself', writes Phyllis Greenacre. Significantly, *Alice* shows an obsession with identity—'Who in the world am I?' the young girl wonders, and later declares, 'I'll stay down here till I'm somebody else'—and the constant switching from child-size to adult-size suggests that the author may have conflated the young girl and himself in the central character. If this were the case, it would explain the preoccupation of Dodgson with mirror images and the desire to pass 'through the looking-glass'.

Viewed in the light of this, Alice's story can be understood as a form of catharsis by which the unsettled Dodgson vented his feelings about Oxford. His discomfort in Christ Church, conscious or unconscious, was transposed to the young girl's experience of a nightmarish world, in which she undergoes the type of physical discomfort and identity crisis that characterise severe stress. In the progress through Wonderland the young rectory boy/girl exhibits all the culture shock of a freshman transposed from home and dropped into college life. The length of the fall down the rabbit-hole speaks of the emotional distance involved, and in the early stages of her time in Wonderland Alice is distraught and disorientated: she feels lonely, longs for her cat, and the first meeting with others takes place in a pool of her own tears. The rites and rituals of the alien world seem to her strange and absurd—'we're all mad here', the Cheshire Cat says—and the young girl is told on more than one occasion how stupid she is because she does not catch on to the new ways. The games and cruelty of Wonderland are like an absurdist extension of *Verdant Green,* whose freshman-hero pulls 'crabs' while rowing and shoots an Honorable's skye terrier when practising archery. But it is in the parodic references to academic life that the university background of *Alice* is most apparent, almost as if Dodgson's unconscious were reprocessing his everyday environment in the manner of dreams. 'It's really dreadful . . . how all the creatures argue', Alice mutters to herself at one point, as if the strain of constant logic-chopping was wearing for the author. His psychic double is put through the academic mill to such an extent that language loses meaning and she fears for her sanity: 'How the creatures order one about, and make one repeat lessons!' she complains. Significantly it is curiosity which motivates the young Alice, as it does academics, and the *Adventures* can be read as a series of verbal and intellectual challenges. There is training in syllogisms at the Mad Hatter's tea-party, in sophistry by the Cheshire Cat, and drawing the moral by the duchess. There are lessons in logic and language, such as meaning what you say and saying what you mean. There is pedantic nitpicking when the duck asks the mouse the meaning of 'it' in the phrase 'even Stigand, the patriotic archbishop of Canterbury, found it advisable'. There are speculative queries, like the riddle of the raven and the writing-desk; there is showing off in the dry speech by the mouse; and there is a parodic instance of academic nonsense in the meaningless paraphrase of 'Be what you would seem to be.' There is even a form of tutorial given by the caterpillar from the top of its mushroom that by its Socratic questioning and long pauses recalls the manner of Benjamin Jowett, with whom Carroll was acquainted. And at the end of the passage through Wonderland there is a final examination of sorts when Alice has to answer for herself at the trial of the stolen tarts, success in which leads to speculation about her future life.

In the very midst of the academic mayhem lies a secret garden. When Alice finally obtains entrance, she finds the King and Queen of Hearts playing croquet, just as the Liddells who ruled over Christ Church played croquet in their own enclosed garden. The resemblance extends to a similarity of character, for Mrs. Liddell was a more forceful figure than her thoughtful and indecisive husband. 'I am the Dean, this Mrs. Liddell / She plays the first, I, second fiddle', ran a verse well-known in university circles. Dodgson's relation with them was polite and friendly, if somewhat formal, for they moved in circles that included Gladstone and royalty, and Mrs. Liddell considered her family to be socially superior to the mathematics don. At one point there was a rift in relations when Mrs. Liddell tore up the letters Dodgson had written to Alice, though what occasioned this is unclear. There may have been an uneasiness in her mind concerning the relationship with Alice, or she may have feared that Dodgson was planning to marry one of her daughters. Viewed in the light of this the queen's constant reiteration of 'Off with his head' takes on macabre overtones, for it may well represent Dodgson's fear of Mrs. Liddell severing his contact with Alice (or in Freudian terms, his manhood). Was the mathematician worried, as others before him, of losing his soul at Oxford? As the real-life Alice passed through puberty, Dodgson may have sensed trouble in Wonderland and decided to terminate the dream before it engulfed him; accordingly, Alice awakes at the end of *Through the Looking-Glass*, free to join adult life but stranding Carroll in his own time-warp. Like the Mad Hatter's tea-party, he was forever stuck at a particular moment in time and unable to accompany the girl he identified with to full maturity—the White Knight escorts Alice to the brook, but he cannot cross it. Though Carroll later wrote *The Hunting of the Snark* (1876) and *Sylvie and Bruno* (1889, 1893), the Wonderland was abandoned and Dodgson clung ever more tenaciously to the adult world of college politics, issuing a circular to the effect that 'He [Mr. Dodgson] neither claims nor acknowledges any connection with any pseudonym, or with any book that is not published under his own name.' Though this was prompted by the desire for anonymity, it may also have reflected a need for cohesion in a fragmented personality.

The presence of *Alice* still lingers in modern-day Oxford. There is the Deanery Garden in Christ Church where Dodgson first met his dreamchild, and a portrait of him hanging in the college hall; opposite the college stands the Old Sheep Shop of *Through the Looking-Glass* where the real-life Alice used to buy Barley Sugar sweets; there is the Treacle Well at Binsey where the dormouse says three little sisters lived; there is even the remains of a dodo, symbol of the stuttering 'Do-do-Dodgson', in the University Museum. Associations with *Alice* have left their mark on the fiction too, and the book had a decisive impact on the course of Oxford literature by steering it in the direction of youthful enchantment and golden afternoons. The appeal of Wonderland contributed too to the tendency of novels to focus on the peculiarity of Oxford: from background the city evolves to form the very subject matter itself. Novels set in Oxford become novels about Oxford, and love in the city turns to love of the city. Delight in *Alice* augments the affection: when the young Keddy goes up to Oxford, he is excited to find that he has passed 'through the looking-glass, and never expected to return', and the students of *Sinister Street* are inspired by a similar notion to set up a magazine entitled *The Oxford Looking Glass*. But it is in the student Wonderland of *Brideshead Revisited* that the influence of *Alice* is most striking, for the Christ Church infatuation of Charles Ryder for Sebastian drew its inspiration from that of Lewis Carroll for Alice.

Shortly before starting to write *Brideshead Revisited* in 1939, Evelyn Waugh had written a review of Carroll's *Complete Works,* and his novel was strongly affected as a result. Like Dodgson, Sebastian suffers from an arrested emotional development and both struggle with the demands of adulthood. Both are also characterised by an almost desperate longing for the sanctuary of childhood and a return to innocence. When Charles Ryder yearns for excitement in the grey city, he finds in Sebastian an invitation to Christ Church and 'that low door in the wall, which others, I knew had found before me, which opened on an enclosed and enchanted garden'. The reference is to the low door in *Alice* which leads into 'the loveliest garden you ever saw'. As sublibrarian of Christ Church Dodgson had had access to a small room overlooking an enclosed garden in which the Liddell children used to play together, and it must have seemed to him a private Eden of childhood innocence from which he as an adult was locked out. Only in the realm of the imagination could he find the golden key. All too aware of the transience of childhood, he made up a story which is full of the dread of passing time. His interest in photography can be seen in the same way as an attempt to capture the passing moment, just as his fantasy traps the dream-child within the pages of a book. Sebastian too tries to overcome time by refusing to grow up, and the title of the Oxford section of *Brideshead Revisited*, 'Et in Arcadia ego', carries the suggestion of pre-lapsarian times which is echoed in the return of Sebastian to his childhood guardian when he takes Charles to visit his nanny. But though Sebastian carries about him the verdant freshness of childhood, he is plagued by the thought of decay: 'I should like to bury something precious in every place where I've been happy and then, when I was old and ugly and miserable, I could come back and dig it up', he says. The child-man clings to his teddy as the child-girl to her kitten, both anxious not to let go of their innocence. 'Ever drifting down the stream / Lingering in the golden gleam' wrote Carroll, and Sebastian wishes for nothing more than to linger in that golden gleam. Youth, dream, love, enchantment, and all bathed in the rosy glow of nostalgia: it was but a step from Wonderland, a glance through a looking-glass—et in Arcadia ego.

CHAPTER 5

A Delightful Lie: The Oxford Myth

'Isn't it all a delightful lie?' he wanted to know. 'Mightn't one fancy this the very central point of the world's heart, where all the echoes of the general life arrive but to falter and die?'

—Henry James, 'A Passionate Pilgrim' (1875)

1865 WAS AN *annus mirabilis* for Oxford literature, for not only was that the year in which *Alice's Adventures in Wonderland* was published, but it was also the year in which Matthew Arnold's influential *Essays in Criticism* first appeared. The latter contained a passage apostrophising Oxford as a 'Beautiful city' and an 'adorable dreamer' which is considered to mark the initiation of the cult of Oxford which flourished in the late nineteenth and early twentieth century. The literary portrayals were such that the name of Oxford was imbued with an aura of mystique unparalleled among its fictional counterparts. Athens, Rome, Venice, Paris . . . such cities resonate with the potency of concepts like culture, power, and art. The Oxford of the myth by contrast is shadowy and elusive: 'Know ye her secret none can utter?' claimed devotees. Venerable with age but blessed with eternal youth, fictional Oxford conjures up not so much a single idea as a host of glittering images—*jeunesse dorée* on college lawn; panelled rooms with mullioned windows; verdant lawn, and stone-wall retreats; Pimms, boaters, and long summer evenings on a languid river; May balls of sumptuous decadence; mulled wine and Turkish coffee; beauty, wit, and brilliance set against a backdrop of dreaming spires.

The 'Beautiful city' of Arnold's imagining was constructed on foundations laid by Elizabethan and Romantic predecessors: Camden prepared the ground, Hazlitt laid the foundations, and Arnold shaped the superstructure. The visionary city he constructed served as a focus of inspiration for the next generation who celebrated Oxford in adulatory terms, both in verse and prose. By championing the Hellenic strand of the national inheritance, Arnold also played an important part in fostering the affinity of Victorians with ancient Greece. Taking their tone from the influential example of Oscar Wilde, students later dispensed with the moral dimension of Arnold in favour of pleasure and the cult of beauty, so that when the cultural élitism of the English Athens was married to the social élitism of upper-class undergraduates, the result was a frothy mix of supercilious wit and superior posing. For the novelists of the early twentieth century Oxford was no longer a physical entity as such but a fictional space in which to flaunt their purple prose, and their novels broke upon the public in two myth-making waves separated by World War I. The first of these included two influential novels which still continue to find a readership: Max Beerbohm's *Zuleika Dobson,* which appeared in 1911, and Compton Mackenzie's *Sinister Street,* which came out three years later. Following World War I, there was a second wave in the brief revivescence of the 1920s, sandwiched between the austerity of war on the one hand and the Great Depression on the other. Beverley Nichols's *Patchwork,* issued in 1921, attempted to reinvoke the spirit of *Sinister Street,* while Gerard Hopkins's *A City in the Foreground,* published in the same year, offered a less intoxicated view. The battering that the national confidence took in World War I can be sensed in both, for on the one hand there was a mood of relief in the aftermath of the war to end all wars, and on the other a realisation that the heyday of Edwardian England had passed forever and things would never be the same again. The satirical and disillusioned tone of Evelyn Waugh's *Decline and Fall* (1928), which begins and ends with Oxford, conveyed a sense of unease with a world out of joint. It is a wickedly funny novel whose satiric humour derives from the discrepancy between the reactionary narrative and the reality of the world in which it is set. Nearly twenty years later, following the social engagement of the writers of the thirties, Waugh wrote the retrospective *Brideshead Revisited* in more sentimental vein. The book was composed during the deprivations of World War II and looked back with a sense of longing to the decadent and carefree 1920s. It represented the culmination of the genre, for by the time the book came out the 'golden age' of Oxford life had passed. From the midst of wartime and middle age Waugh evoked a student paradise in the lost world of his youth by glamorising a small group of the privileged and the well-connected. It was not until the 1950s that Britain began to wake up to post-war realities, but as the country struggled to shake off its imperial inheritance, traditional values came under attack and the Oxford myth increasingly fell out of favour. A process of 'dis-enchantment' set in, as a result of which mythical Oxford stands today in a shaky state of uncertainty, in danger of collapse yet sustained by its own dazzling legacy.

If the English Athens represented Oxford as cultural fountainhead, the Oxford myth portrayed the university in terms of a privileged paradise. The two might seem contradictory, for the former depended on the quality of its achievements, whereas the latter was characterised by indulgence. As the experience of the eighteenth century had shown, 'tippling and toping' were incompatible with maintaining the viability of the English Athens. With the rise of university esteem in Victorian times, however, the literature shows a return to favour of the old Elizabethan notion of the university, furthered on the one hand by the growing confidence of Victorian Britain and on the other by a revival of interest in Greek studies. With the sun never setting on the British Empire, there was a widespread feeling that the country represented a peak of civilisation, fostered by parallels with Darwin's evolutionary theory concerning the survival of the fittest, and parallels were once again drawn with the achievements of fifth-century B.C. Greece. This resulted in part from a greater appreciation of the Greek tradition in the cultural life of the nation, furthered by men such as Arnold and Jowett with their interest in Greek studies. The identification of Victorians with their classical predecessors can be sensed in the claim by John Stuart Mill that the battle of Marathon was a more important event for British history than the battle of Hastings, and in the attachment of figures like James Hill and George Grote to the Greek tradition. For the devotees of Oxford, the university stood in the same relation to the country at large as Athens had to ancient Greece. For Pindar Athens had represented the bulwark of Hellas; Michael Fane of *Sinister Street* pictures Oxford in similar terms and fancies its guiding spirit to be Pallas Athene.

The Victorian version of the English Athens differed in a number of important ways from its earlier counterpart. Firstly, it had a component of cultural nationalism which emphasised the Englishness of the city in contrast with the territorial patriotism of Elizabethan times which derived from attachment to the 'patria', as exemplified by the topographical writings of Camden and Drayton. The advent of romanticism brought a greater interest in cultural identity and the notion that behind the nation-state stood a pivotal ethnic group. Victorian intellectuals were thus concerned to give the sense of Englishness shape and definition, and the Whig view of history promoted by Thomas Macaulay (1800–59) suggested that the national gift for compromise had led to a steady development towards freedom, justice and democracy. This heritage was seen as presaging a glorious future with the suggestion that the country had a unique national destiny to spread the rule of democratic law and order. At the same time the intellectual culture of the country was defined as empirical, pragmatic, individualist and concrete, as exemplified by the tradition of Francis Bacon, Thomas Hobbes, John Locke, John Stuart Mill and Charles Darwin. The tendency towards common sense was contrasted with Continental philosophers, who were seen as theoretical, metaphysical, ideological, contentious and altogether too abstruse. In literature efforts were made to build up a national canon embodying Englishness and a Shakespeare-blessed inheritance—Palgrave's *Golden Treasury of English Verse* (1861) was intended as a 'national anthology', and forty years later Quiller-Couch's best-selling *Oxford Book of English Verse*

(1900) fulfilled a similar function (both men were Oxonians, indicative of the strong patriotic spirit in the Victorian university). A sign of the times was the introduction of English as a subject for study at Oxford, and the first examinations in the subject were held in 1897. The blessings of language and literature was set beside that of the English countryside, which was reenvisaged in Arcadian terms as the physical essence of all that was good in the national tradition. Conservation groups were set up to protect country villages from the inroads of industrialisation, and *Country Life* promoted a picture-book view of the countryside as an idyllic existence in which the graceful balance between humans and nature was accompanied by healthy pastimes and social harmony.

The pride of the English derived its strength from the unparalleled scale of the British Empire, which was acclaimed as the greatest contribution to the spread of civilisation since that of the Romans. The glory the English derived from this involved a distinction between the political state of Britain with its trappings of power and the cultural qualities of the English with their democratic traditions. The multi-ethnic state of Britain was beginning to forge an identity of its own as the tradition was established of a common cause ranged against an untrustworthy and undemocratic Continent, and in the imperial melting-pot it was impractical to insist too strongly on a common ethnicity. Figures like Disraeli, Marx, Wilde, and Conrad were absorbed with little difficulty because of the heterogeneity, and on the northern side of the border Scotland not only had a separate education system but a 'Scottish Athens' of its own in Edinburgh (this had had its 'golden age' during the late eighteenth and early nineteenth century, when it hosted the likes of James Boswell, Robert Burns, Walter Scott, David Hume, and Adam Smith). Nonetheless, though Britannia ruled the waves, it was the 'Queen of England' who stood at the heart of the empire in the minds of the English, and the two words 'England' and 'Britain' were often used as synonyms (as indeed they sometimes still are even today). Nowhere is the cult of Englishness more evident than in the novels of the Edwardian era, in which Oxford is represented as the embodiment of all that is best in the national character. The assumption was that if Britain ruled the world and Oxford represented the cream of the country, then the fictional exploration of the university would illuminate the virtues that had led to global ascendancy. The search for the 'secret' of Oxford thus becomes the search for the key to national greatness. The self-acclamation reaches its apogee in *Sinister Street*, in which Michael Fane declares forthrightly, 'I'm so positive that the best of Oxford is the best of England, and that the best of England is the best of humanity.'

Sinister Street exemplifies a further difference between the Edwardian and Elizabethan conceptions of the English Athens, for whereas Renaissance writers sought to glorify the contribution of the university to the life of the nation, the new version was inspired by the sympathy of college members with the ideals of ancient Greece and the lifestyle of the city-state. This was fostered by the dominance of Greek philosophy, particularly that of Plato, in the late-nineteenth-century university. Shelley had been among the first to be inspired by the philosopher-poet, but it was not until later in the century following the work of men like Jowett and Pater that the influence of Plato became widespread. Students of classics saw in the aristocratic assumptions of the ideal city-state a similarity with their own conditions and a justification of their leisured lifestyle, and when they later came to write of their student days they made use of the philosopher's ideas to underpin their own. According to Jean Fayard, 'the *Republic* lay open on every table and couch in Oxford and the spirit of Plato breathed from its pages like the odour of a cherished flower.' The cult of beauty, the striving for the ideal, the disdain for the ordinary, and the praise of contemplation—all stemmed from Plato. The notion that the virtuous life lay in the contemplation of good held particular appeal for wealthier students at the university, who were free to pursue their interests without even the compunction to pass exams. This was particularly true of Edwardian days, but it still pertained to a lesser extent in the 1920s when Waugh claimed, 'At least half of the undergraduates were sent to Oxford simply as a place to grow up in'. The novels of such students reflect their easy-going ways, and those fictional characters who spend their time studying are the objects of scorn and despised as dullards: Gaveston ffoulkes of *The Oxford Circus*, for instance, is amused by the efforts of those who have to work, for 'they, poor bats and moles, thought of Oxford as a place of learning!' Auberon of *Rough Justice* 'found that the life of most men at St. Mary's was just about as strenuous as lying full length in the sun, with soft music playing. Learning was dross in their sight; base was the slave who worked or was poor.' The code of the upper-class men of Anthony Powell's *A Question of Upbringing* is also to refrain from practical work, remaining aloof like Plato's philosophers, though the search for ultimate truth had become debased to a matter of art for art's sake and the praise of uselessness. Whereas the English Athens of Elizabethan times focussed on achievements, the modern version pictured the secluded groves as a place for privileged youth; in contrast to the contemplative observations of Robert Burton, the students of the myth indulge themselves in the pursuit of beauty and a life of pleasure. The evolution of the Oxford myth in this way out of the tradition of the English Athens is closely connected with the rise to dominance of romanticism, the development of which affected the whole tone of Oxford writings.

FROM ARTIFICE TO ROMANCE

The Oxford myth has its roots in the late eighteenth century, when the first indications appear of a romantic attachment to the city. This was closely bound with the shift in taste away from a preoccupation with classical form to a revaluation of the Gothic in which Oxford remained rich. The transition is exemplified in Thomas Warton's verses 'On Sir Joshua Reynolds's Painted Window at New College Oxford', in which the poet declares that he was 'For long, enamour'd of a barbarous age, / A faithless truant to the classic page' and honours the painter for marrying classical elegance with medieval religiosity.

> Reynolds, 'tis thine, from the broad window's height,
> To add new lustre to religious light;
> Not of its pomp to strip this ancient shrine;
> But bid that pomp with purer radiance shine;
> With arts unknown before to reconcile
> The willing Graces to the Gothic pile.

Warton's stance marks an important change in attitude to Oxford, for appreciation of its medieval aspects led to growing affection for the city. The comments of Horace Walpole (1717–97), another early enthusiast for the medieval, typify the delight taken in the historical atmosphere of Oxford: 'as soon as it was dark I ventured out, and the moon rose as I was wandering among the colleges, and gave me a charming venerable Gothic scene, which was not lessened by the monkish appearance of the old fellows stealing to their pleasures.' The fascination with the past which Walpole exemplifies was allied to an interest among writers in the effect of milieu in shaping sensation, exemplified by the novels of Walter Scott (1771–1832). Meanwhile, literary language was freed from classical conventions, and the urbane conventions of eighteenth-century verse were replaced with a concern to articulate individual reaction. As a result of these developments writers were able to make use of a greater range of expressive terms, and this is reflected in the heightened sense of immediacy and personal investment which mark the descriptions of Oxford in the early nineteenth century.

The Romantic response to the city was coloured not only by its historical appearance, but by the pastoral nature of the setting and the intellectual tradition. Beauty, the past, and the pursuit of truth were a heady mixture for an age whose credo was 'A thing of beauty is a joy forever'. Significantly, part of *Endymion,* in which Keats made his famous declaration, was written in Oxford during the poet's visit in 1817. He was enamoured of the town: 'This Oxford', he wrote to a friend, 'I have no doubt is the finest City in the world'. It was during this visit too that he made up the parody of Wordsworth beloved of anthologists, the first verse of which runs as follows:

> The Gothic looks solemn,
>   The plain Doric column
> Supports an old bishop and crosier.
>   The mouldering arch,
>   Shaded o'er by a larch,
> Stands next door to Wilson the Hosier.

Like Keats, other romantic writers were moved to praise by the city's historical aspect, and Mary Shelley wrote in *Frankenstein* (1818) of how the beauty of the town was heightened by its Civil War associations. The leading essayists of the age—Charles Lamb (1775–1834) and William Hazlitt (1778–1830)—were particularly delighted by the sense of the past, and both portrayed the *genius loci* in terms of the lingering presence of the great minds of earlier times. Lamb 'inhales learning' as he ponders on the spits that might have cooked for Chaucer, while Hazlitt 'imbibes the air of thought' and enthuses about a 'sacred city'. In a poetic outpouring that foreshadows Arnoldian themes, the latter weaves together a dazzling web of words around spires, dreams, enchantment, imagination, and the heroic struggle against barbarism. It is a passage of stunning force which powerfully conveys the light of learning dispelling the dark forces of ignorance, though in Hazlitt's picture, ironically, darkness takes the form of the human element of pre-reform Oxford.

> Rome has been called the 'Sacred City':—might not *our* Oxford be called so too? There is an air about it resonant of joy and hope: it speaks with a thousand tongues to the heart: it waves its mighty shadow over the imagination: it stands in lowly sublimity, on the 'hill of ages;' and points with prophetic fingers to the sky: it greets the eager gaze from afar, 'with glistering spires and pinnacles adorned,' that shine with an internal light as with the lustre of setting suns; and a dream and a glory hover round its head, as the spirits of former times, a throng of intellectual shapes, are seen retreating or advancing to the eye of memory: its streets are paved with the names of learning that can never wear out: its green quadrangles breathe the silence of thought, conscious of the weight of yearnings innumerable after the past, of loftiest aspirations for the future: Isis babbles of the Muse, its waters are from the springs of Helicon, its Christ-Church meadows, classic, Elysian fields!—We could pass our lives in Oxford with-

out having or wanting any other idea—that of the place is enough. We imbibe the air of thought; we stand in the presence of learning. We are admitted into the Temple of Fame, we feel that we are in the sanctuary, on holy ground, and 'hold high converse with the mighty dead.' The enlightened and the ignorant are on a level, if they have but faith in the tutelary genius of the place. We may be wise by proxy, and studious by prescription. Time has taken upon himself the labour of thinking; and accumulated libraries leave us leisure to be dull. . . . Let him then who is fond of indulging in a dream-like existence go to Oxford and stay there; let him study this magnificent spectacle, the same under all aspects, with its mental twilight tempering the glare of noon, or mellowing the silver moonlight; let him wander in her sylvan suburbs, or linger in her cloistered halls; but let him not catch the din of scholars or teachers, or dine or sup with them, or speak a word to any of the privileged inhabitants; for if he does, the spell will be broken, the poetry and religion gone, and the palace of the enchantment will melt from his embrace into thin air!

This then is the Oxford of romanticism—'the palace of the enchantment'. Though Hazlitt uses Rome as the model for his sacred city, his Oxford speaks across the ages to that of Camden and Spenser. The difference from Gibbon's 'palaces of science' could hardly be more marked: in place of detached consideration there is soaring aspiration, and instead of the clear light of day there is moonlight and magic. Though arts and science had hitherto been partners in the common pursuit of knowledge, the two disciplines were fast becoming Two Cultures filled with mutual distrust, and Hazlitt's Oxford exalts imaginative rather than analytic truth. It is an English Athens arrayed with the finery of romanticism, a city above all of 'poetry and religion'.

The notion of Oxford as an imaginative stronghold underpins what many claim to be the best sonnet ever written about the town, 'Oxford, May 30, 1820'—the product of a Cambridge man, William Wordsworth (1770–1850). Though the poet follows Dryden in forsaking his *alma mater*, the apostasy is not simply a rhetorical device but the genuine assertion of a belief in poetic truth. The sonnet contains the famous tribute to the High—'The stream-like windings of that glorious street'—and the lines ring throughout with Wordsworthian significancy.

> Ye sacred Nurseries of blooming Youth!
> In whose collegiate shelter England's Flowers
> Expand, enjoying through their vernal hours
> The air of liberty, the light of truth;
> Much have ye suffered from Time's gnawing tooth;
> Yet, O ye spires of Oxford! domes and towers!
> Gardens and groves! your presence overpowers

> The soberness of reason; till, in sooth,
> Transformed, and rushing on a bold exchange,
> I slight my own beloved Cam, to range
> Where silver Isis leads my stripling feet;
> Pace the long avenue, or glide adown
> The stream-like windings of that glorious street -
> An eager Novice robed in fluttering gown!

The overpowering emotional transport, 'Nurseries' of infant-wisdom, 'blooming vernal Flowers' that embody truth, the loss that comes with time, and the pantheistic overtones of the Isis-led 'Novice' all speak of Wordsworth's visionary view of life and the rejection of rationalism. Though the sonnet is accompanied by another in apparent retraction, 'Shame on this faithless heart!', it is a lesser poem, unable, as it were, to stand against the momentum of his passion. With its air of devotion, the sonnet is an important marker of the growing significance of Oxford during the course of the century, for as commercial and utilitarian values gained in influence, the city served as a symbolic rallying point for those concerned to defend religious and imaginative truths. With the upheavals that accompanied industrialisation, the historical buildings and intellectual tradition seemed to many to represent a cultural oasis of stability and continuity.

Curiously, the Tractarian uproar of the 1830s and 1840s had the effect of strengthening attachment to Oxford, for though the movement turned the city into a religious battleground, it was intrinsically Romantic in nature. In his *Apologia* Newman claimed lineage from such writers as Coleridge, Southey, Wordsworth and in particular Walter Scott, who had drawn attention to 'something deeper and more attractive' in the faith of the Middle Ages. As nursery and stronghold of the Church of England, the university represented for Tractarians 'the very soul of the nation' in a very real sense, and in their concern to defend religious truth members of the movement saw themselves as part of a university tradition which stretched back through the high church Toryism of the eighteenth-century university to the time of Duns Scotus and the medieval founders. The Oxford Movement was thus as much a movement *for* Oxford as a movement *of* Oxford, and the emotional attachment was strong. Newman's comments about his time as a student at Trinity College are worth repeating here: 'There used to be much snapdragon growing on the walls opposite my freshman's rooms there, and I had for years taken it as the emblem of my own perpetual residence even unto death in my University.' In his novel, *Loss and Gain*, the protagonist Charles Reding is almost as attached to Oxford as he is to his faith; the gain of Catholicism only comes at the loss of the city, and the pain this causes can be seen in the passage below. The hero is making a return to Oxford after an absence of two years, and since he is on the point of conversion, he knows that this must be his final visit to the Anglican stronghold. It is as if he is parting from a loved one.

> He had passed through Bagley Wood, and the spires and towers of the University came on his view, hallowed by how many tender associations, lost to him for two whole years, suddenly recovered—recovered to be lost for ever! There lay old Oxford before him, with its hills as gentle and its meadows as green as ever. At the first view of that beloved place he stood still with folded arms, unable to proceed. Each college, each church—he counted them by their pinnacles and turrets. The silver Isis, the grey willows, the far-stretching plains, the dark groves, the distant range of Shotover, the pleasant village where he had lived with Carlton and Sheffield—wood, water, stone, all so calm, so bright, they might have been his, but his they were not. Whatever he was to gain by becoming a Catholic, this he had lost; whatever he was to gain higher and better, at least this and such as this he never could have again.

The strength of the Tractarian affection for Oxford is apparent too in the poems of F.W. Faber (1814–63), a fellow of University College and a follower of Newman. Faber's series of poems—'College Library', 'College Garden', 'College Chapel', 'Oxford in Winter', 'Absence from Oxford'—are strongly coloured by the historical and religious associations of the city's ancient buildings, and in 'Aged Cities' the poet recalls Continental towns he has known and ends with a quatrain that echoes the eulogistic verse of the Elizabethan Dan Rogers.

> Yet have I seen no place, by inland brook,
> Hill-top or plain, or trim arcaded bowers,
> That carries age so nobly in its look
> As Oxford with the sun upon her towers.

In 'College Library' Faber describes how a nearby churchyard lends a haunted air to the library as it seems to fill with dead men's spirits, while the moonlight shadows that flicker on medieval works tell 'Of quiet ages men call dark and drear, / For Faith's soft light is darkness to the world.' The Romantic refuge in the past is here pervaded by a deeply felt yearning for the religious certainty of those who erected the college buildings. Such sentiments only served to foster the notion of Oxford as 'a sacred city'; the movement that began in a college common room ended by sanctifying college stone.

Faber's poetry was in keeping with the shifting taste in architecture, as exemplified by A.W.N. Pugin's influential book *Contrasts* (1836). This championed the Gothic as the genuine expression of religious devotion while downplaying the pagan classical styles of the Renaissance. The writings of John Ruskin, who studied at Christ Church in the 1830s, reflect a similar line of thinking, though he was less sympathetic to the Anglo-Catholicism of the Oxford Movement. In his autobiography, *Praeterita* (1886–89), he relates that as a student he revelled in the medieval and Tudor associations of Christ Church cathedral—'religion unbroken,—the memory of loyalty, the reality of learning'—but was disappointed by his rooms in eighteenth-century Peckwater Quad, considered one of the glories of the university, because he felt deprived of 'an oriel window looking out on a Gothic chapel'. Ruskin worked vigorously to promote appreciation of the medieval, and the Gothic revival of north Oxford, particularly the remarkable University Museum (1855), constitutes the physical part of his legacy. For the Pre-Raphaelites of the next generation, much influenced by Ruskin's ideas concerning the social import of beauty, the medieval associations of Oxford held an almost mystical import. Edward Burne-Jones and William Morris studied together at Exeter College in the early 1850s and were overwhelmed by the romance: 'Oxford is a glorious place; godlike!' Burne-Jones wrote to his mother, 'at night I have walked round the colleges under the full moon, and thought it would be heaven to live and die here.'

By the time that Arnold came to write of Oxford, then, there was a groundswell of affection for the city. At the same time the work of men like Newman, Pattison and Jowett had served to raise public esteem for the university. Earlier in the century the university had been the butt of jibes in the national press, and it had been outshone in international terms by the likes of Edinburgh, Gottingen, and the 'Spree-Athen' of Berlin with its newly founded Humboldt University. But as Oxford underwent reform, its public image was transformed and university spokesmen came to stand once again at the centre of the nation's affairs. By the 1860s university confidence was on the rise, and there was a large measure of public goodwill for a reforming institution, so that the pursuit of excellence could again be trumpeted without cause for derision. At the same time the inroads of industrialisation were beginning to make themselves felt in the city. The railway had arrived in the south, and the rapid expansion of the population led to housing development on the green fringes of the city. For the academic community there was a very real sense of the modern world closing in, both philosophically and physically. It was against such a background, with Oxford cast as a relic from happier times, that Arnold conjured up a visionary city which drew substance on the one hand from romantic affection and on the other from allegiance to a threatened tradition.

ARNOLD'S DREAMING SPIRES

Of all those who have written about Oxford, Matthew Arnold has become the most closely identified with the city, so much so that he is sometimes referred to as its unofficial poet laureate. Not only did he coin the two famous epithets—'city of dreaming spires' and 'home of lost causes'—but his long poems 'The Scholar-Gipsy' (1853) and 'Thyrsis' (1867) have been called the 'two great Oxford poems' and his celebrated prose piece in *Essays in Criticism* is considered the city's finest tribute. For anthologists of Oxford his words take pride of place, for commentators a quotation is indispensable, and for admirers of Oxford his writing takes precedence. Books declare homage in their very titles—Patrick's *Dreaming Spires* (1924), Silver's *Our Young Barbarians* (1935), Liddell's *The Last Enchantments* (1948), and Dawes's *The Last Enchantment* (1960). Scholars and lovers of romance have set off in the footsteps of his scholar-gipsy, many of them eager to identify 'each hallowed spot' of the poems, and when that great benefactor of the university Cecil Rhodes lay dying in far-off Africa, he called for the passage from *Essays in Criticism* to be read out to comfort him. The moonlight, enchantment and dream with which Arnold arrayed Oxford has stuck in the public mind, and the debate he initiated still plays itself out in contemporary accounts of the city.

Matthew Arnold could be said to have inherited the Oxford tradition from his father, the famous Dr. Arnold of Rugby, for before becoming headmaster of the public school, Thomas Arnold had studied at Corpus Christi and been a fellow of Oriel. In 1841, the year before his death, he was appointed regius professor of history and returned in honour to Oxford, where he had acquired a reputation as an outspoken opponent of Tractarianism and defender of a 'broad church'. His son became a student at Balliol in the early 1840s, where according to Lionel Trilling he 'was everything of which his father would have disapproved—jaunty, indolent, debonair, affected'. Like his father, he became a fellow of Oriel and left Oxford to work in education, but he renewed his connection in 1857 when he was elected professor of poetry for five years. He used the position to put forward his views on the edifying nature of literature and the vital role of criticism, and such was the approbation with which the lectures were greeted, both locally and nationally, that he was pressed to continue for a second term of office.

Arnold had written 'The Scholar-Gipsy' shortly before taking up the professorship, and 'Thyrsis' appeared in the year that he relinquished the post. The two poems, though separate in composition, can be considered as a thematic whole, for they are linked by similarity of style, sentiment and subject matter, with the second poem responding to the resigned despair of the first with an upbeat ending. Compton Mackenzie paid tribute to the poems by claiming that Arnold had done more for Oxford than any of the great Cambridge poets had ever achieved for their *alma mater*, yet curiously they contain little by way of description of the city, a mere few lines between them, for the setting is rural and the mood pastoral. For one critic, indeed, they are 'second only to Keats in the poetry of the English countryside'. Nonetheless, behind the nature descriptions can be sensed the spirit of academic Oxford, for the poems derive from the custom of university members to take long afternoon walks. This was an age when many were familiar with the surrounding countryside for up to twenty miles in every direction (the practice was eroded towards the end of the century by increased pressure to work, expanding suburbs, and alternative interests like sports and cycling). Country walking had been invested with a special significance by Romantics following the practice of Coleridge and the Wordsworths, and what had once been a sociable exercise was re-envisaged as a form of spiritual journey. In the encounter of the individual with nature lay the means for personal refreshment, and because the peripatetic led away from civilisation and then back, the walk was seen in terms of a retreat which provided opportunity for reflection and self-examination. For Arnold, as for others, the fullness and vitality of nature contrasted with the aridity of modern urban life. The effect of this in Oxford terms is that the source of wisdom is posited not in the university as such but in the surrounding countryside.

As a student Arnold had been accompanied on country walks by his college friend and fellow-poet, Arthur Hugh Clough (1819–61), and both 'The Scholar-Gipsy' and 'Thyrsis' concern the memory of such walks and the sense of loss—of youth, of conviction, and of friendship. 'The Scholar-Gipsy' was inspired by a passage in Joseph Glanvill's *The Vanity of Dogmatizing* (1661) concerning the legend of an Oxford scholar who forsakes his future for the lure of the gipsies. The story is summarised in the fourth verse of the poem:

> And near me on the grass lies Glanvil's book —
>   Come, let me read the oft-read tale again!
>   The story of the Oxford scholar poor,
>   Of pregnant parts and quick inventive brain,
>   Who, tired of knocking at preferment's door,
>   One summer-morn forsook
>   His friends, and went to learn the gipsy-lore,

> And roamed the world with that wild brotherhood,
>   And came, as most men deemed, to little good,
> But came to Oxford and his friends no more.

The scholar-gipsy is championed in the poem as a seeker of truth who
has foreseken rational knowledge for the inspiriting wisdom of nature.
In contrast to his single-minded devotion to Romany arts and mysteries
(telepathy and fortune-telling in Glanvill's original), the poem posits the
'sick hurry' and 'divided aims' of contemporary life, and the poignancy
of the writing derives from the sense of regret that the modern mind
with its analytic bent is no longer capable of accepting revelation like the
gipsy lore. For Romantics the gipsy was a symbol of pre-industrial life, an
unspoilt noble savage who was untainted by a corrupt society. The longing for the cloister which underlies much Oxford literature is here
reversed as escape from the 'fever' and 'fret' of the world is projected
onto the freedom of the open countryside. The poem follows the spirit
of the seventeenth-century 'drop-out' as he roams the surrounding hills,
allowing the poet haunting vignettes as the scholar is seen

> Crossing the stripling Thames at Bab-lock-hithe,
>   Trailing in the cool stream thy fingers wet
>   As the punt's rope chops round;

or caught on Cumnor range, where he

> Turn'd once to watch, while thick the snowflakes fall,
> The line of festal light in Christ-Church hall

or by Godstow Bridge, where bathers

> Marked thine outlandish garb, thy figure spare,
> Thy dark vague eyes, and soft abstracted air —
> But, when they came from bathing, thou wast gone.

Removed from the throng, the scholar-gipsy is a lone and reserved figure
whose presence, significantly, is only noticed by the young and innocent.
For those consumed by the 'strange disease of modern life', he remains
hidden from view.

   The crisis of faith which underwrites the 'The Scholar-Gipsy' is taken
up again in 'Thyrsis', which was written to commemorate the premature
death of Clough in Florence (in the poem Clough is portrayed as Thyrsis and Arnold as Corydon, names taken from shepherds in Virgil's pastoral). In recalling the walks of the two friends, the poet remembers the
'signal-elm' of which the pair had been fond and which they had
invested with a symbolic importance. It stands at the heart of the poem,

replacing the scholar-gipsy of the earlier poem, and has been called 'the most famous tree in English literature':

> We prized it dearly; while it stood, we said,
> Our friend, the Gipsy-Scholar, was not dead;
> While the tree lived, he in these fields lived on.

Though the tree is used in this way as a symbol of revealed truth, it is also imbued with a mythic stature that draws on ancient models of the tree as a religious and totemic object of devotion. Located on a hill overlooking the city—'Bare on its lonely ridge'—the solitary tree is a lone survivor of the primordial forest that formed mankind's earliest temple. As such it speaks of the divine order and the beneficence of nature; it is a Blakean tree of immortal knowledge, the sight of which provides the poet with a modicum of consolation for the death of his friend. Because it stands on a hill, the path leading up to it involves effort and struggle; moreover, like truth, it can be approached from different directions. For country walkers, its sheltering branches offer respite and an opportunity to look down on the city below in restful contemplation. Conversely, for those in the city mired in the commonplace of everyday life, the tree constitutes a focal point that raises the thoughts of the beholder upwards in the manner of the soaring church spire of medieval times; for an age of doubt the natural feature serves as a more potent reminder of the eternal verities than the clerical structures of the past. The poem thus fashions not so much an elm as a tree of eternal life whose physical form points to a higher truth and mankind's ultimate end.

Though hardly relevant to the effect of the poem, it has been pointed out often enough that the real-life model for the tree is not an elm at all, but an oak. This caused some confusion amongst early enthusiasts, and Edward Thomas wrote in his book on *Oxford* (1903) that 'I know nobody who ever saw, and recognised, Matthew Arnold's tree', though Henry Taunt, the local photographer, pointed out soon afterwards in *The Oxford Poems of Matthew Arnold* (1910) that 'Arnold's Tree is an Oak and not an Elm, but it has always been trimmed in the fashion which Elms often are and at a short distance few could tell the difference. It is generally termed 'The Umbrella Tree', and is seen from many parts of the Cowley Road, Headington Hill, and the higher ground on the East side of Oxford. Once noticed it will not be easily forgotten.' The identification was corroborated by a letter to the *Times Literary Supplement* on November 22, 1917, by the former professor of poetry A.C. Bradley, who wrote, 'About 1877 I asked Matthew Arnold whether the tree thus visible was the tree of "Thyrsis" and he answered without hesitation, "Yes".' Since the poem was written from memory of walks some twenty years earlier, the misidentification of the tree is not the only error, for there are also inaccuracies in the routing and the description of the views. This in no way affects the potency of the poem, and indeed the poetic tradition of the elm suggests an apt choice for a monody; for ancient Greeks it was considered suitable for a funeral grove because it provided no food.

The framework of 'Thyrsis' reflects Arnold's three-fold view of life: first, the innocence of youth in harmony with the world; then alienation and the isolation of the individual in a troubling universe; finally, reconciliation and the sense of acceptance that comes through suffering. As students, the poem suggests, the two young friends had abandoned themselves to the joyful pursuit of truth, but the springtime feelings had given way to doubt and despair. Instead of struggling through to calmer waters, Clough the 'Too quick despairer' is portrayed as giving in too easily and abandoning his friend. Left behind, the solitary poet tries to revisit the tree of their student days, but has to turn back before he can reach it because dusk is approaching. Nonetheless, the inspiring sight of the 'lone, sky-pointing tree' serves at the end of the poem as a reaffirmation of the ideals of youth and renews the poet's determination to continue his quest for truth. Like 'The Scholar-Gipsy', the poem evokes the countryside in terms of romantic attachment, and from the lonely ridge where stands the signal-elm is a view of the city whose description has become the most famous of all the many lines about Oxford.

> And that sweet city with her dreaming spires,
> She needs not June for beauty's heightening,
> Lovely all times she lies, lovely tonight!

The sentiments underlying Arnold's two poems—the urge to escape the present, the romanticising of the past, and an idealisation of the city—are also much to the fore in the celebrated prose passage from *Essays in Criticism*. The collection was based on views put forward in Arnold's Oxford lectures, and the eulogy was added to the preface in appreciation of the university for providing him with a platform. As poet and critic Arnold was well-versed in the tradition of Oxford literature, and he drew on the past in shaping his tribute. Like the early Romantics, he glories in the historical associations of the city and pictures it as a stronghold of the imagination; like the Tractarians, he sees in the Gothic architecture the conviction of faith of earlier times and is filled with a sense of loss. The sceptical reference in the passage to Tübingen University with its reputation for science underscores the rejection of philosophical materialism and the assertion of belief in a higher truth, while the allusion to 'barbarians' and 'Philistines' arises out of Arnold's nomenclature for Victorian society: 'barbarians' for the upper classes concerned with their own enjoyments; and 'philistines' for the narrow-minded middle class with their materialistic and moralistic instincts. (The reference to barbarians is taken from a slight misquotation of Byron's *Childe Harold's Pilgrimage*—'*There* were his young barbarians all at play'; the use of 'philistine' as an uncultured person had been appropriated from the German by Carlyle earlier in the century.)

> Beautiful city! so venerable, so lovely, so unravaged by the fierce intellectual life of our century, so serene!
>
> 'There are our young barbarians, all at play!' And yet, steeped in sentiment as she lies, spreading her gardens to the moonlight, and whispering from her towers the last enchantments of the Middle Age, who will deny that Oxford, by her ineffable charm, keeps ever calling us nearer to the true goal of all of us, to the ideal, to perfection,—to beauty in a word, which is only truth seen from another side?—nearer perhaps than all the science of Tübingen. Adorable dreamer, whose heart has been so romantic! who hast given thyself so prodigally, given thyself to sides and heroes not mine, only never to the Philistines! home of lost causes, and forsaken beliefs, and unpopular names, and impossible loyalties! what example could ever so inspire us to keep down the Philistine in ourselves. . . . Apparitions of a day, what is our puny warfare against the Philistines, compared with the warfare which this queen of romance has been waging against them for centuries, and will wage after we have gone?

The passage has proved beguiling to generations of admirers, but for those intimate with the history of the university the portrait does not bear close examination, one reason no doubt why it is masked in moonlight. It is clearly an idealised view, and Arnold himself was aware of the partiality for he wrote in a letter to his brother, 'I find I am generally thought to have buttered her up to excess for the sake of parting good friends; but this is not so, though I certainly kept her best side in sight, and not her worst.' The question raises itself therefore as to what amongst the vast range of Oxford literature has led the writings of Arnold to stand supreme, for there are other descriptions of equal power, other lines of luminous brilliance, yet none have captured the public imagination in quite the same way. The answer would seem to lie in the scope of the vision that underpins the 'Beautiful city', for it is not the description of Oxford as such that gives the passage its rhetorical force so much as the exposition of an idea—or rather an ideal. At the centre of Arnold's construct stands the classical notion of 'perfection', or self-realisation, as the end of human endeavour, and the tribute to the university was born out of a belief that the means to further that end was through the promotion of culture. The viewpoint was summed up in *Cul-*

ture and Anarchy (1869), in which he spoke of culture as 'a pursuit of our total perfection by means of getting to know, on all matters which most concern us, the best that has been thought and said in the world; and through this knowledge, turning a stream of fresh and free thought upon our stock notions and habits.' For Arnold British society was characterised by the impoverishment of its cultural life and he was particularly concerned to counter the puritanical and commercial instincts of the middle class. To balance the overemphasis on morality and work, which he termed the Hebraic tendency in the national culture, he advocated an injection of the Greek spirit to foster enjoyment of life and the appreciation of beauty. His debt to classical Greece can be seen in the borrowings he made, not just in terms of philosophy but in the actual wording of his vision. His tribute to the 'Beautiful city' owes something to the 'beautiful city' of Plato's *Republic,* and the lyric sweep of the Oxford passage clearly echoes Pindar's words in praise of a wrestling victory.

> Man's life is a day. What is he?
> What is he not? A shadow in a dream
> Is man: but when God sheds a brightness
> Shining life is on earth
> And life is sweet as honey.

The sense of human insignificance which the Greek poet gives voice to was linked in Arnold's mind to the championing of Christianity, and the praise he expressed for Newman stemmed from admiration of his defence of religion against the rationalist tendencies of the age. Yet at the same time there was in Arnold's writings a suggestion that culture could act as an alternative to religion, for he wrote of poetry providing a means of consolation in the modern age as religious writings had done in the past: 'More and more mankind will discover that we have to turn to poetry to interpret life for us, to console us, to sustain us', he wrote in *Essays in Criticism.* The stance put Arnold at odds with the dominant commercial and scientific tendencies of the age, and the elegiac atmosphere of the passage about Oxford derives from its sense of a heroic but losing battle. It is not so much the description of a city as a hymn to transcendence.

The views Arnold put forward were closely identified with Oxford in the public mind, not just because of his professorship there but because of the way in which he proselytised on the university's behalf—'the cause in which I fight is, after all, hers', he claimed expansively. As centres of culture, universities played an important part in his battle against philistinism, and those who worked there he regarded as 'aliens' detached from society and removed from the class in which they originated. As such they were able to propagate what Arnold with his liking for sloganeering called 'sweetness' (beauty) and 'light' (truth and learning)—terms taken from Swift's *The Battle of the Books* (1704). His writings on the subject in *Culture and Anarchy* (1869) illustrate how closely he identified his vision with the university.

> Yet we in Oxford, brought up amidst the beauty and sweetness of that beautiful place, have not failed to seize one truth,—the truth that beauty and sweetness are essential characters of a complete human perfection. . . . I say boldly that this our sentiment for beauty and sweetness, our sentiment against hideousness and rawness, has been at the bottom of our attachment to so many beaten causes, of our opposition to so many triumphant movements.

The lost causes, forsaken beliefs, unpopular names and impossible loyalties were never fully spelt out, but one may suppose that apart from Lollardism, the Civil War, Jacobitism and the Oxford Movement, Arnold had in mind the championing of religion and the humanist tradition. The urgency of his rallying-cry was born of the sense that, handicapped by its privileged and corrupt history, the university was losing the battle: 'Oxford, Oxford of the past,' he wrote, 'has many faults; and she has heavily paid for them in defeat, in isolation, in want of hold upon the modern world.'

With Arnold, then, the Romantic response to Oxford found its supreme articulation, one in which the beauty of the city was wedded to high moral purpose and the heroic defence of truth. His mythopoetic city appealed to deeply rooted human aspirations, and as he was the leading man of letters of his time, the imagery he used carried the stamp of authority. Succeeding writers drew from his writings the material for a golden city: buildings of bewitching beauty, a glorious past, guardian of culture, home of truth, and an other-worldly sense of detachment. The playground of the Bright Young Things, however, would hardly have met with Arnold's approval, for his advocacy of culture had a strong moral dimension, and he insisted on 'high seriousness' in literature. For the Victorian sage appreciation of art was inseparable from the consideration of its effect on conduct, and the 'silver city of dream' conjured up by later novelists took its tone of frivolous superiority from other sources.

By placing Oxford at the centre of his mission, Arnold transformed the dull doings of Wormius and his kind into a noble crusade and the highest of human callings. Academic Oxford by way of response has taken him to its bosom, proclaiming him 'the truest representative of her culture' and 'that prince among dons'. The man who championed

the university was himself championed by the men of the university. The
idealisation of Oxford came at a time when patriotic feelings were rising
across the country as a whole, and the tribute found a ready response
amongst the swelling chests of loyal Oxonians, for in the minds of impe-
rialists the lofty aims were married with the role of the university in providing the rulers of empire. If culture was the means to perfection, ran
the thinking, and Britain represented the best in the world, then it followed that to be educated at the country's leading university marked a
high point of human development. Inspired by such a notion, Cecil
Rhodes set up a scholarship scheme to promote Oxford values throughout the English-speaking world, and William Gladstone made a speech at
the Union in 1890 which illustrates the extent of the filial devotion: 'To
call a man a characteristically Oxford man is, in my opinion, to give him
the highest compliment that can be paid to any human being. I fear I do
not and cannot accept such a compliment. But one part of it I will
accept, and it is this, that, apart from every subject of controversy, there
is not a man that has passed through this great and famous University
that can say with more truth than I can say, "I love her from the bottom
of my heart."'

To his detractors Arnold is little more than a defender of privilege
and an ideologue of élitism. Like his Greek mentors, he believed that
enlightenment was only attainable by a privileged few whose role was
to spread the benefit of their wisdom, and the haughty talk of moral
absolutes and eternal verities has made him a prime target for those
for whom such notions as culture, truth and 'the best' are in themselves suspect. Moreover, in contrast to the current emphasis on plu-
ralism, Arnold insisted on the need for cultural and religious confor-
mity in order to ward off the tendencies in society towards anarchy. Yet
though so much of his social criticism is out of step with modern
thinking, it is worth noting that Arnold's advocacy of culture, like
Oscar Wilde's socialism, was a case of champagne for all. Culture, he
claimed, 'is not satisfied till we *all* come to a perfect man! It seeks to
do away with classes; to make the best that has been thought and
known in the world current everywhere.' His long career as a schools
inspector can be seen as serving the same end, for he hoped to level
society upwards through the vital role of state education in raising
national standards. Indeed, because of his arguments in favour of government intervention, he has even been claimed as a forerunner of
the welfare state. His position as a cultural élitist *and* a democratic liberal confounds modern perceptions, so that both radicals and conservatives have found in him an ally for their cause in the contemporary
debate about culture, education and the canon. It is testimony to the

power of his vision that the concerns he addressed still speak to a society with values of a very different kind. Though much else has fallen, the signal-elm still stands and offers inspiration for those who seek it; though the dreaming spires are obscured by modern constructs, they remain the city's most alluring fiction and the view of Oxford that everyone wants to see.

Nothing Remains but Beauty

In his lines from Shotover stile, the Oriel fellow Arthur Grey Butler (1831–1909) contemplates the faith of those who built the towers and spires of Oxford which glisten in the sunlight below. As he does so, the city becomes slowly wrapped in mist, and the encircling vapours seem to the poet like the mists of doubt which have obscured the former certainty of his faith. 'Nothing remains but Beauty', he bemoans.

As secularisation made headway and Oxford was stripped of its clerical dress by the process of reform, beauty became an article of faith in itself and the yardstick by which the poets measured their response to the city. The poetry of Gerard Manley Hopkins (1844–89) exemplifies the transition. Arriving as a student in 1863, Hopkins was an exhibitioner at Balliol where he studied under Jowett. With a room at the top of the college and a view over the 'towery city', he felt himself at home in the cloistral and clerical atmosphere. He thought canoeing the 'summit of human happiness', enjoyed a succession of breakfast-parties, and made the most of such opportunities as hearing Matthew Arnold lecture in the Sheldonian. In one of his student sonnets, 'To Oxford' (1865), he writes of how his love for the city grows more 'sweet-familiar' with each passing term, declaring it 'my park, my pleasaunce', while in another he presents a fresh and startling perspective of the city's buildings by crouching up against a chapel building and inspecting the ornamental ridge-crest with its circular holes and flag-shaped serrations. Thoughts are here led heavenwards, not by a church steeple, but through the eye of the poet pressed against the side of the wall. In the uncompleted 'Richard', Hopkins went even further in overturning convention by writing of a shepherd moved to exchange the tinkling of his herd's bells for the musical towers of Oxford. The pastoral reversal idealises the cloistered gardens as a place where nature, beauty and spirituality coincide, and from Cumnor Hill Arnold's symbolic focus is relocated to college quadrangle.

While still a student, Hopkins had been received into the Catholic faith by Newman at Birmingham, and after graduating (with a double First) he trained as a Jesuit priest. In late 1878 he was appointed assistant

of the Oxford church of St. Aloysius in Woodstock Road, and in the ten
months he stayed there he produced two of the finest poems ever written
about the city, 'Duns Scotus's Oxford' and 'Binsey Poplars'. Hopkins
found Oxford to be less congenial than in his student days, and his
unease is reflected in the poems. In the Protestant backlash against the
excesses of Tractarianism, some of his old friends seemed distrustful of
his Jesuitism. Moreover, the monastic nature of the university which had
so appealed to him was being eroded by the process of reform; in 1877
there had come a decisive break with the past when dons were allowed to
marry. In addition, the city had added a 'graceless growth' of which he
wrote in 'Duns Scotus's Oxford', where the ugly suburban expansion is
portrayed as the product of commercial values which are inimical to the
harmonious balance of town and nature (William Morris expressed a
similar view in a talk he gave in 1886, 'The Aim of Art', in which he
bemoaned the city's loss of beauty and romance). A similar sense of dis-
may marks 'Binsey Poplars', which concerns the axing of aspens by the
banks of the Thames. For Hopkins the felling of the trees was more than
a mere destructive act; it was the wilful assault on a delicate and divinely
appointed organism, which is compared in the poem to the shocking
image of a needle piercing an eyeball. An entry in his Journal recorded
an earlier reaction to the cutting down of a tree: 'I heard the sound and
looking out and seeing it maimed there came at that moment a great
pang and I wished to die and not to see the inscapes of the world
destroyed any more.' The 'inscape' was Hopkins's term for the intrinsic
character of a landscape, and in his poem he writes of the riverside scene
being 'unselved' by the casual chopping down of the trees and thereby
losing its 'thisness', or 'haeccitas' in Duns Scotus's terms. The delicacy
and fragility of the riverside scene are echoed in the deliberate wording
of the poem, and its very shape is suggestive of the gentle meandering of
the Thames as it crosses Port Meadow. In the first verse the row of trees
is portrayed as a 'rank' of Roman soldiers whose sandal straps cast shadows on the area beneath, and the repetition of 'felled' echoes the brutal
blows of the axe that destroyed them. The subtle nuance and sensibility
make this surely the finest short poem to have been inspired by an
Oxford scene.

> My aspens dear, whose airy cages quelled,
> Quelled or quenched in leaves the leaping sun,
>   All felled, felled, are all felled;
>   Of a fresh and following folded rank
>   Not spared, not one
>   That dandled a sandalled

Shadow that swam or sank
On meadow and river and wind-wandering weed-winding bank.

O if we but knew what we do
When we delve or hew-
Hack and rack the growing green!
Since country is so tender
To touch, her being so slender,
That, like this sleek and seeing ball
But a prick will make no eye at all,
Where we, even where we mean
To mend her we end her,
When we hew or delve:
After-comers cannot guess the beauty been.
Ten or twelve, only ten or twelve
Strokes of havoc unselve
The sweet especial scene,
Rural scene, a rural scene,
Sweet especial rural scene.

In contrast to the 'muscular Christianity' of Tom Hughes, Hopkins here exemplifies an 'aesthetic Christianity' which emphasises the appreciation of beauty as a means to God. Instead of the outward challenge, it looks rather to personal response and the cultivation of the senses. It thus marks an important shift towards introspection and subjectivity.

Whereas 'muscularity' had been transplanted to Oxford from Rugby (it had roots too in the Cambridge of Charles Kingsley), aestheticism was a home-grown variant which had been fostered by the man who tutored Hopkins as a student, Walter Pater. This shy and retiring Brasenose don had an enormous influence on contemporaries both through his teaching and his writings, and among the most ardent of his followers was the young Oscar Wilde, who declared, 'There is no Pater but Pater, and I am his prophet.' Pater's *Studies in the History of the Renaissance* (1873) captured the imagination of a generation of students and shaped their view of the world. For Wilde it was 'the holy writ of beauty' and the 'Golden Book', and for those drawn to aestheticism the conclusion amounted to a virtual manifesto.

Not the fruit of experience, but experience itself, is the end. A counted number of pulses only is given to us of a variegated, dramatic life. How may we see in them all that is to be seen in them by the finest senses? How shall we pass most swiftly from point to point, and be present always at the focus where the greatest number of vital forces unite in their purest energy?

> To burn always with this hard, gemlike flame, to maintain this ecstasy, is
> success in life. . . . Only be sure it is passion—that it does yield you this fruit
> of a quickened, multiplied consciousness. Of this wisdom, the poetic pas-
> sion, the desire of beauty, the love of art for art's sake, has most; for art
> comes to you professing frankly to give nothing but the highest quality to
> your moments as they pass, and simply for those moments' sake.

The ideas achieved such notoriety that Pater dropped the conclusion
from the next edition of the book out of concern for its adverse effect.
Like Arnold, he believed that art was a means of achieving perfection 'in
man's entire organism', which included the moral sense, though this was
overlooked by those who took his theory as a simple platform of art for
art's sake. 'Aesthetics are higher than ethics', Wilde proclaimed defiantly.

In the passage of 'Emerald Uthwart' through Oxford, Pater describes
the attractions of the city in terms of sensual delight: the beauty of the
buildings, the intellectual pursuits, the physique of young males are all
combined in the portrayal of an aesthetic ideal. 'In truth the memory of
Oxford made almost everything he saw after it seem vulgar', runs the
narrative. The air of devotion and the range of expressive language in
the imaginary portrait are taken up by Lionel Johnson (1867–1902) and
by Arthur Quiller-Couch (1863–1944) in poems characterised by a
cultish praise of Oxford. Johnson was an ardent lover of learning, particularly the classics, and in 'Oxford Nights' he describes how the
authors of the past bring him nocturnal joy during his sleeplessness. But
it is in 'Oxford' (1890) that the poet truly finds his voice, for here the
city is celebrated as 'a queen' of beauty which transports the mind in Platonic terms to 'those high places, that are beauty's home'. The delight of
the poet is enhanced by the inspiring presence in the city of a revered
contemporary—Walter Pater. For Johnson as for Wilde, the Brasenose
don was a decisive influence, and in the poem he is referred to not by
name but by a third-person reference—'And there, O memory more
sweet than all! / Lived he'. The influence of Pater can be felt too in the
descriptive language of the poem, which offers a fresh perspective of the
college buildings through its luxuriant sensuality: 'chapels of cedarn fragrance, and rich gloom', purrs the poet, 'Poured from empurpled panes
on either hand'. The aestheticism of Hopkins is here taken to a new
plane. The poem evokes too the name of Arnold, thereby making a link
between the two formative figures of the Oxford myth, one who transformed the city into a 'queen of romance', and the other who promoted
appreciation of its beauty. In keeping with the Hellenic spirit they championed, Johnson wraps the Oxford of his poem in classical garb, and the
Hesperian allusion of the last line refers to the Greek belief in a garden

of golden apples in the Isles of the Blest—the earthly paradise in other guise. Since the isles were located in the West, they had associations with sunset and eventide, and Johnson's Oxford is above all a city of reverie

> Where at each coign of every antique street,
> A memory hath taken root in stone;
> There, Raleigh shone; there, toil'd Franciscan feet;
> There, Johnson flinch'd not, but endured alone.
>
> There, Shelley dream'd his white Platonic dreams;
> There, classic Landor throve on Roman thought;
> There, Addison pursued his quiet themes;
> There, smiled Erasmus, and there, Colet taught.
>
> And there, O memory more sweet than all!
> Lived he, whose eyes keep yet our passing light;
> Whose crystal lips Athenian speech recall;
> Who wears Rome's purple with least pride, most right.
>
> That is the Oxford, strong to charm us yet:
> Eternal in her beauty and her past.
> What, though her soul be vexed? She can forget
> Cares of an hour: only the great things last.
>
> Only the gracious air, only the charm,
> And ancient might of true humanities:
> These, nor assault of man, nor time, can harm;
> Not these, nor Oxford with her memories.
>
> Together have we walked with willing feet
> Gardens of plenteous trees, bowering soft lawn:
> Hills whither Arnold wandered; and all sweet
> June meadows, from the troubling world withdrawn:
>
> Chapels of cedarn fragrance, and rich gloom
> Poured from empurpled panes on either hand:
> Cool pavements, carved with legends of the tomb;
> Grave haunts, where we might dream, and understand . . .
>
> Over, the four long years! And unknown powers
> Call to us, going forth upon our way:
> Ah! turn we, and look back upon the towers,
> That rose above our lives, and cheered the day.
>
> Proud and serene, against the sky, they gleam:
> Proud and secure, upon the earth, they stand:
> Our city hath the air of a pure dream,
> And hers indeed is an Hesperian land.

Johnson's poetic mystification of Oxford was followed six years later
by Arthur Quiller-Couch's 'Alma mater' (1896), in which the author
invests the city with the kind of mystique suggested by his own pen-name
of 'Q'—'Know you her secret none can utter?' teases the opening-line.
Quiller-Couch had entered Trinity in 1882 to study classics, and he wrote
the poem on a return visit fourteen years later. It is infused with the nostalgia of the older man remembering his youth: 'Once my dear—but the
world was young then', muses the poet as memories come to mind of
Bellocian days of rowing, hunting, riding, and reading poetry with fellow
students. Though the Oxford of Johnson is reduced to a single college,
the poem reaches out in the final lines to impart a mythical sacredness to
the city as a whole.

> Still on her spire the pigeons hover;
>   Still by her gateway haunts the gown;
> Ah, but her secret? you, young lover,
>   Drumming her old ones forth from town,
> Know you the secret none discover?
>   Tell it when *you* go down.
>
> Yet if at length you seek her, prove her,
>   Lean to her whispers never so nigh;
> Yet if at last not less her lover
>   You in your hansom leave the High;
> Down from her towers a ray shall hover —
>   Touch you, a passer-by.

Written in the closing years of the century, the lines present a marked
contrast with the literature of its opening years, such as Hogg's account
of Oxford. Where once stood a corrupted and clerical seat of learning,
there now appears a city of glamour and mystique. 'Know you her secret
none can utter?' asked the poets, and the question was seized on by the
novelists of the next generation: Evelyn Waugh acknowledged the debt
by using a phrase from Quiller-Couch's poem 'Never a palinode!' for the
title of the Oxford chapter of his memoirs. Yet though the fictional city
had taken on mythic proportions, it lacked a character large enough to
inhabit such a magical space. In *Zuleika Dobson* Max Beerbohm was to
create an aristocratic paragon who was accomplished in all areas of life
and brilliant enough to capture every prize the university could offer.
The creature of his imagination owed much to a flesh-and-blood exemplar—his friend, Oscar Wilde. As Byron for the Byronic hero, the figure
of Wilde looms large behind the fictional type of mythic Oxford: 'I was a
man who stood in symbolic relations to the art and culture of my age', he
noted in another context. The legend of Oscar and the myth of Oxford

are so inextricably linked together that it is impossible to write of one without the other.

THE INFAMOUS ST. OSCAR OF OXFORD

As with Samuel Johnson, it is not so much for what he wrote but for what he was that Oscar Wilde (1854–1900) is of such importance to Oxford literature. As he said himself, only his talent went into his writings; his genius went into his life. His wit and brilliance represented the aesthetic ideal, and the pose of effortless brilliance he adopted set the tone for those who followed after him. For some he was the model hero, the myth incarnate, the embodiment of all their aspirations, and the story of his student days became the standard by which later fiction took its standards. Just as importantly, he was a key figure in furthering the cult of Oxford and identification with the Greeks, for the teaching of men like Jowett, Arnold and Pater concerning classical ideals was reinterpreted by Wilde for his own purposes. Because of his reputation as a student, his ideas concerning the vital role of beauty spread through the university and were an important influence on the next generation of writers. In shaping himself, Wilde shaped the Oxford myth.

When Wilde began as a scholar at Magdalen in 1874, he was a relatively unsophisticated Irish provincial with a degree from Dublin and a string of forenames: Oscar Fingal O'Flahertie Wills (the splendid set of initials, O.F.O'F.W.W., were scratched on the window-pane of his college room). Within four years the young Irishman had recreated himself as a well-known university figure who went under the title of 'Oscar Wilde, Magdalen College, Oxford.' He set about the remaking of his character in conscious vein; his Irish accent was discarded for a stately and distinctive English, and his Dublin clothes were dispensed with in favour of tweed jackets, tall collars and curly brimmed hats. In his first year he was much influenced by the lectures of John Ruskin concerning art and beauty as a means of furthering moral improvement and appreciation of the divine purpose. Ruskin also held that physical labour enhanced human dignity, and to demonstrate this to his students he initiated a road-building scheme at Hinksey. The project began with enthusiasm, but petered out as the lack of professionalism became plain. 'What became of the road?' Wilde queried. 'Well, like a bad lecture it ended abruptly—in the middle of a swamp.' Thereafter the student of classics turned from the medieval leanings of Ruskin to the more indulgent aestheticism of Walter Pater and his passion for the Renaissance. Though he never forgot his debt to Ruskin, he came to see the Greek way of thinking as much closer in spirit to the modern age than the medieval.

Seizing on the notion of art for art's sake, he adopted a more flamboyant lifestyle and took to wearing extravagant clothing. He decorated his rooms with *objets d'art:* statuettes, Greek rugs, peacock feathers, and a carefully placed easel with an unfinished painting. He made a special feature of lilies, which Ruskin had praised in *The Stones of Venice* (1851–53) as an example of beauty at its most useless, and he held 'beauty parties' at which the conversation had to match the exquisiteness of the clothing and the decor. His reputation began to build, and one of his witticisms—'I find it harder and harder each day to live up to my blue china'—was attacked in a university sermon and quoted in *Punch*. By 1880 aestheticism was established enough to be parodied by Rhoda Broughton in her book *Second Thoughts,* in which a 'long, pale poet' called Francis Chaloner is thought to be modelled after Wilde, and the next year Gilbert and Sullivan gave the movement greater exposure by ridiculing 'lily love' in their operetta *Patience.*

Wilde studied Greats, by tradition *the* Oxford school, and revelled in the opportunity to absorb classical literature and Greek philosophy. 'Greats is the only fine school at Oxford, the only sphere of thought where one can be, *simultaneously,* brilliant and unreasonable', he claimed. As he grew in confidence, he affected a pose of indolence and insouciance; when he studied, it was secretly and in the small hours. For the rest of the time he enjoyed a leisurely lifestyle in the manner of the rich—in the manner because like others his extravagant lifestyle was funded out of debt. His early pursuits included fishing, shooting, boxing, even surprisingly eights, though he soon tired of it and declared, 'I don't see the use of going down backwards to Iffley every evening.' What he enjoyed most was convivial and intellectual conversation, and his charismatic personality ensured him a large circle of admirers. In his second year he had to sit Moderations, which included a compulsory divinity test with a separate paper for Anglicans and non-Anglicans. When asked which one he wanted, he cavalierly replied, 'Oh, the Forty-Nine Articles', and on being told that the Anglican creed only comprised thirty-nine articles, he responded with feigned incredulity. In the *viva* (oral interview) he had the Reverend William Spooner of spoonerism fame, who was a far more conventional figure than his popular image suggests. He took objection to Wilde's supercilious manner and ordered him to write out the twenty-seventh chapter of Acts; when after some time he asked the student to stop, Wilde continued writing as if he had heard nothing.

> 'Did you hear me tell you, Mr. Wilde, that you needn't write any more?'
> 'Oh yes, I heard you, but I was so interested in what I was copying that I

could not leave off. It was all about a man named Paul, who went on a voyage and was caught in a terrible storm, and I was afraid that he would be drowned; but do you know, Mr. Spooner, he was saved and when I found that he was saved, I thought of coming to tell you.'

Spooner was outraged, and Wilde failed. The real test, however, consisted of the classical part of the examinations, and when the results of these were posted, Wilde pretended indifference by refusing to go to see them and only read of his First Class in *The Times* as he breakfasted in the Mitre. Not only had he managed a First without being a 'reading man', but he had managed the best First of his year. Two years later at the final examinations Wilde repeated his display of brilliance by asking for extra paper after the first hour of a three-hour exam, and then walking out ostentatiously half an hour before the end. Again he was awarded a First; again it was the best of the year. There was distinction too when his long poem *Ravenna* won the Newdigate Prize, the prestigious university prize for poetry.

Like the Pre-Raphaelites who preceded him, Wilde was delighted by the appearance of Oxford and described it as 'The most beautiful thing in England'. Worcester chapel particularly appealed to him; Keble College did not. He found his Magdalen surroundings delightful and wrote that 'the dullness of tutors and professors matters very little when one can loiter in the grey cloisters at Magdalen, and listen to some flute-like voice singing in Waynfleete's chapel, or lie in the green meadow, among the strange snake-shaped fritillaries'. He was enamoured too of the literary tradition: one of his best friends was nicknamed Little Mr. Bouncer after the character in *Verdant Green*, he thought Mallock's *The New Republic* 'decidedly clever', and he admired the writings of Newman, which furthered his desire to convert to Catholicism. He made presents of Arnold's poems, and his allegiance to the Arnoldian vision can be seen in a letter he sent to the Hon. George Curzon concerning the vote of the Oxford Union to turn down a book of his poetry: 'Our sweet city with its dreaming towers must not be given entirely over to the Philistines. They have Gath and Ekron and Ashdod and many other cities of dirt and dread and despair, and we must not yield them the quiet cloister of Magdalen to brawl in, or the windows of Merton to peer from.' He affected to despise academics, alleging, 'One cannot live at Oxford because of the dons—in all else it is a most pleasant city', and when asked what he was going to do after graduating, he replied, 'God knows. I won't be a dried-up Oxford don, anyhow. I'll be a poet, a writer, a dramatist. Somehow or other I'll be famous, and if not famous, notorious.' Though the words were eerily prophetic, the pose belied the truth, for on graduating he was disappointed not to be offered a fellowship by his college and made an application to another. Since he followed Plato in believing the speculative life to be superior to the practical, it is hardly surprising that he should wish to remain among the academic groves, nor that in later life he should remember Oxford with affection. To a prospective Oxford student he once wrote in Platonic terms, 'I envy you going to Oxford: it is the most flower-like time of one's life. One sees the shadow of things in silver mirrors.'

Wilde's Oxford writings are small in quantity, and the two poems he wrote which touch on the city are disappointing (when he sent 'Magdalen Walks' to Walter Pater, the Brasenose don advised him to try prose instead with the suggestion that it was a medium more suited to the demands of the age). In 'The Burden of Itys' Wilde showed his classical leanings by imagining ancient Romans in the Oxford countryside comparing it favourably with their homeland, and the musings of the poet are interrupted by Great Tom tolling the nine o'clock curfew across the meadows. Much more eloquent, however, was his prose writing on Oxford in the unlikely context of a play review of a university production of *Henry the Fourth*. The cult of beauty is here wedded to that of Oxford.

> In spite of the roaring of the young lions at the Union, and the screaming of rabbits in the home of the vivisector, in spite of Keble College and the tramways and the sporting prints, Oxford still remains the most beautiful thing in England, and nowhere else are life and art so exquisitely blended, so perfectly made into one. Indeed, in most other towns art has often to present herself in the form of a reaction against the sordid ugliness of modern lives, but at Oxford she comes to us as an exquisite flower, born of the beauty of life and expressive of life's joy.

The delight Wilde took in Oxford was enhanced by the opportunity it afforded him for the appreciation of young men. The idealisation of male beauty in Pater's writings made a strong impression on him and may even have encouraged his own homosexual tendencies. 'Boy worship' was in vogue at the time, and despite the obloquy there was an atmosphere of sublimated male affections: in the undergraduate journal of 1877 an article appeared which attacked aestheticism for its 'Pagan worship of bodily form and beauty'. Inspired by the example of Greeks like Socrates and Plato, Wilde masked his homoeroticism in classical form. Of an undergraduate sportsman he commented, 'His left leg is a Greek poem', and in later life he remarked, 'Young Oxonians are very delightful, so Greek and graceful and uneducated. They have profiles but no philosophy.' The fondness for young males drew him back to Oxford on several occasions, and on one such visit he was introduced by the student-poet Lionel Johnson to his cousin at Magdalen, Lord Alfred Douglas. It proved to be a fateful meeting.

In act 3 of *The Importance of Being Earnest* Wilde writes of Oxford with affectionate mockery: 'Untruthful! My nephew Algernon?' bellows Lady Bracknell, 'Impossible! He is an Oxonian.' In less playful manner, he designated himself later 'the infamous St. Oscar of Oxford, poet and martyr'. The self-canonisation was not devoid of substance, for it was Oxford, the home of aestheticism, that had made him, and it was Oxford that broke him too: the letter read out at Wilde's trial with its 'madness of kisses' was found in Douglas's suit in Magdalen College. 'The two great turning-points of my life were when my father sent me to Oxford, and when society sent me to prison', he wrote from Reading gaol. Yet despite his disgrace, Wilde came to be seen as the student hero writ large. With his aristocratic pose and pretensions, his classical leanings, his delight in Oxford, his wit, charm, and brilliance, he represented the ideal of the university aesthete. Both Lionel Johnson and Max Beerbohm were friends and admirers, and their writings bear testimony to his personal influence. For others his plays were sufficient—'Your conversation was brilliant, but it was simply a rechauffé of *The Importance of Being Earnest*,' says a student in *Patchwork*, in which the prevailing ethos is to be languidly witty in the manner of Wilde. Writing of Oxford in the 1920s, Jean Fayard found that 'Whether one loved or hated him, Oscar Wilde was king.' It could well be argued, in fact, that the Wildean manner became the university norm of the twentieth century, for the literature attests to the pervasive spread of the attitudes he represented. In Wilfrid Sheed's *A Middle Class Education* (1961), a student claims that 'every single bloke up here has a pose of some sort', and in Dacre Balsdon's *The Day They Burned Miss Termag* (1961), a young girl wishing to be an actress decides to take up a place at the university after being told that 'in Oxford acting was a large part of living, if not a substitute for it'. The protagonist of John Fowles's *The Magus* (1966) characterises student life as 'eternal dandyism', and *What's Bred in the Bone* (1985) by Robertson Davies describes a Corpus Christi aesthete and 'the Oxford pretence of doing nothing while in fact getting through a great deal of work'. Nor is the effect confined to the student community, for to the college fellow of John Wain's *Hungry Generations* (1994), the 'obligation to be amusing' is the salient trait of the senior common room. Yet despite all this, and despite his academic brilliance, Wilde goes unhonoured by his college, in contrast to the disgraced Shelley. The odium of conviction undoubtedly played a part in this, but it would seem too that his air of flippancy did not appeal to serious-minded academics, for to men like Spooner the haughty arrogance of the pretentious youth was not just offensive but subversive. Even today Wilde remains an uneasy figure to fit into the literary mainstream, and it seems that Magdalen would rather advertise its association with the more stalwart and Anglican C.S. Lewis. The rooms where Wilde once held his beauty parties (on the kitchen staircase overlooking the Cherwell) are used now as a bar and for storing furniture. How 'St. Oscar of Oxford, poet and martyr' would have relished the irony!

ATHENIAN GROVES AND BEERBOHM'S GODDESS

The Oxford novel of the first half of the twentieth century differs little from that of its nineteenth century predecessor in terms of structure. The formation of a central character is still set against a university background; the setting retains a country house atmosphere; and the cast list, though modified and modernised, is recognisable and essentially unchanged. But with the move from Arnold's moonlight to Pater's sensuous gloom, there comes a great difference in tone. In place of the warnings of vice there is advocacy of pleasure, and instead of the striving against sin there is a spirit of experimentation. Protestant righteousness is replaced either by a pagan universe as in *Zuleika Dobson,* or agnosticism as in *Sinister Street,* or a decadent Catholicism as in *Brideshead Revisited.* Above all, Oxford in these novels is glorified in a way not seen since the days of the Elizabethans, and the notion of the 'English Athens' once again comes into its own.

The Greek connection fostered by Arnold, Pater and Jowett was taken up by the students of Greats who drew parallels between their lifestyle and the secluded groves and philosopher-guardians of the *polis.* Plato's ideal city-state has been described by Lewis Mumford as 'small, isolated, self-contained, enclosed', and the description could equally be applied to the Oxford colleges of this period. 'College life', wrote Andrew Lang, 'is somewhat, as has often been said, like the old Greek city life. For three years men are in the possession of what the world does not enjoy— leisure; and they are supposed to be using that leisure for the purposes of perfection.' The colleges liked to pride themselves too on their small 'democracies', and Edward Thomas for one claimed that 'Oxford is one of the most democratic places in Europe'—democratic, that is, because as in Athens the franchise extended only to a social élite of eligible males.

Identification with the achievements of ancient Athens was furthered by the wealth of writers in and around the city at this time. It had its own Parnassus in Boar's Hill where lived a number of outstanding poets— Robert Bridges, John Masefield, Robert Graves, and Edmund Blunden, the first two of whom were successive poet laureates. Bridges was a friend of Hopkins who lauded Oxford in Arnoldian terms in his 'Invitation to the Oxford Pageant, July 1907' and whose crowning achievement, *The Testament of Beauty* (1929), celebrated the countryside round Boar's Hill and was described by Stephen Spender as akin to 'a brilliant paper written on aesthetics for Greats'. W.B. Yeats also lived for a short time in the city, and in 'All Souls' Night' (1920) he wrote of necromancy in his Broad Street residence—'Midnight has come, and the great Christ Church Bell / And many a lesser bell sound through the room; . . . A ghost may come'. Meanwhile, out at Garsington Manor the colourful Lady Ottoline Morrell hosted a literary salon from 1915 to 1927 which was frequented by most of the leading figures of the day, including her lover Bertrand Russell and various members of the Bloomsbury set. The Morrells had strong connections with the university, and the manor included among its visitors such promising young undergraduates as Aldous Huxley, Cyril Connolly, Peter Quennell, L.P. Hartley, Harold Acton, Anthony Powell, and A.L. Rowse (the latter, son of a Cornish stonemason, proved more congenial to her than his upper-class contemporaries at Christ Church. Both Lawrence in *Women in Love* [1920] and Huxley in *Crome Yellow* [1921] portray the eccentric hostess in unkind terms, and she was so upset by Lawrence's caricature of her as Hermione Roddice that she did not write to him for the next ten years. Huxley also touched on Oxford life in *Those Barren Leaves* [1925], and in *Eyeless in Gaza* [1936] he presents the development of Anthony Beavis from a student eager for knowledge to revolutionary adventurer and advocate of selfless love.) Also at the university during the 1920s were a group of poets known collectively as 'MacSpaunday'—Louis MacNeice, Stephen Spender, W.H. Auden, and Cecil Day-Lewis. As a student the authoritative Auden dominated the literary scene, and Spender writes in his autobiography of the way in which contemporaries were summoned to his rooms for instruction. 'You came away from his presence always encouraged', was MacNeice's view of the experience. Novelists too were represented among the students of the 1920s, not just in the form of Waugh but in the Green(e)s, Henry and Graham (Henry Green was the pseudonym of Henry Yorke. Graham Greene's memoirs of his student days in *A Sort of Life* [1971] are as lurid as any of his novels, with tales of Russian roulette, foreign espionage, and drunken appearances before the dean.) Meanwhile, out at Elsfield John Buchan hosted the literary-minded at his Sunday afternoon teas when T.E. Lawrence, working on *The Seven Pillars of Wisdom* (1926) at All Souls, would turn up on his motorbike or Robert Graves would drop by from nearby Islip, where he had moved with the American poet, Laura Riding. And to complete the picture of a creative powerhouse, Oxford was also host in this period to a group of writers known as the Inklings, amongst whom were two of the greatest fantasy writers of the twentieth century in C.S. Lewis and J.R.R. Tolkien. The group used to meet in Lewis's rooms in Magdalen College's New Buildings, and in his spiritual autobiography, *Surprised by Joy* (1955), Lewis wrote of his loss and rediscovery of Christianity there. The key moment came while he was at work in his study: 'You must picture me alone in that room in Magdalen, night after night, feeling whenever my mind lifted even for a second from my work, the steady, unrelenting approach of Him whom I so earnestly desired not to meet. That which I greatly feared had at last come upon me. In the Trinity Term of 1929 I gave in, and admitted that God was God, and knelt and prayed: perhaps, that night, the most dejected and reluctant convert in all England.' Tolkien, a Catholic, played a key part in the conversion. Such figures served to enhance the literary reputation of Oxford, and between them the 'peculiar race of artist-scholars, scholar-artists' maintained a steady stream of imaginative works which reinforced the notion of the city as the 'seat of the English muses'.

The novelists of the age, in consequence, dwelled at some length on the 'starlit spires and Athenian groves of the dream-bound colleges', to which the rest of the city merely served as prop. Until World War I it was assumed that the privilege to enjoy the sheltered groves belonged, in Oxford as in Athens, to those of noble birth, for according to Plato it was the right of the well-born to lead a speculative life. For Max Beerbohm the aristocratic manner was integral to the spirit of Oxford, and in his affectionate parody *Zuleika Dobson* he plays with the idea to great effect. (Beerbohm was particular about the pronunciation of his heroine and sent a telegram to the BBC stipulating 'Zuleika speaker not hiker'; the model was thought to be the actress Constance Collier, to whom Beerbohm was briefly engaged, though the author himself maintained that the character was based on a young woman he had known who died of consumption.) The book's protagonist, the duke of Dorset, is cast as the epitome of the Oxford type: rich, well-bred, superior, affected, charming, noble, handsome, brilliant, witty, nonchalant, leisured, cultured, philosophical, and with a due sense of leadership and *noblesse oblige*. The young Adonis affects the manner of a dandy and takes to Oxford as a peacock to a park. He gains a brilliant First in the first part of his Greats, wins the Newdigate and every other university prize, and his natural air of authority is such that when he is temporarily sent down for overseeing a student dispute, the warden of the college puts his own landau at the duke's disposal. As an aesthete par excellence, the duke is concerned above all with the effect of his appearance, and his dress and manner are carefully calculated as in a work of art. Form is all-important. When he drowns himself for love of Zuleika, his plumed hat remains on the surface to mark his aquatic grave; it is in both senses a noble death, and the perfect posthumous pose. Others do their best to live up to his example, though his attributes have to be shared out. There is dandyism in the affected Gaveston ffoulkes of *The Oxford Circus;* charm and beauty in the aristocratic Sebastian of *Brideshead Revisited;* brilliance and wit in the self-centred Ray Sheldon of *Patchwork.* When the latter tries on a new bowler-hat, he is told by a friend, 'I shouldn't be seen with you in that.' 'I quite agree', retorts Sheldon, 'No one would look at you. Besides, a second party would ruin the effect. I shall walk down the middle of the road ploughing solitary furrows.' The legacy of Wilde is all too clear.

As a student Max Beerbohm knew and revered Oscar Wilde, referring to him as 'the Divinity' and adopting his languorous manner. He was once asked if he was going down to the river for Eights Week and replied affectedly, 'What river?' Years later, when he came to write his own novel of Eights Week, he styled it after the playful triviality of *The Importance of Being Earnest.* The central theme concerns the illusory effect of beauty and its power to enthral. Zuleika herself is so radiant that she makes sweat appear on the brows of the emperors whose stone busts surround the Sheldonian, and all who meet her fall under her spell (to emphasise the point, she is also a trained magician). As the embodiment of beauty, this 'adorable goddess' is also in a sense the personification of Oxford, for as suggested by the ambiguous subtitle of the novel—'an Oxford love story'—this is as much a story about love *of* Oxford as about love *in* Oxford. The city stands at the very heart of the story, and the mass suicide of students at the end is as much an act of surrender to Oxford as to Zuleika. The book won great popularity among loyal Oxonians in the first half of the century, who treasured it as much for its affectionate ribbing of their *alma mater* as for the delicacy of the writing. Though the florid prose and self-conscious snobbery have passed out of fashion, the rhetorical polish still commands respect, and the wit retains a Wildean sparkle. 'Oh, I never go in motors', says Zuleika, 'They make one look like nothing on earth, and like everybody else.'

The devotional worship of Oxford is echoed in other novels of the age, for sated on the literature of Arnoldian glamour, writers line up to worship at the shrine of a sacred city. *Patchwork's* Ray Sheldon is filled with 'the desire to taste to the full the life of Oxford at its best', and Evelyn Waugh in his memoirs wrote, 'My imagination was aglow with literary associations. . . . it seemed to me there was a quintessential Oxford which I knew and loved form afar and intended to find.' For some the search for the spirit of Oxford becomes an obsessive quest in which the city takes on a mythic, Shangri-La quality. Indeed, when the High Lama in James Hilton's *Lost Horizon* (1933) asks if there is anywhere similar in the West to Shangri-La, he is told by way of reply, 'Well, yes, to be quite frank, it reminds me very slightly of Oxford, where I used to lecture.' Elsewhere the praise is couched in prose of studied opulence. 'Sometimes dreaming in the sun, sometimes dappled by rain, sometimes unnaturally white under a decrescent moon—today a fairyland of frost and spangled snow. What was it about this city that troubled so exquisitely one's senses?' wonders Ray Sheldon. On occasion the mystification reaches self-parody: 'Somewhere in the silent college the thing unknown was waiting', writes Dickinson as if of a monster. At other times it impresses by its earnestness. None are more eager than the devotee Michael Fane, who believes 'Oxford should be approached with a stainless curiosity. Already he felt that she would only yield her secret in return for absolute surrender.' Through his devotion Fane is granted glimpses of the 'unutterable secret'—the study of classics, which have no practical value but train a man to be a gentleman; May morning, when from the top of Magdalen he views the city 'imprisoned in a crystal globe'; the Grid, an élitist club with an atmosphere of good-fellowship; 'The Oxford Looking Glass' with its quick-witted intellectualism; Venner's office, where the old college servant imparts wisdom to the young; and above all, in the group of male friends, good, true and artistic, that he collects around him.

Other writers offer other visions. For Henry James in *English Hours,* the *genius loci* was characterised by 'the peculiar air of Oxford—the air of liberty to care for the things of the mind assured and secured by machinery which is in itself a satisfaction to sense'. For the French visitor Hippolyte Taine, it was the organic interaction of architectural feature with natural phenomenon. For James Hilton the oriental utopia with its everlasting youth consisted like Oxford of a cloistered life amidst beautiful surroundings untouched by the outside world of pointless struggle. For Edward Thomas, as for Evelyn Waugh, Oxford offered the chance of a second childhood in sheltered surroundings, a childhood 'as blithe and untroubled as the first, and with this advantage over the first: that it is not only good, but he knows that it is good.' And for Gerard Hopkins in *City in the Foreground,* as for Lamb and Hazlitt before him, simply being at Oxford was enough in itself, for 'It's just because Oxford teaches nothing in particular that she is such a priceless possession. She has all the treasures in the world hidden in the fold of her garments, and he who is lucky enough to be able to search for them and find them has the greatest education the world can give. . . . It doesn't matter what the professors teach, it's what the *place* teaches, it's the young spirit that breathes in the hearts of those who are taught.'

The mystification of Oxford goes hand in hand with values that for the modern reader are at best hard to swallow and at worst repugnant. The duke of Dorset is 'the most awful snob' that Zuleika has ever met, and Mackenzie's Michael Fane defends such snobbishness as the concomitant of excellence. The exclusiveness is all-pervasive: women do not belong; foreigners belittle the spirit of Oxford; the 'lower orders' are inherently ridiculous. In *Zuleika Dobson* the duke of Dorset maintains that while Americans have a right to exist, they should refrain from exercising that right in Oxford, and the students of *Sinister Street* hold similar notions about those from the lower classes. An unfortunate Cockney named Smithers is picked on in that novel 'not from any overt act of contumely, but for his general bearing and plebeian origin'. Those of leftish leanings are also given short shrift, and in *Sonia* the radical Manders is debagged and hurled into Christ Church's Mercury fountain. Yet though the egalitarian tendencies of the twentieth century conflict with the values of the Oxford myth, the novels continue to enjoy popularity, and, to the consternation of modern academics, the image of the university they project has proved remarkably enduring. To have youth, talent and wealth, to enjoy the opportunity for self-development in beautiful surroundings, to spend one's prime amidst gifted contemporaries, to lead a life of leisurely study with access to lawn and river and meadow—this is indeed the stuff of dreams.

It is above all the language of the Oxford myth that beguiles. The rich cadences, the consummate artistry, the glittering phrases, the sparkling images—only the most obtuse could completely resist such siren sentences. One of the most sumptuous of the stylists is Compton Mackenzie, whose favoured adjectives include verdurous, decrescent, golden, luminous, shimmering, entrancing, poignant, supreme, exquisite, tranquil, languid, and magical. In two short paragraphs on Oxford he writes of 'a tender city of melting outlines', the 'wan aggregation of immaterial domes and spires', the 'moist heart of England', and 'the wraithes of mist destroying with their transmutations the visible fabric'. Rising to the supreme challenge for the romanticist, he even veils the dull drizzle of a depressing Oxford February with the semblance of allure.

> February was that year a month of rains from silver skies, or rains that made Oxford melodious with their perpetual trickling. They were rains that lured him forth to dabble in their gentle fountains, to listen at the window of Ninety-nine to their rippling monody, and at night to lie awake infatuated.

Other writers are equally seductive. 'So each of his terms told off, in a delicious reverie of idle adoration, its rosary of golden days', purrs Montague in effortless elegance. 'Some clock clove with silver the stillness of the morning', adds Beerbohm with incomparable delicacy. 'Oxford, in those days, was still a city of aquatint', muses Waugh. Arnoldian enchantment is combined with Pater's aestheticism to produce writing that is rich in adjective, ornate in structure, and florid in style. It is the language of moonlight and dream, of romance and mystique, of myth and magic. It is, in short, the language of a delightful lie designed to appeal to the deep, almost desperate urge of human beings to believe in an earthly paradise.

WAUGH'S ENCHANTED GARDEN

No other Oxford generation has so stamped its mark on the public's imagination as that of the early twenties, for many *the* Oxford generation. It is *their* drunken exploits, *their* social pretences, *their* leisured affluence, *their* dinner clubs, *their* college escapades, and *their* pursuit of pleasure that colours still the image of Oxford as a fabled land of decadent youth. Champagne and plovers' eggs for lunch; clumsy clamberings over college walls; cavorting in Mercury fountain; dinner-suited drunkenness: the images spring quickly to mind, etched in a novel of the 1940s that has sold over a million copies. Like Scott Fitzgerald's portrait of the Roaring Twenties, the fiction has become fact in the collective consciousness and moulds the way in which the present generation perceives the past. The story has enjoyed a remarkable double life, for apart from its initial success in book form, it won international acclaim and a worldwide following when it was adapted for television by Granada in 1981. Scripted by John Mortimer, the series featured Jeremy Irons as Charles Ryder, Anthony Andrews as Sebastian, and a glittering support cast which included John Gielgud, Laurence Olivier, and Diana Quick.

As with *Sinister Street,* Oxford is only part of a wider canvas, but it is the part that everyone remembers. Its portraitist was Evelyn Waugh, whose imagination was 'aglow with literary associations' from the moment he entered Hertford College in 1922. He knew by heart the 'Beautiful city . . .' of Arnold, quoting it to good effect in his scholarship essay, and had steeped himself in *Zuleika Dobson* and the Oxford section of *Sinister Street.* He claimed indeed to have read every Oxford novel he could get his hands on, from *Verdant Green* to *Patchwork.* Quiller-Couch's 'Alma Mater' was one of his favourite poems, and he liked too the verse of Belloc and Flecker, the latter of whom had won favour among Oxford *aficionados* for his lines from *The Dying Patriot:*

> Proud and godly kings had built her, long ago,
> With their towers and tombs and statues all arow,

With her fair and floral air and the love that lingers there,
And the streets where the great men go.

Fired by what he had read, Waugh arrived in Oxford with high expectations and the conviction that somewhere in the city lay an Oxford of romance and mystery; in his novel he invests Charles Ryder with similar feelings. The freshman starts his Oxford life in pleasant enough fashion with rooms on the ground floor of his college quadrangle filled with the fragrance of gillyflowers, but it is a 'grey' existence in a 'grey' city with the nagging feeling that something is missing. The college is unspecified, though it is presumably based on Hertford, where Waugh studied (the fictional counterpart in *Decline and Fall* is unkindly referred to as an 'ugly, subdued little College'). Michael Fane would not have categorised it as the *real* Oxford as represented by Christ Church, and the entry for Ryder to the 'holy of holies' comes in unexpected manner after Sebastian accidentally vomits through his window. The invitation to lunch which follows takes Ryder to Sebastian's rooms in the Meadow Buildings of Christ Church and the beginning of a whole new way of life.

The style and content of *Brideshead* owe much to the conventions of the Oxford novel, though the book is as much a celebration of the upper classes as of Oxford: for once the collegiate splendour is outmatched by the baroque grandeur of Brideshead, which is given the transposed epithet of 'enchanted palace'. The aristocratic tone is reflected in the condescending attitude of the snobbish students toward the university, which is looked down on as faintly ridiculous for taking study seriously, and the representative Oxford don is the unlikeable social climber, Samgrass. The 'adorable dreamer' of the book is the beautiful and upperclass Sebastian Flyte with his captivating charm and innocence (modelled after Waugh's student friends, Hugh Lygon, second son of Earl Beauchamp, and Alastair Graham, both of whom failed to live up to the promise of their student days). There is about Sebastian a 'nursery freshness', and from his infant-like vomiting to his ever-present teddy-bear (based on Betjeman's Archie), he is characterised by childlike behaviour. In the first raptures of affection he takes Charles to meet his nanny, and his continual drunkenness constitutes a means of clinging to childhood by rejecting the responsibilities of adulthood. His religion too is childlike, for it consists of a wide-eyed belief in a beautiful story. 'It seems to me', comments Ryder in retrospect, 'that I grew younger daily with each adult habit that I acquired.' Under the spell of his friend Charles is able to enjoy the happy childhood of which he had been deprived by war, temperament and bereavement. That summer term the two friends clamber their way back into a youthful paradise.

Like his mentors, Waugh looks to the Greeks for inspiration and takes an Arcadian motif for his Oxford section. Sebastian's life in the city is marked by a bond with nature, though significantly this is unlike the Romantic view in being cultivated rather than wild: he shows his repentance for vomiting by filling Charles's rooms with flowers; his lunch-party features a large nest of moss placed for effect in the centre of his table; he surprises Charles by championing butterfly and flower over art and architecture; and he insists on taking Charles to visit the Botanic Garden without which he claims he would be lost in Oxford. In the most pastoral scene of the novel the pair turn off the road on the way to Brideshead and stop at a sheep-cropped knoll, where they eat strawberries and drink wine under a clump of elms. They had little need to roam so far afield, for as Auden wrote of Christ Church, 'Nature is so close'. Sebastian had but to step out of his Meadow Building room onto the balcony, like the poetry-declaiming Anthony Blanche, to be faced with bucolic scenes, and within the college too there was the open green of Tom Quad, where the waters of Mercury, alias Hermes, sang of Arcadian pastures. Deeper still within the secluded preserves there lay Alice's enchanted garden.

The closeness to nature, it is suggested, represents a closeness to God. The city as a whole is pervaded by a 'cloistral hush', and when Charles makes his way from Broad Street to Christ Church on the last Sunday of the academic year, it is to the sound of church bells and 'through a world of piety': past church-goers of half a dozen different sects, past church-bound boy scouts, past the begowned mayor and corporation heading for a city church, and past a crocodile of choir boys on their way to the cathedral. Even the wayward Sebastian is at mass. This is the city of Newman, the narrative reminds the reader, thereby linking the Anglicanism of Christ Church with the Catholicism of Sebastian.

The childlike innocence, the verdant surrounds, and the closeness to God evoke the 'terrestrial Elysium' of Lockhart's very first Oxford novel, but the rapture of Charles and Sebastian cannot last. In their second year the pair withdraw into a world of their own, cutting themselves off from their friends. Sebastian's drinking becomes increasingly desperate, and his moroseness undermines the couple's happiness. The summer magic has gone, autumnal shadows lengthen, and the state of grace is less apparent. As his name suggests, he is doomed to martyrdom, and like St. Oscar of Oxford his downfall has to do with the orientation of his sexuality (both the historical and fictional character could be charged with insouciance). Sebastian is eventually removed from Christ Church, and in the latter part of the book the restless youth searches desperately for sanctuary, first in a house in Tangiers with a German deserter, then in a nearby cloistered monastery. The protective community offers him a replacement for the country house to which he can no longer return. 'He longed for some home in which he could regain the blitheness and the security of childhood. . . . He wanted warmth, children's games, children's talk, the enclosed universe of the nursery'—Maurice Bowra's view of Waugh is here instructive, for it would seem the author, stimulated by associations of Alice and her Wonderland, projected his childhood fantasy onto Sebastian and Christ Church, combining the notion of the enchanted garden with that of religious grace to create a collegiate Eden. It is an Arcadia with Christian morality, Hellenism with an Hebraic code, Paradise Gained and Lost in an English Athens.

Brideshead Revisited thus marks the culmination of the Oxford myth in more than one sense, for the enchantments of Arnold's Middle Ages are extended back beyond ancient Greece to the dawn of time itself. The power of the Oxford section lies not in its depiction of the 1920s as such but in its transcendence, for the novel rewrites the universal dream of a golden past in the form of a college story. Waugh himself was a great believer in fictions, both religious and mythical; writing of Quiller-Couch's fictional 'secret', he claimed in Grail-like terms that 'It is not given to all her sons either to seek or find this secret, but it was very near the surface in 1922.' Those students who led lives of a different hue knew of no such secret, nor indeed did the circle of moneyed aesthetes all share Waugh's intoxicated view. Even Harold Acton, who was part-prototype for Anthony Blanche, did not think the book an accurate portrait of the period. (Acton was a larger-than-life character of cosmopolitan background with rooms in the Meadow Buildings, from the balcony of which he declaimed poetry at passers by.) Other accounts of the period present a mixed picture: the memoirs of Osbert Lancaster have something of the same élan, but Anthony Powell's fiction and the memoirs of Graham Greene and A.L. Rowse provide a different impression. The matter was best put in perspective by Waugh's friend Christopher Hollis, who stated, 'It would be of course absurd to pretend that the story of Evelyn Waugh was the story of all Oxford in the 1920s. Our clique was a very small clique and our existence quite unknown to the great majority of undergraduates.'

The myth-making of the small clique was much enhanced by the best-selling verse memoirs of John Betjeman, *Summoned by Bells*, which appeared at the beginning of the 1960s. He had had his first taste of Oxford as a public-school boarder at the Dragon School in Oxford, where he spent his free time exploring the city by bicycle—'Take me, my Centaur bike, down Linton Rd.'—and where he first developed a passion for church architecture. After studying at Marlborough, he returned to

Oxford as a student at Magdalen and had rooms in the New Buildings next to the deer park. He affected the air of an aesthetic *bon viveur,* mixing with high church circles and cultivating the friendship of the well-born, and in *Summoned by Bells* he writes of the luncheon-parties, dining-clubs, pranks and indulgences of his student days—'I cut tutorials with wild excuse, / For life was luncheons, luncheons all the way'.

> Balkan Sobranies in a wooden box,
> The college arms upon the lid; Tokay
> And sherry in the cupboard; on the shelves
> The University Statues bound in blue,
> *Crome Yellow, Prancing Nigger,* Blunden, Keats.
> My walls were painted Bursar's apple-green;
> My wide-sashed windows looked across the grass
> To tower and hall and lines of pinnacles.

The hectic socialising which Betjeman enjoyed led to the great lover of churches failing the compulsory divinity exam, and to his devastation he was sent down from the 'sweet hothouse world of bells' to which he was so attached. When he went to see his tutor, C.S. Lewis, he was told to his chagrin that he would only have got a Third in his finals anyway. The pain of it all can still be felt in the lines he wrote fifty years later, and as in the writing of Waugh there is anguished regret for the loss of a youthful paradise. Afterwards the 'genius of the *genius loci*', as Harold Acton put it, wrote fondly of Oxford and of the donnish suburb of North Oxford in terms that helped reinstate its unfashionable Victorian Gothic. His verse conjures up an area of gabled gothic houses, lace curtains, and sundry old professors at a time 'When rents were lower in Rawlinson Road'. The Betjemanesque touch combines a lightness of tone with topographical detail, as can be seen here in 'May-Day Song for North Oxford', in which the jaunty lines give a fresh facelift to the solid and staid Victorian houses.

> Belbroughton Road is bonny, and pinkly bursts the spray
> Of prunus and forsythia across the public way,
> For a full spring-tide of blossom seethed and departed hence,
> Leaving land-locked pools of jonquils by sunny garden fence.

Like the small clique of Brideshead fame, the Oxford myth too derives from a small and closely connected group of writers. These drew inspiration from the teachings of Arnold and Pater, and they in turn drew inspiration from the philosophers of fifth-century B.C. Athens. Arnold wrote of being 'stuffed with Greek and Aristotle' at Oxford, and it was from that philosopher that he derived his notions of perfection;

Pater, more inclined to Plato, was strongly influenced by Arnold's ideas in the formulation of his own and knew 'The Scholar-Gipsy' by heart. The ideas of the two men were transmitted to students like Wilde, Johnson, and Beerbohm, the latter of whom confessed to being unable to read anything prior to Arnold with pleasure: 'he, in small doses, pleases me and inspires me with a sort of affection. Had I never been at Oxford I don't suppose even Arnold would waken anything in me', he confessed. One sees just how narrow the horizons were. The next generation included Compton Mackenzie, who admitted to the influence of Arnold in writing *Sinister Street,* and his novel invokes the names of Quiller-Couch, Beerbohm, Belloc and, most reverentially of all, Walter Pater, whose works bound in thick sea-green cloth and stamped with a golden monogram are the first items to adorn the shelves of Michael Fane. After Mackenzie came Waugh, for whom Beerbohm was a literary idol. He once addressed him as 'Master', just as Beerbohm before him had called Wilde 'The Divinity' and Wilde had written to Pater with 'Homage to the great master'. Waugh was the last of a line, and the nostalgic quality of his writing reflects an awareness of the decline and fall of an era.

The Oxford myth was of an age, and like the youth of which its authors wrote, awareness of its passing transience served to heighten the poignancy of the writing. Even as Arnold was writing of the last enchantments, the modern age was closing in, and with each accretion of urban development the romance was eaten away. For John Buchan in the 1890s, when the university remained half-monastery and half-playground, there was an uneasy feeling of 'the outer world at its gates'. Within the city too stood a Trojan horse containing William R. Morris, later Lord Nuffield, who rose from his humble East Oxford bicycle shop to the design and production of Morris-Oxford cars in premises on Longwall Street. The operation was then transferred to Cowley, where he produced munitions during the war, after which he was able to cash in on the car boom of the 1920s. By 1926 the company was the most important volume producer in the British motor trade and the 'city of dreaming spires' had become an important industrial centre. 'Welcome to Oxford, Home of Pressed Steel' declared a poster at the train station. Since Cowley lay on the fringe of Oxford, the tranquillity of the central area remained for some time unaffected, connected to the outer world, as Beerbohm put it, only by way of its suburbs. The Brideshead generation of the mid-twenties was by all accounts the last able to indulge in the type of conspicuous consumption that marked the Edwardian era. As the number of grammar-school students at the university increased, study took on a more central role in the life of undergraduates, and utilitarian

values replaced those of the upper class. In *City in the Foreground* a group
of marginalised working-class students living in the Iffley Road question
the whole ethos of the university: not for them 'a life of beautiful uselessness' that the idle rich of *Sonia* have in mind, for 'They wished not to
fling wide the city gates, but to demolish her very walls, to tear down her
buildings stone by stone that they might build they knew not what.' The
reaction against the unabashed élitism of Waugh's university can be felt
too in a venomous poem, 'The Oxford Voice', by D.H. Lawrence in *Pansies* (1929) which attacks the superior tones of the university accent.

> For every blooming bird is an Oxford cuckoo nowadays,
> you can't sit on a bus nor in the tube
> but it breathes gently and languishingly in the back of your neck.
>
> And oh, so seductively superior, so seductively
>   self-effacingly
>   deprecatingly
>   superior. —
> We wouldn't insist on it for a moment
>   but we are
>   we are
>   you admit we are
>   superior. —

Meanwhile, the university responded to the change in social conditions by introducing reforms that struck at the roots of the traditional
university. Compulsory Greek was abolished, women were granted
degrees, and for the first time in its history the university became depen-
dent on government money. The era of aristocratic pleasures, of gaiety,
frivolity, and aesthetic indulgence was drawing to an end, to be replaced
by middle-class values of work, efficiency, usefulness, and a concern for
morality. In 1907 there had come a fierce attack on the study of classics
in *Massacre of the Innocents*—'Let no man in future read the works of
Cicero, Paley and Demosthenes, and their ghastly commentators, as a
preparation for holding the reins of the British Empire'. The theme was
taken up in Louis MacNeice's long poem *Autumn Journal* (1938), in
which he gives an ironical account of his time at Merton studying Greats
which is far removed in tone from the earnest defence of the subject in
Sinister Street.

> We learned that a gentleman never misplaces his accents,
>   That nobody knows how to speak, much less how to write
> English who has not hob-nobbed with the great grandparents of English,
>   That the boy on the Modern Side is merely a parasite
> But the classical student is bred to the purple, his training in syntax

Is also a training in thought
And even in morals: if called to the bar or the barracks
   He always will do what he ought.

There is here a disagreement with Newman's *The Idea of a University*, in which it is argued that the disciplining of the mind through study of the humanities prepared a person for decision-making jobs. The poem speaks of a radical shift in values which was to mark the end of the university as a place of leisure where men acquired the accomplishments of a gentlemen.

Even as a student of Greats MacNeice had held a distrust of philosophical systems, and he came to reject Platonic absolutes in preference for 'The drunkenness of things being various'. He saw the escape into the past as an attractive but disreputable escape from uncomfortable realities, and he was suspicious of the praise of contemplation for the same reason. The poet was particularly concerned with the failure of the old way of thinking to address the wrongs of the world, and in the *Autumn Journal* he castigates ivory tower dons for sanitising ancient Greece, which is portrayed in the poem as a society whose vitality is built on the backs of the oppressed. On the eve of World War II, MacNeice proclaimed his own call to arms in a passage which marks the end of Oxford's love affair with Plato. It highlights by contrast the wistful nature of *Brideshead Revisited* in wishing to return to the old values of the 1920s before Auden, Orwell, Priestley and others ushered in the age of the common man.

So blow the bugles over the metaphysicians,
   Let the pure mind return to the Pure Mind;
I must be content to remain in the world of Appearance
   And sit on the mere appearance of a behind.
But in case you should think my education was wasted
   I hasten to explain
That having once been to the University of Oxford
   You can never really again
Believe anything that anyone says and that of course is an asset
   In a world like ours;
Why bother to water a garden
   That is planted with paper flowers?
. . . .
Good-bye now, Plato and Hegel,
   The shop is closing down;
They don't want any philosopher-kings in England,
   There ain't no universals in this man's town.

G.A. Kolkhorst, or 'the Colonel' as he was known, was one of those colourful characters who enliven the pages of university memoirs. Like Sligger, he had a circle of student friends, though he was not always taken seriously, and they met in his rooms in 38 Beaumont Street, where his literary allegiance was declared by a prominent photograph of Walter Pater (on which Osbert Lancaster mischievously scrawled 'Alma Pater'). John Betjeman provides an instant portrait of the aging aesthete in *Summoned by Bells*.

> I see you pouring sherry—round your neck
> A lump of sugar hanging on a thread
> 'To sweeten conversation': to your ear
> A trumpet held 'for catching good remarks.'

Kolkhorst held strong views on the state of Oxford literature, and in a paper for the St. John's Society given in 1952 he expressed the opinion, 'One may no longer be novelesque about Oxford. Conversely, Oxford is no longer a fit subject for a novel. It must be taken seriously. The Oxford novel is finished.' It was not so much the Oxford novel that was finished, however; it was the novel of the Oxford myth. By the 1930s the Oxford of *Brideshead Revisited* no longer existed in its moral climate, and by World War II it no longer existed even in its physical aspect. Waugh himself recognised this by having Ryder say of the city of his youth that it is 'submerged now and obliterated, irrecoverable as Lyonnesse'. Beerbohm evidently concurred, for writing in the next year in the preface to the 1946 edition of his novel he claimed that *Zuleika Dobson,* though a fantasy, 'was far more like to the old Oxford than was the old Oxford like to the place now besieged and invaded by Lord Nuffield's armies'. For the postwar generation the notion of an English Athens did not seem so appealing, and for the 'angry young men' of the 1950s the lie was distasteful rather than delightful. The walls of the enclosed garden could no longer keep out those who for so long had been excluded, and those on the inside no longer wished to assert their superiority. The Oxford myth was seen as an anachronism, the pretensions of which were absurd—'the famous Oxford culture, the English Athens and all that crap', sneer the students of Sheed's *A Middle Class Education,* the title of which speaks for itself (in Belloc's *A Moral Alphabet* [1899] Oxford is put down in upper-class fashion as a 'Malarial Spot' where 'with decent application, / One gets a good, sound, middle-class education'). For Oxford literature World War II heralded a more significant break with the past than had World War I, and *Brideshead Revisited* was the last major work of its type. Written during the war, the novel came out at its end when the luxuriant and exuberant tone of the writing stood in contrast to the privations of wartime. In the rationing of the postwar period the book's sense of loss echoed that of its readership, who relished it for a lifestyle of which they could only dream. Maurice Bowra, warden of Wadham, is said to have coined the phrase 'the Waugh to end Waugh'; viewed in such terms, *Brideshead Revisited* could be considered the Great Waugh that marks the end of an era.

CHAPTER 6

The Writing on the Walls:
From Premodern to Postmodern

They wandered at random, choosing the narrower ways and coming suddenly on colleges and long old walls.

—John Galsworthy, *End of the Chapter* (1934)

Oxford has been often portrayed as a city of bells. It is no less a city of walls. While the bells ring out in fictional tintinnabulation, the college walls act as lines of demarcation which run like faultlines through the literature, and over the course of the centuries they have acted as a means of seclusion for those on the inside, sheltering them from the world without. Although student had consorted with carpenter in Chaucer's pre-collegiate university, the retreat behind college walls brought division and insularity. As gown cut itself off from town, the monastical institutions turned inwards, feathering their nests and setting up the privileged retreats of pre-reform Oxford. These self-contained worlds delighted those who saw in them a life of ease combined with that of the mind; in the words of Henry James it offered a 'charmed seclusion'. For some it seemed the perfect place for contemplation, for others a protective environment within which to indulge their fancies. Seen from a different perspective, however, the walls appeared less appealing, for they represented the physical boundaries of a socially privileged society and served as a reminder that to generations of outsiders Oxford stood not so much for excellence as for exclusion. The almost unknown Wye Saltonstall (fl. 1630s) first gave this expression in one of his Characters, 'A Townesman in Oxford', who is depicted as 'one that hath liv'd long by the well of knowledge, but never sipt at it'. Remarkably it was not until the end of the nineteenth century that the theme was taken up again. The publication of Thomas Hardy's *Jude the Obscure* in 1895 represented an important landmark, for it was the first sustained examination of the university from the viewpoint of the downtrodden. Walls play a prominent part in the novel, and the writing on the walls takes both a literal and figurative form, for the biblical quotation Jude scrawls along the front of Biblioll college reinforces the implication contained in the book that the university could not maintain its privileged ways and restricted intake. In place of the dreaming spire Hardy posits an alternative motif for the city—that of the long wall.

In the early part of the twentieth century the pressure for change was considerable, but the university responded with a reluctance that irritated even some of its own members. The conservatism meant that the small number of women and those from poorer backgrounds who were admitted found themselves confronted by attitudes that ranged from grudging tolerance to outright disapproval. The struggle of women students is documented in Vera Brittain's *The Women at Oxford* (1960), which begins with the establishment of the first women's colleges in the 1870s. Yet even though women had gained colleges of their own, they were marginalised in university life, not allowed full degrees until 1920, and restricted in number until 1956. Memoirs tell of the strict rules governing their behaviour; chaperones were required for all social functions, and when hosting members of the opposite sex students had to place their beds outside the room in the corridor. The male student caught clambering over the wall of the women's college in Dorothy Sayers's *Gaudy Night* (1935) was committing a serious breach of discipline, and in Nina Bawden's Oxford of the 1940s guests are not allowed before lunch or after six. By contrast change comes relatively quickly in the postwar period, for in Leo Bellingham's *Oxford: The Novel* (1981)—set in the 1960s—male and female move in and out of each other's colleges with little hindrance. Twenty years later, in a social revolution beyond the imagining of earlier generations, colleges became coeducational and women lived alongside their male counterparts. The speed of the transformation was remarkable. In 1961 the Exeter fellow Dacre Balsdon was spinning a humorous fantasy about a men's college being taken over by women in his novel, *The Day They Burned Miss Termag*; not long afterwards there were no men's colleges. Of the thirty-seven colleges that now exist only one remains committed to a single-sex intake, and that, ironically, is a women's college, St. Hilda's.

The liberalisation of the twentieth century led not only to gains in women's education but to a widening social intake among men. In the early part of the century those not from public schools found themselves socially isolated in the élitist atmosphere of the university; at its most extreme, as in the Christ Church of *Sinister Street*, even public-school men feel out of place if they are not from the big four of Eton, Winchester, Harrow, and Charterhouse. Writing of his student days in the 1920s, Stephen Spender noted that 'Oxford was not as I had imagined it would be: I soon discovered that I was a new boy among public-school boys, who thought that not to come from a public school was as ridiculous as to be a foreigner.' The class consciousness was all-pervasive. In Paul Harrison's *Oxford Marmalade* (1946) Alistair Chester from Stratton Secondary finds himself isolated amongst peer and landed gentry at Christ Church, while

Jack, the coal-miner's son of Julian Mitchell's *Imaginary Toys* (1961), is another instance of a working-class student made to feel an outsider. In *Path of Dalliance* (1963) by Auberon Waugh (son of Evelyn), public-school boys are told that working-class types are there to broaden the outlook of those like themselves who have come to Oxford in the normal manner, and the snobbish Sillery of *A Question of Upbringing* ogles the north country son of a builder (part-inspired by the critic Cyril Connolly) as if he is a type of exotic animal. Such attitudes led to the resentment of figures like the working-class eponym of Dennis Potter's *The Nigel Barton Plays* (1967), who is full of hatred for the superiority and social *mores* of his privileged contemporaries. The class divisions and social tensions of the mid-century university are explored at greater length in novels like Philip Larkin's *Jill* (1945), Julian Mitchell's *Imaginary Toys* (1961), Raymond Williams's *Second Generation* (1964), and Wain's *Where the Rivers Meet* (1988).

The two world wars were significant though contrasting markers in the modernising process. In *Goodbye to All That* (1929) and *Testament of Youth* (1933) Robert Graves and Vera Brittain described the effect of World War I on their unfortunate generation. It was a devastating period: the 1,400 undergraduates enrolled in 1914 were reduced to 369 by 1918. When C.S. Lewis went to University College as a student that year, he found only five others in residence; before the end of his first term he too was commissioned. Many of those going to fight were fired with an idealism that led them to identify with a passage from book 12 of the *Iliad* quoted in their letters and diaries—'Because we are privileged,' says the hero Sarpedon, 'because we have the best estates and the foremost seats and the choicest food and drink, therefore we must fight in the front rank, and kill or be killed.' Hundreds and hundreds of the young students did just that, and a whole generation was laid waste in the nightmare of mud across the Channel. Among those who lost their lives in the war were Julian Grenfell of Balliol, author of 'Into Battle', which was published in *The Times* on the day he died at Ypres, and Edward Thomas, graduate of Lincoln College, who died at Arras. The American philosopher George Santayana, was in Oxford for the whole of the war and he described the flavour of the period—college-hospitals, daily casualty lists, cadets in quadrangles, the whirr of aeroplanes over Port Meadow—in the introduction to his *Soliloquies in England* (1922). Laurence Binyon too wrote of Oxford in wartime, musing on the desolate air of the deserted colleges.

> It is as if I look on the still face
> Of a Mother, musing where she sits alone.

> She is with her sons, she is not in this place;
> She is gone out into far lands unknown . . .

The tragic losses incurred during the war proved a terrible blow to the confidence of the ruling classes, and the sense of waste and futility described by the likes of Siegfried Sassoon (another student sent off to the trenches) fired a widespread determination never to let such a catastrophe happen again. Curiously, though, when students returned to Oxford after the war, the university returned to its old ways as if nothing had changed. It made for an uneasy time for the war veterans, hardened and embittered, who were made to feel out of place. 'The young men up from school think we have come to clean the windows when they see us', C.S. Lewis wrote. 'Survivors Not Wanted' was how Vera Brittain entitled the section of her memoirs. As if indifferent to their feelings, the post-war aesthetes set about recreating the lifestyle of their Edwardian predecessors and the Brideshead generation made merry. By the 1930s, however, the shadow of economic depression and political repression made for a far less frivolous atmosphere. The infamous vote by the Oxford Union in 1933 not to fight for king and country reflected a more worldly view of political developments, and the outbreak of war was consequently not greeted with the same innocent enthusiasm which characterised the rush to the trenches earlier in the century.

World War II brought a familiar scenario of diminished numbers, casualty-lists and war wounded, but it did not have the devastating effect on university life as had been the case earlier in the century. The bells hung in silence, there were few undergraduates over nineteen, and the Home Guard drilled in Christ Church Meadow, yet in his recollections of the war years, the novelist and playwright John Mortimer claims that the Oxford of earlier times was maintained in spirit, even if rationed out on coupons; students with bow-ties and powdered chins still went out for dinner, and late-comers still had to climb over walls to get back into college. Among the undergraduates at the time were Philip Larkin, Kingsley Amis and John Wain, and the drama society, OUDS, flourished with members like Peter Brook and Richard Burton, the latter of whom went to study at Exeter College in 1944 on a special course while attached to the R.A.F. Those who died in the war included Keith Douglas (1920–44), a promising young poet who had studied at Merton College under Edmund Blunden, and the opening verse of the poem he wrote in 1941 entitled 'Oxford' takes on added poignancy in the light of his death three years later.

> At home, as in no other city, here
> summer holds her breath in a dark street

the trees nocturnally scented, lovers like moths
go by silently on the footpaths
and spirits of the young wait
cannot be expelled, multiply each year.

The changes that followed the war, paradoxically, were more radical and profound than those after World War I. The widespread expectation of a new social order was signalled by the electoral preference for Labour at the expense of the war-hero Churchill, and the university had to make efforts to cater for a more egalitarian society. There was a rapid expansion in student numbers; the central university assumed greater authority as colleges had their powers cut back; and the level of the entrance examination was raised dramatically to exclude applicants whose sole qualification lay in their 'college connections'. At the same time there was active recruitment among less prestigious schools which had never entered candidates, with the result that the social composition of the university began to change, albeit slowly. In the 1860s the top twenty public schools supplied an estimated 46 percent of Oxbridge undergraduates; by 1955 this had dropped to 23 percent. As the university struggled towards meritocracy, efforts were made to dispel the traditional image of upper-class élitism, and writers too showed a concern to counter the former exclusiveness. The social levelling brought with it the demise of the English Athens as a viable concept, for not only had the assumption of superiority that underwrites the notion passed out of fashion, but modern Oxford with its practical efficiencies and traffic-jams made mockery of the 'dreaming spires' of tradition. This led to a change in the nature of Oxford writings in the latter part of the century, and postmodern fiction portrays the university as simply one part of a multifaceted city, and not necessarily the best part either. No longer can an Oxford story be called a collegiate story, and among those now featured in the pages of contemporary fiction are the obscure men and women of the city to whom Thomas Hardy first gave voice and identity over one hundred years earlier. Written at the close of the nineteenth century, *Jude the Obscure* can be viewed with hindsight as a pivotal work which is at one and the same time steeped in the past and suggestive of the future. The walls described in the book, figurative as well as literal, shape the agenda of the twentieth century.

HARDY'S NEW JERUSALEM

The city of *Jude the Obscure* is Christminster, not a real city at all but a fiction, a vision, and an illusion. As its name suggests, it is a city that speaks of Christ, and it is one marked by a cross—that set in Broad

Street. Jude's first meeting with the woman who is to be his undoing takes place, ominously, over the very spot where the three Protestant bishops were burnt to death. Far from presaging the triumph of faith over death, the encounter leads to hardship, suffering and an untimely end. It is a Greek tragedy in Christian guise which takes its tone from that other strand of the university, the clerical seminary that stretches back through Newman and the Tractarians, through Wesley and the Methodists, through Cranmer and the martyrs, through Wyclif and the Lollards, back indeed to the clerks and the very origins of the university. Like the poor of medieval times, Hardy's hero aspires to better himself through a career in the church. The university on which he pins his dreams treats him with cold indifference, however, for the home of Hebraism is swamped by a Hellenic band, and the poor are 'elbowed off the pavement for the millionaire's sons'. Christminster is no English Athens; it is a New Jerusalem—no less a mythic city, but one informed by martyrdom.

Despite his lowly background, the young Jude Fawley is an earnest and studious youth who is inspired by the example of the village school-teacher to set his heart on a place at Christminster, where parsons are raised 'like radishes in a bed'. The ambition is so much above his station that he keeps it to himself: 'It is a place much too good for you ever to have much to do with', the youth is told by the great-aunt by whom he is brought up. His dream is such that he becomes 'so romantically attached to Christminster that, like a young lover alluding to his mistress, he felt bashful at mentioning its name'. His first sighting of the city is visionary in nature. Straining from atop a barn roof on Ridgeway crest some twenty miles from the city, his view is obscured by mist, and he prays for it to clear. For a tantalising quarter of an hour he keeps vigil, then spire and dome appear fleetingly before him like a mirage, before once more being veiled in mist. The experience is clothed in the language of reve-lation: there is a 'halo' of glowing light in the darkness; 'the voice of the city' speaks to him through its distant bells; and to Jude the city appears the heavenly Jerusalem itself, making him lose all sense of his physical self. Image and reality remain blurred thereafter for the young idealist, and his failure to distinguish between the two leads to disaster. Models and representations form a recurring motif in the novel: at one point Jude is fascinated by a miniature recreation of Jerusalem, and at another he becomes obsessed with forming cakes in the shape of Christminster. The biblical city and the university town overlap in his mind, for his view of Christminster is informed by the Book of Revelation and medieval notions concerning the spirituality of scholarship. Steeped in the writ-ings of the church fathers, Jude sees the university as 'the tree of knowledge' and 'the paradise of the learned'. It is a paradise from which he is forever locked out.

Dreams and broken dreams permeate the Christminster sections, as if in mockery of Oxford's self-image (Hardy was much influenced by Arnold's poetry and prose). When the young innocent arrives in the city for the first time, it is significantly evening-time, and he walks around the city centre in the darkness communing with the spirit of illustrious figures from the past. The long list of names reveals his intimacy with the literature of the university (though not, significantly, with the novels), and among the figures he reverently recalls 'the most real to Jude Fawley were the founders of the religious school called Tractarian'. This is the city, the reader is reminded, of Newman, Keble, and Pusey, influential figures for the young believer. As he stands in the darkness on the outside of the walls, the solemn youth is reminded too of Arnold's eulogy, and the notion of a 'Beautiful city' calling humans to perfection hovers in the evening air. Next morning the clear light of day brings the first moments of disenchantment, however, when the college walls which had appeared so beguiling in the darkness are revealed to be rotten and gnawed by the damp of the Christminster climate. Jude takes lodgings in a working-class part of the city named Beersheba (Jericho), and the 'raw and cold air' of the nearby meadows is indicative of his reception in the city. Though he finds work as a mason and sends letters of applications to the colleges, he calculates that it will take him fifteen years to save enough money to afford the university fees and that without the advantage of a coach, he has no chance of winning a scholarship. Later he receives a solitary reply to his letters of application in which the master of Biblioll (thought to represent the plain-speaking Jowett of Balliol) states tersely that as a working-man the mason should look to succeed in his own sphere of life. Far from being a citadel of enlightenment, it seems that the university is concerned only with those of its own kind, and the values it represents appear little better than the rotten walls that protect it. Dismayed, the mason climbs despondently to the top of the Christminster Sheldonian where, in Hardy's words, he 'awoke from his dream'. The phrasing is significant, for the city of dream cannot accommodate that of a working man. Jude's cousin, Sue Brideshead, realises the irony of this when she tells him, 'You are one of the very men Christminster was intended for when the colleges were founded; a man with a passion for learning, but no money, or opportunities, or friends.'

Jude's obsession with the university is interlaced in the book with his tragic personal life—of the book's six sections only two are set in Christminster—and romance conspires with learning to humble and humiliate him. Though he is married to an earthy country woman named Arabella, Jude is abandoned by her, and his affections turn instead towards Sue, who is by contrast a creature of the city—overly cerebral and lacking in physical warmth. Wilful and ethereal, she is a 'bride' who is unable to give of herself completely because she is ruled by her 'head'. When Jude arranges a job for her with Phillotson, his old school teacher, she marries the older man out of spite at Jude's marital involvement. The marriage proves unhappy, however, and she returns with her husband's consent to Jude, whose wife has emigrated to Australia. Defying convention, the couple set up house together, and in addition to little Father Time (Jude's son from his marriage to Arabella) they have two children of their own. Unable to rid himself of his obsession with Christminster, Jude returns there with his family after an absence of some eight or so years. Their arrival in the city coincides with the university's annual Remembrance Day (Commemoration), and as they join the crowd waiting for the procession of university dignitaries, Jude's tragedy is underscored by his undiminished love of learning. The idealism of the young worker stands in marked contrast to the indifference of the gowned figures as they pass him by with lack of interest. When town too turns against the impoverished family by its unwillingness to house them, the situation becomes too much for little Father Time, who feels responsible for the desperate situation, and he is found hanging alongside the two younger children—'Done because we are too menny' runs the suicide note. The shock of this is too horrific for the couple to bear, and Jude finds Sue not long afterwards prostrate with guilt in the high church of St. Silas in Beersheba (Jericho's St. Barnabas), for she sees the death of her children as a punishment from God for leaving her marriage. Soon afterwards, as if in penitence, she returns to a man she does not love, and Jude's isolation is made complete. Not only has he been rejected by the university he aspired to, but he has lost the children he cared for and the woman he loved. Far from perfection, the 'Beautiful city' has led him to futility, and his spiritual malaise is mirrored by a physical decline. When Arabella makes an unexpected return into his life, he has little strength to resist her, and as he wanders half-dazed around the city he summons up the spirits of the past, though this time with a crucial difference—disenchantment with Christminster has brought disillusionment with Christianity.

> I don't revere all of them as I did then. I don't believe in half of them. The theologians, the apologists, and their kin the metaphysicians, the high-handed statesmen, and others, no longer interest me. All that has been spoilt for me by the grind of stern reality.

If broken dreams mark one of the ways in which Hardy subverts traditional notions, another is in the ironic undercutting of the conventions
of the *Bildungsroman*. Instead of using the university as background for
the formation of character, Hardy exploits the city as a setting in which
to portray the disintegration of a young man. This is seen at its starkest at
the end of the novel, for just one year after his return to the city Jude's
health gives way altogether during the annual festivities for Remembrance Week. As he lies dying, all around there is bustling activity and
festive preparation; from one side comes the swelling sounds of an organ
concert, from the other hurrahs from the river. The communal excitement contrasts with the isolation of Jude, who is left to die alone after
Arabella negligently slips out to view the celebrations. Not yet thirty, the
young man has been betrayed by life, and he dies a martyr to his youthful idealism. Even after death he is hounded by the university, for as he
lies under a white shroud, 'the joyous throb of waltz entered from the
ball-room at Cardinal'. Two days later, while he is laid out in his coffin,
there comes the bitterest irony of all: the sound of rejoicing at the con-
ferring of honorary degrees on the duke of Hamptonshire and 'a lot
more illustrious gents of that sort'. As if to add insult to injury, bells of
joyous celebration ring out, and the voice of the city that seemed to
beckon to Jude at the start of the book is shown at the end to be cruelly
indifferent.

Hardy's Christminster is very much a tale of two cities, town and gown,
and the division between them is enforced by the walls which loom large
in the book. These are lent force by the mason's eye of the protagonist;
age, condition, and design are all carefully described. Their symbolic
role in the novel is apparent from Jude's very first evening in the city, for
when Great Tom sounds his 101 strokes, the college gates slam closed
and the villager is shut out from the world he aspires to. Later he hovers
on the outside of the walls as if awaiting a divine arm to lift him inside:
'Only a wall divided him from those happy young contemporaries of his
with whom he shared a common mental life; men who had nothing to do
from morning till night but to read, mark, learn, and inwardly digest.
Only a wall—but what a wall!' When he takes work as a mason, Jude finds
himself working on the very walls behind which he so yearned to study—
an ironical twist—and along the 'freezing negative' of Biblioll he writes
a quotation from the Bible: 'I have understanding as well as you. I am not
inferior to you: yea, who knoweth not such things as these?' The walls
play a key role too when Jude returns to Christminster with his young
family, for while the heads of houses and learned doctors sit inside in
comfort, the lover of learning has to stand outside in the rain. Eager to
catch some of the Latin oration, he creeps under the open windows, but

it is in vain, for he cannot hear anything. Again it is only a wall that separates him: 'Well—I'm an outsider to the end of my days!' he bemoans. Wet and homeless, he and his family look for lodgings, but the search for accommodation among the dingy back alleys only serves to emphasise the family's standing in the 'city of light'.

> They started in quest of the lodging and at last found something that seemed to promise well, in Mildew Lane—a spot which to Jude was irresistible—though to Sue it was not so fascinating—a narrow lane close to the back of a college, but having no communication with it. The little houses were darkened to gloom by the high collegiate buildings, within which life was so far removed from that of the people in the lane as if it had been on opposite sides of the globe; yet only a thickness of wall divided them.

Because accommodation proves impossible to find for the family as a whole, Jude is forced to take separate lodgings, and Sue stays in 'an old intramural cottage' cast in shadow by the 'four centuries of gloom, bigotry, and decay' from the nearby college. To little Father Time the colleges look like gaols, but with a vital difference. Rather than preventing escape, their 'scholared walls' seem designed to prevent entry.

With gown obscured from view in this way, town and townsfolk dominate the 'City of Colleges'—one more example of the many ironies in which the book abounds. There are the stoneworker colleagues of Jude; the ecclesiastical suppliers for whom Sue works; the customers at the 'obscure and low-ceiled tavern up a court'; the landlords and ladies of Beersheba; and the pork and sausage shop which Arabella's father sets up. The institution at the centre of this city is not Cardinal College but the railway station, and the lives of the townsfolk interact with gown only at grand festive occasions like degree-giving celebrations and boat races. The dingy and smelly alleyways of Jude's city stand in stark contrast to the moonlit gardens of Arnold, and the reversal of focus is mirrored by a reversal of values: 'It [Christminster] is an ignorant place, except as to the townspeople, artisans, drunkards, and paupers. . . . They see life as it is, of course; but few of the people in the colleges do', Sue remarks at one point. For ordinary citizens the academics are of marginal interest, 'the Dons, magistrates, and other people in authority being sincerely pitied for their shortcomings'. Hardy thus sets up a paradigm that stands in stark contrast to that of the Oxford novel, and *Jude* redraws the mythological map of the city by championing the 'shabby purlieu which he [Jude] himself occupied, unrecognized as part of the city at all by its visitors and panegyrists'. When the young mason first comes to Christminster, he is blind to everything but the university, but later he comes to see that the yard where he works is every bit as worthy as the best of the colleges. The 'secret' he discovers is not hidden in the depths of a college, but lies at the city's central crossroads of Fourways (Carfax).

> He began to see that the town life was a book of humanity infinitely more palpitating, varied, and compendious, than the gown life. These struggling men and women before him were the reality of Christminster, though they knew little of Christ or Minster. That was one of the humours of things. The floating population of students and teachers, who did know both in a way, were not Christminster in a local sense at all.

By contrast with the positive light in which the town members are depicted, the university of Hardy's Christminster presents a startling contrast with the praise being lavished on Oxford in this period: prison in place of paradise; gloom instead of moonlight; bigotry rather than sweetness and light. The paganistic Sue delivers the most damning statement about the Christian stronghold when she describes it as 'a nest of commonplace schoolmasters whose characteristic is timid obsequiousness to tradition'. Hardy's portrayal of the university is all the more remarkable for appearing in the decade of Wilde, Lionel Johnson, and Quiller-Couch; it was the height of the British Empire and a time when Gladstone was proudly declaring that to be a characteristically Oxford man was the highest compliment that could be paid a human being. Outrage at the attack on one of the nation's most cherished institutions fuelled the hostile reactions to the book, which was roundly condemned for its immorality, pessimism and atheistic attitudes. The bishop of Wakefield burnt a copy, and Hardy was supposedly so hurt by the criticisms that he gave up novel-writing altogether (though the real reason may have been that his financial independence by this time allowed him to return to his preferred option of writing poetry). In the 'biography' which he dictated to his second wife, Hardy shows annoyance at the misunderstanding of his novel, and he is at pains to emphasise that his purpose was to make a philosophical statement rather than to promote reform of the university or the divorce laws. Jude's death in the sacred city rewrites the martyrdom of Christ in a way that signifies the bleakness of the human condition. In the construction of his New Jerusalem Hardy drew on elements of Greek drama, as is suggested by the remorseless manner in which his protagonist is hounded by fate and the ironic contrast between the title of 'Jude the Obscure' and that of 'Oedipus Rex'. Viewed in the light of this, *Jude* can be seen as marking the final outcome of the nineteenth-century novels of faith set in Oxford, for the crisis precipitated by the Tractarians set in motion a series of fictional explorations which led by the end of the century to the despairing death of an isolated individual in an indifferent universe.

The exclusion of Jude serves then as a means to describe 'the grind of harsh reality', and though the university is cast as the villain of the piece, there is nonetheless a sense of underlying respect for the tradition of learning it represents. The problem for Jude lies in access, not with the scholarly endeavour, and the attitude of Hardy's hero is telling in this, for even after all his misfortune he retains an affection for what is termed a 'unique centre of thought and religion—the intellectual and spiritual granary of this country'.

> I love the place—although I know how it hates all men like me—the so-called Self-taught,—how it scorns our laboured acquisitions, when it should be the first to respect them; how it sneers at our false quantities and mispronunciations, when it should say, I see you want help, my poor friend! Nevertheless, it is the centre of the universe to me, because of my early dream: and nothing can alter it.

There is undoubtedly something here of Hardy's own feelings, and *Jude* is generally held to be the most autobiographical of his novels. Not only does Jude's rural background mirror Hardy's—the author too was self-taught, considered becoming a priest at one point, and regretted not having attended university—but Hardy's father had been a mason and he himself an architectural assistant. (There has even been unfounded speculation that in his youth Hardy may have received a letter of refusal from the university similar to that of Jude.) Though the novel is set temporally in the 1880s, the prevailing atmosphere suggests that it more properly belongs to the 1860s when Hardy himself would have been of student age and under the influence of the Tractarian teachings which affect his hero. In a letter to a friend in 1926 the author admitted as much when he wrote that Christminster 'is not meant to be exclusively Oxford, but any old-fashioned University about the date of the story, 1860–70, before there were such chances for poor men as there are now.' This was a time when there was considerable discussion of the future course of the university, with Jowett championing the training of an élite in keeping with Platonic notions of higher education while others argued in favour of opening up entrance to a wider social intake. Hardy had himself attended a talk on the subject in 1858 by his friend and mentor Horace Moule (whose later suicide is thought to have prompted the writing of the novel) and at one point in the book Jude makes a vague reference to a movement for reform when he says, 'I hear that soon there is going to be a better chance for such helpless students

as I was. There are schemes afoot for making the University less exclusive, and extending its influence.' One example of such endeavours were
the extension lectures started in 1878 which were given to groups of
ordinary men and women up and down the country. It would seem,
then, that the attitudes of the book hark back to pre-modern times, and
the few descriptions that are given of academic types reinforce the retrospective view of the university, for the pompous doctors and the gown-
less students illicitly buying bull-pups come straight out of *Verdant Green*.
Onto the university of his student days Hardy grafted the physical setting
of 1890s Oxford, and to ensure credibility the author paid a visit to the
city shortly before embarking on his novel. (The visit took place in June
1893 during Encaenia, the awarding of honorary degrees, which allowed
Hardy to witness first-hand the rituals and festivities described in the
book.) There are several topographical discrepancies between Christminster and its real-life counterpart, some of them no doubt deliberate,
and it has been pointed out that Jude's sighting of the city from the
Ridgeway barn is technically impossible, for the view is obscured by Boars
Hill. As a result Christminster represents a prime example of the 'city of
the mind' which hovers tantalisingly in the interspace between print and
referent. By name and construct it is clearly imaginary and exists, as
Hardy himself pointed out, only between the covers of a book; yet at the
same time the locations are easily recognisable from real life, and it
requires little effort to recognise the likeness of Cardinal College to
Christ Church, of Chief Street to the High, of Fourways to Carfax, and of
Beersheba to the Oxford suburb of Jericho (St. Silas, the 'Church of Cer-
emonies' in Beersheba, was based on the Anglo-Catholic church of St.
Barnabas, the designer of which was Hardy's former employer, A.W.
Blomfield).

The renaming of Oxford locales by Hardy served to emphasise the
fiction of his fictional city, and though he professed to be disinterested in
the matter of university exclusion, the author must nonetheless have
been pleased by the contribution his novel made to widening student
intake at Oxford. In a postscript to the preface of the novel added in
1912, he noted—not without pride one presumes—the suggestion to
give Ruskin College, founded for working men in 1899, the name of
'College of Jude the Obscure'. For their part university authorities were
inclined to ascribe the Oxford of *Jude* to the pre-reform past, and when
it was learnt in 1920 that Hardy was due to visit a production of *The
Dynasts* by the university dramatic society (OUDS), it was quickly
arranged for the author to be awarded an honorary degree. This was followed two years later by the award of an honorary fellowship at Queen's
College. For a man who had written so harshly of the sense of exclusion,

there must have been a bitter-sweet feeling at finding himself in old age on the inside of the college walls; it was, to borrow his own phrase, one of 'life's little ironies'. By all accounts he greatly enjoyed himself, and interestingly, on both occasions he made a particular point of going to visit the Martyrs' Memorial in St. Giles, as if it stood at the symbolic centre of his city. Erected by Protestant loyalists in 1841–43 in reaction to the Tractarian furore, the memorial commemorates the death of the three martyrs in nearby Broad Street, and its neo-Gothic pinnacles speak of the Christian tradition of the city. From college quadrangle and dreaming spire, Hardy had relocated the spiritual heart of the city in a manner which refuted the whole notion of the English Athens and its academic groves.

The singularity of Hardy's achievement is no less striking in other areas, for not since Chaucer had an Oxford story been set in town, and there was no precedent in all English literature for a major work with a working-class hero. Of other Oxford novels only *Tom Brown at Oxford* can compare in terms of humanity, though as far as structure is concerned the two books could hardly be further apart, for the well-ordered oppositions of Hardy's novel make Hughes's book seem unplanned and shapeless. The hardships of Hardy's protagonist were for long eclipsed in the public mind by the decadence of well heeled aesthetes, and the martyrdom of Jude was overshadowed first by that of St. Oscar and later by that of Sebastian. Yet though the obscure mason was elbowed aside by his more privileged contemporaries, there are signs that he is pushing back, for as memory fades of the upper-class university, a new Oxford is being created in the fiction of the contemporary city that is closer in spirit to *Jude* than *Brideshead*. There has been a significant upsurge of interest in Hardy's novel in recent years, and books such as Jennifer Dawson's *Judasland* (1989) proudly advertise their allegiance (Judasland is Jude's land, Jericho). Indicative of the current trend, a pub in Oxford's Walton St. was renamed after the novel (its location is near the cemetery of St. Sepulchre where Jude's children are presumed to have been buried), and to mark the centenary of Hardy's book a film was released in 1996 directed by Michael Winterbottom and starring Christopher Eccleston and Kate Winslet. (For the purposes of the film Christminster was represented by Edinburgh, the grime and starkness of which were felt to be closer to the atmosphere of the novel than the more mellow colours of modern Oxford; when Hardy wrote his book the college walls were in a bad state of disrepair.) The tributes to *Jude* in recent times are an acknowledgment of the way the values of the book resonate with those of the modern age. By adding the dispossessed to the mythology of the city Hardy redefined the 'home of lost causes' and created an alternative to the Arnoldian tradition that was only taken up by writers in the second half of the twentieth century. Jude and Sue believe themselves to be fifty years ahead of their time; the novel itself could be said to have been a hundred years ahead of its.

DON'S DELIGHT: A GOLDEN AGE OF MURDER

The first half of the twentieth century saw the emergence of a flourishing new subgenre of the Oxford novel in the form of detective fiction, and the old witticism that Oxford consisted of the 'quick and the dead' (quick wits and dead souls) took on a new meaning as the fictional city was filled with 'clever dicks' and academic corpses. The ties between Oxford and the detective story are remarkable, not simply for the amount of crime set in the city but for the number of Oxonians who have been avid readers—and writers.

> 'Oh, detective stories!' said the Dean. 'Well, of course, I'm very fond of a good thriller . . .'
>
> 'And notice,' continued Dr. Browning, who had fallen into his remorseless lecture-room manner, 'how much of that literature has been written by Oxford graduates—Dorothy Sayers, Edmund Crispin, Michael Innes, C. Day Lewis, J.C. Masterman and so on. Not only are they graduates,' his voice became low and dramatic, 'many of them are at this moment senior teaching members of the University.'

To the names mentioned by Timothy Robinson, writing here in *When Scholars Fall* (1961), could be added those of G.D.H. Cole, a reader in economics who collaborated on a number of detective novels with his wife and ran an influential socialist circle, and W.H. Auden (at one time a member of the Cole group) who wrote a poem 'Detective Story' suggesting that 'Someone must pay for / Our loss of happiness, our happiness itself' and who claimed to have served as model for Nigel Strangeways, the detective-hero of his friend Cecil Day-Lewis, alias crime writer Nicholas Blake. (In more recent times too the tradition of donnish interest in the genre has been maintained by T.J. Binyon of Wadham, John Fuller of Magdalen, and Peter Levi, former professor of poetry.) One may wonder at the fascination of academics for an apparently light-hearted genre, but A.M. Quinton claims, 'This is a perfectly intelligible state of affairs. The classical detective story is, in an appropriately narrow sense of the word, pre-eminently intellectual. It calls on its author for out-of-the-way knowledge, for extended interest in the articulation of mistaken theories and for the ability to manipulate complex interlockings of times, places and movements. To compensate it does not require anything very refined in the way of characterisation.' It might also be pointed out that research and detection have much in common: the pursuit of truth, the painstaking search for evidence, the close attention to detail, the need for patience and perseverance, and the use of logic tempered by flashes of inspiration. Small wonder then that according to T.J. Binyon, 'Academics form by far the largest group of amateur detectives'. Edmund Crispin (pseudonym of Robert Montgomery [1921–78], a contemporary of Larkin and Amis at St. John's) played on the similarities by mirroring his Oxford academic/detective, Gervase Fen, with an Oxford detective/academic, Sir Richard Freeman (Fen was based on Will Moore, Montgomery's French tutor at St. John's). The mirroring technique of a university professor who takes up detective work and a city policeman who writes literary criticism not only exemplifies the duality of Oxford town and gown but allows Crispin to entertain the reader with literary allusions, bookish repartee, and wide-ranging quotations. The tone was taken from Innes, as was the pseudonym (from a character in Innes's *Hamlet, Revenge!* [1937]), and both authors share a taste for playfulness and the bizarre. The donnish school of detection, as such writing has been named, is characterised by its erudite murderers and well-read detectives. Books and libraries play key roles. 'Oxford murders are literary murders. To deal with them you need to have literary policemen', comments a knowing character in Robinson's *When Scholars Fall*.

The interwar period of the early twentieth century has been called the 'Golden Age of crime' when a profusion of works sharing common characteristics enjoyed widespread public popularity. The books were typified by their air of genteel escapism and upper-middle-class backgrounds, and they revolved around a common pattern: a 'bloodless' murder which spared the reader any unpleasantness; a closed setting such as a remote house or an island; a crime 'puzzle' involving a limited number of suspects; an idiosyncratic amateur detective in the tradition of Sherlock Holmes; and a summing up which revealed the unexpected truth. The upshot, as Julian Symons has pointed out in *Bloody Murder* (1972), was an intellectual diversion which offered cosy reading and a source of reassurance, for the fiction of an ordered universe in which good always triumphs and justice is always done appeals to the desire for security. The underlying presumption is that the disruption caused by the crime will be temporary and that, armed with reason and intuition, the detective will be able to right wrongs and restore the *status quo*. Given the human dread of change (and death is the biggest change of all), the light-hearted playfulness is deeply reassuring in that it promotes the notion that all will be well in the end. Viewed in this light the genre can be seen as symptomatic of the social insecurity in the interwar period as

the ruling classes lost power both at home and abroad. This holds true of
the university too, for the traditional order of academics were worried
about being usurped by a more earnest and professional generation.
The Oxford of detective fiction is a remote and cabbalistic world of
intriguing academics, a rarified world which is barely accessible to the
ordinary person, and the books have a strong mythologising function in
that they celebrate insularity and superiority. It is perhaps no coincidence that the golden age of detective fiction should overlap the period
of the 'Oxford myth', for closed settings and self-containment are integral to both.

   University crime begins with the 'most famous man who never lived'
when Sherlock Holmes goes to the amalgamated 'Camford' in 'The
Creeping Man' and 'The Three Students'. Though he talks of his time as
a student, Holmes does not specify which university he attended, and
speculation on the subject has generated a number of articles, several of
which focus on the fact that Holmes mentions being bitten by a dog
while on his way to morning chapel. The debate was initiated by the
Catholic chaplain of Oxford, Ronald Knox (1888–1957), who argued
that the aristocratic connections and indolent ways of Conan Doyle's
detective meant that he must have been at Christ Church. Knox was a
cleric with a literary bent, and his passion for detective fiction led him to
form a Detection Club which promoted the idea that the genre should
be primarily an intellectual exercise based on logic and fair play. One of
his own attempts, *Footsteps at the Lock* (1928), holds the distinction of
being the first of the Oxford murders. The story centres around two
cousins studying at the university who take a canoe trip up the Thames,
with only one returning. The students are contrasting types, one a hearty
and the other an aesthete with a gift for epigrams—'Photography, he
held, was the highest of all the arts, because the camera never tells the
truth.' The lightness of tone allows for a refreshing view of the city;
Oxford, for instance, is cast as a once-beautiful city 'breathing out from
her gas-works all the disenchantment of middle age'. There is also a
barely suppressed sense of smugness, as in this account of high table:
'Who is this man next to you, to whom you have not been introduced? Is
he a mere guest like yourself, or is he a Fellow? In the latter case, presumably, there is some subject on which he is a European authority'. The
focus here, as elsewhere in detective fiction, is on the senior community;
yet though the subject-matter differs from the undergraduate dramas of
the Oxford novel, the two types of book share common values. The literary bond was cemented in Knox's ties with Evelyn Waugh, personal as
well as religious, and it is perhaps not without significance that the

author of *Brideshead* should have been literary executor and biographer
of the city's first crime writer.

One year after Knox's publication, Adam Broome's *The Oxford Murders*
(1929) brought the killings into the very heart of the city by having the
regius professor of Latin murdered in Wellington Square, the reader in
French in the Turl, and a philosophy tutor on Port Meadow. This initiated an outbreak of Oxford crime with a triplet of golden age classics: Sir
John Masterman's *An Oxford Tragedy* in 1933; Dorothy Sayers's *Gaudy
Night* in 1935; and Michael Innes's *Death at the President's Lodging* in 1936.
All three won favour with critics, and Innes's book in particular was
singled out as setting new standards for the genre. These 'old masters'
were followed by a younger generation, amongst whom Edmund Crispin
with three Oxford stories in the 1940s, Robert Robinson with *Landscape
with Dead Dons* (1956), and Timothy Robinson with *When Scholars Fall*
(1961) wrote of criminal capers in their *alma mater* to particularly good
effect. In recent years the crime wave has continued unabated, and to
many people today Oxford is no longer the city of dreaming spires, or of
Brideshead Revisited, but that of Inspector Morse . . . *mors* . . . death.

Though Crispin set a trend for town murders, the title of
Whitechurch's *Murder at the College* (1932) captures the spirit of the early
fiction, since for writers in the interwar period, as for many of their suc-
cessors, the college provided an obvious addition to the list of 'closed settings' which included the manor, the ship, the island, the hotel, the
train, etc. The small circle of suspects could be easily transposed from
country house to college quadrangle, and as Michael Innes observed in
characteristic language, the college 'offers such a capital frame for the
quiddities and wilie beguilies of the craft'. For tactful reasons the colleges where the crimes take place are imaginary in name and sometimes
implausible in setting; Sayers's Shrewsbury College situated on Balliol
cricket ground is a prime example. The fictional college allows for history and traditions to be written to taste, and this is either done with
painstaking realism as in the case of J.C. Masterman, or with barely con-
cealed ridicule as in the case of Robert Robinson (his college boasts a
clock called Iscariot that betrays midnight by sounding thirteen). Of particular importance in college layout are the means of ingress (the classic
golden age murder comes complete with a map). The scene of the murder might be limited to a single staircase and a locked room, as in *Murder at the College,* or the murder can take place 'in the only College in the
University as no one can climb into', as in *Landscape with Dead Dons.*
Another possibility is for the circle of suspects to be restricted to the few
fellows who possess keys to the principal's garden, as in *Death at the Presi-*

dent's Lodging. In cases where clambering over walls allows the possibility of an outside job, favoured spots can be carefully monitored by murky figures in the dark, as in *When Scholars Fall.*

The college also offered scope for the kind of jealousies and enmities that underlie the surface pleasantries of golden age novels such as those by Agatha Christie (though the 'queen of crime' lived not far distant in Wantage, she never wrote of the university). Not only did the polite and ordered college society contain potential for imaginative characterisation, but the daily round with its set features of high table, college meetings and common-room drinks provided the likes of Innes and Masterman with opportunity to display their mastery of donnish discussion. The range of topics at such functions is shown to be intimidating for outsiders untrained in academic pleasantries.

> The Master was finding it heavy going; for Jennings responded only in monosyllables to his conversational openings. The Master tried the arts of primitive Africa, the prevention of noise in modern England, the doctrinal differences between the Anglican and the Orthodox churches, and several other no less enthralling subjects, with uniform lack of success.

The semi-formal conventions, politely mannered conversation and concern to maintain decorum in the tight-knit academic community all militate against the expression of genuine emotion, and only in the investigation which follows the murder do the suppressed feudings of high table come to light. Beneath the corporate harmony there brood unkind thoughts, and within the ivory tower fester hatred, envy and resentment. Senior tutors are frustrated heads; fraudulent researchers cover up misdeeds; political differences lead to hatreds; occasionally even rivalry in love causes the cerebral dons to harbour murderous intentions. 'Close confinement in colleges, sometimes for life, differences of opinion, academic rivalry—all have contributed', notes Dr. Browning of the enmities in *When Scholars Fall.*

Amongst the castlist of detective Oxford are intriguing heads of houses, ambitious junior tutors, resentful deans, and scheming scientists. Many of the types are recognisable from the Characters of the early seventeenth century, particularly a Pretender to Learning, and the bookish eccentric is guaranteed a star turn. The college porter also comes into his own, for as guardian of the lodge he is a key witness who knows more about the college than anyone else. For Crispin the porter is 'the uncrowned king of the college' whose ambiguous role as monitor enables him to combine expressions of servility with an authoritative and intimidating manner (Tom Sharpe plays on the same idea in his humorous accounts of Cambridge). 'A good Porter', writes Dacre Balsdon, 'is the centre of the whole nervous system of a College. He sees the first scout come in the morning and he sees the last undergraduate go out at night. There is hardly a question about the College and its members which at any moment he may not be called on, and expected, to answer.' The practical common sense of this working-class figure contrasts with the philosophical abstraction of the senior common room, and his down-to-earth manner acts as a breath of fresh air in a world of prevarication: 'I see them come and I see them go. What do you suppose I'm put 'ere for, sir?' queries Robert Robinson's forthright representative.

The murders themselves are often gruesome and invariably academic. There is a corpse whose head is wrapped in a gown surrounded by a library of over eight thousand books *(Death at the President's Lodging);* a woman's head delivered to a don more concerned about his lecture than informing the police *(Off with Her Head);* a tutor shot to death in a dean's room *(An Oxford Tragedy);* a body with a Jacobean slogan written nearby *(When Scholars Fall);* a dead don propped among the statues of the college roof *(Landscape with Dead Dons).* Dealing with these intricate webs of intrigue requires all the ingenuity of a first-class brain, and the detective is invariably called on to pick his way through a thicket of scholarly obfuscation and literary allusions. As often as not the great detective is a member or former student of the university, either a don such as Crispin's Gervase Fen, or a visiting lecturer such as Masterman's Brendel, or a former student such as Innes's Appleby. These detectives are not only learned, but possess a degree of erudition that passes all normal understanding: Appleby, for example, is conversant with different editions of *The Deipnosophists.* Occasionally too there is a complete outsider such as the Coles' Inspector Fairford, which allows for the induction and language lessons of the Oxford novel.

> 'The other thing I wanted to ask was, how free am I to go about asking questions in college? I don't know how many I shall need to ask, but I don't want to be more of a nuisance than I have to be.'
> 'That's very thoughtful of you, inspector. Naturally, the whole thing is very painful to us. Do you mean the men, or the servants?'
> 'Aren't the servants men? I thought they were. Of course if they include women . . .'
> The Master giggled. 'We usually speak of the undergraduates as "the men",' he said.

The outcome of the investigation is a lengthy summing up in the best traditions of the golden age which takes place—how else?—with all the fellows assembled in the senior common room. Occasionally apprehension of the criminal proves awkward and the villain has to be chased through the streets of Oxford, or, more imaginatively, through the subterranean stacks of the Bodleian, as in *Operation Pax* (1951). In Crispin's *The Moving Toyshop* (1946) the chase sequence winds its way from St. Giles through the science area to Parson's Pleasure, the stretch of the Cherwell formerly reserved for naked bathing. This is given greater exposure, so to speak, by Robert Robinson in a grand finale in which naked males pursue the culprit around the streets of Oxford, observed by high churchmen who suppose them to be Baptists, heads of houses who dismiss them as an advertising campaign and philosophy dons who take them as hypothetical.

The puzzle-solving and game-like essence of the genre lend the proceedings an air of levity ideally suited to enliven an environment in which fusty dons bat philosophical abstractions back and forth. The narrative tone may be urbane, as with the dons Masterman and Innes, or it may be irreverent, as with former students like Crispin and the Robinsons, but the books all share a common subtext in that they are written to entertain. The Robinsons take particular delight in the freedom this allows by caricaturing stock characters and parodying traditional values. Robert recycles McKenna's *Sonia* jest to good effect: 'Your refusal to face facts reminds me of the two Christ Church men. One bet the other five pounds there was no such College as Wadham', states one character. 'Who won?' comes the mock-innocent reply. Timothy too enjoys himself by playing with Oxford's traditional bias.

> 'You aren't a scientist or anything like that, are you?'
> He [Inspector Mild] looked at Blakelock with incipient distaste.
> 'No, Greats actually.'
> 'Thank goodness for that! You gave me quite a turn.'

Scientists are always suspect in the Oxford novel; in detective fiction they are doubly so.

The Oxford of the detective novel thus inclines to the fantasy tradition, more *Zuleika Dobson* than *Sinister Street*, for it draws on notions of an academic Wonderland in which manic professors mix with absent-minded dons in a realm of antiquated customs, peculiar practices and strange language. From *Verdant Green* to *Landscape with Dead Dons* is but a short step that makes mockery of the intervening hundred years, a period that had seen the stock of Oxonian peculiarity added to by Brandon Thomas's *Charley's Aunt* (1892) and Laurel and Hardy's *A Chump at Oxford* (1940) (which followed the huge success of Robert Taylor's *A Yank at Oxford* [1937] in which an overconfident young American gets into all kinds of trouble at the university but ends up a true blue). 'It is true that the ancient and noble city of Oxford is, of all the towns of England, the likeliest progenitor of unlikely events and persons', states Crispin in mitigation of his homicidal japers, and the Alice-like sense of unreality which hovers over Oxford proceedings is acknowledged by the Coles in the titular reference of *Off with Her Head*. It is a setting which is unconducive to outsiders like Routh of Innes's *Operation Pax* (1951), who thinks of Oxford as

> a collection of colleges and a row or two of shops, and as a place where everybody went about in a sort of uniform, so that one might be awkwardly conspicuous in ordinary clothes. And he had somewhere read that there were officials of the University who might stop you in the street and ask your business, and who had the power to have you turned out of the place if they didn't like you. He wished he had got to Reading, which was the sort of town he earned his living in and understood.

For David Lodge all campus fiction is essentially escapist because of the remoteness of academic life, both in terms of its campus location and its other-worldly occupation, and this may well explain why detective fiction seems so at home in Oxford. The whole construct teeters on the fringe of normality. It is a world in which professors speak Old Norse in their sleep (Farrer's *The Missing Link*); a murdered head of college is carted around college in a wheelbarrow *(Death at the President's Lodging);* and not simply a body but a whole shop goes missing *(The Moving Toyshop)*. The enclosed and institutional nature of the college is seen as encouraging psychoses which are unable to flourish in a more open society. 'You never know where you are with these college people', remarks the Coles' bewildered Scotland Yard inspector: 'Everything about the place is designed to encourage lunacy', agrees a character in *When Scholars Fall*. Within the cloistered retreat murderous thoughts brood below the surface. In the moonlit quadrangle a begowned Doctor struggles with a Hyde. Death stalks the staircase of the ivory tower. Murder will out. The don must die.

With or without alliteration, dons, death, and detection remain a potent concoction in the postwar period, as a list of Oxford murders indicates: *Don among the Dead Men* (Vulliamy, 1952), *Coffin in Oxford* (Butler, 1962), *Death of a Don* (Shaw, 1982), *Masterstroke* (Heald, 1982), *Oxford Blood* (Fraser, 1985), *The Adventures of Speedfall* (Fuller, 1985), *Grave Witness* (Levi, 1985), *Professor in Peril* (Lejeune, 1987), *Death and the Oxford Box* (Stallwood, 1994). But of all the Oxford murders, none can rival the extraordinary success achieved by those of Colin Dexter (ironically, a Cambridge graduate). His books had already won critical approval when his detective, Inspector Morse, became a household name in the early 1990s following the production by Central Independent Television of a highly acclaimed series. The programmes starred John Thaw as the Wagner-loving Morse and Kevin Whately as his Gilbert-and-Sullivan sidekick, and they were scripted by writers of the calibre of Julian Mitchell (author of *Another Country* [1981]) and Anthony Minghella (director of *The English Patient* [1996]). The series won a worldwide following, and its success was firmly rooted in the traditions of the golden age. Puzzle-solving lies at the base of Dexter's books: not only are the plots sophisticated brain teasers, but the stories are filled with cryptic word games and crossword clues. Much is made, for instance, of Morse's brilliance in being able to finish off *The Times* crossword in a matter of minutes (Dexter was himself a crossword prize-winner and took the name for his detective, with its implication of 'coded' meanings, from a rival competitor). In 1996 the twelfth novel in the series, *Death Is Now My Neighbour,* gained front-page coverage in the national press when the detective's closely guarded first name was revealed to be Endeavour, signalled earlier in the series by reference to his family's Quaker sympathies and interest in Scott of the Antarctic (Endeavour was both a Quaker name and the ship on which Scott sailed). The clues reflect the game-like nature of the books, and Dexter's debt to the golden age is acknowledged in a revealing reference when the hospitalised Morse takes up a book to read, for he had 'always enjoyed Agatha Christie: a big fat puzzle ready from page one. Perhaps it might help a little with the big fat puzzle waiting for him in the world outside the Radcliffe Infirmary'.

The popularity of Dexter's books owe much to the off-beat character of Inspector Morse, who is formed in the mould of the golden age great detective. Not only is he intellectually acute and a literary detective *par excellence,* but he is a quirky and unconventional character. Described as 'arrogant, ungracious, vulnerable, lovable', the curmudgeonly inspector is clever both in a learned and intuitive sense, though his flashes of brilliance do not always lead in the right direction. The waywardness is coupled with a distaste for police procedure which makes him lean on the stolid and reliable Lewis, a partnership which clearly derives from the Holmes-Watson template of Conan Doyle. Lewis struggles to keep up with the acumen of his inspector, and he is 'not unaccustomed to hearing Morse make some apposite quotation from the poets between draughts of beer'. Yet though Dexter's detective is able to quote effortlessly from Aristotle and to recognise a parody of seventeenth-century verse, he is also a man of demotic tastes, more at home in the back bar of a pub than at high table. Nonetheless, the beer-loving bachelor has tastes which are defiantly old-fashioned. He refers to women students by the derogatory term of 'undergraduettes', thinks Matthew Arnold much underrated, and his bedside reading reflects his traditionalism—*The*

Road to Xanadu, A Selection of Kipling's Short Stories, The Life of Richard Wagner, and *Selected Prose of A.E. Housman.* His taste in architecture is equally revealing. Though he is keenly appreciative of the architectural wealth of the city—the solution to one of the cases (*The Way through the Woods*) even depends upon his recognition of the roofs of houses in Park Town—his delight does not extend to 'the hideous structures they've put up in Oxford since the war', and he harbours a violent contempt for 'the vandals who sit on the City's planning committees'. The narrative too looks to the past and plays on the Oxford tradition. Morse is a former student of Greats, and the assumption is that his mental brilliance is closely allied to his academic discipline. If investigations take him into college, it is either Christ Church (renamed Wolsey) or the imaginary Lonsdale College in Radcliffe Square, whose city centre location places it in the same ancient bracket as his own college of St. John's. Yet though the books are steeped in the literary tradition, they inevitably reflect the times in which they are written, and Morse's Oxford, in contrast to that of pre-war detective fiction, is one in which gown is submerged in town. The series of murders take Morse into parts of the city unrecognised in earlier times: he works in Kidlington, has a bachelor pad in North Oxford, and the titles of *Last Bus to Woodstock* and *The Dead of Jericho* indicate the extent of his boundaries. Enquiries lead seamlessly from University Schools to the Churchill hospital, and even those investigations which involve academics are more concerned with terrace houses than college rituals. There is as much narrative interest in the Cutteslowe Wall as in Walter Pater's grave in Holywell cemetery, and the origin of Jericho gets more space that that of the university. Though scheming academics are well represented, the key character in a Dexter novel is as likely to be a girl on the game as a Chaucerian scholar who describes his garden as 'agrestal'. The view of Oxford that emerges is consequently quite different from that of earlier detective fiction. No longer is the university at the centre of the action, nor is it held in such high regard. Morse's standing as a former student who left without a degree plays a key role in this, for the detective is at once a part of, and apart from, the academic community. Since he never graduated (because of an aborted love affair), he has an insider-outsider status that enables him to cast a wry but knowing eye on the university. Though he delights in high culture and the acquisition of knowledge, he scorns 'the futility of academic preferment', and the dons with their servants, oak-panelling, and college rituals seem to him to live in 'cloud-cuckoo land'. Yet at the same time he himself is something of a pedant and a pedagogue, obsessed with exactitude in spelling and forever pointing out to Lewis the limited horizons of his knowledge. Dexter thus manages to have it both ways, for though the short-tempered and opinionated Morse is portrayed sympathetically, the university figure of *The Jewel That Was Ours* is cold, superior, and a sufferer of 'the Oxford Disease—that tragic malady which deludes its victims into believing they can never be wrong in any matter of knowledge or opinion'.

Like the porter at the Randolph who has come to doubt the superiority of the English, the books take a questioning attitude to the romance of Oxford. Significantly, for all his learning, Morse has never once read *Zuleika Dobson*. The narrative too refuses to yield to a colour calendar view of the city, and the once proud college buildings are shown to be hemmed in by supermarkets, hamburger shops, and ugly housing blocks. Typically, when the American tourists of *The Jewel That Was Ours* get stuck in a traffic jam, 'a litter-strewn patch of ill-kempt grass beside a gaudily striped petrol station lent little enchantment'. Like Morse's health, the city is in long-term decline and has seen a downturn in the quality of life. Yet taken all in all, the detective is grateful to have spent his career in such a pleasant university town—and that, finally, is the picture of Oxford that emerges. It is a city blessed with real-ale pubs, suburbs of distinctive character, remarkable buildings, and a diverse and fascinating population with more than its fair share of intellectuals; 'we're all of us overqualified in Oxford', Morse claims at one point. The books may have served to further mythologise Oxford as a city of brains, but Dexter's city is no English Athens. Like his Soho-haunting Greats detective, it is a mix of the coarse and the cultured.

STEWART'S HIGH TABLE

One of the golden age's most golden murders, *Death at the President's Lodging*, was greeted on publication as a breakthrough for the genre. Its author, the prolific Michael Innes, went on to write nearly fifty other detective and mystery novels, and he has since been credited with playing a key role in the transition of the detective story from intellectual diversion to crime novel. 'I don't know why there has never been a serious study of him', said Philip Larkin, 'he's a beautifully sophisticated writer, very funny and now and then very moving.' (A serious study now exists, George L. Scheper's *Michael Innes* [1985].) That Innes was in fact the Christ Church don J.I.M. Stewart (1906–94), is hardly a mystery, for the pseudonym was not intended as a disguise but as a means of distinguishing the writer of entertainments from the serious academic (Stewart's second initial stood for Innes). Writing under his own name, he produced several critical studies which included books on Shakespeare, Kipling, Hardy, and Joyce, as well as a volume for the *Oxford History of En-*

glish Literature entitled *Eight Modern Writers* (1963). And as if all that were not enough, he was also a novelist of distinction who produced some twenty books written under his own name on themes ranging from art to Englishness. In terms of fiction his real name has not achieved the fame of his pseudonym, yet amongst the novels he wrote is a body of work set in Oxford which amounts to a sustained exploration of university life. It is a remarkable achievement, and one which comes closest to doing for Oxford what Trollope did for Barchester and C.P. Snow for Cambridge.

Stewart's novels offer the reader a gourmet feast of fine writing served in copious portions, with each course an unexpected and often aston-ishing delight. It is a feast, moreover, shared with the most erudite of companions, whose conversation sparkles with wit and learning. For some tastes the combination may be too rich, too self-consciously supe-rior, but for others it makes for a deeply satisfying enjoyment. The books beckon the reader into a world of well-meaning dons with well-appor-tioned lifestyles in well-endowed colleges, and the commentary that accompanies the guided tour is reflective, urbane, and droll. In the pas-sage below taken from the beginning of *Stop Press,* Stewart in his guise as Innes introduces the reader to his fictional Oxford in a paragraph which evokes all the traditional features of the *genius loci*—age, culture, beauty, history, continuity, Hardy's masons, Beerbohm's vapours, Pater's sensu-ousness, Arnold's dreams and Warton's tutelary deity all seem to find a place within the rich texture of the writing. The measured pace, the lex-ical range and the unexpected imagery mark the writing out at once as unmistakably Stewart's.

> It was a November evening in October and the air was stagnant, raw and insidiously chill. Vapours—half-hearted ghosts on the verge of visibility played desultory acoustic tricks about the city, like bored technicians flick-ing to and fro the sound screens in a radio station. A wafter of caten stone, loosened by a last infinitesimal charge of condensing acid, would slither to the ground with disconcerting resonance. The masons' mallets, making good in random patches centuries of such mellow decay, tapped like so many tiny typewriters in an engulfing silence. The sky, a sheet of lead rapidly oxidizing, was fading through glaucous tones to cinereous; lights were furred about their edges; in the gathering twilight Gothic and Tudor, Palladian and Venetian melted into an architecture of dreams. And the hovering vapours, as if taking heart of darkness, glided in increasing con-centration by walls and buttresses—like the first inheritors of the place, robed and cowled, returning to take possession with the night.

Stewart's Oxford—the Oxford whose first inhabitants were monks—is here implicitly equated with gown: at the centre of his world lies the uni-versity, and at the centre of his university lies the college. Though the 'gluttonous, bibulous dining-clubs that dons love' recall those of Warton, Stewart's college differs from its eighteenth-century predecessor in being a caring community concerned with academic standards and personal fulfilment. Tutors worry over students in their charge and are at pains to shape their development, even to the extent of making sacrifices on their behalf. For their part students are seen to mature as they pass through the college, though the one glaring failure, the upper-class and dissolute Iwo Mumford, suggests that the men of the Oxford myth no longer belong in a meritocratic university.

Like the London of Dickens, Stewart's college is cast in a larger-than-life dimension and celebrated in all its aspects. There are dazzling discussions at high table; lovingly reconstituted architecture; carelessly scattered erudition; measured, self-reflective thought; and lurid characterisations. The portrayal is underpinned by an outlandish sense of humour that borders on the absurd. In *The Guardians* (1955) a tramp with the sole of his shoe repaired by tape and a hat covered with mould turns out to be Stringfellow, an old college tutor, and the American woman who strains from the Ridgeway to see Oxford glimpses not the dreaming spires as she imagined but the steaming towers of the Atomic Energy Research Establishment at Harwell. The gaping lunacy that lurks beneath the polished surface of Stewart's world is revealed all of a sudden in *The Gaudy* (1974), when the avuncular proceedings of an after-dinner speech inexplicably take on a farcical and surreal air.

> The eminent Swede reached his peroration at last. Oxford, and this the most prominent of its colleges, were, most properly, well to the fore. So were Roger Bacon, Robert Boyle, Newman, Shelley, and Matthew Arnold. The distinguished physicist had been doing his home-work well. 'Beautiful city!' he bellowed, and seized the microphone with both hands. I found myself wondering how he was going to cope with the overtone of irony which Arnold's celebrated apostrophe carries. 'Home of lost grouses,' he suddenly shouted, 'and unpopular games, and impossible royalties!' He sat down.
>
> Had I, as I listened, invented this incursion into the world of *Finnegans Wake*? Perhaps I had, since nobody seemed startled and nothing except the regulation applause succeeded.

Stewart the author here directs a narrator who wonders if he has invented a Swede misquoting Arnold in the manner of Joyce. It is a compounded fiction, and one that serves to remind the reader of the artifice, and artfulness, of the writing. As literary don and man of letters, Stewart was more than usually aware of the vital force of literature in shaping perceptions, and the power of imaginative fiction is often referred to in his writings. Typically, for Shefford in *Vanderlyn's Kingdom* the moors around Haworth achieve a greater reality through the writings of Emily Brontë than they do by their physical presence. Similarly, one senses in Stewart's novels a concern to rewrite reality in more compelling form, for the rhetorical skills at his disposal are used to bedazzle the reader and compel admiration for an institution he evidently loves and reveres.

Stewart's most ambitious work is the five-volume *A Staircase in Surrey* (1974–78), which covers some thirty years of college life. The series is structured around the inhabitants of a staircase in Surrey quadrangle (also featured in *Death at the President's Lodging*), and the technique proves surprisingly effective, for through flashback and the return of an ex-student Stewart manipulates three different generations and three different social classes, all bound together by a scout pointedly named Plot. From the narrow focus of a single staircase the books span outwards to embrace first the rest of the college, then contingent areas like fellows' wives and students' families, and finally the world at large through excursions to Scotland and Italy. The ambiguous title connects the college staircase with the home county from which many of its inhabitants originate, and prompts the inference that this is as much an examination of middle England as of the university, for the college is posited as a microcosm of the country at large. Isolated and enclosed, the college represents a cultural island in much the same way that Shakespeare's 'demi-paradise' is protected on all sides by the sea, and the qualities of its members are equated to those of the population at large: tolerant, decent, civilized, witty, sophisticated and charming on the one hand, snobbish, insular, hypocritical, self-seeking, awkward and aloof on the other.

If Newman informs the structure, Arnold directs the purpose of Stewart's college, for the overriding concern of the fellows is to strive for excellence and to transmit what is best to the next generation. Significantly, the guardian of the traditional order is named Arnold Lempriere, and his first name hints at the values he represents. He also provides a personal link with the nineteenth century, for in his youth he had studied under the elderly Lancelot Phelps at Oriel (as Stewart himself). Phelps was a figure from another age who knew Newman and Arnold personally as a young man and the connection serves to reinforce the communal sense of continuity. It is an aspect of college life on which the author lavishes affection—'the appearance of a medieval centre of learning sailing pristine through the centuries can be breathtakingly beautiful', he writes in *The Aylwins* (1966). Stewart's college is not a bureaucratic institution but an organic body that adapts and evolves to changing circumstances. Its manifestation at any one moment is not an arbitrary assemblage, but the considered result of an historical process involving a great many forebears. Students may come and go—*The Gaudy*—individuals are mortal—*The Memorial Service*—but the college continues on serenely. At the end of *Full Term,* the end indeed of the quintet, the deceased Lempriere is remembered at a service in the college chapel where earlier in the day an infant had been christened. Personal, annual and academic circles all come full term as the aged congregation gather outside and a group of young men in rowing kit head down to the river, indifferent to the concerns of their elders. The flow of youth marks the beginning of a new academic year, and the college renews itself even as its oldest members die off. Change within continuity is the keynote of Stewart's college, just as diversity within unity is the keynote of the university.

When Arthur Aylwin of *The Aylwins* has to choose between a university chair and college headship, he plumps for the latter. It is a significant choice, for his allegiance to collegiate education is stronger than that to his academic subject and it reflects the author's sympathies with Newman and his views concerning the civilizing and humanising effect of small communities. Indeed, Stewart's novels can be read as the fictional exposition of *The Idea of a University,* for the celebration of college life is central to his concern, and his books comprise the most imposing literary monument ever raised to the institution. Given the plenitude of Stewart's gifts, it may seem surprising that he has never achieved the popularity of fellow Oxonians like John Fowles and Iris Murdoch. It may be that the style and values are too old-fashioned, too Jamesian in style and Edwardian in tone, to appeal to modern readers, for like the characters the books hark forever backwards. By contrast the novels of Fowles and Murdoch range far beyond the college confines and raise the issue of what happens to the gifted youth once they go out into the larger world and seek its glittering prizes. Stewart's college preoccupations can seem stifling at times, a feeling oddly enough which even his own characters seem sometimes to share: 'I surveyed the quadrangle around me', notes the narrator of *The Aylwins,* 'a place of modest proportions, and easily to be sensed as claustrophobic in moments of discontent'. Given the closed world of which he writes, it is hardly surprising that Stewart so enjoys insider jokes. The misunderstanding in *Vanderlyn's Kingdom* about the meaning of 'president' (for the Englishman the head of college, for the American the head of state) is a nod in the direction of Innes's *Death at the President's Lodging,* the title of which had to be changed for U.S. consumption to *Seven Suspects.* This in turn contains a college fellow called Gott who writes detective novels under a pseudonym—a reference to authorial omnipotence. Given such in-jokes between Stewart and his pseudonym, the title of his autobiography—*Myself and Michael Innes* (1987)—seems peculiarly apt. The intertextual references are accompanied by a style whose elaborateness adds to the sense of constriction. 'It could be overpowering at times', states the narrator of *Vanderlyn's Kingdom,* 'you could fairly accuse the place of laying it on a bit thick', a charge which might be equally applied to the writing. The lush prose, the ponderous thoughts, the lavish meals, the sumptuous architecture, the privileged circumstance, the erudite wit, the obscure quotations: the fare is so unremittingly rich that without the spice of an Innes mystery the risk of surfeit, as at high table, is never far absent.

For the college fellow of *The Aylwins* there is a 'tendency to regard oneself as impressively circumstanced in relation to the world outside'. Inside, outside; within, without—Stewart's world is dichotomous. Reality resides in college, and the city of Jude is not just obscure but discounted: 'Anything characteristic of Oxford has faded away by the time you get to Linton Road', states the narrator of *The Madonna of the Astrolabe* as if to clarify the fictional boundaries. Stewart's Oxford is limited to that cluster of ancient and central colleges from which Jude was excluded, and Hardy's walls here form a protective shield for a 'learned and patrician paradise'. As the rising new order of postwar Britain hammered at the gates, the whole notion of a patrician paradise became increasingly difficult to defend. For some the insularity was distasteful, while for others the patrician style was symptomatic of authoritarianism and male bias. For all the splendour of Stewart's high-table fare, it smacked of an outmoded tradition which was unappealing to an age which sought greater informality and inclusiveness. It was a feast which was increasingly resented, because many felt themselves unwelcome and uninvited.

SAYERS'S PARADISE, GAINED AND LOST

The scarcity of women writers in the canon of Oxford literature can be partly attributed to the long historical absence of females from the university. Before 1878 there were no women dons, no women students, and no women's colleges. Except for the wives and daughters of those allowed to marry (heads of college, canons of Christ Church, and university professors), there was barely a woman to be seen inside the college walls at all and consequently few with sufficient personal experience to participate in an 'insider' genre. Nicholas Amhurst noted in the early eighteenth century that there were women who liked to eat of the apple of knowledge from out of their brother's pockets, and during the course of the nineteenth century there was mounting pressure for the introduction of female students. There were red faces in 1873 when A.M.A.H.

Rogers won an exhibition to Worcester College but had to be rejected after the initials were found to stand for Annie Mary Anne Henley. An Association for the Education of Women in Oxford was formed to press for the establishment of women's colleges, and amongst those who lent their support were liberals such as Benjamin Jowett, T.H. Green, Mrs. Humphry Ward, and the Pattisons, husband and wife. These were opposed by die-hard reactionaries like J.W. Burgon (1813–88), vicar of St. Mary's (remembered curiously for a single line from a Newdigate Prize–winning poem describing Petra as 'A rose-red city—"half as old as time"'). 'Inferior to us God made you, and inferior to the end of time you will remain', proclaimed the vicar to a group of women attending New College chapel, adding enigmatically, 'But you are none the worse for that!' Such ecclesiastical opposition was not enough to stem the tide, however, and the latter part of the century saw the establishment of a succession of women's colleges: Lady Margaret Hall in 1878, Somerville in 1879, St. Hugh's in 1886, and St. Hilda's in 1893.

By the beginning of the twentieth century women undergraduates were an established feature of the university, though they were separated and chaperoned. Male Oxford remained at best suspicious and at worst hostile. For the novelists of the Oxford myth they were 'virgincules', ridiculed for their lack of beauty, their studiousness, and their primness. Writing of his student days in the 1920s, Waugh noted, 'It was a male community. Undergraduettes lived in purdah.' The words of Michael Fane—'The great point of Oxford, in fact the whole point of Oxford, is that there are no girls'—seem all the more provocative given the thirty-year history of the women's colleges, and the Canadian humorist Stephen Leacock articulated what for many lay at the base of such attitudes when he wrote, 'There is no doubt that unless Oxford puts the women out while there is yet time, they will overrun the whole university.' Dacre Balsdon played on such fears in *The Day They Burned Miss Termag* by having a feminist commission toy with the idea of making Oxford all-female and sending the men to—of all places—Cambridge.

Meanwhile, the growing confidence of women students was reflected in a remarkable group of novelists to emerge from Somerville in the interwar period, inspired perhaps by the example of an earlier Somervillian, Rose Macaulay, whose novels such as *Potterism* (1920) featured Oxford-educated women. Among the younger generation of novelists were Vera Brittain (1893–1970), Dorothy Sayers (1893–1957), Margaret Kennedy (1896–1967), and Winifred Holtby (1898–1935), and the writers explored a common theme—the role of the educated woman, torn between the compromises of marriage and the desire for fulfilment. As in the writings of male authors, college days viewed in ret-

Merton's medieval Mob Quad —
small, enclosed, inward-looking
and the model for all other
quadrangles

The college gate, offering a
glimpse into an inner world
which only the privileged may
enter

College buildings offer a Wonderland of strange creatures, mysterious openings, and secret gardens

Princess Frideswide, founder and patron saint of Oxford, here in a detail carved on her tomb in Christ Church cathedral

Geoffrey Chaucer, father of
Oxford literature (by an
unknown artist c.1400)

The cross set in Broad Street which marks the spot
where the burnings of the Oxford martyrs took place

THE BURNING OF BISHOP RIDLEY AND FATHER LATIMER: WITH DOCTOR SMITH PREACHING.

The burning of Ridley and Latimer (from a woodcut of 1837)

The palatial confines of Christ Church, viewed from the air

The bust of Robert Burton, alias Democritus Junior, in Christ Church cathedral, together with the horoscope he drew up foretelling the day of his death

Oxford in the Civil War. 'Never perhaps has there existed so curious a spectacle as Oxford presented in these days'.

Anthony Wood, Oxford antiquary and 'wonderful pryer'

John Aubrey, one-time collaborator of Anthony Wood and author of *Brief Lives*

Thomas Warton, poet, wit, and literary historian (painted by his friend, Joshua Reynolds)

Samuel Johnson's rooms above Pembroke College gate. 'The lovers of learning will ever regard it with veneration'.

The Reynolds window in New College praised by Thomas Warton.
'Reynolds, 'tis thine, from the broad window's height, / To add new lustre
to religious light'.

John Newman, spiritual leader and novelist

Mark Pattison, author of some startling *Memoirs* and prototype for the fictional don

All the flavour of the traditional Oxford novel — student heroes, male
bonds, and country house setting

Shelley's Memorial in University College

Center, Benjamin Jowett, master of Balliol and a dominating influence in the late Victorian university

Francis Urquhart, universally known as Sligger, whose shadowy presence haunts the literature of the early twentieth century

The Birmingham-Oxford coach
transporting Verdant Green
(seated beside his father) to a
different realm. Four-in-hand
Fosbrooke is at the reins, and little Mr. Bouncer is blowing his
bugle at passing villagers. (From
Edward Bradley's original illustration.)

Town and gown fight, as illustrated by Edward Bradley.
'There's a smasher for your
ivories, my fine fellow! There's a
crack on your snuff-box'.

Tom Brown giving a 'wine' in his rooms for his father. The squire is placed tactfully by his radical son with his back to the death warrant of Charles I. (From the original illustration.)

Charles Dodgson alias Lewis Carroll, here posing for one of his own photographs

Alice Liddell in a photograph taken
by Charles Dodgson

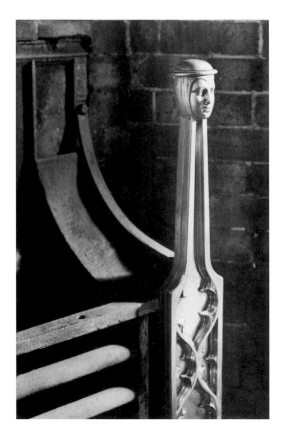

A detail from the fireplace in the hall
of Christ Church, one of the many
associations in the college with *Alice in
Wonderland*

Matthew Arnold, poet, eulogist, and myth-maker

Arnold's signal-tree — 'the most
famous tree in English literature'

The view from Arnold's tree over the 'dreaming spires' and 'home of lost causes'

View of the city centre from the east. G.M. Hopkins was dismayed by the 'graceless gro[...] that was beginning to obscure the 'pleasau[...] of his youth.

Binsey Poplars by the river Thames. The trees are replacements for those felled at the time of Hopkins.

Walter Pater of Brasenose College, a formative influence on Hopkins and Wilde

Porträt Oscar Wildes etwa aus dem Jahre 1878,
als er in Oxford war.

Oscar Wilde as a student, in or around 1878

Max Beerbohm in a self-portrait. 'I was a
modest, good-humoured boy, it is Oxford
that has made me insufferable'.

Zuleika Dobson, from a fresco in Beerbohm's
room in Merton College

Eights Week in the past, a highlight of the social year and often a literary highlight too

The 'English Athens' as seen from the air — cloistered walks and academic groves

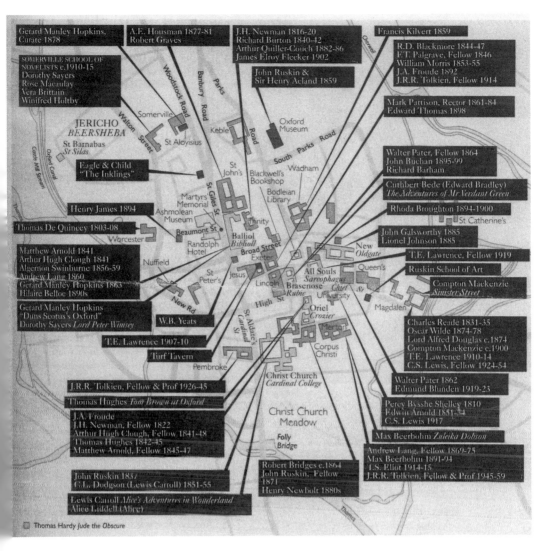

Gerard Manley Hopkins, Curate 1878

A.E. Housman 1877-81
Robert Graves

J.H. Newman 1816-20
Richard Burton 1840-42
Arthur Quiller-Couch 1882-86
James Elroy Flecker 1902

Francis Kilvert 1859

R.D. Blackmore 1844-47
F.T. Palgrave, Fellow 1846
William Morris 1853-55
J.A. Froude 1892
J.R.R. Tolkien, Fellow 1914

SOMERVILLE SCHOOL OF
NOVELISTS c.1910-15
Dorothy Sayers
Rose Macaulay
Vera Brittain
Winifred Holtby

John Ruskin &
Sir Henry Acland 1859

Mark Pattison, Rector 1861-84
Edward Thomas 1898

JERICHO
BEERSHEBA
St Barnabas
St Silas

Somerville

Oxford
Museum

Keble

Walter Pater, Fellow 1864
John Buchan 1895-99
Richard Barham

St Aloyisius

St John's

Blackwell's
Bookshop

Wadham

South Parks Road

Cuthbert Bede (Edward Bradley)
The Adventures of Mr Verdant Green

Eagle & Child
"The Inklings"

Bodleian
Library

Rhoda Broughton 1894-1900

St Catherine's

Henry James 1894

Martyrs'
Memorial
Ashmolean
Museum

Trinity

John Galsworthy 1885
Lionel Johnson 1885

Thomas De Quincey 1803-08

Beaumont St.
Worcester

Balliol
Biblioll

Broad Street

New
Oldgate

T.E. Lawrence, Fellow 1919

Matthew Arnold 1841
Arthur Hugh Clough 1841
Algernon Swinburne 1856-59
Andrew Lang 1860
Gerard Manley Hopkins 1863
Hilaire Belloc 1890s

Randolph
Hotel

Nuffield

Exeter

Jesus

St
Peter's

Lincoln

All Souls
Sarcophagus
Brasenose
Radc
High St.

Queen's

University

Ruskin School of Art

Compton Mackenzie
Sinister Street

Gerard Manley Hopkins
"Duns Scotus's Oxford"
Dorothy Sayers Lord Peter Wimsey

W.B. Yeats

New Rd.

St Aldate's
Cardinal St.

Oriel
Crozier

Magdalen

Charles Reade 1831-35
Oscar Wilde 1874-78
Lord Alfred Douglas c.1874
Compton Mackenzie c.1900
T.E. Lawrence 1910-14
C.S. Lewis, Fellow 1924-54

T.E. Lawrence 1907-10

Turf Tavern

Merton

Corpus
Christi

Walter Pater 1862
Edmund Blunden 1919-23

Pembroke

J.R.R. Tolkien, Fellow & Prof 1926-45

Christ Church
Cardinal College

Percy Bysshe Shelley 1810
Edwin Arnold 1851-54
C.S. Lewis 1917

Thomas Hughes Tom Brown at Oxford

J.A. Froude
J.H. Newman, Fellow 1822
Arthur Hugh Clough, Fellow 1841-48
Thomas Hughes 1842-45
Matthew Arnold, Fellow 1845-47

Christ Church
Meadow

Folly
Bridge

Max Beerbohm Zuleika Dobson

Andrew Lang, Fellow 1869-75
Max Beerbohm 1891-94
T.S. Eliot 1914-15
J.R.R. Tolkien, Fellow & Prof 1945-59

John Ruskin 1837
C.L. Dodgson (Lewis Carroll) 1851-55

Robert Bridges c.1864
John Ruskin, Fellow
1871
Henry Newbolt 1880s

Lewis Carroll Alice's Adventures in Wonderland
Alice Liddell (Alice)

Thomas Hardy Jude the Obscure

'Seat of the English Muses' — map of Oxford in the nineteenth and early
twentieth centuries. (Reprinted from the *Atlas of Literature*, ed. Malcolm
Bradbury [De Agostini, 1996].)

Compton Mackenzie, whose *Sinister Street* glamourised the Edwardian university

Christ Church Meadow Buildings. From the first-floor balcony Anthony Blanche declaimed poetry to the passers-by.

Evelyn Waugh, whose *Brideshead Revisited* marks the culmination of a genre and the end of an era

133 Outside Queen's Lodge

Gowns, smokes, and the narrow opening which led into a privileged
and all-male world

Thomas Hardy after receiving his honorary doctorate — on the inside at last

Death stalks the ivory towers — the cover of *Masterstroke*

A scene from the film of *Jude the Obscure,* made to celebrate the centenary of the book

Oxford detectives, *right,* Inspector Morse and, *left,* Sergeant Lewis as they appeared in the television series

Right, J.I.M. Stewart in a Christ Church setting with Cecil Day-Lewis

Dorothy Sayers in 1928 —
Christian apologist, detective
writer, and champion of the
women's college

C.S. Lewis in the Magdalen
College rooms where his conver-
sion took place and where the
Inklings used to meet

The English Athens now —
tourist site and functioning
museum

rospect take on a golden glow and are seen as havens of security in a forbidding world. Those novels actually set in college—Brittain's *Dark Tide* (1923), Renée Haynes's *Neapolitan Ice* (1928), and Doreen Wallace's *A Little Learning* (1931)—tell a different story, however, for alongside the compassion and friendships of college life are the feuding, rivalry, cliques and competitiveness of a large community. There is too a sense of underlying frustration, for the fictional students are aware of their disadvantages by comparison with their male contemporaries. This is exemplified in the physical aspect of their college, which is remote, poorly endowed, architecturally undistinguished, and lacking in the qualities of beauty, age and tradition lauded by the poets. The women are every bit as familiar with Oxford writings as the men, and the knowledge of what they are missing heightens their dissatisfaction. Sylvia Verney of *Neapolitan Ice*, for example, reveres 'the pile of books that had inspired her ideas of Oxford' but is disappointed to find her college room 'desolate looking' and to have her social life constricted by 'chap rules' (chaperone rules). Disillusionment begins on the very first page of Vera Brittain's *Dark Tide* when the heroine arrives in her 'magic city' only to find gasworks obscuring the dreaming spires. The students of these early novels are anxious not to be taken for dowdy bluestockings and miss out on glamorous love affairs, and variations of the Pygmalion theme soon lead away from the college environment to the wider world. The fear of failure which haunts the students is not that of the exam schools, but that of failing to find a husband; the glittering prizes available to the men are simply not on offer.

Meanwhile in Cambridge Virginia Woolf was making public her views about the disadvantages suffered by women in two lectures entitled 'Women in Fiction' which were given at Newnham and Girton. These were written up as *A Room of One's Own* (1929), since hailed as a feminist classic, in which it was argued that until women achieved material independence they would be unable to express themselves freely and creatively. In paying tribute to the women writers of the past, Woolf noted that their achievements were all the greater for being set against social prejudice and discouragement. One instance of which she herself was keenly aware was the educational disadvantage of women compared with their male peers, for the education of sons was often at the expense of the daughters (in her own family males such as her father, Sir Leslie Stephen of the *Dictionary of National Biography* fame, were educated at public schools and Cambridge while the girls were educated at home). There are some tart observations about the male orientation of Cambridge: she is turned away from Trinity College library because ladies have to be accompanied by a college fellow (and this despite the fact that her father had donated a Thackeray manuscript to the library), and the description of an opulent lunch enjoyed in a men's college is followed by that of a spartan dinner in a women's college. The disparity leads her to ponder on

> the organ booming in the chapel and of the shut doors of the library; and I thought how unpleasant it is to be locked out; and I thought how it is worse perhaps to be locked in; and, thinking of the safety and prosperity of the one sex and of the poverty and insecurity of the other and of the effect of tradition and of the lack of tradition upon the mind of a writer, I thought at last that it was time to roll up the crumpled skin of the day, with its arguments and its impressions and its anger and its laughter, and cast it into the hedge.

The nearest Oxford equivalent to Woolf in feminist terms was Vera Brittain (1893–1970), whose autobiographical writings were better suited than fiction to her cathartic style of writing. Brittain had gained an exhibition to Somerville in 1914 and was impressed by the atmosphere of work at the college, though like others she chafed at the strict rules. The *mores* of the time were exemplified in an incident that occurred when the college was commandeered during World War I as an army hospital and the students had to move into a quadrangle of Oriel. The male students of that college opened up a hole one evening in the wall dividing the two communities, and after urgent consultation the heads of the respective communities felt decency obliged them to keep watch over the situation and for the rest of the night they zealously guarded the opening, seated on either side of the wall to prevent the possibility of nocturnal contact. Meanwhile, over in France, the war to end all wars was taking place and Oxford students were being mowed down in the trenches alongside their compatriots. Vera Brittain volunteered as a nurse and served in army hospitals both in Britain and abroad. It was a harrowing time, compounded by the deaths of her brother and boyfriend, and *Testament of Youth* describes how the disillusioning nature of the experience turned her from patriotism to pacifism. With the return to peace, Brittain resumed her studies, but the war had changed her and, like others, she found it difficult to settle back into an unchanged university. The postwar university comprised an uneasy mix of types which Brittain divides into three distinctive groups. The first group consisted of the older dons, for whom the war had been remote and who were anxious about the influx of unruly war veterans; the second was made up of returnees like herself for whom the discipline of study was hard and college regulations petty and absurd; the third comprised young entrants fresh from school and eager to enjoy student life.

Between them lay resentment and incomprehension. War veterans like Brittain were particularly alienated by the lack of understanding shown for their predicament, and in *Testament of Friendship* (1940) she describes the importance of Winifred Holtby in helping her recover her purpose and idealism. Holtby was younger but the only other college member with war experience, and the bond of shared hardship united the pair in the face of indifference and lack of sympathy. There was also the added annoyance of 'dusty old dons and proctors who exact the same from women as from men and yet treat us sometimes as if we were strangers in a strange land'. The rivalries and resentments made for a volatile community, and Brittain blamed the restrictions of the women's college for not allowing an adequate outlet. In the preface added in 1941 to the reprint of her novel *Dark Tide*, she claimed that the fractious relationships described in the novel were a fair representation.

> You cannot take a hundred young women at an emotional age, enclose them within the walls of a modern cloister, deny them normal unsupervised friendship with their masculine contemporaries, and submit them to overwork and competition which, for economic reasons and through limitation of numbers, has always been fiercer among Oxford women than Oxford men, without producing certain qualities of pettiness, cruelty, hysteria and a tendency to the disproportionate exaggeration of trifles, which seldom exist among women who live in a more natural society.

The argument which Brittain here advances is one addressed by Dorothy Sayers in *Gaudy Night*, undoubtedly *the* novel of the women's college. Sayers (1893–1957) was an unconventional character, notorious as a student for walking down the High grandly smoking a cigar, and she was among the first women ever to receive a degree at the university, getting a First in modern languages. She was later prominent in the field of Christian apologetics and detective fiction, and her hero Lord Peter Wimsey became one of the most celebrated of the golden age great detectives. *Gaudy Night* centres around mysterious acts of vandalism that take place in Shrewsbury College (modelled on Somerville). Unusually for detective fiction there is no murder and no violence. Instead there is a feast of fine writing, rich in descriptive passages and literary allusions, and for the first time the issues facing women academics are subjected to serious fictional scrutiny. At the beginning of the book the detective novelist Harriet Vane returns to Oxford for a college reunion—the gaudy of the title. She looks on the college as a scholastic sanctuary free of the troubles of the outside world, and it becomes clear that her idealistic view is shaped by her immediate past when she was accused of murder. At the same time she sees the college as a possible alternative to mar-

riage, a subject which exercises her mind since she is being pressed by
the eminently eligible Lord Peter Wimsey to marry him. As she looks
around her at the gaudy, she sees on the one hand the dons of Shrewsbury, dedicated to the life of the scholar and for the most part single,
while on the other there are her contemporaries, many of them 'promising scholars, distinguished in their studies and subsequently extinguished by matrimony'. For Vane and her contemporaries a choice has
to be made between intellectual and emotional fulfilment: 'head' or
'heart' is how the book poses the dilemma. When the former student is
invited to investigate the acts of vandalism which have taken place in the
college, she welcomes the opportunity to sample college life, and it is not
long before the question arises as to whether the destructive acts result
from the emotional suppression of the single-sex community.

> The warped and repressed mind is apt enough to turn and wound itself.
> 'Soured virginity'—'unnatural life'—'semi-demented sisters'—'starved
> appetites and suppressed impulses'—'unwholesome atmosphere'—she
> could think of whole sets of epithets, ready-minted for circulation.

The tradition of the hysterical female is so strong that even the dons
themselves are concerned about it, and the book posits an opposition
between the 'unnatural woman' who ignores human sentiment and the
'womanly woman' who subordinates her intellectual aspirations. College
opinion differs not only about this, but about women's place in the university in general. When Harriet brings in the more experienced Lord
Peter to help in the investigation, the most stridently anti-male fellow
provides evidence of emotional imbalance by falling absurdly in love
with him. The theme is brought to a paradoxical end, however, for when
the criminal is finally identified she turns out to be a married woman
whose motive has to do with an excess of feeling. Ironically enough, the
vandalism is caused not by emotional repression and the overuse of intellect, but by a lack of restraint which might have been supplied by a
greater use of intelligence.

The college emerges from all this triumphantly vindicated, for in
withstanding the series of unsettling attacks it shows great corporate
strength. In his final summing up Wimsey is moved to comment on this
when he notes that 'the one thing which frustrated the whole attack
from the first to last was the remarkable solidarity and public spirit dis-
played by your college as a body. I think that was the last obstacle X
expected to encounter in a community of women.' Harriet too comes to
appreciate the support system that the academic community offers, and
she is strongly drawn to join the college herself. Instead she turns to
Wimsey in the knowledge that he offers her both affection and the free-

dom to develop. Her reluctance to accept his proposals had stemmed from a fear of loving too much, but she is told by one of the college fellows, 'You needn't be afraid of losing your independence; he will always force it back on you.' It makes for an oddly ambiguous ending, for while the college is championed as an alternative to marriage Harriet happily anticipates wedding bells.

The title of *Gaudy Night* can be read more as a declaration of intent than a description of the contents, for the college reunion to which it refers occupies merely an introductory role in the story. As the heroine of Haynes's *Neapolitan Ice* notes, 'words seemed to be badges of admission, badges that she "belonged"', and the titular use of 'gaudy' functions in the same way to signify the inclusion of women in the Oxford tradition. It is no coincidence that the same word is used by that most insider of writers, J.I.M. Stewart, for one of the titles in his Oxford quintet. Another way in which Sayers positions her book in the mainstream of the Oxford tradition is through the profusion of quotations from university authors, and the descriptive passages in her novel are every bit as fanciful as the writers of the myth. She even adds a mythic touch of her own: 'One day she [Vane] climbed up Shotover and sat looking over the spires of the city, deep-down, fathom-drowned, striking from the round bowl of the river-basin, improbably remote and lovely as the towers of Tir-nan-Og beneath the green sea rollers.' Panoramas of dreaming spires, punting trips between willow-lined banks, clambering over college walls, chases by university bulldogs, basking on the college lawn—Sayers wallows in the opportunities for lyrical display and filial devotion. The imagery is affectionate, the language poetical, the atmosphere romanticised.

> April was running out, chilly and fickle, but with the promise of good things to come; and the city wore the withdrawn and secretive beauty that wraps her about in vacation. No clamour of young voices echoed along her ancient stone; the tumult of flying bicycles was stilled in the narrow strait of the Turl; in Radcliffe Square the Camera slept like a cat in the sunshine, disturbed only by the occasional visit of a slow-footed don; even in the High, the roar of car and charabanc seemed minished and brought low, for the holiday season was not yet; punts and canoes, new-fettled for the summer term, began to put forth upon the Cherwell like the varnished buds upon the horse-chestnut tree, but as yet there was no press of traffic upon the shining reaches; the mellow bells, soaring and singing in tower and steeple, told of time's flight through an eternity of peace; and Great Tom, tolling his nightly hundred-and-one, called home only the rooks from off Christ Church Meadow.

By adopting the idiom of the Oxford tradition, Sayers makes the point that women participate on equal terms, as is illustrated by the cameo

scene at the end of the book as the couple linger in New College Lane
near the still heart of the university. When Lord Peter proposes and Harriet accepts, the pair are not pictured as two amateur detectives but as
Wimsey of Balliol and Vane of Shrewsbury in full academic dress. Moreover, the proposal is couched in the Latin of the degree-giving ceremony.
To the astonishment of a passing proctor, Wimsey marks the acceptance
of the proposal with a kiss, and the symbolic embrace of academic
female by male signifies a fictional seal of approval on a coeducational
university. The final sentences of the book seem to imply that though
this might be distasteful to the traditional guardian of order, it is beyond
his control.

> With a gesture of submission he [Wimsey] bared his head and stood
> gravely, the square cap dangling in his hand.
> '*Placetne, magistra?*'
> '*Placet.*'

> The Proctor, stumping grimly past with averted eyes, reflected that
> Oxford was losing all sense of dignity, but what could he do? If Senior
> Members of the University chose to stand—in their gowns, too—closely
> and passionately embracing in New College Lane right under the War-
> den's windows, he was powerless to prevent it. He primly settled his white
> band and went upon his walk unheeded; and no hand plucked his velvet
> sleeve.

At the beginning of *Busman's Holiday* (1937), the sequel to *Gaudy
Night,* Harriet and Lord Peter are married in St. Cross Church at Holywell, which had been associated with the university since the thirteenth
century. The maternal role of the college is given public recognition as it
acts *in loco parentis,* for Harriet is given away at the ceremony by the
female head of Shrewsbury, in contrast to the traditional model in which
the bride is given away by the father. It serves to reinforce the overthrow
of convention which characterises *Gaudy Night* as a whole. Not only is it a
detective story with no murder, but Wimsey apart, the key roles are taken
by a female detective, a female criminal, and female suspects. By rewriting Oxford detection in this way, Sayers established the women's college
as an idealised counterpart to that of the men. From the realm of purdah
women had established a 'grey-walled paradise' of their own.

The literary arrival of women came even as the shadow of World War
II was closing in, and in the changing social climate which followed the
war writers concerned with the position of women took a less romanticised view of the university. Barbara Pym's *Crampton Hodnet* (1985), written during the 1940s but published posthumously, locates the university
in the English class system and subtly caricatures the upper-middle-class

mores of North Oxford. Pym (1913–80) was a student at St. Hilda's, and in recent years her reputation has soared on the back of enthusiastic recommendations from such figures as Philip Larkin, John Betjeman, and John Bayley. Her heroine, Barbara Bird, has a tendency to take off on flights of fancy, and when the tutor on whom her heart is set asks her out, an unwelcome note of reality is introduced into her fantasy affair. The couple discreetly spend time together, and the anxieties of the young female are described with comic understatement. When the couple go punting with a bottle of wine, the prospect of a romantic interlude is shattered with a sudden splash as she is precipitated into the water—symptomatic of the way life pours cold water over youthful illusions. Thereafter the tutor turns back to the comforting embrace of his academic muse. The light-hearted tone and romantic misadventure are also in evidence in *Jane and Prudence* (1953), the beginning of which features a group of former students who return to college for a reunion. They talk of the three possibilities open to them in future: marrying clergymen; marrying others; and finding fulfilment through work. It is a deft touch which restates the dilemma for women posed by Sayers in an age when career and marriage were seen as incompatible.

With the rise of feminism during the 1960s, there was growing resentment of the marginalisation of women in university life, and though Rachel Trickett's *The Elders* (1966) expressed guarded sympathy for the comforting support of the women's college (the author was a fellow, and later principal, of St. Hugh's), American writers were more vocal in denouncing an unreconstituted university and championing integration over segregation. Muriel Beadle's look at Oxford through transatlantic eyes, *These Ruins Are Inhabited* (U.S. 1961; U.K. 1963; and remarkably still in print thirty years after publication), provides an account of the author's year at Oxford accompanying her Nobel Prize–winning husband. They arrived with high expectations—'To an American academic family, coming to Oxford was like coming to Olympus'—but first impressions proved a shock, for their Headington house was damp and inconvenient, while going to the city centre was something of an ordeal because of the traffic. She was particularly dismayed to find that, in contrast to American ways, she was excluded from the social events put on by her husband's college. Yet when her friends come to visit she takes them on guided tours and proudly points out the hidden beauties of the city. There are some striking vignettes of the artistic and architectural treasures of the city, and as the year progresses she moves from disappointment to affection. By the end of the book it is clear the author has grown to love the 'inhabited ruins' of the old college buildings.

Later Americans were less inclined to be so forgiving, and the attacks grew more embittered. In Carolyn Heilbrun's *The Question of Max* (1976), written under the pseudonym of Amanda Cross, the detective Kate Fansler is 'besotted with the idea of Oxford' as an academic though as the protagonist of a leading feminist she is repulsed by the 'hideously masculine quality of life'. In an early example of political correctness, domesticated wives of university dons are disparaged for their matrimonial devotion while the Somerville novelists of the 1920s are lauded for their sense of independence. Like Fansler, the female professor of Marilyn French's *The Bleeding Heart* (1980) also harbours mixed feelings towards the university, at once in awe of a monument to scholarship and alienated by the aura of masculinity. The story concerns two Americans who have an affair in Oxford, and the female-male opposition is compounded by the woman being literary and academic while the man is scientific and business-minded. Echoing Hardy, French portrays the women shopping in Cornmarket as more representative of the 'real Oxford' than the unseen inhabitants of college precincts immersed in speculation.

Jennifer Dawson's *Judasland* goes further in its identification with Hardy, for it explores the same territory as *Jude the Obscure* both topographically and thematically. Not only is the novel set in Jericho, but it tells of exclusion—that of the Indian Dr. Hari, who works at a practice in Jericho; that of a socialist don named Conroy, more attuned to the ways of Birmingham than Oxford; and above all, that of Clare, secretary-cum-dogsbody for Sanctus Spiritus College. Clare's life is divided between college and Jericho, and in both she finds herself surrounded by 'Oxford's self-infatuated people'. College life turns out to be far from the glamorous social round which her parents had eagerly foreseen for her, for 'her life had more connections with banging pipes and toilet-roll invoices than with *Brideshead Revisited*'. The willing female is surrounded by demanding males typified by a self-important expert on Icelandic dialects. The college rituals too fail to impress her, as exemplified by the meaningless charade of Benediction Night when a junior fellow has to chant a long Latin prayer and offer five eggs in a kind of soap-dish to the vice-regent, though nobody knows why. To Clare it seems designed to reinforce masculine ties by recalling the all-male community of the monkish past. Though Jericho by contrast provides a more human environment in the remnants of the working class for whom the area was originally built, the gentrification of the area has resulted in an influx of students whose self-confident conversation comes floating up from the streets in snatches that capture the flippant, superior, know-all attitudes of the speakers. The poetic style of the narration piles up images in the manner of an impressionist painting, and the picture that emerges is of

an inhospitable and indifferent city. As its name suggests, Judasland
betrays those who come to live there. English insularity closes out Dr.
Hari; the socialist don commits suicide; and Clare grows to despise the
academics by whom she is surrounded. 'It's a pity Oxford's pursuit of
excellence by its very definition automatically excludes it from accepting
strangers, the foreigner, the other', the book asserts, and it makes plain
its allegiance in an ending which sees Clare and Dr. Hari move to Tower
Hamlets for a new life together in a pluralistic and multicultural future.

In 1994 the college which had provided the model for *Gaudy Night*'s
Shrewsbury College went coeducational and accepted male students for
the first time. Somerville did not take the step lightly, and the decision
proved controversial among its members, generating protests and con-
frontations. The move also initiated a national debate about women's
education, and the participation of former students like Mrs. Thatcher
led to widespread media interest. Those who wished to preserve the single-sex status spoke of the tradition of success: apart from Indira Gandhi
and Dorothy Hodgkin (Mrs. Thatcher's teacher and a Nobel Prize winner for chemistry), this was most evident in the field of literature, for the
novelists of the 1920s had been followed by authors of the calibre of Iris
Murdoch, Margaret Forster and Michèle Roberts. With Somerville turning coeducational, St. Hilda's now remains the sole surviving women's
college, and there are female students at all the former male colleges. Yet
though the position of women has been transformed, it has not ended
the sense of ambivalence felt by some, for writing in *The Oxford Women's
Handbook 1991* the novelist Jeanette Winterson stated that 'as women we
do not inherit the grandeur that moves us or the scholarship that makes
the University famous. We are not heirs, we are claimants.' For some the
whole tradition of the university is predicated on an unsound foundation, and books like Adriana Cavarero's *In Spite of Plato: A Feminist Rewriting of Ancient Philosophy* (1995) seek to address the issue at its source in
classical Greece. Given such suspicion towards the original Athens, it is
perhaps unsurprising that feminists should feel such unease about its
English counterpart. Cast out of Sayers's 'grey-walled paradise', they find
themselves adrift in a world not of their making.

THE LESS DECEIVED

'I thought it [Oxford] was the most lovely place on earth. And then suddenly I realised it was wrong—it was all lies. I'd been living in a dream,
making up sonnets, and playing soft music, and wandering about in the
moonlight. It wasn't real.' When Ray Sheldon of Nichols's *Patchwork*
wakes from his *Sinister Street* enchantment and wonders, 'Would Oxford

ever again be like that? Had it ever been like that, or had it only existed, a silver city of dream and shadow, in the mind of a novelist?' he echoes the awakening of Jude from his Christminster illusion. In a city of dream these are significant indicators which mark a change of consciousness and the desire to shed illusions. The shift away from moonlit romance during the course of the century formed part of the social adjustment being made by the country as a whole as it was forced to wake up to the new realities about its declining role as a world power. In Oxford terms this led to a rejection of romanticised notions about the university and a determination to rewrite the city in more sober terms, a trend which was initiated by Philip Larkin's *Jill*. The novel was written just before *Brideshead Revisited,* though it appeared a year later in 1946, and the university it portrays is the antithesis of Waugh's—deprivation not decadence is the keynote. Indeed, taken together the two books are like chalk and cheese, and Larkin's novel can be read as a wartime assault on the Oxford myth using such weapons as irony, understatement, deflation, contrast, and bathos.

The undercutting of convention begins with the arrival of the 'student-hero' John Kemp by train (the name itself is a declaration of sorts: John signals ordinariness, Kemp is northern dialect for a contender). Because the nameplates have been removed from the station, the 'sacred city' is just another nameless town, and Kemp is unimpressed—'What he could see did not look very remarkable'. When Zuleika Dobson arrives in Oxford, her uncle awaits her in the first-class waiting-room and takes her in escort to his college. When Gaveston ffoulkes arrives, he imperiously orders a hansom. But when the unprepossessing John Kemp arrives, he cannot even summon a cab and is unceremoniously brushed aside by a driver who is going off for tea. His reception at the college is equally deflating. For the upper-class figures of the Oxford myth the college is simply a replacement of the country home in which they grew up, and the young men stride grandly about the college quadrangles giving orders to college servants as if they were family retainers. Gaveston ffoulkes, for example, crosses the threshold of his college in nonchalant manner, 'nodding kindly to the bewhiskered porter's obsequious welcome'. John Kemp by contrast is completely ignored when he enters the college, for the porter is busy talking to two young men. He is also better dressed than Kemp. 'Yes, sir?' he finally deigns to ask the newcomer.

> John swallowed, and the two young men turned to look at him.
>   'Er—I've just arrived-er-can-you-er-my rooms—'
>   'What, sir,' snapped the little man, bending an ear nearer. 'What d'you say?' John was speechless. 'A fresher, are you?'

'Yes -'
'What name?'
'Er-Kemp-er-'
'Kent?'

The porter picked up a list and ran his thumbnail down it: the two young men continued to look at John as if he held no particular significance for them. It seemed hours before the porter exclaimed:

'Kemp! Kemp, are you? Yes, room two, staircase fourteen. With Mr. Warner. That's you, sir,' he repeated as John did not move. 'Fourteen, two.'

'Er- where?-'

'Founder's Quad-second arch on the left. Staircase fourteen's on the righthand side. You can't miss it.'

John backed out, murmuring thanks.

Who was Mr. Warner?

As Kemp makes his way across the quadrangle, the matter-of-fact narration, bereft of adjectival colour, stands in contrast to the sumptuous descriptions of Stewart. There is no sense of awe, no evocation of the past, no reflection on the insignificance of the individual—merely the matter of settling in. Kemp's room-mate, Mr. Warner, turns out to be a confident, breezy, boozy public-school boy, and the difference in lifestyle and attitude between the two men is marked. 'Come from Town?' asks the Londoner. 'Yes,' replies the northerner, 'From Huddlesford.' Kemp's working-class origins are so far beyond the perceptual boundaries of his room-mate that he refuses to believe them, and the public-school boy assumes charge from the outset, choosing the best bed, ordering the scout about, and decorating the room with his school photos. Kemp by contrast is uncertain and knows no one. His feelings of isolation are deepened by his first dinner in Hall, typically an occasion of some moment in the Oxford novel when the splendour of the surroundings, the dons at their high table and the excitement of first meetings have a heady effect on the student hero. For Kemp, however, the rite of passage proves something of an ordeal: 'During the meal John hardly lifted his head. . . . He finished the three courses very quickly, waited till someone else left, then walked out himself.' While others carouse and socialise, Kemp sits in his room, dejected and depressed. His sense of alienation is heightened by the drinks parties Warner gives, for he feels excluded from the public-school chatter, and by way of compensation he invents a female named Jill to whom he pens letters of the Oxford he is unable to enjoy. He writes in borrowed terms of the 'frisson' of putting on a big, black gown and of how he lounges around for the most part, only occasionally deigning to do some work.

> What do we all do? We are kings in our nutshell. It is so pleasant simply to exist, to breathe the air, to inspect the architecture, to walk beneath the trees, to see the sky reflected in puddles. One could spend a whole morning walking the length of one street—High Street, for instance.

Fantasy and reality become disconcertingly caught up with each other when Kemp comes across the embodiment of his imaginary Jill, and his pursuit of her is marked by all the clumsiness of inexperienced adolescence. So disastrous are his attempts at seduction that the whole affair turns out a hopeless non-romance—just like his student life in a wartime Oxford. In the end Kemp incinerates his Jill-inspired writings, preferring the clear light of truth, however harsh, to illusions and delightful lies. His goal thereafter, in the words of Larkin's 1955 collection of poetry, is to be 'The Less Deceived'.

The anti-romantic tone of *Jill* is also much in evidence in two of Larkin's poems which concern return visits to the university. Retrospective verse of student days is traditionally the occasion for nostalgic memories of golden days, but for Larkin in 'Poem about Oxford' there are only memories of 'blacked-out and butterless days' from which the poet was glad to escape—'Unlike the arselicker who stays'. As for the much-lauded architecture, there is 'Dull Bodley' and a dismissive comment to the effect that 'the old place hadn't much tone'. In 'Dockery and Son', another poem concerning a college reunion, the return is far from being imbued with Quiller-Couch mystique, for it brings only unpleasant realisations. As he leaves the city, ignored and dejected, it is not with fond memories that the poet is preoccupied, but with the thought of mortality; the Oxford of poetic dream does not even rate a mention. Nothing could be further from the self-importance of the Apollonian men of the myth than Larkin's pose of self-belittlement, and the drabness of his world is the very antithesis of Brideshead extravagance. For Larkin, Waugh's world was riddled with pretentiousness and sentimentality, and in a compelling metaphor for the attitude of the 'angry young men' of postwar Britain to their predecessors, he wrote of wanting to stuff Sebastian's teddy-bear down his throat.

As the social barriers of wealth and class came under attack in the 1950s, the rising new order gave voice to a sense of frustration with a society whose values were weighted in favour of those at the top. Since universities played a key part in propping up the established order, they too came under suspicion, and novels by Mary McCarthy and Randall Jarrell set the trend for modern campus fiction. Such works were characterised by a distrust of intellectualism, the denigration of non-utilitarian education, and the portrayal of self-seeking academics. The classic

British exemplar, *Lucky Jim* (1954), was written by Larkin's college contemporary and lifelong friend, Kingsley Amis (1922–95). Underlying
the storyline is a deep antagonism to the pretensions and phony sophistication of the ruling classes. The belittling of traditional attitudes can be
seen in a passage in which the historian Jim Dixon hits out at the
enchantment of the Middle Ages: 'Had people ever been as nasty, as self-
indulgent, as dull, as miserable, as cocksure, as bad at art, as dismally
ludicrous, or as wrong', he wonders to himself. Alienation also provides
the keynote of *Hurry on Down* (1953) by John Wain (1925–94), a contemporary of Larkin and Amis at St. John's, which features the career of
the Oxford-educated Charles Lumley as he hurries down the social ladder from promising graduate to window-cleaning, begging, and crimi-
nality. His downward trajectory is born of the search for a life free of
hypocrisy and a distaste for the class-based society into which he is born.
Englishness emerges as little more than 'small snobberies and appearances' supported by deference, deception, and a mute compliance with
convention. Those who succeed in society are either crass or dishonest,
mouthing platitudes in which they do not believe, and Lumley refuses to
conform. His attitude threatens the social order, and he is publicly
attacked at a party for not sticking to his class origins and career path—
the same idea used to oppress Jude almost a hundred years earlier and
indicative of how little had changed. Lumley ascribes his predicament to
the fact that 'He had been equipped with an upbringing devised to meet
the needs of a more fortunate age, and then thrust into the nineteen
fifties', and the blame for this is laid at the door of a university which promotes 'the smug phrases, the pert half-truths, the bland brutalities' by
which the ruling classes maintain their grip on power. When the anti-
hero returns to his college with a girl in tow, the romantic idyll he had
hoped for is spoilt by the intrusion of priggish dons and loafish students.

> The formal beauty of the groves and flower-beds, set off by the breath-tak-
> ing perfection of the grey stonework of the College itself, strove to the
> limit of its power to soften and contain their boorishness, but was defeated
> by their appalling mental and physical ugliness as they sprawled on the
> ground or loafed coarsely to and fro, smoking cigarettes and scattering
> stubs, empty packets, and match-sticks on the velvety turf.

The university of *A Perfect Spy* (1986) by John Le Carré (pseudonym of
Oxford-educated John Cornwell [1931–   ]) conjures up just the kind of
attitudes against which figures like Lumley were in revolt. The book is
fashioned around the making of a double agent, Magnus Pym, whose
career begins with spying on socialists and Marxists while a student.
Looking back on the Oxford of his youth, he describes it as 'a conven-

tional sort of place' where 'The college scouts doubled as the Dean's Joes
[spies] and ratted on us if we broke the rules.' Eager to curry favour in
his new surroundings, the freshman quickly adapted to the ruling ethos.

> With his first cheque Pym bought a dark blue blazer with brass buttons,
> with his second a pair of cavalry twill trousers and a blue tie with crowns
> that radiated patriotism. After that there was a moratorium because the
> third cheque took a month to clear. Pym polished his brown shoes, sported
> a handkerchief in his sleeve and groomed his hair like a gentleman's. And
> when Sefton Boyd, who was a year ahead of him, feasted him in the exalted
> Gridiron Club, Pym made such strides with the language that in no time
> he was talking it like a native, referring to his inferiors as Charlies, and to
> our own lot as the Chaps, and pronouncing bad things Harry Awful, and
> vulgar things Poggy, and good things Fairly Decent.

Ved Mehta's stylish memoir, *Up at Oxford* (1993), also portrays the
1950s university as steeped in the traditions of upper-class England. As
'seen' by the blind Indian (the book is curiously full of visual descriptions), it is a hierarchical world of ties, tweed jackets and gowns where
one-upmanship is as common as stammering (the habit is cultivated
deliberately, it is suggested, to signify the painstaking process of turning
thought into speech). Prewar attitudes prevail; classics are advocated as
the best mental discipline, American education is ridiculed, and Mehta
is accused of not being a gentleman for trying to change his specialisation three times. For an outsider the unstated rules and assumptions of
the class-based society are baffling, and Mehta's account is peppered
with entertaining anecdotes that seem certain to enter Oxford folklore—the absent-minded don who stops to converse and forgets in
which direction he was heading; the tutor who insists that his pupil continue reading out his essay while he goes to the toilet; and an hilarious
account of Handshaking (interview at the end of term) when the bad
acoustics force the author to make wild guesses as to the questions he
was being asked, following which, to his bemusement, rather than his
hand being shaken his little finger was gently wagged. The mannered
ways and snobbishness (including that of the author) are a notable feature of the memoirs, as are the number of breakdowns and suicides in
Mehta's gifted circle, and though never stated as such the book suggests
a crisis of adjustment to a world in which Britain and Oxford are no
longer guaranteed primacy. (It may not be altogether fanciful to interpret the desperate struggle of William Golding's hero in *Pincher Martin*
[1956] to survive on his mid-Atlantic rock in the same light, for the
dying sailor clings forlornly to his Oxford inheritance of Education and
Intelligence to see him through. The college scene he recalls would

seem to be based on the Brasenose of the Nobel Prize winner's own student days.)

Among the senior figures in the university at this time were J.R.R. Tolkien (1892–1973) and C.S. Lewis (1898–1963), whose friendship was decisive in shaping the study of English at Oxford. Tolkien was Merton professor of English language and literature, and his book *The Hobbit* (1937) had gained him a measure of fame in the wider world. A Catholic and a conservative, Tolkien once described himself as 'a hobbit in all but size. I like gardens, trees and unmechanized farmlands. I smoke a pipe and like good plain food (unrefrigerated), but detest French cooking.' Perhaps his most distinguishing trait was his love of the English language, for he revelled in the sound, sight, and origin of words. 'He could turn a lecture room into a mead hall', commented J.I.M. Stewart, 'in which he was the bard and we were the feasting, listening guests.' Another student inspired by his enthusiasm for old English was W.H. Auden, who wrote to Tolkien in later life, 'I don't think I have ever told you what an unforgettable experience it was for me as an undergraduate, hearing you recite *Beowulf*. The voice was the voice of Gandalf.' In 'A Short Ode to a Philologist' (1962) Auden paid tribute to the 'bard to Anglo-Saxon' whose imaginary world he loved so much, and another former student, U.A. Fanthorpe, also celebrated his creative powers in a poem called 'Genesis' (1986)—'The sage sat. And middle-earth / Rose around him like a rumour'.

Tolkien first met Lewis in 1926, and the two men soon became close friends, discussing literary matters and exchanging views on each other's creative output. Ironically, Lewis was an Ulster Protestant and a literature specialist with a bias against Catholics and philologists, yet he was attracted by the older man's love of Scandinavian sagas and shared his distaste for modern literature (Tolkien hated modernism and Lewis did not think anything after Wordsworth a fit subject for study). Tolkien played a key role in the conversion of Lewis to Christianity in 1931, and they met regularly throughout the 1930s both on an individual basis and through the twice-weekly gatherings of the Inklings. Together they were instrumental in reshaping the English syllabus towards the study of early literature and the promotion of established notions of Englishness— Tolkien for instance spoke in terms of the patriotic study of philology, and Lewis subscribed to a view of literature which was much in keeping with the tradition of Quiller-Couch and the Whig conception of history. (As a result twentieth-century literature barely featured on the Oxford syllabus until 1970 and Anglo-Saxon was a compulsory subject; this was much resented by students like Larkin and Amis, who referred to their Old English texts as 'ape's bumfodder' and other obscenities.) With his remarkable memory and oratorical skills, Lewis became the biggest draw in the English department during the 1930s, and during World War II he achieved a wider fame as a Christian apologist through his talks for the BBC, which were heard by over a million people, and through the publication of books like *The Problem of Pain* (1940) and *The Screwtape Papers* (1942). His ability to put over the Christian viewpoint in clear and forceful manner won him a wide following in the United States too, and such was the impact he made that in 1947 he was featured on the front cover of *Time* magazine. Lewis by this stage was a comfortable middle-aged bachelor living with his brother at The Kilns in Headington (in a curious arrangement he had earlier cohabited with the mother of his best friend). The Oxford he inhabited was the one depicted in *Shadow-lands*—a male world of tweed jackets, pipes, Anglican dons, cloistered surrounds, sherry parties, and intellectual repartee. It was one into which Joy Gresham burst with such startling consequences, for following the death of his mother when he was aged nine, Lewis had developed an emotional shield which prevented a close involvement with women.

Lewis and Tolkien had remained the closest of friends up until around 1940, when the introduction of Charles Williams into the Inklings upset the balance of their relationship. Nonetheless, the two men remained on good terms and continued to provide critical support for each other's writings. The relationship had something of a boyish public-school affection to it, with the two men competing to see who could produce better smoke-rings and sharing common pursuits like country walking. Their conversations were filled with word games, riddles and fanciful speculation, and their imaginations were fired by the world of male adventure (significantly they were bound by participation in World War I, in which Lewis had been wounded and Tolkien had fought in the battle of the Somme). At the heart of the epic quests which they loved stood the heroic struggle of good against evil, and inspired in this way they turned to fantasy in their writings to celebrate a hierarchic, Christian and ritualistic world of myth and magic which they believed had been lost in modern life. Out of Beowulf and Beer emerged Middle Earth and Narnia. Lewis was such a fluent writer that works poured out of him in astonishing number and variety. Remarkably, *The Lion, the Witch, and the Wardrobe* (1950), written for children (sales top 100 million worldwide) was followed by volume 3 of *The Oxford History of English Literature,* entitled *English Literature in the Sixteenth Century, excluding Drama* (1954), in which he claimed to have proved that there was no such thing as the Renaissance in England. Yet though he was known throughout the English-speaking world, Lewis lacked popularity among his colleagues, some of whom were alienated by his combative manner and sharp debating skills, while others thought it inappropriate for a specialist in English literature to act as an amateur theologian and to talk in evangelical terms of miracles. In 1951 he lost the professorship of poetry to C. Day-Lewis, and despite the efforts of Tolkien the university refused to offer him a chair in literature, with the result that he took up an offer by Cambridge in 1956 and transferred his place of work from Magdalen College, Oxford, to Magdalene College, Cambridge (though he kept The Kilns as his place of residence). The ease with which Lewis wrote made for a startling contrast with Tolkien, who was a painstaking perfectionist worried about every sentence he produced (tellingly, *The Silmarillion* which he began in his youth was only published posthumously in 1977). The older man had for many years been working on a follow-up to *The Hobbit* aimed at an older audience, and he later acknowledged that without the encouragement of Lewis he might never have completed it. *The Lord of the Rings* came out in two parts in 1954–55 and, boosted by enthusiastic reviews by Lewis and Auden on either side of the Atlantic, it gradually established itself as the great classic of twentieth-century fantasy with the result that like Lewis (who was virtually sanctified in some American circles) Tolkien became the centre of a transatlantic cult. The book was adopted by the student movement of the 1960s, leading on the one hand to popular graffiti such as 'Gandalf for President' and 'Tolkien is hobbit-forming' and on the other to the Headington home of the Oxford professor being besieged by admiring fans.

Although Lewis and Tolkien differed from their upper-class predecessors, they were nonetheless characteristic of the conservative and retrospective attitudes still very much in evidence at Oxbridge at the end of the 1950s. The two ancient universities were seen as lagging behind the needs of a technological society—'Outdated, relics, living on the past. I'd abolish them', says the vacuum-cleaner salesman of Graham Greene's *Our Man in Havana* (1958). As in the eighteenth century, satire was used to prick at the smug complacency, and Dacre Balsdon's entertaining fantasy *The Day They Burned Miss Termag* exposes the anti-women, anti-black, anti-working-class tendencies of the university. In the Nigel Barton plays of Dennis Potter the working-class hero views with repugnance the baying voices and superior assumptions of his contemporaries. To radicals the university was little more than a bastion of privilege shored up by a scholarly heritage, and in Wilfrid Sheed's *A Middle Class Education,* which came out in 1961, there are doubts about the value of a university education at all—'four years footled away completely, while the assistant office boys are surging up the ladder' is how one student sees it. Nobody in Sheed's university subscribes to traditional notions except the American Fosdike, who wanders about bewilderedly in quest of the English

Athens and its fictional secret. When he probes his contemporaries, the response he gets is as Larkinesque as the myth itself was Wildean.

> 'Have you gotten something out of Oxford?'
> 'Good Lord, I don't know. I've never thought about it. No, I don't suppose I have. I daresay one would have been equally drunk and fatuous anywhere. As a matter of fact, it's pretty much the sort of life I lived in the Army, and at school too—only with broader vistas, of course.' . . .
> 'Do you think that maybe the whole thing is an elaborate hoax, that there really isn't anything here to get?'
> Browning yawned. This was getting entirely too far from the important things. 'I really don't know. I think the chaps who throw bread at each other down at Black's may get something out of Oxford, and the women who smoke cigars, and all the numberless weeds who dive fully clothed into various bodies of water up here—I expect they all get something, though I haven't the faintest idea what. Anyway, they're the ones who write the delirious books about Oxford when they go down.'
> This obviously had nothing to do with Athens. It could go on just as well at Lord Squashhead's estate or at Tootle's American Bar, or any damn place where there was bread to throw and water to dive into. Fosdick was no wiser.

Sheed's protagonist, destined for a career in soap, feels ill at ease in a college described as 'Small, undistinguished sort of place, fit only for the humble work of polishing up its quota of rural deans and minor officials', and the outmoded practices of the academic community are illustrated by some delightful vignettes. The affable but eccentric warden wanders around college in khaki shorts and straw hat (though a nasty rumour has it that he is only pretending to be eccentric), and the college chaplain is a mild-mannered man uncertain as to his authority: 'I implore you to lay aside the tools of violence' is his ineffectual response to a student melée. The old order is mercilessly pilloried in the person of Inglenook-Mackenzie, a pre-war dandy who returns to give the Junior Common Room a no-nonsense pep-talk. 'I have recently come across a disgusting and loathsome habit', he blusters, 'of referring to undergraduates as students, instead of undergraduates. Now that may be all very well at the red-brick universities, and among our colonial friends, but it's not good enough for Oxford. Nothing like good enough.' When he gets together with his cronies, they deplore the drop in standards and boast of how they used to smash window panes every night. They are particularly outraged at hearing that sales of port have fallen off and complain indignantly, 'Chaps without the money to do it properly shouldn't come to Oxford in the first place.' It is symptomatic of an institution out of touch with the real world, and by the time the hero goes down his youthful idealism has been curbed by the sense of being unprepared for life. Though the university is trying to adapt, as the building of new college accommodation suggests, it has yet to take on board that its graduates will have to survive in a competitive world by the mettle of their wits rather than the strength of their class connections.

Julian Mitchell's *Imaginary Toys* (1961), published in the same year, goes even further in its portrayal of students concerned to break free of the suffocating mould society has prepared for them. Far from glorying in their role as a future élite, his undergraduate-heroes are rebels in defiance of middle-class conventions and what it means to be English. The novel declares its radicalism at the very outset, for in place of induction and mystification the book starts with rejection in the form of a rose thrown into the middle of the road. Scholarship is treated with scant respect—postgraduate study is written off as a 'racket'—and the university as a whole is shown to be self-serving and removed from the needs of society. As an institution it is characterised by its repressive sexual atmosphere and ridiculed for housing 'more virgins of both sexes than any comparable community in the British Isles'. There is anger too at the treatment of a working-class student who has to 'fight every inch of the way to get past people who think he hasn't got quite the right background, don't you know'. Published at the beginning of the 1960s, the book is indicative of the decade's libertarian and egalitarian tendencies, and the determination to write off the old order is nowhere clearer than in the epilogue.

> And so we leave the city of dreaming spires, where learning is learnt and learned, and the dons swill the profits on their High Tables, and the undergraduates are all exactly as Max Beerbohm described them in *Zuleika Dobson,* all dukes or faintly undesirable Americans or absolutely spineless members of the lower orders: city of crumbling stone where the moss gathers and is cherished by comical men in bowler-hats, called 'porters', characters to a man, and the young gentlemen idles away his days, preparing himself for the rigours of a life of politics or the law, or often, simply, of looking after his estates, so sadly diminished, in so many cases, by the tragically class-directed death-duty tax, a noble city, founded with a noble purpose, which it nobly fulfils.

The drive towards greater personal freedom during the 1960s was by its very nature anti-institutional, and the hierarchical nature of college life with its boarding-school restrictions proved the cause of great resentment. In Michael Dibdin's *Dirty Tricks* (1991) the university of the protagonist's student days is portrayed as one in which learning and tradition are thrown out of the window in a whirl of pop and liberation.

Studying for a degree is seen as a denial of the spirit of the times—the college library is abandoned for swinging London and the pursuit of truth for the pursuit of women. For the revolutionary fellow of *Death of a Don* the college is a bourgeois institution which he is determined to destroy from within, yet even without such subversion the traditional college was being undermined by external forces, and the literature attests to a remarkable change in lifestyle. Whereas for Waugh's generation the institution had provided both lodging and in-house education, the inability of colleges to accommodate the rapid increase in numbers after World War II had led to nearly half their members living out, while science laboratories and centralised faculties led to much of the teaching becoming extramural. At the same time social resentment of college wealth and prestige led to measures to limit their power, and following the Franks commission of 1966, rationalisation of the university led to a weakening of college autonomy. This was accompanied by more liberal attitudes as the authorities were forced to adapt to the changing social climate, and in 1969 the Family Reform Act lowered the legal age of responsibility to eighteen, which meant in effect that colleges were no longer acting *in loco parentis*. Looking back at the period in *Hungry Generations,* Wain's college fellow remarks that 'the floodgates of the 1960s and 1970s opened and all rules and regulations simply danced away like bits of matchwood on the flood-tide'. Prominent among the changes was a loosening of the restrictions concerning college access, such that students were freer to come and go as they liked. No longer was there a need as in Mehta's day for the newcomer to be instructed as to which window to climb through when returning late from a night out on the town.

The upshot in *Death of a Don* is a college in which all sense of community has been lost and most of the members prefer to live out. Those in residence are uncomfortable with the archaic formalities, and college rules are resented or ignored. Overnight guests go unchecked, and the small number of dons who huddle together at high table dispense with the customary rituals. Once the hub of the college, chapel consists only of a handful of lonely types. Even the physical fabric of the institution is in decay, for the expenditure needed for repair is beyond the college budget. It is not so much the *Death of a Don* as the death of a college, and in *The Healing Art* (1980) A.N. Wilson administers the *coup de grace* by setting fire to the whole institution and burning it down (an act of literary revenge against New College, it is said, for not extending his contract). It marked Oxford's belated response to the 'burn, baby, burn' ethos of the 1960s and the public-school revolution of films like *If* (1968) in which youth declared war on the social *mores* of the times. If nothing else, it signified that the college in its traditional guise was in serious trouble, and in an introduction to *Jill* written for an American edition in 1976 Larkin claimed historical value for his novel in portraying a rapidly vanishing mode of life.

> One wonders, in fact, how long the collegiate system will last: legislation by a succession of socialist or quasi-socialist governments has severely diminished college incomes from investment or property, while the rise in labour and other costs in running these academic hotels has been equally damaging. Furthermore, nobody really wants to live in them: dons and students alike prefer domesticity, houses and wives on the one hand and flats and mistresses on the other. Finally, left-wing agitation is striving to unite all Oxford students into a single political force that would be hostile to the collegiate system and the spirit it engenders. Recently a fellow of my own college said he gave it ten years.

The prediction might have been wildly wrong—the college had after all survived seven hundred years and was unlikely to come to a sudden end—but an important transformation had taken place as a result of which the college no longer dominated the lives of its members as in former times. At the same time diminishing budgets meant that the once resplendent living conditions no longer compared favourably with those elsewhere. Ved Mehta, for instance, was appalled at the quality of the facilities at Balliol by comparison with what he was used to in America. For his staircase of ten bed sits and law library there was a single unheated and smelly toilet; the food was unappetizing, even on a good day; and the showers were so distant and inadequate that most undergraduates did not bother to use them. At one point the expatriate student was hauled up in front of a flabbergasted master to explain why his gas bill was higher than his college fees: 'The explanation was simple: I left the gas fire on when I was out of the room. Even so it did little to dispel the permanent Arctic chill that hung about the room. The chill seemed to me to press home the point that comfort was an enemy of good scholarship.' The fall in standards provides a running subtheme in postwar literature. In Rachel Trickett's *The Elders* one of the characters complains of high table that the food is foul and the company awful, and in *Jake's Thing* (1978) by Kingsley Amis the college offers packaged food as in railway canteens. When the female scout of *The Healing Art* contemplates the carpetless stairs, distant toilets, cold draughts and gloomy furniture of the rooms in her charge, she is moved to pity those who have to live in such conditions—a far cry from Brideshead opulence.

The downturn in standards followed the cuts forced on the university by a Labour government during the 1960s, and colleges had to adapt to market forces by opening themselves up to tourists and conference-goers. The loss of seclusion which this entailed affects the tone of the literature, for in contrast to the sheltered environments of prewar Oxford, the college begins to seem more like a sightseeing venue in which tourists are as much at home as fellows. In *When Scholars Fall* a timid don caught in a narrow passageway by a group of sightseers bolts back to his medieval room like a startled rabbit, and in *Jake's Thing* a college fellow is chased across a quadrangle by a multilingual horde looking to photograph the genuine article. For Amis's don in *Jake's Thing* the college provides little in the way of community; students are hidden away in private occupations (consuming drugs, fornicating and writing poetry, it is suggested), and male camaraderie is threatened by an influx of women. The loosening of college ties constituted a serious diminution in Oxford's sense of distinctiveness, for the communal lifestyle which had shaped Newman's idea of a university was no longer central to an Oxford education. The account by Martin Amis, son of Kingsley, of his time as a student is telling in its use of metaphor: 'My Oxford is likely to seem rather shapeless—even rather jangling and unassimilated—compared to reports of it by my predecessors there. This is because my Oxford, the Oxford of 1968–71 (and presumably everyone else's Oxfords thereafter), did not feel like an experience which had shape, point, a clear structural place in one's life.' The result in terms of fiction is that the college becomes increasingly marginalised. The paralysed law student of Michael Stewart's *Monkey-Shines* (1983) (made into a film with a non-Oxford setting) has lodgings in town and dealings with the laboratory from which he obtains his task-performing monkey, but little mention is made of a college. The Oxford of this classics-trained author has nothing in common with that of his Greats predecessors, and with the demise of the college the way was opened up to new ways of viewing the city. The same forces that had fostered the desire to shed the conventions of the past led also to a radical reevaluation of Oxford. Even as the process of dismantling the English Athens was underway, a new city was being raised in its stead.

THE REWRITING OF OXFORD

The change in the literary image of Oxford during the course of the twentieth century has owed itself to a number of developments, primary amongst which has been a growing disinclination to favour any one particular section of society. This has led on the one hand to the literary spotlight being turned away from the university and onto other parts of the city, and on the other hand to the greater participation of previously neglected figures such as town citizens and women. The trend has been most noticeable in recent detective fiction where works like Joan Smith's *A Masculine Ending* (1987) and Veronica Stallwood's series of Oxford crimes (*Oxford Fall* [1996] was the fifth) feature women detectives, a pluralist city and a determinedly female point of view. The Oxford of such books is far removed from the self-congratulatory tone and insider perspective of earlier fiction.

The change in the nature of the literature has resulted in part from the changes in the character of Oxford itself, for a city of dreaming spires was transformed during the course of the century into a city of screaming tyres. John Betjeman had already noted on the eve of World War II that the city consisted of three parts which sat in uneasy alliance with each other: the academic heart around the city centre; the car works and East Oxford; and Christminster, Jude's old market-town. Of the three, Motopolis, the second part, was in the ascendant. The wages at the Cowley factories drew scouts from their staircases, and the roar of the cars they produced disturbed the college quadrangles. University poets took their revenge in print on the car-making Lord Nuffield, who as William Morris the second had destroyed their Earthly Paradise. 'Before he came', writes John Wain,

> the country and the town
> Had settled down to something like accord.
> A river slow but deep enough to drown:
> Roads, markets. Barns where harvest could be stored. . . .
>
> Against this treaty Nuffield launched his war:
> His weapons progress, profits, trusts and banks:
> His prizes sales, promotions, more, more, more:
> The cars rolled through the streets like tinny tanks.

When Muriel Beadle arrived in the city in 1957 in expectation of a taste of paradise she found to her horror that the city centre, far from suggesting a sleepy university town, was more like 'a cross-town street in Manhattan at high noon'. W.H. Auden was similarly horrified at the traffic when returning from America in 1972, and after being robbed he claimed that Oxford was not only noisier but more dangerous than New York. In the bestselling *Not a Penny More, Not a Penny Less* (1976) by Jeffrey Archer (the blurb misleadingly boasted a Brasenose background for an author who never went to university), Oxford is characterised as 'a city blocked solid with juggernaut lorries and full of unintelligible one-way systems'. The surrender by the city authorities to the tyranny of the combustion engine was accompanied by the kind of urban redevelopment and in-filling so detested by Inspector Morse, with the result that a once quiet backwater became a bustling centre of commerce. The city was in addition a magnet for visitors drawn in increasing numbers from around the world by the tourist sights and educational facilities. Institutions unattached to the university were able to profit from the name of Oxford, and as language schools and tutorial colleges mushroomed the city centre changed in appearance. Restaurants and bars opened to serve the influx of young people, and a city formerly dominated by the university evolved into a world educational centre catering for a cosmopolitan clientele. In a sign of the times the medieval room in the church of St. Mary's where the very first university meetings were held was turned into a cafe serving day-trippers and other occasional customers. As 1980s Thatcherism reached even into the deepest recesses of the ivory towers, the new Oxford ethos became marketing and servicing customer's requirements, as a result of which dons had to acquire a sharp-minded and practical frame of mind. Present realities are reflected in posts like the Virgin Atlantic Research Fellowship in Entrepreneurship at Templeton College and in the funding of two huge new institutions at the time of writing, one a business college and the other an Islamic centre, and both stemming from hard work by the university authorities in attracting Arab money.

Taken all in all, the changes in university and city life meant that Oxford no longer exuded a sense of other-worldly remoteness. To the students of the 1980s the whole idea of a 'city of dream' seemed absurd—'there is more of a sense that one is a student, much like a student from any other university, studying in a largely ugly town much like any other ugly town, which contains the odd purple patch', was a characteristic response in *The Oxford Myth* (1988), a group of essays edited by Rachel Johnson. The comment reveals a value system in which the bond of shared ordinariness is preferable to the privilege of inhabiting a 'sacred city'. Distinctiveness had become a disease, and postwar literature attests to the erosion of Oxford 'uniqueness' in all walks of life. In his *Autobiography* (1964) Compton Mackenzie wrote of the decline in college character and how modern undergraduates were more concerned to look alike than to look different. For others there was no longer any magic in the city: 'Once you stop following the architectural lines upwards,' wrote Martin Amis in *Rachel Papers* (1973), 'it's just like anywhere else'. The university too had lost its élan: 'Modern Oxford is grey, grim and serious', complained Dacre Balsdon. Worst of all in the minds of many, the dons were no longer spectacular or eccentric—'We are all becoming standardised and normal, Nigel', confesses a fellow in Crispin's *Gilded Fly*—and the fellows of A.N. Wilson's *Unguarded Hours* (1978) 'know surprisingly little about their own subjects and nothing about anything else'. In a poem on 'Their Oxford' Kingsley Amis looked back nostalgically to the legendary figures of his student days and bemoaned the trend toward ordinariness.

> In my day there wer]e giants on the scene,
> Men big enough to be worth laughing at:
> Coghill and Bowra, Lewis and Tolkien.
> Lost confidence and envy finished that.

In literary terms the loss in distinctiveness was offset by a gain in plurality. It was a trend which had started early in the century and was born of a desire to challenge tired clichés, as is made explicit in the opening lines of James Elroy Flecker's 'Oxford Canal'.

> When you have wearied of the valiant spires of this County Town,
> Of its wide streets and glistening museums, and black monastic walls,
> Of its red motors and lumbering trams, and self-sufficient people,
> I will take you walking with me to a place you have not seen -
> Half town and half country—the land of the Canal.

The generation of modernists were similarly concerned to reimagine the city, and one of the favourite walks of W.H. Auden as a student was by the gas-works and municipal rubbish dump not far from Christ Church, where the last enchantments of the Middle Ages gave way to the imagery of modern times. In George Santayana's *The Last Puritan* (1935) the American eponym lives for a while in Iffley, and the church there is given the type of treatment usually reserved for the city centre, but the area to gain most literary favour was North Oxford, unsurprisingly perhaps since it represented the residential extension of the university. Among the novels set in North Oxford are Barbara Pym's *Crampton Hodnet,* Robert Liddell's *The Last Enchantments,* and Brian Aldiss's *Forgotten Life* (1988), in which the small dramas of the leafy suburb are set in contrast to the aggrandizing adventures of the young. Pym's sleepy academic adjunct is as yet untouched by the developments of the postwar period. It is a place where curates lodge with spinsters; where polite undergraduates do their best to mask their boredom at tea-parties; where gossip is rife about university affairs; where hen-pecked dons fantasise about female students; and where Miss Morrow will have peace as long as Miss Doggett remains upstairs. It is a world of hypocrisies and pretences, yet the human follies are described in a manner which manages to convey a warm affection for the donnish suburb: 'It was not difficult, Miss Morrow thought, to imagine that heaven might be something like North Oxford.' Liddell's *The Last Enchantments,* which came out in 1948, occupies a similar if less lighthearted space (as a student at Corpus Christi, he belonged to the same circle as the younger Pym and remained a lifelong friend). The quiet concern with the morality of personal relationships has won the book praise from critics who like to refer to Liddell in such terms as 'the most unknown major author of the century', though the slow narrative pace and elegance of expression hark back to an earlier age. The book shows a disdain for the eye-catching antics of the Oxford novel by adopting Hardy's name for the city in conscious opposition to that of the Bright Young Things: 'A "Christminster novel" is always about the loves and hatreds and rivalries of the young—and very boring they generally are, and not always quite proper.' Being 'proper' is important to Liddell's gentle folk, whose manner of behaviour is informed by the past no less than the buildings they inhabit—not so much the 'last enchantments' of the Middle Age as of the middle-aged. The personal story at the heart of the novel reveals caring souls within the suburb's large anonymous spaces whose support provides a measure of compensation for the inadequacies of family life. 'I should like to spend my eternity in Christminster as a beneficent and loving ghost' is the narrative response to the spirit of place. Family problems lie too at the heart of Brian Aldiss's *Forgotten Life,* in which the death of the older brother of a psychology don has an unsettling effect on his sense of self. (The prolific Aldiss, best-known for his science fiction, worked as a book-seller in Oxford, an experience which provided the material for his first book, *The Brightfount Papers* (1955), before becoming literary editor of the *Oxford Mail.*) The story leads via the writings left behind by the dead man to an unloved childhood and war years in the Far East, and the revelations prompt a mid-life crisis in the younger brother which is compounded by marital insecurity. As the certainties of the don crumble, the forgotten life of the past has to be integrated into his present. As might be expected from an author who is a long-term resident of the city, there are some deft topographical touches, as in this description of Banbury Road: 'The great houses, behind their great trees, lay back from the thronging cars, blind, wounded, extinct—yet living on, their carcasses turned over to contemporary fashion and lusting estate agents.' There are some telling asides too about the university and a note of irritation with the mannered self-irony which prevails in academic circles—'That's the Oxford manner. Everything's effect, effect is everything. . . . Doesn't matter how foolishly you behave, as long as what you say is either frivolously intellectual or intellectually frivolous.'

For some writers the division of Oxford into town and gown represented a subject in itself, and family connections provided a convenient means of bridging the gap. In *Second Generation* (1964) Raymond Williams attempted to wed labour to culture by bringing Welsh mining families to work at the car-factory. One of the sons enters the university,

where his sense of identity is threatened by the alien ethos, then after
graduation he goes to work at the factory, where his learning is put to use
on behalf of his family and class. The technique of spanning the cultural
divide though family connections was taken up with greater effect by
John Wain in an ambitious trilogy which charts the development of
Oxford between the 1930s and the 1960s, when the city passed irre-
versibly from sleepy backwater to bustling industrial centre. The human
interest is hung around the lifestory of the two sons of the landlord of an
Osney pub (based on the Waterman's). In the first of the novels, *Where
the Rivers Meet* (1988), the sons grow up and go their separate ways, with
Brian working in the motor trade and Peter entering Episcopus College,
a mere seven minutes from his lower-middle-class home. In *Comedies*
(1990) Brian becomes involved with MG racing cars, while Peter marries
and becomes a history don. The war years bring a more sombre tone as
the lives of the two brothers go amiss: Brian attempts suicide after losing
his wife and job, while Peter falls in love with another woman. *Hungry
Generations* (1994) focuses on the post-war years and recovery—of Brian
from his personal misfortunes, and of Peter from divorce and the death
of his son in a racing accident. Set around the story of the two brothers
is that of the city 'where the rivers meet', and the narrative is full of
points of information and historical digressions. The authorial love of
place is all too clear, though this does not extend to the city's planning
committee nor to W.R. Morris, the villain of the piece, who is held personally responsible for turning a once pleasant environment into 'the
grimy detritus of a car-industry'. The story is narrated by Peter Leonard,
the brother who becomes a don, and he is at pains to emphasise his local
origins and allegiance to town: 'Show me one respect in which Episcopus
College, as a human environment, is superior to the Bargeman's Arms,
Oseney Town', he challenges. Similarly, when his uncle becomes a scout,
he is held up as 'a man as worthy of respect as Canon Jenkins, and as
pure an expression of the traditional essence of Oxford'. Nonetheless,
Leonard's career path means that the narrative inevitably favours the
university, and, like Stewart, Wain is concerned to uphold the tradition
of humanist scholarship (primarily a man of letters, Wain lived in
Oxford and was associated with the university as a fellow in creative arts
at Brasenose [1971–72] and as professor of poetry [1973–78]). On the
one hand, the trilogy strives to undo the image of unearned privilege by
stressing the hard work done by ordinary students and teachers; on the
other hand, there is a running argument with utilitarian detractors who
belittle the value of disinterested research. The somewhat priggish narrator (anti-business, anti-socialism, anti-frivolity, anti-hedonism but pro-
goodness) sees himself as a natural scholar who, despite his social

difficulties when he first enters the university, forms an integral part of its backbone.

> Ultimately, I and my kind were the reason why Oxford University had come into existence over 700 years previously and why it was still in existence. We had been there all along and we would still be there when the tiny posturing smart set of snobs and hard-faced social climbers whose exploits got into the newspapers had vanished like a puff of scented smoke.

The trilogy ends with an uncharacteristically visionary moment when the well-tended college garden seems to dissolve and give way to scenes of disorder, warfare and barbarism. The implication is that just as nature is controlled and regulated by the college gardeners, so social chaos is held in check by the civilised order that academic work serves to further. It is an unmistakable nod in the direction of *Culture and Anarchy,* and the vision emphasises that even at the end of the twentieth century the Arnoldian tradition remains alive, if beleaguered. The picture of Oxford which emerges is, perhaps not surprisingly, one of decline as the city moves from an age of certainties and measured beauty down a steepening slope towards consumerism, business values, anti-humanists and the whole 'rat-infested rubbish tip' of modern Britain.

The concern for inclusiveness that led Wain to write of both town and gown was taken further by others for whom the division of the city into two was in itself an anachronism. Recent fiction has posited instead a pluralist city of different parts with differing realities which coexist and overlap. Characters like Inspector Morse shuffle in and out of the different Oxfords with an ease and fluidity which would have been impossible in earlier times. In Michael Dibdin's *Dirty Tricks* the constituent parts are seen in class terms, and the book champions the radical chic of East Oxford over the moneyed conservatism of the North with Magdalen Bridge marking a symbolic crossing point between these states of mind: warmth and vitality lie on one side, calculation and murder on the other. Reality is thus relocated from college quadrangle to terraced house, and an American once again serves as the innocent dupe on whom is hung a belief in the superiority of Oxford culture, the response to which is unmitigated scorn—'In England, that kind of patriotism is something you do with other consenting adults under the covers with the lights out, and usually comes with various unpleasant side-effects such as xenophobia, anti-semitism, Anglo-Catholicism and so on.' The book is a detective story of sorts with a truncated reference to Morse in an Inspector Moss, and as such it can be read as an attempt to subvert the comforting world of Dexter's murder-puzzles by putting the criminal in charge of the nar-

rative. While the dirty tricks of the title apply as much to the manipula-
tions of the rich as to the shady doings of the narrator, it could be said
that the author also has a few of his own in the all-too-evident concern to
do down academe and the privileged classes. The 'unwriting' of the English Athens in this way serves as a means to attack traditional notions of
Englishness. Others rewrite the city in quieter fashion by simply setting
their fiction in an Oxford untouched by university life. Joanna Trollope's
The Men and the Girls (1992) provides a prime example, for the Oxford it
portrays is one of tutorial colleges whose most attractive feature is
Osney—'this little water-girt place, these cottage streets of brick and
painted stucco with their oddly, unmistakably foreign air, an island of distinct character protected from the surrounding schools and factories
and newspaper offices by the quiet, olive-green barriers of river and
canal'. The description illustrates the way in which the different parts of
late twentieth-century Oxford clamour for attention, as if each in its way
were a little cultural 'island of distinct character' waiting to be recognised. With Trollope, then, the marginalisation of the university is complete, and ironically the only acknowledgement in the book of its existence is an erroneous reference to cutting through Christ Church to get
to the river.

The fragmentary nature of contemporary Oxford arises out of the dis-
persal of shared beliefs in modern times, and as such it can be seen as
marking the outcome of a historical process charted by Ronald Knox in
a remarkable book entitled *Let Dons Delight* (1939). This portrays the
breakdown in a common culture by recreating the conversations of the
senior common room of the fictional college of Simon Magus between
1588 and 1938. The conversations take place at fifty-year intervals and in
each case the junior member becomes the senior member of the next
conversation. Amidst the theological discussions and donnish pedantry
are sketches done in the style of the time: those from 1588 and 1638, for
example, purport to be biographical sketches from Anthony Wood's
Athenae Oxonienses, while following the conversation of 1738 there is a
dialogue between Boswell and Johnson as they travel by coach back to
London. Though the theological disputes drag at times, these are leav-
ened by the many light touches. 'You will not teach the potato to grow in
Ireland', pronounces one of the members on hearing of Walter
Raleigh's attempts, 'it is very marshy and boggy there.' A later don
claims, 'You will find Elkanah Settle's name is still remembered when
Dryden's is quite put out of men's minds.' And in 1738 while complain-
ing of how the building of Radcliffe Camera is ruining the middle of
Oxford, the dons make reference to an 'idle scamp' at Pembroke called
Samuel Jackson (*sic*) whom they are sure will come to a bad end. The

clerical discussions continue in such convivial fashion into the nineteenth century, when the first hint of a challenge to the unified belief system comes with the introduction of non-Anglicans. Soon afterwards scientists introduce a completely new vocabulary. And in 1938
communication virtually ceases altogether when a philosopher refuses to
discuss anything until it is first defined. The break-down in the communal atmosphere is symptomatic of the profound differences concerning
the nature of truth. Fifty years after Knox wrote his book doubts were
being raised as to whether there even was such a thing as truth.

The desire to divest Oxford of glamour in recent fiction can thus be
seen as part of a wider social process involving a distrust of authority
rather than a downturn in the quality or achievement of the university.
Indeed, all the evidence points the other way and suggests that Oxford
remains as much 'a seat of the Muses' as it has ever been. Writing in volume 8 of *The History of the University of Oxford,* Val Cunningham surveys
the contribution of Oxford figures to the literary life of the nation in the
late twentieth century and notes, 'The Oxford dominance in this scene
is all too obvious'. Among the novelists he lists, quite apart from those
already mentioned, are such Oxonians as Penelope Fitzgerald, D.M.
Thomas, Julian Barnes, Alan Hollinghurst, Timothy Mo, William Boyd,
Sarah Maitland, Vikram Seth, Penelope Lively, Gabriel Josipovici, and
Maggie Gee. Leading poets include Tom Paulin, Mick Imlah, Adrian
Mitchell, John Heath-Stubbs, Al Alvarez, Alan Brownjohn, U.A. Fanthorpe, Geoffrey Hill, Anthony Thwaite, and George Mitchell. 'Martian
poetry' originated at Oxford with Craig Raine and Christopher Reid, a
relationship paralleled at Magdalen where John Fuller acted as mentor
to the present professor of poetry, James Fenton. The city too continues
to host a wealth of writers drawn by its bookish culture—Ian McEwan is
a notable example—while other writers live nearby on account of their
university connections: Susan Hill is married to the Shakespearean
scholar Stanley Wells, Barbara Trapido to a fellow of Lincoln, Angela
Huth to a history don at Corpus Christi, and Candia McWilliam to an
English tutor at St. Catherine's. P.D. James, like Dorothy Sayers, was born
in the city and still owns a house there (she studied at Cambridge). And
in addition to all the writers, there are a large number of Oxonians active
in other areas of literature. The faculty of English, for example, provides
some of the weightiest reviewers for the national press in such figures as
John Carey, Peter Conrad, Val Cunningham, Terry Eagleton and his predecessor, John Bayley (the husband of Iris Murdoch and himself a novelist). The *Times Literary Supplement* is described by Cunningham as a
'welcoming home-from-home for very many Oxonians', and both the
London Review of Books and the *Literary Review* were founded and run by

Oxford men. At one time or another A.N. Wilson has been literary editor of the *Spectator*, Anthony Thwaite of the *Listener* and the *New Statesman*, and Martin Amis of the *New Statesman*, where Julian Barnes was his
assistant. Craig Raine and Andrew Motion have been influential poetry
editors; Humphrey Carpenter has been a one-man publishing venture;
Marina Warner has been prominent amongst feminist commentators
and Melvyn Bragg among presenters—the list could be easily extended.
Indeed, charges have been made of an Oxford 'literary mafia' with a
stranglehold on the national culture.

It would be wrong, then, to suggest any falling off in Oxford talent,
just as it would be wrong too to suggest that the pluralist city of modern
fiction no longer has room for the traditional viewpoint. The charm of
Brideshead cannot be easily dismissed, for it hovers over the post-war
period like the glow from a fading sunset. The question of what happens
to the Bright Young Things once they go out into the world to seek their
'glittering prizes' (a phrase taken from Auden's 'Oxford') was taken up
by two of the modern university's outstanding novelists, Iris Murdoch
(1919–) and John Fowles (1926–). The latter's humanist novel,
Daniel Martin (1977), explores the condition of Englishness in a variety
of settings which include 'the most English of all cities. Mother Oxford,
Venus-Minerva, triple-haunted, hundred-tongued'. The generation of
1940s students lead a charmed life of punting parties where champagne
bottles are tossed nonchalantly into the Cherwell. Yet after going down
the students fail to fulfil their potential and opt for cosy jobs in the
media and education where they produce or review the creative works of
others. By comparison with their vigorous American counterparts, the
Oxonians seem paralysed by guilt about an imperial past and a privileged background; rather than engage with life, they hide behind a cynical pose of world-weariness and know-it-all superiority. The concerns of
Iris Murdoch, by contrast, are more with moral and personal matters
than with career choices. Though the former philosophy don resides in
Oxford, the city hardly features in her works (possibly because the local
setting would prove restrictive; an earlier resident, Joyce Cary, similarly
preferred to write of other places). Nonetheless, her cerebral characters
often have about them the air of the senior common room, and several
have university connections. The author's Platonic notions concerning
virtue and the need for self-knowledge would seem to place her firmly in
the Oxford tradition, and this is borne out by the few references in her
novels to the university; the college of *An Accidental Man* (1971), for
example, is described in nineteenth-century terms as 'not quite a small
Athenian state'. At the beginning of *The Book and the Brotherhood* (1987)
a group of outstanding students (all with First Class degrees) revisit their

college for a commemoration ball of revelry, debauchery and mayhem. It is a mad, crazy midsummer night during which the group relive the irresponsibility of youth shielded by college walls and a protective darkness. Moonlight, dream and romance—the college is once more cast in other-worldly terms. Daylight on the other hand brings 'remorse, regret, the tarnished hope, the shattered dream, and all the awful troubles of ordinary life'.

There is something of Murdoch's world of sophisticated talk, complex relationships and bizarre happenings in the Gothic construct of Robertson Davies's *Rebel Angels* trilogy. Though only one of the sections of *What's Bred in the Bone,* the second of the three books, actually takes place in Oxford, the whole atmosphere is steeped in the alchemy of the medieval past, and the story is constantly reaching out across the Atlantic from its setting in the Toronto University College of St. John and the Holy Ghost (Spook, for short). Beerbohm cartoons play a key part; the urbane warden was at Balliol (as was Davies himself); and there is a clear Wildean implication in the sinister Urquhart McVarish, who studied at Magdalen being 'sodomised' to death. The erudition, intellectual wizardry and high-table wit flash with brilliance, and in the observation made by one of the characters that 'Oxford will strengthen whatever is bred in the bone' there is the suggestion of a titular acknowledgement to the author's English *alma mater.* Known for his jocular sense of humour, the Canadian also manages some light-hearted digs—'Gunfire in Oxford is uncommon. The University Statutes strictly forbid it'; there is reference to 'the Oxford pretence of doing nothing while in fact getting through a great deal of work'; and on reading an obituary in *The Times* one of the characters is moved to exclaim, 'Do you notice they say he went to school in Canada but was educated at Oxford? . . . God the English!'

Like *The Book and the Brotherhood,* Davies's book came out at a time when the *Brideshead* image had been revived in the public mind by the television series of Waugh's novel and by a drugs and death scandal involving the daughter of a government minister and her upper-class circle. Antonia Fraser's *Oxford Blood* (1985) tried to feed off this through a detective story featuring Golden Girls and Boys centred around a drunken aristocrat—a 'blood' whose blood group is germane to the plot. The book reflected the continued interest in privileged decadence at Oxford, much resented by the senior community for its adverse effect on the concerns of serious scholarship. On the fly-leaf of volume 8 of the official *History of the University of Oxford* dealing with *The Twentieth Century* (1994) there is a statement declaring that the whole weighty multi-authored tome of scholarship is dedicated to proving 'how misleading is

Evelyn Waugh's *Brideshead Revisited* to modern Oxford'. It is a remarkable testimony to the potency of imaginative fiction, coming as it does fifty years after publication of the novel. It reflects too the sober-minded nature of the contemporary university and its determination to maintain its standing in a meritocratic world by dispensing with the frivolity of the past. Though colleges continue to provide a haven of peace in a traffic-thronged world, glorification and idealisation are hard to find these days. 'Magical' appears to be the furthest the senior community will allow themselves (influenced perhaps by the vogue for magical realism), as in the description of a college garden by Peter Levi as 'a magic circle of privacy and anonymity' and Val Cunningham's reference to 'the magnetic hold on the imagination of a magical place, this formative Oxford matrix'. Though the poems of John Fuller tell of 'college beano' and 'Veuve du Vernay in the gutter', there is little sense of the self-congratulation and decadent revelling that marked the writings of earlier times. Instead of looking down from well-stocked ivory towers, contemporary dons such as the Marxist Terry Eagleton seem more concerned to look askance at their institution, as if to distance themselves from the taint of privilege. In Fuller's poem 'Gone to Ground' the distancing is physical as the poet goes off on his summer vacation, while in *Where I Fell to Earth* (1990) the Australian Peter Conrad portrays himself as a visiting alien at Christ Church, perplexed and dumbfounded by the peculiarities he encounters. The role of college member is only one of his multiple existences, the others of which take place in the interstices of his Oxford life, and the comparison this occasions leads to a Carrollian view of the city. 'Here in this moist, stifling labyrinth between two rivers and inside a circle of hills, people were turned inside out by thinking. Brains as squashy and unarmoured and tentacular as jellyfish dodged in front of buses on the High Street or furiously pedalled those wobbling bikes.' Such a city continues to offer rich pickings for writers of the Oxford novel, though perhaps it takes a foreigner to exploit it these days. In the much acclaimed *All Souls* (1989; Eng. trans. 1992) Javier Marías explores the spirit of place through a love affair between a visiting lecturer and the married wife of a don (the Spaniard was himself a visiting lecturer). Like Beerbohm's Oxford, the city is characterised by its lethargy, as if the heavy-hanging air and life of abstraction deprive the bodies of physical life and make them 'all souls'. The narrator lives in a pyramid-shaped house off Walton Street, where he is entombed, as it were, in a moribund state—like the rest of the city. Though on the surface all is flux and fluidity, it is a 'static city preserved in syrup', a phrase which recurs in one form or another no fewer than five times during the course of the novel as if to emphasise how its inhabitants are trapped in the past. Even the tramps who frequent the city centre with its book-shops and pervasive sense of history seem affected. The spirit of place is brilliantly personified in the eccentric Will, a senile porter at the Taylorian who lives in temporal shifts all of his own, greeting people with the names of those long dead and shuttling at random between the different periods of his life.

The air of unreality which hangs over the city of *All Souls* emanates from the academic community at its heart. 'Any university is a spiritual pyramid,' writes Jan Morris, 'a thing of cumulative shades and evocations, and Oxford in particular possesses this quality of inheritance'. Perhaps this is why the city has always been associated with the abstract—truth, beauty, the past. Ideas play such a large part in Oxford that the dream-city can seem more real than the real city, and Peter Ackroyd took up this theme in an article in the *Spectator* in which he dwelled on the imaginative inheritance of the city.

> There is an air of insubstantiality about it all. This is odd since the physical fact of the place is clearly the most important: the bridges, the libraries, the gardens and the quads are, as it were, the doughnut round the hole. . . . Oxford is insubstantial because it lives off myths, it is a clutter of broken images.

Insubstantial—all souls—disembodied intellects; literary Oxford is in more than one sense a city of the mind. It is an imaginative space in which exist eccentric academics and beautiful youth; ancient buildings and enchanted gardens; dreaming spires and broken dreams. It is at one and the same time a city of colleges and a city of cars, paradise regained and paradise lost, the English Athens and not the English Athens. The multiple authorship of this urban palimpsest stands in contrast to the pastoral creations known and loved as Hardy's Wessex, Wordsworth's Lake District, and the Brontës' moors, yet it has just as distinct and recognisable a character. Six hundred years after Chaucer first wrote of the city it remains one of the most eye-catching features in English literature, a fictional locus where a student named Nicholas still plans the seduction of the sprightly young wife of a carpenter and Sebastian Flyte still charms a freshman by the name of Charles Ryder. Even in a city of walls the imagination remains unbounded, for dream transcends both space and time, and the rewriting of the city is a constant and ongoing process. The story of Oxford is one without end.

Conclusion: An Englishman's House

Friends, we will let our final visit be
Oxford's epitome:
The place they call the House.
           —John Betjeman, *Summoned by Bells* (1960)

ON MARCH 10, 1675, the astrologer William Lilly (1602–81) caused consternation in Oxford by predicting the destruction of the city. He had a formidable reputation in astrological matters, and his authority was based on an influential book, *Christian Astrology* (1647), in which Oxford is positively identified with the sign of Capricorn (December 22–January 21). The hardships of winter and the death-rebirth cycle of nature associated with the sign are held to produce seriousness, conservatism, discipline, hard work, self-control, dryness, and a need to be sanctioned by the authority of the past. Whatever one thinks of astrology, as a description of academic Oxford such terms might be considered peculiarly apt. Moreover, Capricorn is ruled by Saturn, which as the planet of hardship and endings is closely associated with melancholy—and in Robert Burton Oxford nurtured the author of the greatest book ever written on the subject. In a sense melancholy underlies the whole flow of literature, for the connection between Saturn and the scholar is close and has been often commented on: it may be no coincidence that Thomas Warton wrote a long poem 'The Pleasures of Melancholy' (1747)—'O come then, Melancholy, queen of thought'—and that Oxford's greatest detective, Inspector Morse, is also prone to the condition. Furthermore, Burton's long treatise, *The Anatomy of Melancholy*, could be considered a classic example of the Capricorn propensity to labour in the land of the dead, for the book looks back to the figures of the past for comfort and guidance to counter the threat of despair. It may be that the heavy-hanging air of Oxford, described so graphically by Beerbohm, owes itself as much to the astrological as the geographical lie of the land and that the slow-moving populace is struggling as much with the burden of Saturn as with the micro-climate of the river valley. The turning inwards which characterises depression leads to a withdrawal from an emotional involvement with life, as in the monastic tradition of Oxford and the cult of Platonic contemplation. This results in a dryness of character, which in the case of academics is compounded by a preference for books and libraries over activity and people. The dry-as-dust scholar and the dried-up don are familiar characters: 'It is as though the genius of the city dries up the sap in you', notes Jan Morris. Swinburne thought nobody in Oxford could be said to die, 'for they never begin to live', and T.S. Eliot, who spent a year in 1914–15 studying philosophy at Merton College, disliked the lack of vitality and observed that Oxford was all right but he did not like 'being dead'. Perhaps this is why P.D. James chose Oxford as the setting for her futuristic fantasy *The Children of Men* (1992), based around global infertility and the death of mankind. The repressed emotions of the academic and the determination to tie down loose ends in footnotes and references create an environment in which fantasy and spontaneity, when they do burst into the open, often emerge in outrageous and startling form. The humour of J.I.M. Stewart furnishes one example, but it is in the imaginary worlds of Lewis Carroll, J.R.R. Tolkien and C.S. Lewis that the pent-up urges are given their most complete expression. Interestingly, these alternative worlds exist on the far side of depth and darkness, for Hobbits like Wonderland belong at the bottom of a hole while Narnia is reached through the hidden recesses of a wardrobe. It is as if the emotionally repressed dons were reaching deep down into their subconscious to extract childhood fancies that make mockery of their adult world of rectitude and pedantry. Even Waugh's collegiate idyll, locked away behind a low doorway, exists in a different dimension from that of grown-up society.

The plumbing of depths associated with Saturn can lead towards spirituality and a concern with transcendental truths, and there is a tendency towards the construction of religious and philosophical systems as if to provide sanctuary from black thoughts — the theologising of medieval monks and the religious attachment of Oxford are apposite in this regard. Yet the desire to construct is not limited to the intellectual plane, for the building of structures can take material form too—significantly, the very first Oxford story features both a carpenter and a student of astrology. The desire for security leads also to a strong attachment to place, and the college buildings with their solid walls of thickly hewn stone can be seen as a determination to provide structure and impose continuity on a world that constantly threatens to give way. The structured routine of college life with its reassuring round of daily rituals works to the same effect, as does the insistence on adhering to tradition. There is too a need to combat the sense of disintegration by keeping up appearances and achieving set goals, as if the abyss that lurks at the bottom of the Capricorn soul can be avoided by climbing up the ladder of worldly success. Viewed in this light, the pursuit of excellence could be construed as the avoidance of despair.

With its air of authority and concern for tradition, Capricorn carries strong patrician overtones and is often identified with the principle of the Father (the biblical God of the Old Testament presents a prime example). The paternalism inherent in the star sign is reflected in the masculine character of Oxford literature, while the pursuit of the feminine arts of truth and wisdom by the scholarly community has led to an idealisation of the Other. From the medieval monks who cherished a virgin saint to the writers of the Oxford myth who championed Pallas Athene, the literature is characterised by a tendency to romanticise and mystify the feminine (both the foundation of the city and the act of creativity represent aspects of giving 'birth'). That the making and remaking of the 'English Athens' took place under the two most celebrated queens in English history may be historical coincidence, yet it is worth noting the devotion of the academics to Elizabeth and Victoria who in their guise of the virgin queen and the faithful widow constituted two popular female icons (Victoria did not apparently return the affection, for she is said to have referred to Oxford as 'that old monkish place which I have a horror of'). Even the city itself was dressed in female form by Oxford writers and worshipped for her beauty; in the sentimental outpouring of affection some imagined her as a beautiful dreamer, others as a goddess—adorable but unattainable, ever seductive but never willing to yield her secret. It was imagery that depended on a distancing effect to lend enchantment, and one that with its Platonic rationale bears the Capricorn stamp of a philosophical framework.

If Robert Burton suggests the archetypal type of the melancholy scholar, then his college of Christ Church is the representative House—preserver of mysteries in the enchanted garden and the symbolic heart of the English Athens. It was through college members like Burton and Camden that the notion of the English Athens was first promoted, and it was from Christ Church that the writers of the Oxford myth took their tone and inspiration. For literary pilgrims it represents a treasure-trove of historical associations which lead through the pages of the past. From Carfax, the Fourways that lies at the centre of Jude Fawley's city, the college stands but a three-minute walk southwards along St. Aldate's. Short as it is, the walk cannot be called pleasant, for the twentieth century has conspired against the narrow streets of the medieval city, and the incessant traffic that roars indifferently past sets up a background cacophony and poisons the air. Here in the centre of modern Oxford there is little of peace, or dream, or enchantment, and like Hilaire Belloc's stranger the visitor might well wonder,

> Is it from here the people come,
> Who talk so loud, and roll their eyes

> And stammer? How extremely odd!
> How curious! What a great surprise.

Those who join the jostling multilingual throng passing down St. Aldate's will soon come to Pembroke Square, where there is a small backwater of relative calm enabling contemplation of the college opposite. Solid and stern, the balustraded walls of Christ Church cast an imposing frontage on the world. Here is the sequestered vantage from which Democritus Junior scoffed at the world hurrying by. Here too is 'the long front, and its windows with lifted eyebrows' which expressed surprise at the effrontery of Jude. From its midst Wren's elegant tower rises to an ogee top housing the six-ton Great Tom, which some fondly believe to be honoured in the lines of Milton's *Il Pensoroso:*

> Oft on a plot of rising ground,
> I hear the far-off curfew sound
> Over some wide-watered shore,
> Swinging slow with sullen roar.

Still it strikes its 101 mighty notes each evening, an archaic ritual from its days of dominion, and still it bears the name of Thomas Clusius, a reminder of its origins in Oseney Abbey and of Chaucer's carpenter who worked there. From the top of the tower the eyes are drawn downward along the pinnacles to the windowed niche that bears the statue of the formidable Wolsey, cardinal of this Cardinal college, then further down to the huge arched gateway in which the original oak doors, massive and enduring, stand ever ready to slam shut on the outside world. In the opening presented is visible a man in a bowler hat, and behind him a glimpse of secluded lawn in the middle of which, mounted on a pedestal, stands a statue whose forward motion with upraised arm and heavenward gaze suggests a figure in flight. This is Mercury, Arcadian Hermes in other guise, messenger of the gods and master of the word. Together the two guardians of the college, the bowler-hatted gentleman and the statuary figure, combine to present the very picture of an English Athens complete with academic grove and cloistered walks.

To pass into that other realm one must walk further down the street, for the gentleman who guards the entrance to this Renaissance citadel will turn away the unauthorised in firm but polite manner. At a point, then, a little further down the street not far from the shop where the young Alice Liddell went to buy sweets and where thousands now go to buy memorabilia, visitors can cross over the busy road and enter through the iron-gated entrance into the Christ Church War Memorial Garden. Here at the entrance continuity is written into the physical fabric, literally, for inscribed in the paving is a quotation from Bunyan: 'My sword I give to him that shall succeed me in my pilgrimage.' The path through the quintessentially English garden passes by Trill Mill Stream as it emerges from its subterranean passage, which T.E. Lawrence while a student at Jesus navigated in a canoe all the way from Hythe Bridge Street. The path leads to the northern edge of Christ Church Meadow, fronted on the left by the eleven pinnacles of Christ Church hall whose 'festal light' was visible to the scholar-gipsy on far-off Cumnor range. To the right stands the Brew House, where W.H. Auden lived after his return from America; it was his third spell with the college following his residence as a student and later as a beslippered professor of poetry. Nearby the imposing vista of Poplar Walk laid out by Dean Liddell, father of Alice, stretches down to the Thames where the boat races of *Zuleika Dobson* took place, and on the other side is the imposing Victorian Gothic of the Meadow Buildings where lived Sebastian Flyte of *Brideshead Revisited*. Following the sumptuous lunch-party to which Charles Ryder was invited, Anthony Blanche stepped out onto the balcony and declaimed lines from *The Waste Land* to hearties headed for the river.

On payment of the requisite sum—for in an age of commercialism the college is not averse to marketing its secrets—entrance is gained through the tourist entrance of the Meadow Buildings by passing through a turnstile which revolves like a Tibetan prayer-wheel as if to mark the transaction between one world and another. The wide-ranging meadows give way to narrow archways and alleyways leading into a Wonderland of locked doors and dark openings, one of which gives onto to a tiny cloistered square bounded on one side by a souvenir shop, on another by a cathedral, and on a third side by an area boasting a ceiling of delicate fan tracery and a flight of stately stairs. The door at the top bespeaks little of the magnificence of the dining-hall within, the high ceiling and imposing length of which is more suggestive of a chapel than a communal refectory. For Charles I it made a ready parliamentary building, the centre of the royalist kingdom in those heady days of Civil War. The solid wooden tables running lengthways lead the eyes to the far end where, set at a right-angle to the rest, stands the raised high table. Empty, the room seems cold and stark: filled with the babble of student and don it offers a different prospect. 'Sir, it is a great thing to dine with the Canons of Christ-Church', observed Samuel Johnson, a great thing indeed to judge by the meals of ritual and circumstance that pepper the novels of J.I.M. Stewart. From the panelled walls bear down the faces of former college members, stern and contemptuous of the passing parade of transients, and among their number the distinctive wrinkles of W.H. Auden and the dreamlike features of Charles Dodgson are prominent.

Outside in the sunlight stands Tom Quad, the most magnificent, the most stately and the most aristocratic of Oxford quadrangles. In Elizabethan times the likes of Philip Sidney, Richard Hakluyt and William Camden strode about the cloistered walks in excited conversation. Here is Waugh's Arcadia, in which Anthony Blanche sported and pranced for the college bullies. Here too an inebriated Bertie Wooster once thought of diving into Mercury fountain in the belief he was a mermaid. In the far-left corner, to the right of Tom Tower, lived Charles Dodgson in his bachelor quarters, ordering his life in well-filed notes, issuing pamphlets on assorted topics, and entertaining his young visitors at photographic sessions in a rooftop studio. The flow of tourists leads towards the tower in the northeastern corner where they pass under the statue of the former Dean of the college Dr. John Fell, who as a boy of twelve had been expelled from the deanery along with his royalist father (also Dean) by the Puritan visitation following the Civil War. In reaction, when he became Dean following the Restoration, John Fell showed a strong bias towards the monarchy and upper classes which led him to expel the philosopher John Locke from the college (who had fallen into political disfavour). He also expelled William Penn, founder of Pennsylvania, and is remembered as a strict disciplinarian in a verse written about him by a student named Thomas Brown (1663–1709), later a pamphleteer and satirist.

> I do not love thee, Dr. Fell,
> The reason why I cannot tell;
> But this I know, and know full well,
> I do not love thee, Dr. Fell.

Beyond the opening lies Peckwater Quad with its eighteenth-century Palladian buildings where the arrogant aristocrats of the nineteenth century cracked their whips. Here ragged the drunken lords mentioned in Cox's *Recollections* on that evening in 1831 which ended with the fatal 'blow' suffered by his parents when they received the news of their dead son. Here too lived the vexed John Ruskin, disappointed at having to view the regimented features of the classical buildings. On the southern side stands the library, which houses Cardinal Wolsey's hat in a display case made by Horace Walpole. From the upper floor of the building where he worked as librarian Charles Dodgson looked down on his dream-child playing innocently beneath the chestnut tree in the Deanery Garden below.

The picture gallery with its da Vinci prints, which lies just beyond the library, marks the end point of the tourist trail, and the way back leads along the eastern side of Tom Quad to the far corner where a double archway knocked through the house of a former canon marks the entrance to the cathedral, dwarfed and seemingly misplaced amidst its lordly surroundings. The building serves at once as the smallest cathedral in the country and chapel to the largest college; it is a relationship of such peculiarity that the complex has been called 'a theoretically impossible place'. With the cathedral on one side to preach of Christ and Mercury in the middle to spread the Word, the collegiate purpose laid down by Henry VIII 'to maintain the service of God and literature' is made physically manifest. Yet at the same time the scene speaks of the strain of absurdity in Oxford literature, for as the bowler-hatted Englishman poses for photos beside oriental tourists, the grotesques above the dining-hall grin and grimace while across the quad the spirit of the former mathematician still seems much at home. 'Insanity is rooted in the air of Oxford', wrote Dacre Balsdon in *Freshman's Folly*.

Inside the cathedral lies the spiritual heart of Oxford. The young Jude followed Sue Brideshead here to observe her at prayer, and the degradation of Archbishop Cranmer took place here in the account by John Foxe. To John Ruskin the cathedral architecture represented 'an epitome of English history' and the choir 'virtually the navel' of the nation. His description in *Praeterita* celebrates the pre-eminence of the college in the life of the nation (thirteen prime ministers have studied here, though most for short periods at a time of patronage politics). It serves as a reminder of the unabashed élitism of former times.

> There remained in it the traditions of Saxon, Norman, Elizabethan, religion unbroken,—the memory of loyalty, the reality of learning, and, in nominal obedience at least, and in the heart of them with true docility, stood every morning, to be animated for the highest duties owed to their country, the noblest of English youth. The greater number of the peers of England, and as a rule, the best of her squirealty, passed necessarily through Christ Church.

Laced with Victorian certainties, Ruskin's account speaks of the history embedded in the fabric of the building and of how the mind is drawn back in time by the surrounding features. Back to the Oxford Movement by the bust of Pusey, an early ally of Newman; back to Robert Burton by his bust and melancholy countenance surmounted by the horoscope forecasting the time of his death. The fifteenth-century vaulting on the roof of the choir, the fourteenth-century Latin chapel, the thirteenth- and twelfth-century nave and transepts lead further back in time, back to the mid-twelfth century when work on the building first began and the medieval town of Oxford knew not a single college. One feature leads back even beyond this to Saxon times and the very origins of the city, for in the north-eastern part of the cathedral, not far from the altar, stands the shrine of St. Frideswide, a virgin saint who gave birth to a city as Pallas Athene before her. On the side of the shrine is a carving which depicts a face peering out from between oak leaves, a curiously pagan element in a house of Christ, for the Druidic sacred tree was also a symbol of Zeus, the god of lightning which plays such an important part in the legend. In the east window of the Latin Chapel is the stained-glass recreation of the story by Edward Burne-Jones which features Frideswide's assailant being struck blind, together with the treacle-well at Binsey from which sprang the water with which his eyes were bathed. It is a Christian story wrapped around with pagan import and mythic association—the story, in short, of an English Athens. Here by the shrine it is possible to pause in contemplation and commune with the spirit of place. 'I do not envy', wrote Falconer Madan, 'the disposition of a person who can stand at this Place of Pilgrimage and remain unmoved.'

Outside the cathedral the college walls speak of confinement. 'It was a matter of architecture more than anything else', writes Sheed of the college type, an observation which might be equally applied to the literature for its character is writ large in the physical structure: the dreaming spires and privileged circumstance; the insularity and eccentricity; the ivory tower and the exclusivity; the architectural magnificence and the self-satisfaction; the academic grove and the enchantment; the cloistered utopia and the dreamlike existence; the closed world and the absurdity; the sense of the past and of continuity. 'The individual passes, but the college goes on' runs the last sentence of J.C. Masterman's *An Oxford Tragedy*. It could serve as literary epitaph. Yet beyond this one senses something deeper in the literature struggling to be heard, something more prophetic and more compelling. The English Athens; seat of the English Muses; the terrestrial Elysium; the sacred city; the enchanted garden; the New Jerusalem; a patrician paradise; Tir-na-nog; the Hesperian Isles; Shangri-La; lotus-land; Wonderland—what lies behind this hyperbolic *mélange* of utopian vision and golden age analogue? What indeed is the unutterable secret that yearns to be told? C.S. Lewis, the man who for many Christians held all the answers, suggests an answer here also.

Lewis was very much a traditionalist for whom myth, symbol and magic were an important means of getting at deeper truths, and his writings were fed by a fertile imagination (as with Lewis Carroll, this may have been linked to a disturbed subconscious stemming from repressed emotions). Because of his gift for lucidity, Lewis was able to order the products of his imagination in a manner which speak simultaneously to different levels of reality, and this gives his writings a powerful resonance. This can be seen in one of his lesser-known novels, a spiritual thriller entitled *That Hideous Strength* (1945) written under the influence of Charles Williams, which draws on the 'Matter of Britain' to depict the forces of good as heirs to the Arthurian tradition in opposition to those driven by a modern, mechanistic view of life. Of the two institutions in this mythopoeic world one is a sinister scientific institution and the other an academic college whose description in the passage below is full of potent signification.

> If you came in from the street and went through the College. . . , the sense of gradual penetration into a holy of holies was very strong. First you went through the Newton quadrangle which is dry and gravelly; florid but beautiful. Georgian buildings look down upon it. Next you must enter a cool tunnel-like passage, nearly dark at midday unless either the door into the Hall should be open on your right or the buttery hatch on your left, giving you a glimpse of indoor daylight falling on panels, and a whiff of the smell of fresh bread. When you emerged from this tunnel you would find yourself in the medieval college: in the cloister of the much smaller quadrangle called Republic. The grass here looks very green after the aridity of Newton and the very stone of the buttresses that rise from it gives the impression of being soft and alive. Chapel is not far off: the hoarse, heavy noise of the works of a great and old clock comes to you from somewhere overhead. You walk along this cloister, past slabs and urns and busts that commemorate dead Bractonians, and then down shallow steps into the full daylight of the quadrangle called Lady Alice. The buildings to your left and right were seventeenth-century work: humble, almost domestic in character, with dormer windows, mossy and grey-tiled. You were in a sweet, Protestant world. You found yourself, perhaps, thinking of Bunyan or of Walton's *Lives*. There were no buildings straight ahead on the fourth side of Lady Alice: only a row of elms and a wall; and here first one became aware of the sound of running water, and the cooing of wood pigeons. The street was so far off by now that there were no other noises. In the wall there was a door. It led into a covered gallery pierced with narrow windows on each side. Looking out from these you discovered that you were crossing a bridge and the dark dimpled Wynd was flowing under you. Now you were very near your goal. A wicket at the end of the bridge brought you out on the Fellows' bowling-green, and across that you saw the high wall of the Wood, and through the Inigo Jones gate you caught a glimpse of sunlit green and deep shadows. . . .
>
> Half a mile is a short walk. Yet it seemed a long time before I came to the centre of the Wood. I knew it was the centre, for there was the thing I had chiefly come to see. It was a well: a well with steps going down to it and the remains of an ancient pavement about it. I did not step on it, but I lay down in the grass and touched it with my fingers. For this was the heart of Bracton or Bragdon wood: out of this all the legends had come and on this, I suspected, the very existence of the College had originally depended.

The journey to the heart of the college follows an architectural path which leads from the present to the well of prehistory, and the physical description of the college evokes a gnostic vision. The well at the centre of the wood is consecrated to the memory of Merlin, and each warden of Bracton drinks a draught of water on the day of his election in a Grail-like chalice which invokes the spirit of Arthur's advisor. Like the wine of holy communion, it marks a sacramental pledge. The 'hidden strength' transmitted from generation to generation is drawn both literally and metaphorically from deep within the native soil, and in the waters of the ancient well of knowledge lies the essence of Englishness. Nature is seen here in romantic terms as the motherland which gives birth and nour-ishment to the national character, for the wood around the well has associations with divine knowledge, while water carries connotations with the unconscious and intuitive wisdom. Taken together, the phallic trees and vulvic well denote the conception and birth of the native cul-ture. Tellingly, the progressive element in college wish to sell off the wood, for they only see its material value. To the defenders of tradition this is tantamount to selling off the national birthright.

Lewis was not the first to give expression to such ideas, and indeed they have roots in the earth magic of ancient times and esoteric cults like the priests of the Delphic oracle. In medieval times too, when enquiry into the world was considered in teleological terms to lead closer to heaven, the university was seen as a magical locus of hidden knowledge, and in one of his sermons the poet John Donne extolled the university in terms borrowed from the biblical imagery of the Song of Solomon.

> The University is a Paradise, Rivers of Knowledge are there, Arts and Sci-ences flow from thence. Counsell Tables are *Horti conclusi,* (as it is said in the Canticles) *Gardens that are walled in,* and they are *Fontes signati, Wells that are sealed up;* bottomless depths of unsearchable Counsels there.

Donne's secret gardens and sealed wells speak to Lewis's vision in that both are based on an exclusive view of knowledge. The mystification of learning served to confer an aura of power on initiates, for others had to literally take their word, be they king or peasant. The favouring of the university in medieval times after the riots between town and gown illus-trates the practical benefits that accrued from the possession of knowl-edge, and it was because the stakes were so high that scholarly rivalry was intense and accusations of heresy widespread. A little learning could indeed prove dangerous.

In Fowles's *Daniel Martin,* interestingly, it is suggested that the desire to withhold is a national characteristic exemplified by Newman and his followers, who felt 'the necessity of hiding inner religious mysteries and feelings from the vulgar'. This, it is claimed, was 'very English' and an indication of how 'quintessentially English the Oxford Movement was'. It is a notion which taps into the current of Oxford literature. From its earliest beginnings, from Chaucer's saintly clerk indeed, Oxford as guardian of the national culture has been a reiterated theme—seat of the Muses in Elizabethan times, royalist capital in the seventeenth century, home of the imagination for Romantics, soul of the country for the Oxford Movement, the navel of the nation for Ruskin, the best of England for Edwardians, 'the most English of all cities' for John Fowles, and for Jan Morris 'Oxford is always a mirror of England. She draws her inspiration from the genius of the nation, and all her faults and virtues, all her scars and pleasures, are but microcosms of a greater model.' Literary Oxford, then, is posited as lying at the heart of England, at once an abstraction of its salient features and a summation of its achievements. This book has shown that the equation can be further reduced, for at the heart of the word-city lies the college, and one college in particular. 'In Oxford there is no need to make a microcosm', writes Peter Conrad. 'It is ready-made for one in the form of Christ Church, the largest college in the university and the most imposing, a city or little England in itself.' Here then is the construct the literature would have its readership subscribe to—Oxford's epitome is the nation's. The college is the House the nation built to honour God and literature.

The equating of Christ Church in this way with the myth of the English Athens has little to do with merit or talent (judged on those terms, Balliol would be a more obvious choice). It suggests rather a national propensity for exclusivity and cliquishness (at least among the ruling classes), for as Linda Colley has noted, 'Oxford colleges, like those of Cambridge, have always represented much more than material wealth. They are rather a prime expression of what Tocqueville rightly diagnosed as the stereotypical English institution—the club.' Though the ostensible purpose of clubs is purely social, historically they have also served as an important means of male networking and power-broking which has been achieved at the expense of those who are excluded from membership. The desire for greater openness in recent times has led to a reaction against such clubbishness, and starting with Hardy writers have shown a concern to offer more inclusive visions of Oxford. The process of demythologising which has accompanied this has been part of a wider move in postimperial Britain to shake off the past, and rejection of the English Athens can be seen as part of the process of discarding outworn myths. 'Yes / You have come upon the fabled lands where myths / Go when they die', writes James Fenton of 'The Pitt-Rivers Museum' (1983), though the lines might be applied more widely. Discontinuity

has become the great theme of the times, and grandiose pronounce-
ments about a major cultural turning-point are all too common in the fin
de siècle atmosphere. Even the classical tradition which was once held
sacrosanct has come under increasing attack, and the sentimental ties
with ancient Greece are no longer what they once were. The prolifera-
tion of 'post-' as the favoured prefix for current movements suggest that
though the future may become post-industrial, post-Christian, post-
humanist (even, alarmingly post-human in some book titles), the present age has yet to take proper shape and find a definition of its own. This
may be because of the rapidity with which horizons are shifting as new
ways emerge of seeing the world. In cultural terms the traditional sense
of Englishness has been shown to be a social construction favourable to
the ruling élite, and this has led to a sense of unease about the national
sense of self. On the one hand there is a desire to move away from the
privileged past, but on the other a reluctance to jettison an inheritance
which is widely admired. The debate about the heritage industry illustrates the dilemma which the country faces in terms of forging a new
identity, for attachment to the past remains one of the salient national
characteristics. Traditional images often present a more comforting picture than the disturbing alternatives offered in their stead, and given the
choice most people would seem to prefer a Merchant-Ivory view of the
country to that of Derek Jarman whose *The Last of England* (1987), for
example, juxtaposes heroic images of wartime Britain with sinister
scenes of state exploitation and authoritarianism. As the country at large
wrestles with the national destiny, a similar discourse is playing itself out
in the literature of Oxford, where the traditional city is being reimaged
as one that accommodates a diverse and heterogeneous population.
Interestingly, this new city has more in common with its medieval
antecedent than with the Oxford myth of college-bound stories and
utopian visions. As the millennium draws to a close, it is hard to resist the
feeling that the shift of focus signifies an important historical development. If, as Capricorn implies, the death of the old is a necessary prelude
to renewal and rebirth, then the present period surely signifies the
labour pains of a new order. In the undoing of the English Athens there
lies the making of an altogether different kind of Oxford.

Appendixes

A Glossary of Oxford Terms

The Act   The former name for the degree-giving ceremony and festivities at the end of the academic year. The rituals included the satirical performance of *Terrae Filius* which upset John Evelyn when he heard it in 1669. The last Act took place in 1733 when Handel played in the Sheldonian Theatre, since which time Encaenia has taken its place.

A Blue   An award given to a sportsman or woman who has taken part in an officially sanctioned match against Cambridge University. The Oxford colour is dark blue and that of Cambridge light blue (a tradition which dates back to the 1836 boat race).

Bulldogs   University police who work under the proctors. The term suggests the tenacious courage or fierceness of the animal and dates back to the beginning of the nineteenth century, though the police existed long beyond that. In *Verdant Green* Bradley accompanies his description of a town and gown fight with an illustration depicting the intervention of a proctor in cap and gown accompanied by three beefy bulldogs with top hats, buttoned coats, and sticks. (The bulldogs subsequently adopted bowler hats.)

Cambridge   Traditionally referred to as 'the other place' and still put down for being an off-shoot of Oxford ('ford' comes before 'bridge', it is pointed out). Following riots in Oxford in 1209 when two clerks were killed, many university members resettled in Cambridge, since which time the two universities have engaged in friendly rivalry symbolised by the sporting matches and annual boat race. Until 1826 and the launch of London University, Oxford and Cambridge were the only institutions of higher education in England (Scotland had its own universities), and though they developed in tandem, they had distinctive traditions—Thomas Hardy claimed that Oxford was the romantic university and Cambridge the intellectual. Oxford was associated with the humanities, Anglo-Catholicism, and 'lost causes'; Cambridge with science, Protestantism, and the many poets it produced. Cambridge was also more progressive in some matters, such as the admission of Dissenters (non-Anglican Protestants) in the early nineteenth century which Oxford strongly resisted. In the twentieth century, matters have changed, and Oxford now rivals Cambridge as a centre of science while Cambridge has also been prominent in literature (when C.S. Lewis transferred from Magdalen [Oxford] to Magdalene [Cambridge] in the 1950s he spoke of moving from a culture of philosophy [logical positivists] to one of criticism

[Leavisites]). For an account of Cambridge literature, see Graham Chainey, *A Literary History of Cambridge* (first published in 1985 and recently revised).

Canons of Christ Church   Members of the clergy who are part of the cathedral chapter and who also serve on the governing body of the college. There are six altogether, four of whom are theological professors at the university and one the archdeacon of Oxford (the first lay canon was recently appointed). In pre-reform times they were allowed to marry, and some such as John Fell rose to become Dean. The most colourful of the canons was the geologist William Buckland (1784–1856), whose rooms in a corner of Tom Quad contained fossils, rocks, and a menagerie of owls, ferrets, hawks, guinea pigs, a bear, a pony, and a jackal. (Buckland later became dean of Westminster.)

Chancellor   A position which is now largely honorific but which in former times represented the real authority in the university. The office dates back to the early thirteenth century, and until Elizabethan times the chancellor was a guiding force in university matters. Robert Dudley, earl of Leicester, was the first to appoint a vice-chancellor, and after the Restoration the office of chancellor became restricted to ceremonies. The office holder is elected for life by all those Oxford masters of arts who turn up in person to vote. In 1987, there were 8,309 votes out of a potential 40,000, resulting in the election of Roy Jenkins, the present chancellor, over Edward Heath and Lord Blake. Past chancellors include Robert Grosseteste (c. 1224–1231), who taught Roger Bacon and was a noted translator from the Greek; Archbishop Laud (1630–41), who revised the university statutes; Oliver Cromwell (1650–57), who was refused permission to take a book out of the Bodleian (as it is a non-lending library); Edward Hyde, the earl of Clarendon (1660–67), author of the *History of the Rebellion;* and the victor of Waterloo, the duke of Wellington (1834–52), who originated the well-known maxim, 'Publish and be damned'.

Clerk   The term was originally applied to all those in holy orders, but as they were the only people allowed to study at the medieval university, it took on the added meaning of a learned or educated person (and by a further extension in modern times, any kind of clerical worker). Chaucer's Clerk of Oxenford is the model representative.

Clubs   Of the many university clubs and societies (two hundred or so registered at present), a few date back to the nineteenth century and have achieved prominence in literary terms. The **Bullingdon Club,** a socially exclusive dining club with a membership of about twenty, is caricatured by Evelyn Waugh as the Bollinger Club at the beginning of *Decline and Fall.* The dinner-jacketed, upper-class members (often old Etonians) were notorious for their riotous and drunken dinner parties which invariably attracted the attention of the Proctors. (The club, which meets once a term, took its name from the Bullingdon Point-to-Point with which it used to be connected.) The **Gridiron Club,** which Compton Mackenzie's *Sinister Street* brackets in the same class as the Bullingdon, was founded in 1884 by Lord Cranbourne as an intercollegiate dining-club. Unlike the Bullingdon, the Gridiron (or 'Grid' as Fane calls it) had its own premises, which in Edwardian times used to be in High Street. In 1913 its members included the Prince of Wales, the crown prince of Norway and the prince of Serbia as well as Harold Macmillan and Ronald Knox. Another notable university club is **Vincent's,** now housed in Broad Street, which started as a club for a hundred outstanding university men but has since become associated with sports. In the survey of clubs in *Sinister Street,* Michael Fane observes that Vincent's is the 'last stronghold of muscular supremacy'; that OUDS fosters a 'premature worldliness'; that the Bullingdon 'had too much money and not enough unhampered humanity'; that the Union was 'too indiscriminate'; and that the Grid to which Michael Fane attaches himself is 'the abode of discreet good-fellowship'. In *Zuleika Dobson* Max Beerbohm parodies the exclusivity of such clubs in the imaginary Junta of which the duke of Dorset in his second year becomes the sole member since no one else is considered good enough to be elected.

College   An independent and autonomous institution to which senior and junior members of the university are attached. There are thirty-seven at present (for a listing see appendix B). Until 1878 all colleges were for males, though now all are coeducational except for St. Hilda's, which is for female students only. Colleges cater for a range of different subjects, and their buildings form a 'mini-campus' on which typically there is a dining hall, a chapel, a library, common rooms, and gardens. Accommodation is usually arranged vertically around staircases. Until recent times colleges were self-contained and their members were subject to strict rules of dress and behaviour. There was also a curfew when the college gates shut, and latecomers had to climb over walls or in through windows—the Oxford novel is full of such incidents. The means of ingress were well-known even to the authorities, and when Ved Mehta was at Balliol in the 1950s the dean of the college himself pointed out to how to enter after lock-up.

Commemoration   The former week-long celebration at the end of Trinity Term which included degree rituals, balls and rowing-races in memory of the founders and benefactors of the university. Two ceremonies still survive, Encaenia and the service for the university's benefactors, as do the Commemoration Balls. These are held by colleges on a three-year cycle so that each undergraduate member might have an opportunity to attend once during their student career (some colleges have abandoned the tradition in recent years). Verdant Green attended a Commemoration Ball at his college (based on Brasenose) in 1853, and Hardy's Jude Fawley dies against a background of Commemoration festivities.

Commoner   Traditionally, a member of a college who pays for board and lodging, unlike those 'on the foundation' such as fellows and scholars. Before the Elizabethan period commoners were few in number, but their number increased rapidly thereafter until they formed the bulk of the undergraduates. The **gentle-**

man-commoner paid extra fees in return for certain privileges (such as sharing amenities reserved for fellows). With their leisured ways they came to dominate the social life of the university until the reforms of the nineteenth century abolished the distinctions between commoners. Today the same charges are levied on all undergraduates, whether scholars or commoners, and are met by grants, loans or personal funding.

Dean   At Christ Church this refers to the head of the college, who is also head, or dean, of the cathedral. Famous holders of the office include Dean Liddell, father of the real-life Alice. At other colleges 'dean' is the title of the fellow responsible for disciplinary and advisory matters. As dean of Balliol, Francis Urquhart (Sligger) is said to have used his position to cultivate a large circle of admirers. (To distinguish between the two meanings, a capital letter is used in the text when referring to the Dean of Christ Church.)

Don   A teacher at the university (taken from the Latin *dominus,* master). Until the reforms of the late nineteenth century, dons were in clerical orders, unmarried, untrained and unsackable (only professors and heads of houses were allowed to marry). In such conditions eccentricity flourished, and in 'Lines to a Don' Hilaire Belloc attacked a 'Remote and ineffectual Don' and compared him unfavourably with 'Dons Admirable! Dons of Might!' in a verse which ends, 'Dons perpetual that remain, / A landmark, walling in the plain.'

Eights Week   Formerly a week, this is now four days of inter-collegiate rowing races which take place on the fifth week of Hilary Term. It marks one of the highlights of the social calendar with students lining the banks to cheer on their college crews, with Pimms, strawberries, and straw hats much in evidence. (In former times some stately college barges moored along the side of the Thames made for an even grander occasion. These have been replaced by a row of college boat-houses.) The races date from around 1815, and the name derives from the eight rowers who together with a cox comprise the crew. Boats are entered from each college and race at timed intervals with the purpose of 'bumping' the boat in front and so starting ahead of it the next day. The order of boats is held over from year to year, and the boat at the top of the first division is known as Head of the River. The finale of *Zuleika Dobson* is set in Eights Week, when not only the duke of Dorset but the whole student population drown themselves for love of the heroine.

Encaenia   The ceremony for the giving of honorary degrees which takes place in the ninth week of Trinity Term at which prize-winning compositions, including the Newdigate, are recited. The word is taken from the Latin *encaenia* meaning dedication, a reference to that of the Sheldonian Theatre in 1669, when the ceremony was transferred there from the University Church. Encaenia features as a background to the laying out of the corpse of Jude Fawley.

Fellow   A person who has been elected to the governing board of a college. He or she will usually have teaching duties, though not necessarily. In the pre-reform university many fellows had little to do with their college except for attending the occasional meeting. For those in residence (only some of whom were employed as tutors) college life could be agreeable; Thomas Warton celebrated the joys in *The Progress of Discontent,* in which he writes of fellows living like 'petty kings'. The reforms of the mid–nineteenth century abolished sinecures and family connections, and further changes came in 1878 when fellows for the first time were allowed to marry, as a result of which many set up home in North Oxford rather than live in college. Thereafter fellowship became more attractive as a long-term career, and the average age increased dramatically from pre-reform times. The number of fellows varies from college to college: in 1987 All Souls had sixty-four fellows, twelve visiting fellows, two readers and lecturers (the latter being few in number since the college has no students); Trinity on the other hand had twenty-four fellows, four junior research fellows, and twenty-two lecturers. An **honorary fellow** enjoys dining rights and certain other privileges. The election of Thomas Hardy to an honorary fellowship of Queen's College is a case in point, though that of John Betjeman to the college from which he failed to graduate, Magdalen, is also noteworthy.

First/Second/Third/Fourth Class degree   This refers to the classification of the honours system introduced in the nineteenth century for undergraduate degree courses. Candidates are judged according to their performance in their final examinations: the top classification is a First, and the large majority of students receive Seconds (since 1986 this has been divided into an Upper Second and a Lower Second). The Fourth Class was abolished in the 1960s, and those not considered worthy of an honours degree receive a simple pass. (By a curious anomaly arising from medieval times, students who have passed B.A. can proceed to their M.A. with no examination and the payment of a small fee seven years after matriculation.) The first class lists were for Literae Humaniores and Mathematics in 1807, with Natural Science, Law, and Modern History following in 1853. Theology, Oriental Languages, and English Language were introduced before the end of the nineteenth century. There are now thirty-seven schools of study in nineteen faculties. Oscar Wilde distinguished himself by getting a double First (a First in both Mods and Greats). W.H. Auden, on the other hand, got a Third, as did Evelyn Waugh, who later expressed annoyance at wasting his summer term studying, as he would happily have settled for a Fourth. Others leaving without a degree include P.B. Shelley, who was expelled, Thomas De Quincey, who disliked the examination system, Algernon Swinburne, who was occupied with other matters, and John Betjeman, who failed the compulsory Divinity Examination (later abolished). A.E. Housman failed his finals altogether but later became professor of Latin at Cambridge!

Gaudy   A college reunion which allows former students to meet at seven- to ten-year intervals. The word derives from the Latin *gaudere,* to rejoice, and its usage dates back at least to Elizabethan times, when it simply referred to a (commemorative) feast. Both Dorothy Sayers *(Gaudy Night)* and J.I.M. Stewart *(The Gaudy)* made use of the term to signify the collegiate content of their books.

Go up, be up, go down   Terms for entering, attending, and leaving the university. It is said that the origin lies in the notion of education as a means of going up in the world or of improving oneself spiritually (going up to the 'heights' of Oxford), though some have suggested it is connected with the geographical position of Oxford in relation to London. Correct usage of the terms conveys a sense of belonging (and some would say superiority). When an innocent freshman in *Patchwork* asks, 'By the way, d'you go back to Oxford to-morrow?' he is put in his place by the curt retort, 'I go up.' The title of Ved Mehta's memoir, *Up at Oxford,* suggests through its choice of language an identification with the university.

Greats   The final examination for Literae Humaniores and also the name by which the school of study is known. Greats was the preferred subject in the late Victorian university, and among those who distinguished themselves by getting Firsts were G.M. Hopkins, Oscar Wilde and John Buchan.

Head of house   This is used to refer to the head of a college, a position which carries considerable prestige. The head is housed separately within the college in accommodation which is often set in a walled and private garden. In pre-reform times, unlike other members of the college, the head was allowed to marry and was an important person socially who set the tone for the college as a whole. Figures like Benjamin Jowett and Mark Pattison single-handedly transformed the reputation of their colleges. The appellation of the head varies from college to college as follows: 'master'—University, Balliol, Pembroke, St. Peter's, St. Catherine's, and St. Cross; 'warden'—Merton, New College, All Souls, Wadham, Keble, St. Antony's, Nuffield, and Green College; 'rector'—Exeter and Lincoln; 'provost'—Oriel, Queen's, and Worcester; 'president'—Magdalen, Brasenose, Trinity, St. John's, and Wolfson; 'principal'—Brasenose, Jesus, Hertford, Lady Margaret Hall, Somerville, St. Hugh's, St. Hilda's, St. Anne's, St. Edmund Hall, and Linacre; 'Dean'—Christ Church.

The House   This is used to refer to Christ Church (in the sense of distinguishing it from the other 'houses' or colleges). The expression is said to derive from the Latin title for Christ Church, *Aedes Christi* or House of Christ. In earlier times students attached great kudos to use of the term: when Mackenzie's Fane says to a fellow freshman, 'You seem to have found out a great deal about Christ Church already,' he is immediately corrected and told of the 'proper' term for Christ Church.

Literae Humaniores   The faculty for classics, philosophy, and ancient history, the course in which takes four years (nearly all others take three years). It is divided into two parts, Mods and Greats (by which term the course is also known). In Victorian and Edwardian times this was considered the most prestigious course, and for Mackenzie's Michael Fane it represented the very essence of the university.

Matriculation   The official enrolment of a student into the university. (The word derives from the Latin *matricula*, a roll.) From 1420 onwards this has involved a ceremony of some kind before the chancellor or vice-chancellor. In the pre-reform university matriculants had to take an oath of supremacy and subscribe to the Thirty-nine Articles (this was to ensure that all members were Anglicans). The modern ceremony is performed in the Sheldonian Theatre shortly after the beginning of Michaelmas Term, when new college members are presented to the vice-chancellor by their senior tutor or dean of degrees.

May morning   A festivity peculiar to Oxford when hundreds of people gather at six o'clock in the morning to hear choristers sing an invocation to summer from the top of Magdalen College Tower. The custom dates back at least to the early sixteenth century, when it may have begun as part of an inauguration ceremony. In Victorian times Holman Hunt's painting, *May Morning on Magdalen Tower*, brought the event to national attention, and it became fashionable to stay up all night and celebrate the morning singing in punts moored beneath the tower (this was later banned after rowdy behaviour resulted in mishaps and damage to the punts). In recent years streets have been closed to traffic to allow Morris dancing, busking and impromptu performances to take place. In *Sinister Street* there is a description of the Edwardian celebrations when Michael Fane experiences an epiphany as he listens to the pagan invocation on the top of the Tower and views the city 'imprisoned in a crystal globe'. 'For Michael the moment of waiting for the first shaft of the sun was scarcely to be endured: the vision of the city below was almost too poignant during the hush of expectancy that preceded the declaration of worship. There flashed a silver beam in the east: the massed choir boys with one accord opened their mouths and sang just exactly, Michael said to himself, like the morning stars.'

Mods (Classical Honour Moderations)   The first examination in a school of study (such as Literae Humaniores) taken in the first or second year of study. Oscar Wilde read of his First in Mods while reading *The Times* during breakfast at the Mitre. In Beerbohm's *Zuleika Dobson* the duke of Dorset shows his effortless brilliance by taking a First in Mods without studying.

Newdigate Prize   The university competition for English verse composition on a set subject. It dates back to 1806 when it was begun by Sir Roger Newdigate of University College. The competition is judged by the professor of poetry and a panel of judges, and the winning entry is read out by the author at Encaenia. Past winners have included John Ruskin (1839), F.W. Faber (1836), Matthew Arnold (1843), J.A. Symonds (1860), Oscar Wilde (1878), Arthur Waugh (1888), Laurence Binyon (1890), John Buchan (1898), Julian Huxley (1908), John Bayley

(1950), Jon Stallworthy (1958), John Fuller (1960), James Fenton (1968), and Andrew Motion (1975). There are several other university awards, such as the Hertford in Latin, the Gaisford in Greek, and the Chancellor's Prizes, which date back to 1768. Past winners for the latter include: for Latin Verse, R.A. Knox (1910); for Latin Prose, John Keble (1812), Thomas Arnold (1817), E.B. Pusey (1822), and Benjamin Jowett (1841); and for the English Essay, John Keble (1812), Thomas Arnold (1815), J.A. Froude (1842), J.A. Symonds (1863), and C.S. Lewis (1921). Beerbohm's duke of Dorset enjoys a glittering undergraduate career in *Zuleika Dobson* and wins four university prizes, including the Newdigate. In recent years prizes have lost their former prestige—multiple prizewinners such as R.A. Knox, who won four separate prizes, used to be celebrated figures in university circles.

Oxford University Dramatic Society (OUDS)   Founded in 1884, this flourished in the inter-war years, when professional directors were often involved. Compton Mackenzie was an early and enthusiastic member. From 1935 onwards a guiding hand was taken by Neville Coghill (1899–1980), fellow of Exeter, translator of medieval literature, and the tutor of W.H. Auden and Richard Burton (the latter of whom attended a special war-time course while attached to the R.A.F. and gave an outstanding performance in an OUDS production of *Measure for Measure*). Among the students involved in inter-war productions were Terence Rattigan, Raymond Massey, George Devine, John Betjeman, Osbert Lancaster, and Peter Fleming. The 1933 production of *A Midsummer Night's Dream* on the slopes of Headington Hill was considered particularly memorable, but even this was outdone by Coghill's production of *The Tempest* in 1949 by Worcester College lake, which ended at dusk with Caliban returning to his submerged tank, Prospero drowning his books and sailing off with the others into the darkness, and Ariel appearing to dart across the water and run up among the trees to disappear in a flash of light. Among those starring in OUDS following World War II were John Schlesinger, Tony Richardson, Kenneth Tynan, Robert Robinson, Shirley Williams, Ronald Eyre, Lindsay Anderson, and Michael York. Coghill had founded the Experimental Theatre Club (ETC) in 1936 for more adventurous productions, and he was also instrumental in the acquisition of the Oxford Playhouse by the university in 1961 and in the establishment of the Taylor-Burton Rooms in 1974 with money donated by film stars Richard Burton and Elizabeth Taylor (they also raised funds through a production of *Doctor Faustus* at the playhouse in 1966). Diana Quick became the first woman president of OUDS in 1968, and two of the *Monty Python* team (Michael Palin and Terry Jones) as well as Rowan Atkinson were involved as students in university drama productions. In recent years the establishment of a Cameron Mackintosh Chair of Contemporary Theatre Studies (present holder Richard Eyre) has served to further interest in drama at the university.

Oxonian   (A member) of Oxford University (also used sometimes to refer to a citizen of Oxford). The word is used both as a noun and adjective and derives from a Latinized form of the old name of the city, Oxen(ford). The secondary meaning as a citizen is relatively uncommon, and books such as L.R. Farnell's *An Oxonian Looks Back* (1934) clearly imply a university connection.

To plough/be ploughed   To fail an exam. Henry Bouncer of Bradley's *Verdant Green* maintains that as a man from Harrow he should not be ploughed.

Proctors   University officers elected from among college fellows to be in charge of discipline and administrative matters. The office dates back to the thirteenth century, and in the pre-reform university proctors held wide-ranging powers, even over townspeople. Accompanied by bulldogs, the proctor patrolled Oxford streets at night looking for errant students. Miscreants were asked for their name and college, and the following day they would be summoned to answer for themselves. When Cecil Rhodes, already a successful entrepreneur, was accosted by a proctor in 1873, he allegedly gave the information required of him and then demanded, 'Now, sir, may I ask *your* name and college?' Though their powers have lessened in recent time, proctors remain important officials within the university.

Professors/readers/lecturers   Faculty members whose duties include giving lectures, supervising graduates, and research. Within each of the university's nineteen faculties there are departments, the chair of which holds the title of professor (regius professorships refer to those founded by a ruling monarch). Other departmental members are ranked as readers or lecturers. In the pre-reform university teaching was not regarded highly and emoluments were honorary; college fellowship was of greater importance. As regius professor of Greek the respected scholar and Dean of Christ Church, Thomas Gaiford (1779–1855), never taught or gave a single lecture. Following the reforms of the nineteenth century, professorships grew in importance and in number: in 1800 there were only 21 professors; by 1900 the number had risen to 54; and by 1990 there were over 150. In recent years it was decided to open the title up to a much larger number of academics, so as to be more in keeping with the American model.

Professor of Poetry   A position with a nominal stipend lasting for five years which was established in 1708 by Henry Birkhead. Unlike other professorships, it was left untouched by the reforms of the nineteenth century. All Oxford masters of arts are eligible to vote in the election for the professorship by turning up in person. Past holders have included Thomas Warton (1718–28), John Keble (1831–41), Matthew Arnold (1857–67), C. Day-Lewis (1951–56), W.H. Auden (1956–61), Edmund Blunden (1966–68), John Wain (1973–78), Peter Levi (1984–89), and Seamus Heaney (1989–94). James Fenton is the holder at the time of writing.

Punting   The punt is a narrow river craft (about three foot by twenty-five foot), propelled by a long pole thrust against the river-bottom. Punting for pleasure developed after the 1860s, though the modern form of punt with four seats facing inwards was not introduced until the 1880s. Punting takes place on both the Cherwell and the Thames, and it remains one of Oxford's most popular summer activities. In *Those Barren Leaves* Aldous Huxley wrote of the attractions of punting on a summer evening: 'A yellow moon as large as a pumpkin shone overhead; there were gleamings on the crests of the ripples and in the troughs of the tiny waves, left in the wakes of the punts, shadows of almost absolute blackness. The leaves of the willow trees shone like metal. A white mist lay along the meadows.'

Rhodes Scholarships   Founded by Cecil Rhodes (1853–1902) to promote justice, liberty and peace through the benefits of an Oxford education. Since Rhodes wished to foster a union of English-speaking peoples, the scholarships were restricted to former colonies, though Germany was also included because of its influence and power at that time. The first Rhodes scholars arrived in Oxford in 1903 (their arrival is welcomed in Mackenzie's *Sinister Street* as proving that Oxford is the 'home of living causes'), and there are now over seventy drawn from some eighteen countries (more than a third come from the United States). The scale of the operation necessitates about one hundred selection committees around the world, and former scholars have included Edward de Bono, Kris Kristofferson, President Clinton, and several overseas prime ministers. American Rhodes scholars are treated by Beerbohm in *Zuleika Dobson* as an exotic addition to Oxford's social life, distinguished by a 'splendid native gift of oratory, and their modest desire to please, and their not less evident feeling that they ought merely to edify, and their constant delight in all that of Oxford their English brethren don't notice'.

Royal commissions/reform   Because of the reluctance of a conservative-minded university to reform itself in the nineteenth and early twentieth century, change was imposed by Parliament following the establishment of royal commissions. The first of these was appointed in 1850 by the prime minister, Lord John Russell. The university refused to cooperate, though some liberals such as Henry Liddell offered evidence in a written report. The areas of investigation included a restricted curriculum; the high cost; incompetent fellows; bad teaching; and the exclusion of non-Anglicans and the poor. The result was the **University Reform Act of 1854,** which owed itself in large measure to W.E. Gladstone, aided by Benjamin Jowett. This introduced a new constitution, revisions to college statutes, changes in the fellowship system, new honours schools, and the acceptance of non-Anglicans as undergraduates. Thereafter university conservatives struggled to maintain the clerical and classical character of the university by insisting on religious tests and compulsory Greek. This led to the setting up of another royal commission in 1871 which resulted in the **University Reform Act of 1877.** Its main features were the promotion of research; the creation of new laboratories; the financial contribution of richer colleges to a common university fund; and the removal of religious restrictions for fellows, including the requirement for celibacy. Thereafter demands for further reform were resisted until after World War I, when falling agricultural revenues led to financial difficulties and the university applied for a government grant. This occasioned another royal commission under H.H. Asquith which led to the **University Reform Act of 1923,** when faculties and the professorial system were reorganised; greater weight was given to the university over individual colleges; and a form of university entrance examination was introduced (colleges were formerly responsible for their own intake). Following World War II, the university showed how much its attitude had changed by itself appointing the **Franks Commission** of 1964 to suggest improvements and maintain its international standing in the face of increased competition. Recommendations concerned administrative and financial reform, the nature of expansion, reform of the admission system, and the setting up of a Council of Colleges. (At the time of writing the **North Commission** is reviewing university operations, though it has yet to report its findings.)

Rusticated   To be temporarily expelled from the university, e.g., for one or two terms (from the Latin *rusticari*, to live in the country). The explorer Richard Burton (1821–90), translator of *Arabian Nights* (1885–88), *The Kama Sutra* (1883), and *The Perfumed Garden* (1886), was frequently in trouble with the authorities at Trinity and was rusticated in 1842 for attending an expressly forbidden race-meeting. He took the opportunity to give up the university altogether and left in a horse and carriage, driving over the college flower beds and ostentatiously blowing kisses at the women in the High Street.

Scholar   In medieval times nearly all members of a college were scholars since they received free board and lodging 'on the foundation'. In time the term 'scholar' became synonymous with an academic or learned person, even if the person concerned was paying fees. Nowadays the term is used in both senses, referring both to those who have been awarded a scholarship by their college (nowadays a nominal amount) and to those steeped in learning. C.S. Lewis, for example, was first a scholar at University College and later a respected scholar of English literature while a fellow of Magdalen. Oscar Wilde held a 'demyship' at Magdalen, a scholarship which is half *(demi-)* the full amount.

Schools   As well as denoting the different schools of study, this refers to the Examination Schools in High Street and by extension the final examinations for degree courses which are held there. Examinations have to done in 'sub-fusc' (required clothing also for matriculation and degree ceremonies), which comprises dark suit, white shirt and white bow tie for men; black skirt or trousers, white blouse and black tie for women. At the end of the last paper of the final examinations it is customary for students to be met outside by friends with a celebratory bottle of champagne. Oscar Wilde is remembered for his ostentatious display of walking out noisily half an hour before the end of an examination and still getting the best result of his year.

Scout   A term dating back to the eighteenth century for college servants assigned to individual rooms. Traditionally they were responsible for particular staircases, and their duties included waking up their charges, slopping out, laying fires, clearing up after parties, making beds, waiting at table, and any other extras demanded (for which they might be given a sum of money). Their heyday was in the nineteenth and early twentieth centuries when personal service was in vogue. When Michael Fane of *Sinister Street* arrives at his college, the porter greets him like a family butler and announces, 'Your servant is Porker'. To some students the personal connection was like a lifeline, and dependency on the scout is a notable feature of the genre. With the coming of electric lights, gas fires, and piped hot water after World War I the trend reversed, and as personal service falls out of fashion during the course of the twentieth century, the role of the scout in the life of the student—and of the Oxford novel—diminishes in significance. In recent literature the scout is replaced or relegated to the role of a cleaner and bedmaker. Notable scouts in fiction include *Verdant Green*'s Filcher, keen on his 'perquisites', and the scout of Charles Ryder in *Brideshead Revisited,* who is a fierce guardian of the college tradition and claims it is a pleasure to clear up the vomit of a gentleman like Sebastian Flyte.

Sent down   To be expelled from the university. A number of notable figures have been sent down in the past, including Nicholas Amhurst of *Terrae Filius.* P.B. Shelley and Thomas Hogg provide the most well-known examples. The poet Charles Stuart Calverley (1831–84) is said to have been sent down after throwing a stone through the master of Balliol's window while showing guests around the college and telling them, 'That is the Master's window. And now, unless I am much mistaken, you will see the Master himself.'

Servitor   The lowest class of undergraduate, who performed duties in return for reduced fees, such as running errands, making fires, and serving fellows or richer undergraduates. The servitor was phased out in the reforms of the mid–nineteenth century which levelled out the distinctions between undergraduates. A fictional exemplar is Hardy of *Tom Brown at Oxford,* who plays an important part in saving the hero from perdition.

Student/student   Whereas senior members of most colleges are called 'fellows', at Christ Church they are called Students (to avoid confusion this is spelt with a capital letter). Robert Burton, for instance, was a student at Brasenose before becoming a Student of Christ Church. Charles Dodgson, on the other hand, was first a student and then a Student of Christ Church.

Terms   There are three terms of eight weeks each during the academic year. **Michaelmas Term** starts at the beginning of October and ends in early December. **Hilary Term** starts in early January and ends before Easter. **Trinity Term** begins after Easter and ends in the middle of June. Oxford terms are known for being short and intense, requiring long vacations in order to recover. On the other hand, it has also been said that the social and cultural life is so all-consuming that the vacations are needed for study. The summer holidays, known as the long vacation, have traditionally been the occasion for Continental study trips and reading parties. There is an account of a reading party in Clough's *The Bothie of Tober-na-Vuolich* (1848), and the reading parties of Francis Urquhart, or Sligger, achieved a special place in university folklore. These were held for forty years between 1891 and 1931 at his chalet near Chamonix in Switzerland, and among those attending as students were H.H. Asquith, Ronald Knox, Julian Huxley, Cyril Connolly, Quinton Hogg, and Harold Macmillan.

Terrae Filius An officially sanctioned satirist who in former times was part of the university degree ceremonies. Appointed by the proctors, his role was to provide a light-hearted commentary on university matters. Sometimes the fooling went too far, and the individual concerned was reprimanded or even expelled. On one occasion, in 1658, the Terrae Filius was forced to apologise on his knees before the governing body. Names are known from 1591 to 1763, though the performance was apparently suppressed in the early eighteenth century. Nicholas Amhurst, who in 1721 started the broadsheet *Terrae Filius*, never officially held the position himself.

Tutorials An hour-long lesson which has changed in nature over the course of the centuries. In former times students were taught in small classes by college tutors who gave instruction across the curriculum. There is an amusing account of one such tutorial in *Verdant Green*, in which the tutor Slowcoach is so uninspiring that the students resort to playing pranks on each other. During the course of the nineteenth century, largely under the influence of men like Newman and Jowett, the tutorial was transformed into a one-to-one session in a specialised subject. Typically, a weekly essay would be set and read out to the tutor, who would comment on and question the contents with the aim of disciplining the mind of the student. This remains the basis of the tutorial in the contemporary university, though there is a tendency towards the teaching of two and occasionally three students at a time. The relationship between tutor and student is crucial and can lead to lifelong friendship—or hatred. Evelyn Waugh harboured an obsessional dislike of his Hertford tutor, Crutwell, and an unpleasant character bearing that name appears in several of his early novels. Anecdotes about tutorials abound in Oxford folklore, several of which concern the tutor falling asleep or failing to respond. Jowett was notorious for his long silences and the severity of his questioning, while William Spooner was once on his way to a dinner party when he suddenly remembered a student he had left behind in the middle of a tutorial. Writing in the 1920s, the Canadian humorist Stephen Leacock suggested that the system was based on the idea that after being systematically smoked at for three years a student would turn into a ripe scholar.

The Union The university debating society, which was founded in 1825 and is considered the largest and oldest of the university's clubs. Since the 1850s it has had its own buildings in St. Michael's Street, at which time William Morris and Edward Burne-Jones, then undergraduates at Exeter College, invited their friend Dante Gabriel Rossetti to Oxford and with others painted Arthurian scenes on the walls of the debating hall (now the Old Library). Over the next century the Union established itself as a training-ground for Parliament, and many of its office-holders rose to national prominence (including five prime ministers: Gladstone, Salisbury, Asquith, Macmillan, and Heath). Among those remembered for their brilliance and wit are F.E. Smith (Lord Birkenhead), Norman St. John Stevas, and Kenneth Tynan. Former presidents include Tariq Ali and Benazir Bhutto, and guest speakers have featured celebrities ranging from film stars to heads of state (the choice has sometimes proved controversial—as with Richard Nixon and O.J. Simpson). The most famous debate in the Union's history remains that of February 1933, when the Union supported a pacifist platform and voted against fighting for 'king and country'.

Vice-chancellor From the sixteenth century onwards the vice-chancellor has been the administrative head of the university. The office is held for a set term (now fixed at four years). Traditionally the office-holder was chosen from among the heads of houses, though this is not necessarily the case nowadays. Both Henry Liddell and Benjamin Jowett served as vice-chancellors, and among those who have held the post this century have been the warden of Wadham, Maurice Bowra, who published and translated works on ancient Greek, and John Masterman, provost of Worcester and author of *An Oxford Tragedy* and *To Teach the Senators Wisdom*.

Visitations With the changes in the religious regime of the country during the sixteenth and seventeenth centuries, the university was subject to a series of visitations (or purges). The first followed the Dissolution of the Monasteries, when **Henry VIII's visitation** was carried out by Richard Layton, who tightened the code of discipline, opposed scholasticism, promoted Greek, Latin, and Civil Law, and recommended that writings by Duns Scotus be consigned to the town's latrines. The university's five monastic colleges were spared but did not long survive. The **visitation under Edward VI,** Henry's son, was much more brutal, with interrogations, the removal of college heads and fellows, the revision of statutes, and the imposition of measures designed to secure Protestant loyalty. Following the reign of the Catholic Mary, an **Elizabethan visitation** involved the removal of Roman Catholics and the reinstatement of Protestants, though this was carried out in moderate fashion which won the new queen much favour. Thereafter there was no further visitation until the end of the Civil War and the defeat of the royalist cause, which the university had supported. The **Parliamentary visitation** dismissed most of the top university officials, including the vice-chancellor, Samuel Fell (father of John Fell), and others had to agree to submit to the authority of Parliament. Over three hundred members were expelled, and changes were made to the curriculum and discipline to enforce a more Puritan code. Following the return of the monarchy in 1660, however, the **Restoration**

visitation reinstated ejected fellows and restored the former regime. Though there was a move in the early eighteenth century to introduce a Hanoverian visitation, this never materialised, and Oxford was spared state intervention again until the royal commissions of the nineteenth century.

APPENDIX B

Chronological List of Colleges

College	Year of foundation
University	1249
Balliol	1263
Merton	1264
Exeter	1314
Oriel	1326
Queen's	1341
New College	1379
Lincoln	1427
All Souls	1438
Magdalen	1458
Brasenose	1509
Corpus Christi	1517
Christ Church	1546
Trinity	1555
St. John's	1555
Jesus	1571
Wadham	1612
Pembroke	1624
Worcester	1714
Hertford	1740
Keble	1868
Lady Margaret Hall	1878
Somerville	1879
St. Hugh's	1886
St. Hilda's	1893
St. Anne's	1952
St. Antony's	1953
St. Edmund Hall	1957
Nuffield	1958
St. Peter's	1961
St. Catherine's	1963
Linacre	1965
St. Cross	1965
Wolfson	1966
Green	1977
Kellogg	1990
Harris Manchester	1996

Appendix C
Population Figures

The most noticeable feature of the table below is the rapid growth of the city during the nineteenth century, when the population quadrupled. Early figures are approximate and are taken from Christopher Hibbert, ed., *The Encyclopaedia of Oxford* (Macmillan, 1988).

Year	Population
1086	c. 4,500
1297	c. 6,000
1580	c. 5,000
1630	c. 10,000
1801	c. 12,000
1851	28,000
1901	49,000
1951	98,000
1981	116,000

The number of students at Oxford University in 1996 totalled over 15,000 of whom more than a quarter were graduates. Senior members of the university engaged in teaching, research, and administration numbered about 3,200.

Notes

All titles are published in Britain unless otherwise stated.

The epigraph quotation is taken from Peter Conrad, *The Everyman History of English Literature* (Dent, 1985), 92.

Introduction

p. 1) The opening quotation is taken from J.I.M. Stewart, *The Aylwins* (Gollancz, 1966), 49.

p. 1) 'Oxford! The very sight of the word printed, or sound of it spoken, is fraught for me with most actual magic': Max Beerbohm, *Zuleika Dobson* (Penguin, 1952), 137.

p. 1) The quotation from Naipaul, 'No City or landscape is truly rich unless it has been given the quality of myth', is taken from Gillian Tindall, *Countries of the Mind* (Hogarth, 1991), 10.

p. 2) Information about the number of Oxford novels is taken from Judy G. Batson, *Oxford in Fiction: An Annotated Bibliography* (New York: Garland, 1989).

p. 2) 'The literature devoted to Oxford and its Colleges is probably greater than that relating to any other University . . .': William Knight, *The Glamour of Oxford* (Blackwell, 1911), v. For a bibliography of Oxford writings, see E.H. Cordeaux and D.H. Merry's *A Bibliography of Printed Works Relating to the University of Oxford* (Oxford University Press, 1968) and *A Bibliography of Printed Works Relating to the City of Oxford* (Oxford University Press, 1976).

p. 3) 'For an Oxford man, Oxford is primarily his college': Dacre Balsdon, *Oxford Life* (Eyre and Spottiswoode, 1957), 251.

p. 3) 'Please, sir, can you tell me where is the University? . . .': Dacre Balsdon, *Oxford Now and Then* (Duckworth, 1970), 235.

p. 3) 'Oxford and Cambridge, as establishments for education, consist of two parts, of the *Universities proper,* and of the *Colleges*': William Hamilton, 'Addenda ad Corpus Statutorum Universitatis Oxoniensis,' *Edinburgh Review* 53 (1831): 384–427.

p. 4) 'A college is not simply a place or organization where certain kinds of teaching and research take place . . .': Peter Snow, *Oxford Observed* (John Murray, 1991), 88.

p. 4) 'We all react, consciously and unconsciously, to the places where we live and work . . .': Tony Hiss, *The Experience of Place* (New York: Knopf, 1991), i.

p. 5) 'Inside the gates of such a community you can feel most comfortably insulated': Jan Morris, *Oxford* (Oxford University Press, 1965), 64.

p. 5) 'Most all, perhaps, it is the gardens that keep the heart of Oxford . . .': Jan Morris, 'Is Oxford Out of This World?' *Horizon* 5, no. 3 (January 1968): 86.

p. 5) 'Lands for centuries never molested by labor . . ..': Herman Melville, *Journal up the Straits* (New York: Cooper Square, 1971), 173.

p. 5) Hawthorne's reference to the 'grassy quadrangles, where cloistered walks have echoed to the quiet footsteps of twenty generations' comes from Nathaniel Hawthorne, *Our Old Home* (Columbus: Ohio State University Press, 1970), 191.

p. 5) The supposition by James that the fellows of All Souls must be the happiest of people, 'having no dreary instruction to administer . . .' can be found in Henry James, *English Hours* (Oxford University Press, 1981), 122.

p. 5) 'When to the exhibition of so much of the clearest joy of wind and limb . . .': Henry James, 'A Passionate Pilgrim', in *Novels and Tales,* 13:416–17.

p. 7) For the reference to the Irish man's despising Oxford as 'a symbol of everything he hates . . .' and the dialogue that follows which begins, 'Does he actually know anything about Oxford?' see John Wain, *Hungry Generations* (Hutchinson, 1994), 254–55.

p. 8) 'Oxford is at heart an intensely English city . . .': Jan Morris, *Oxford,* 3d ed. (Oxford University Press, 1987), 270.

Chapter 1

p. 9) The opening quotation, 'A clerk hadde litherly biset his whyle,' is taken from Chaucer's 'The Miller's Tale' and can be found in F.N. Robinson, ed., *The Works of Geoffrey Chaucer* (Oxford University Press, 1957), 49.

p. 9) 'Different places on the face of earth have different vital effluence . . .': D.H. Lawrence, *Studies in Classic American Literature* (Heinemann, 1967), 301.

p. 9) 'Half her beauty lies in her setting . . .': John Buchan, *Memory-Hold-the-Door* (Dent and Sons, 1984), 75.

p. 10) Spenser's reference to Oxford's rivers in *The Faerie Queene* [(Oxford University Press, 1912), 269] runs as follows:

The Ouze, whom men doe Isis rightly name;
Full weake and crooked creature seemed shee,
    And almost blind through eld, that scarce her way could see.

    Therefore on either side she was sustained
Of two smal grooms, which by their names were hight

The *Churne,* and *Charwell,* two small streames, which pained
Them selues her footing to direct aright,
Which fayled oft through faint and feeble plight.

p. 10) Drayton's lines of poetry, 'So lovely Isis comming on . . .', are taken from *Polyolbion,* argument to song 15. See John Buxton, ed., *The Poems of Michael Drayton* (Routledge and Kegan Paul, 1953), 2:615.

p. 10) The claim that the Cherwell is the true Oxford river, 'doomed as the Thames is to forget in the smoke of London the clear fancies of Oxford', can be found in Jean Fayard, *Oxford and Margaret* (Jarrolds, 1925), 80.

p. 11) Baskerville's description of Oxford as 'sweetly hugged in the pleasant arms of those two pure rivers . . .' can be found in Thomas Baskerville, *Account of Oxford* (1683–86). See *Collectanea* (Oxford Historical Society, 1905), 4:179.

p. 11) 'For the millionth time I found reason to bless the semi-rural character . . .': John Wain, *Comedies* (Hutchinson, 1990), 84.

p. 11) Daudet's reference to 'Le rheumatisme vert' is taken from Jan Morris, *The Oxford Book of Oxford* (Oxford University Press, 1984), xi.

p. 11) For Wood's reference to 'sweet wholsome and well-tempered aire', see Anthony Wood, *Survey of the Antiquities of the City of Oxford,* ed. Andrew Clark (Oxford Historical Society, 1889–99), 1:50.

p. 11) 'Certainly Oxford's no good air': Andrew Clark, ed., *The Life and Times of Anthony Wood* (Oxford Historical Society, 1891–1900), 2:399.

p. 11) 'River valleys have their own distinctive intellectual "climate"': J.A.W. Bennett, *Chaucer at Oxford and Cambridge* (Oxford University Press, 1974), 21.

p. 12) 'Yes, certainly, it is this mild, miasmal air . . .': Max Beerbohm, *Zuleika Dobson* (Penguin, 1952), 139. The suggestion as to the meaning of 'inenubilable' is made in L. Danson, *Max Beerbohm and the Act of Writing* (Oxford University Press, 1989), 133. Concerning his use of neologism, Beerbohm is quoted in David Cecil, *Max* (Constable, 1964), 104, as saying, 'At times there is no word in the English dictionary by which I can express my shade of meaning. I try to think of a French, or Latin, or Greek one. If I can't, then I invent a word—such as "pop-limbo" or "bauble-tit"—often a compound of some well-known English word with an affix or prefix to point its significance. Sometimes I invent a word merely because the cadence of a sentence demands it.'

FRIDESWIDE AND THE LEARNED IMPS

p. 13) Regarding the site of the original ox ford, Hall and Frankl (*Oxford* [Pevensey, 1981], 1) state that this was at Magdalen Bridge; Andrew Clark's notes in his edition of Anthony Wood, *Survey of Antiquities,* 1:46, support a western location, as does a deed of 1352 quoted in Christopher Hibbert, ed., *The Encyclopaedia of Oxford* (Macmillan, 1988), 282, which refers to land at Bullstake Mead as being just to the north of 'the ford called Oxford, hard by the bridge which leads towards North Hincksey'; Salter's endorsement of Hinksey Ferry is in H.E. Salter, *Medieval Oxford* (Oxford Historical Society, 1936), 1; Thomas's claim for Folly Bridge is in Edward Thomas, *Oxford* (Block, 1922), 25.

p. 13) With regard to the origins of Oxford, most commentators are inclined to see some truth in the Frideswide legend, though H.E. Salter in *Medieval Oxford,* 4–8, rejects the notion that the town grew up around St. Frideswide's foundation and suggests instead that the town's rectangular shape centred on Carfax indicates that it was deliberately planned at a later date. The medieval historian John Rous, concerned to invest the city with mythic status, claimed that Oxford was founded in 1009 B.C. by King Mempric, fifth in line after Brute, who had first settled the kingdom named after him after fleeing from Troy. See Wood, *Survey of Antiquities,* 1:41.

p. 13) Information about the Frideswide stories is drawn from John Blair, *Saint Frideswide: Patron of Oxford* (Perpetua, 1988).

p. 13) The anonymous account of the Frideswide legend is taken from Arnold Mallison, *Quinquagesimo Anno* (Dugdale, 1974), 180.

p. 14) 'Legend usually crystallizes round a nucleus of genuine tradition . . .': Falconer Madan, *Oxford outside the Guide-Books* (Blackwell, 1925), 11.

p. 15) The quotation from Carroll, 'Once upon a time . . .', and the information about the 'treacle well' at Binsey are taken from Martin Gardner, ed., *Lewis Carroll: The Annotated Alice* (Penguin, 1970), 100. The visit of Henry VIII to Binsey is mentioned in Jan Morris, *Oxford* (Faber and Faber, 1978), 257.

p. 15) The quotation and translation from the Anglo-Saxon Chronicle are taken from James Parker, *The Early History of Oxford (727–1100)* (Oxford Historical Society, 1884), 116.

p. 16) The quotation from Spenser, 'so many learned imps . . .', is taken from book 4, canto 11, stanza 26 of *The Faerie Queene,* 2:142.

p. 16) The description of Bacon as 'a braue scholler . . .': Robert Greene, *Frier Bacon and Frier Bungay* in A.B. Grosart, ed., *Robert Greene: The Life and Complete Works* (Russell and Russell, 1964), 13:11. The contest of magicians is ibid., 61–63.

p. 16) Information about Bacon is taken from A.L. Rowse, *Oxford in the History of the Nation* (Weidenfeld and Nicolson, 1975), 24–25; Charles Edward Mallet, *A History of the University of Oxford* (Methuen, 1924–27), 1:66; and Cecil Headlam, *Oxford and Its Story* (Dent and Sons, 1926), 101.

p. 16) Samuel Pepys's visit to Friar Bacon's Study took place on June 9, 1668.

p. 17) The lines from Chaucer, 'Man sholde not knowe of Goddes pryvetee . . .', are taken from lines 3454–56 of *The Canterbury Tales,* in *Works of Geoffrey Chaucer,* 51.

p. 17) 'I said I was a poor scholar of theology, on my way to Oxford . . .': James Hogg, *The Private Memoirs and Confessions of a Justified Sinner* (Oxford University Press, 1969), 230.

p. 17) For an example of a modern 'reinvention' of Dr. John Dee, one-time fellow of Trinity College, Cambridge, see Peter Ackroyd, *The House of Doctor Dee* (Hamish Hamilton, 1993).

p. 18) Information about 'Duns Scotus's Oxford' is drawn from Norman H. MacKenzie, *A Reader's Guide to Gerard Manley Hopkins* (Thames and Hudson, 1981), 113, 231.

p. 19) Warton's reference to 'a sort of inspiring deity . . .' is taken from *The Idler*, no. 33, December 2, 1758.

p. 19) 'Where at each coign of every antique street . . .': Lionel Johnson, 'Oxford', in *Ireland with Other Poems* (Elkin Matthews, 1897), 32.

CHAUCER'S CLERKS OF OXENFORD

Acknowledgment is gratefully made to J.A.W. Bennett, *Chaucer at Oxford and Cambridge* (Oxford University Press, 1974) for much of the background information used in this section.

p. 20) Resentment between town and gown is described in W.A. Pantin, *Oxford Life in Oxford Archives* (Oxford University Press, 1972), 68–75.

p. 20) The assertion that 'there is probably not a single yard of ground in any part of the classic High Street that lies between St. Martin's and St. Mary's which has not, at one time or another, been stained with blood' is taken from Hastings Rashdall, *The Universities of Europe in the Middle Ages,* ed. F.M. Powicke and A.B. Emden (Oxford University Press, 1936), 3.87.

p. 20) The description of the St. Scholastica's Day riot, on Tuesday, February 10, is taken from Anthony Wood, *The History and Antiquities of the University of Oxford,* ed. J. Gutch (1792–96), 456. The passage about Thursday, February 12 which begins, 'the said Townsmen about sun rising . . .' is ibid., 459–60.

p. 21) 'It was generally the chronic indiscipline of the scholars that caused the town-and-gown battles': Pantin, *Oxford Life in Archives,* 75.

p. 21) Information about the original sources of 'The Miller's Tale' is taken from Bennett, *Chaucer,* 28.

p. 22) Examples of the sunny nature of 'The Miller's Tale' might include Nicholas's sweet-smelling herbs; his psaltery and singing; the attractive young Alisoun with her embroidered and colourful clothes; the 'jolif and amorous' dandy Absolon with his dancing 'after the scole of Oxenford'; the bright moonlight; the merry love-making; the laughter of the neighbours; and the frequent use of such words as 'joly', 'light', 'sweete', and 'mery'.

p. 22) Information about student accommodation and astrolabes is taken from Bennett, *Chaucer,* 33, 35.

p. 22) Though the Clerk is posited as academic standard-bearer, his academic status is unclear and he is described in terms that suggest he is well advanced in his studies—'unto logyk hadde longe ygo'. F.N. Robinson in *Works of Geoffrey Chaucer,* 658, supposes that he was pursuing his master's degree, while Bennett, *Chaucer,* 14, thinks it more likely that he had already obtained it. The basic course of instruction in the medieval university took seven years (based on the apprenticeship of the guilds); the first four years led to the bachelor of arts, after which a period of further study for three years together with some teaching requirements led to the master of arts. (Through a debasement of this, Oxford students in the twentieth century could gain a master's degree by paying twenty-five pounds four years after receiving their bachelor's degree.) To gain a doctorate students needed to spend another six or seven years in the higher faculties of Law, Medicine, and Theology. As for Nicholas, it would appear that he too is at some stage of the seven-year apprenticeship, for he 'Hadde lerned art, but al his fantasy / Was turned for to learne astrologye'. Presumably he had already studied the seven liberal arts—the *trivium* of grammar, logic, and rhetoric, and the *quadrivium* of music, arithmetic, geometry, and astronomy—but had become distracted by the allure of astrology.

p. 23) The lines about the Clerk of Oxford's book collection, 'Twenty bookes, clad in blak or reed . . .' are taken from lines 294–95 of *The Canterbury Tales,* p. 20. The evaluation of the Clerk's books is taken from G.G. Coulton, *Chaucer and His England* (Methuen, 1921), 99. Falconer Madan, however, in *Outside the Guide-Books,* 52, notes that unbound books could be obtained much more cheaply.

p. 23) The lines about the Clerk of Oxford, 'Yet hadde he but litel gold . . .' are taken from lines 298–302 of *The Canterbury Tales,* p. 20.

p. 24) The description of Jankyn, 'som tyme was a clerk of Oxenford . . .', is taken from lines 527–28 of *The Canterbury Tales,* p. 81.

p. 24) The assertion that 'not a detail . . . can be faulted . . .' in Chaucer's account of Oxford is taken from Bennett, *Chaucer,* 18.

p. 24) For an example of an imaginative biography that sends Chaucer to be educated at Oxford, see Regina Z. Kelly's *Young Geoffrey Chaucer* (New York: Lothrop, Lee and Shepard,1952). Scholars are inclined to think that this is mere wishful thinking and that Chaucer's learning resulted either from his training in either the Inns of Court or as part of his court training under Edward III (see Derek Pearsall, *The Life of Geoffrey Chaucer* [Blackwell, 1992], 29–34).

p. 25) Oseney Abbey was dissolved in 1546. In 1643 John Aubrey visited the ruins and later described his impressions: 'In February following, with much ado I got my father to let me to beloved Oxford again, then a garrison for the king. I got Mr Hesketh, Mr Dobson's man, a priest, to draw the ruins of Osney two or three ways before 'twas pulled down. Now the very foundation is digged up.'

John Aubrey, *Brief Lives,* ed. Richard Barber (Boydell, 1982), 8. Over a century later, in the summer of 1754, Samuel Johnson on one of his Oxford visits viewed the ruins in silent indignation, for the destruction upset his high church and Tory sentiments. See James Boswell, *Life of Samuel Johnson* (Oxford University Press, 1953), 193. All that remains today of the once mighty abbey is a small fifteenth-century structure off the Botley Road in the west of the city.

p. 25) Information about the number of students is taken from Pantin, *Oxford Life in Archives,* 104.

p. 25) 'If all the colleges had been dissolved in 1400, it would not have been a crushing blow to the University': Salter, *Medieval Oxford,* 37.

p. 25) The 1410 statute is quoted in Pantin, *Oxford Life in Archives,* 10. Facts about the number of halls and colleges are taken from the same source.

p. 25) The case for college supervision remained consistent through the centuries. When proposals were made to allow students to take lodgings in town because of college overcrowding, Dr. Pusey (quoted in Pantin, *Oxford Life in Archives,* 13) was adamant in his opposition, and his arguments might almost have been based on a reading of 'The Miller's Tale': 'Lodging-houses are the worst forms of temptation. Elsewhere, men themselves (if they fall) seek for temptation; in lodging-houses temptation besets them. . . . The facility of easy and familiar intercourse at any hour, day by day; the necessity of being *solus cum sola,* when meals are brought and removed, the habit of those who keep the lodgings to allow the door to be opened by the maid servant, when they are gone to rest, and too frequently the thoughtlessness or lightness of the class of servants, who are, I believe, often employed not as regular servants but by the term only, and whose wages are eked out by the lodger, are perils from which the young should be shielded.'

FOXE'S MARTYRS AND A CARDINAL DEVELOPMENT

p. 26) Information about *The Jests of Scogin* and *The Merie Tales of Skelton* is taken from Samuel Hulton, *The Clerk of Oxford in Fiction* (Methuen, 1909), 48, 51–58, 366–71.

p. 26) 'Oxford had reached the height of its prosperity in the fourteenth century . . .': Headlam, *Oxford and Its Story,* 221.

p. 27) For Foxe's reference to 'the great Antichrist . . .', see W. Grinton Berry, ed., *Foxe's Book of Martyrs* (Grand Rapids: Baker Book House, 1987), 70.

p. 27) Foxe's description of Wyclif as 'the morning star . . .' and of Tyndale as excelling 'especially in the knowledge . . .' are taken from Berry, *Foxe's Book of Martyrs,* 49, 135.

p. 27) 'We do object to thee, Nicholas Ridley, and to thee Hugh Latimer, jointly and severally . . .': John Foxe, *Actes and Monuments,* ed. Stephen Reed Catley and George Townsend (Seeley and Burnside, 1837–41), 7:526.

p. 28) 'Be of good comfort, master Ridley, and play the man . . .': : Foxe, *Actes and Monuments,* 7:550.

p. 29) 'And now I come to the great thing, which so much troubleth my conscience . . .': Foxe, *Actes and Monuments,* 8:88.

p. 29) 'Here the standers-by were all astonied, marvelled, were amazed, did look one upon another, whose expectation he had so notably deceived . . .': Foxe, *Actes and Monuments,* 8:88.

p. 30) With regard to Cranmer's motives, Diarmaid MacCulloch's *Thomas Cranmer* (New Haven: Yale University Press, 1996) provides an instance of the modern historian's uncertainty, for the book concludes that the mind of a devout and exhausted man facing death is impossible to fathom, and that the crisis of conscience may have been due to a variety of factors.

p. 30) Facts about Oxford's taxable wealth are taken from Hall and Frankl, *Oxford,* 10.

p. 30) The description of Wolsey as the 'the last great medievalist' is taken from Rowse, *Oxford in History,* 60.

p. 31) Though authorship of *Henry VIII* is disputed, it is often attributed to Shakespeare (many commentators believe it to be a collaborative work with John Fletcher). Shakespeare would have known Christ Church well, for he is said to have stayed overnight nearby at Crown Tavern on his journeys from London and Stratford. The Crown, part of the Golden Cross complex in the centre of Oxford, was a tavern rather than an inn, which means that Shakespeare would have stayed there as a guest of the landlord, John Davenant. According to Aubrey, Shakespeare was a close friend of the Davenants and acted as godfather to their son, William Davenant (1606–68), who himself became a playwright and boasted of being Shakespeare's illegitimate son. It seems strange in the light of all this that Shakespeare barely makes mention of Oxford in his writings, though A.L. Rowse makes the unsubstantiated claim that the playwright was present on the occasion of Elizabeth I's visit to Oxford and that reference is made to this in *A Midsummer Night's Dream* (see Rowse, *Oxford in History,* 75).

p. 31) As regards to Wolsey's time at Oxford, Aubrey states in *Brief Lives,* 'He was a fellowe of Magdalen Colledge in Oxford, where he was tutor to a young gentleman of Limmington, near Ilchester, in com. Somerset, in whose guift the presentation of that church is, worth the better part of 200 *li* per annum, which he gave to his tutor, Wolsey.' According to the *Dictionary of National Biography,* however, Wolsey was given the living by Thomas Grey, the first marquis of Dorset and father of three sons in Wolsey's charge at Magdalen College school.

p. 31) Richard Corbet's poem is taken from J.B. Firth, *The Minstrelsy of Isis* (Chapman and Hall, 1908), 292. Great Tom rings 101 times at five past nine every evening. The number of strokes equals the original hundred students who had been increased by one in 1663. Five past nine equals nine o'clock local time, for Oxford lies five minutes behind Greenwich Mean Time.

p. 32) Information about the authority of gown and the right of college heads to search town houses is taken from Pantin, *Oxford Life in Archives*, 62.

Chapter 2

p. 33) The opening quotation is taken from Thomas Seccombe and H. Spencer Scott, *In Praise of Oxford* (Constable, 1910–11), 1:vii.

p. 33) 'I have found in Oxford so much polish and learning . . .': Desiderius Erasmus, *Collected Works* (Toronto: University of Toronto Press, 1974), 1:235–36.

p. 34) Information about the trend towards a collegiate university is taken from Charles Edward Mallet, *A History of the University of Oxford* (Methuen, 1924–27), vol. 2; and James McConica, 'Elizabethan Oxford: The Collegiate Society', in *The History of the University of Oxford*, ed. J. Catto (Oxford University Press, 1984–94), 3:645–732.

p. 34) Aubrey's quotation is taken from 'The Idea of the Education of Young Gentlemen', in the Bodleian Library (Aubrey MS 10). Acknowledgment is gratefully made to Lawrence Stone, who quotes the passage in 'The Size and Composition of the Oxford Student Body 1580–1909', in *The University in Society*, vol. 1, *Oxford and Cambridge from the 14th to the Early 19th Century*, ed. L. Stone (Princeton: Princeton University Press, 1975), 50.

p. 35) Peacham's 'Parents take their sons from school, as birds out of the nest . . .' is taken from Samuel F. Hulton, *The Clerk of Oxford in Fiction* (Methuen, 1909), 106.

p. 35) 'The university was now, from the late sixteenth century onwards, to be governed by a tight little body of heads of houses . . .': W.A. Pantin, *Oxford Life in Oxford Archives* (Oxford University Press, 1972), 40.

p. 36) 'In the afternoon she left Oxford, and going through Fishstreet to Quatrevois, and thence to the East Gate . . .': Andrew Clark, ed., *The Life and Times of Anthony Wood* (Oxford Historical Society, 1891–1900), 1:454.

SEAT OF THE ENGLISH MUSES

p. 36) The wording of the passage from *Britannia*, 'Where the Cherwell flows along with the Isis . . .', is taken from Edward Thomas, *Oxford* (Black, 1903), 258. The Latin original can be found in William Camden, *Britannia* (George Bishop, 1594), 280.

p. 37) Gower's description of London as the new Troy can be found in his Latin work *Vox Clamantis* (c. 1376–81), 1:979 ff.

p. 38) The verse by Dan Rogers, 'He that hath Oxford seen . . .' is taken from J.B. Firth, ed., *The Minstrelsy of Isis* (Chapman and Hall, 1908), 2.

p. 38) The lines from Spenser beginning 'Ioy to you both, ye double noursery . . .' are taken from book 4, canto 1, stanza 26. See Edmund Spenser, *The Faerie Queene* (Oxford University Press, 1909), 142.

p. 38) The lines of verse beginning, 'Renowned Oxford built to Apollo's learned brood . . .', are taken from Michael Drayton, *Poly-Olbion*, song 11. See Michael Drayton, *Poly-Olbion*, ed. J. William Hebel (Blackwell, 1933), 4:403–5.

p. 39) 'That lordly are the buildings of the town . . .': Robert Greene, *Frier Bacon and Frier Bungay*, in A.B. Grosart, ed., *Robert Greene: The Life and Complete Works* (Russell and Russell, 1964), 13:6.

p. 39) The observation 'that Colledges in *Oxenford* are much more stately for the building, and *Cambridge* much more sumptuous for the houses . . .': John Lyly, *Euphues, the Anatomy of Wit*, in R.W. Bond, ed., *The Complete Works of John Lyly* (Oxford University Press, 1902), 2:193.

p. 39) The quotation from Henry Vaughan, 'for every book is thy large epitaph', is from the poem 'On Sir Thomas Bodley's Library; the Author being there in Oxford'. See L.C. Martin, ed., *The Works of Henry Vaughan* (Oxford University Press, 1957), 633.

p. 39) The quotations about the 'Tree of Knowledge' and 'the Muses' Paradise' are taken from 'Ode. Mr. Cowley's Book presenting itself to the University Library of Oxford'. See A.R. Waller, ed. *Abraham Cowley: Poems* (Cambridge University Press, 1905), 409.

p. 39) 'I am not poor, I am not rich . . .': Robert Burton, *The Anatomy of Melancholy* (Duckworth, 1905), 29.

p. 40) For the claim that 'literature is a reconstructed mythology', see Northrop Frye, *Fables of Identity: Studies in Poetic Mythology* (New York: Harcourt Brace Jovanovich, 1963), 38.

A YOUNG GENTLEMAN AND OTHER CHARACTERS

p. 41) The quotations from Overbury are taken from the facsimile reproduction of *Sir Thomas Overbury His Wife (1616)*, in James E. Savage, ed., *The 'Conceited Newes' of Sir Thomas Overbury and His Friends* (Gainesville: Scholars' Facsimiles and Reprints, 1968). 'A Meere Scholler' is 120–23, and 'A meere Fellow of an House', 146–48.

p. 41) 'His smacking of a Gentle-woman is somewhat too savory . . .': John Earle, *Microcosmography*, ed. Gwendolyn Murphy (Golden Cockerell Press, 1928), 33.

p. 41) The description of 'A Young Gentleman' who goes to Oxford 'to weare a gown . . .': Earle, *Microcosmography*, 42.

p. 42) The quotation from Latimer, '[The Devil] gets him to the University . . .', is taken from Sermon the Sixth of 'Seven Sermons Preached Before King Edward VI'. See *Sermons by Bishop Latimer*, ed. G.E. Corrie (Cambridge University Press, 1844), 1:203.

p. 42) 'Whereas they were given to maintaine none but the poore only, now they maintaine none but the rich onely . . .': Philip Stubbes, *The Anatomie of Abuses* (New Shakespeare Society, 1882), 2:20.

p. 42) The charge that 'for double fees / A Dunce may become a Doctor' comes from a verse by Richard Corbet quoted in Hulton, *Clerk of Oxford*, 95.

p. 42) 'The time ha's got a veine of making him ridiculous, and men laugh at him by tradition . . .': Earle, *Microcosmography*, 34.

p. 43) 'I (for the most part) enjoyed the greatest felicity of my life (ingenious youths, as rosebuds, imbibe the morning dew) . . .': John Aubrey, *Brief Lives*, ed. Richard Barber (Boydell Press, 1982), 9.

p. 44) For Wood's reference to the coffee-house of Jacob the Jew, see Clark, *Anthony Wood*, 1:168.

p. 44) The passage from Evelyn, 'I ever thought my Tutor had parts enough . . .', is taken from his entry for May 29, 1637. See E.S. Beer, ed., *The Diary of John Evelyn* (Oxford University Press, 1959), 10–11.

p. 44) 'In summer time to Medley, / My love and I would go' is taken from the third verse of 'A Love Sonnet' in *The Poetry of George Wither*, ed. Frank Sigwick, vol. 1 (Bullen, 1902).

p. 44) For Wither's reference to 'wholesome nursery of wit', see George Wither, *Juvenilia*, vol. 1, *Poems 1625–33* (Spenser Society, 1871), 30. The quotation, 'For I his meaning did no more conjecture . . .' is ibid., 32.

p. 45) The passage from Lyly beginning, 'such playing at dice, such quaffing of drinke . . .': Lyly, *Euphues*, 1:273.

p. 45) For Clarendon's removal from the university because of 'the custom of drinking being too much introduced . . .', see Hugh Trevor-Roper, ed., *Selections from Clarendon* (Oxford University Press, 1978), 12.

p. 45) The text of Laud's revisions is taken from Christopher Hibbert, ed., *The Encyclopaedia of Oxford* (Macmillan, 1988), 215.

p. 46) A portrait of Falkland's Great Tew is given in Charles Edward Mallet, *A History of the University of Oxford* (Methuen, 1924–27), 2:307–10. For Graves's description of Lord Falkland as 'the most sympatique character of the period', see Robert Graves, *Wife to Mr. Milton* (Cassell, 1943), viii. For Clarendon's description of the atmosphere 'as in a college situated in a purer air', see Trevor-Roper, *Selections from Clarendon*, 51.

REBELLION, RESTORATION, AND THE LIFE OF ANTHONY WOOD

p. 47) For Aubrey's comments on the death of Ralph Kettell, see Aubrey, *Brief Lives*, 186.

p. 47) 'Never perhaps has there existed so curious a spectacle as Oxford presented in these days . . .': Cecil Headlam, *Oxford and Its Story* (Dent and Sons, 1926), 319.

p. 48) For Wood's account of the Civil War, see Clark, *Anthony Wood*, 1:53–56.

p. 48) For Wood's comments on the state of the university, see Anthony Wood, *Athenae Oxonienses*, ed. Philip Bliss (Ecclesiastical History Society, 1848), 1:33.

p. 49) For Wood's account of the visitation, see Clark, *Anthony Wood*, 1:144. The reference to his brother is on pp. 166–67.

p. 49) The quotations from *Of Education*, 'pure trifling at Grammar and Sophistry' based on 'the Scholastick grossness of barbarous ages': F. Patterson et al., eds., *The Works of John Milton* (New York: Columbia University Press, 1931), 4:278–80.

p. 49) The attack by Hobbes on university studies can be found in *The Leviathan*, book 4, chap. 46.

p. 49) 'After all this, surprising as it may seem, we are on the threshold of the most brilliant decade . . .': A.L. Rowse, *Oxford in the History of the Nation* (Weidenfeld and Nicolson, 1975), 118.

p. 49) Evelyn's Oxford visit took place July 7–13, 1654: see *Diary of John Evelyn*, 339–41.

p. 49) For Aubrey's reference to Robert Boyle, see Aubrey, *Brief Lives*, 48.

p. 50) Wood's reference to his 'insatiable desire of knowledge' comes from Wood, *Athenae Oxonienses*, 1:68.

p. 50) For Hearne's description of Wood as a 'wonderful pryer . . .', see Wood, *Athenae Oxonienses*, 1:338.

p. 50) Prideaux's reference to Wood as a 'good bowzeing blad' can be found in Humphrey Prideaux, *Letters to John Ellis 1674–1722*, ed. Edward Maunde Thompson (Camden Society, 1875), 12.

p. 50) 'Poore folks' sons study hard, and with much adoe obtaine their degrees . . .': Clark, *Anthony Wood*, 2:276–77.

p. 50) The remark of Wood's friend that he 'never spoke well of any man' can be found in Wood, *Athenae Oxonienses*, 1:182. The comments on Samcroft (1:201) and Prideaux (3:266–67) are taken from the same source.

p. 51) For Wood's description of Aubrey as 'a shiftless person . . .', see Clark, *Anthony Wood*, 2:117.

p. 51) The observation that for Aubrey 'friendship was the essential basis of his life' comes from Anthony Powell, *John Aubrey and His Friends* (Hogarth, 1988), 199. The quotations from Aubrey's letters to Wood are from pp. 150–51.

p. 51) For the quotation from Wood, 'in New College common-chamber . . .', and his account of the Clarendon affair, see Wood, *Athenae Oxonienses*, 1:384–87.

p. 51) For Wood's dealings with Doctors South and Rawlinson, see Wood, *Athenae Oxonienses*, 1:355.

p. 52) The quotations from Hearne's tribute to Wood are taken from Wood, *Athenae Oxonienses*, 1:331–37. The tribute is commented on by Headlam in *Oxford and Its Story*, 330.

p. 52) Wood's comments on the courtiers, 'high, proud, insolent . . .', can be found in Clark, *Anthony Wood*, 2:68.

p. 53) 'Oxford mighty fine place and well set and cheap entertainment.': R.C. Latham and W. Matthews, eds., *Pepys* (Bell and Hyman, 1983), 227.

p. 53) 'Oxford's a place, where Wit can never sterve' and the quatrain beginning, 'Oxford to him a dearer Name shall be . . .', can be found in James Kinsley, ed., *The Poems and Fables of John Dryden* (Oxford University Press, 1962), 310–11.

p. 53) The quotation from Dryden's 'Prologue, To the University of Oxon' beginning, 'Here too are Annual Rites to *Pallas* done . . .' can be found in James Kinsley, ed., *The Poems and Fables of John Dryden* (Oxford University Press, 1962), 305.

p. 53) The quotation from Dryden's 'Epilogue' (1681) beginning, 'This Place the seat of Peace, the quiet Cell . . .', can be found in *Poems and Fables*, 183.

Chapter 3

p. 54) The opening quotation is from C. Day Lewis and Charles Fenby, *Anatomy of Oxford* (Jonathan Cape, 1938), 73.

p. 54) 'Were it not for the important colleges, the place [Oxford] would be not unlike a large village': W.H. and W.J.C. Quarrell, eds., *Oxford in 1710 from the Travels of Zacharias Conrad von Uffenbach* (Blackwell, 1928), 2.

p. 54) 'A Director or Scull of a College is a lordly strutting Creature . . .': Nicholas Amhurst, *Terrae Filius* (1721), no. 13.

p. 55) Information about the number of fellowships is taken from W.A. Pantin, *Oxford Life in Oxford Archives* (Oxford University Press, 1972), 31, and Christopher Brooke and Roger Highfield, *Oxford and Cambridge* (Cambridge University Press, 1988), 273.

p. 55) Information about the number of college members at Corpus Christi is taken from Geoffrey Faber, *Oxford Apostles: Character Study of the Oxford Movement* (Faber and Faber, 1933); information about the number of college members at Lincoln College is taken from V.H.H. Green, *Oxford Common Room: A Study of Lincoln College and Mark Pattison* (Edward Arnold, 1957), 16.

p. 55) Information about the duration of fellowships is taken from Dacre Balsdon, *Oxford Now and Then* (Duckworth, 1970), 81.

p. 56) Information and statistics about the number of poor students at the university are taken from Lawrence Stone, 'The Size and Composition of the Oxford

Student Body, 1580–1909' in L. Stone, ed., *The University in Society*, vol. 1, *Oxford and Cambridge from the 14th to the Early 19th Century* (Princeton: Princeton University Press, 1975), 28–38.

p. 56) 'The Oxford freshman entered a highly structured society . . .': V.H.H. Green, 'The University and Social Life', in *The History of the University of Oxford*, ed. J. Catto (Oxford University Press, 1984–94), 5:317.

p. 56) Eldon's account of his examination is treated by G.V. Cox as a 'post prandium joke': see C.V. Cox, *Recollections of Oxford* (Macmillan, 1868), 160. On the other hand, historians such as Charles Edward Mallet in *A History of the University of Oxford* (Methuen, 1924–27), 3:163, and D. Patterson in 'Hebrew Studies', in Catto, *History of the University*, 5:546, are inclined to accept it as true. More importantly, the university commissioners of 1850 accepted it at face value and included it in their report on p. 50.

AN AGE OF DETRACTION

p. 57) The wording of the passages from Gibbon are taken from Edward Gibbon, *Memoirs of My Life*, ed. Georges A. Bonnard (Nelson, 1966), 46, 50.

p. 58) Information about Hearne is drawn from Mallet, *History of the University*, vol. 2. For Hearne's comments on college clubbishness and neglect, see C.E. Doble, ed., *Hearne's Remarks and Collections* (Oxford Historical Society, 1884–1918), 9:149. The comments on his contemporaries are as follows: Dr. Charlett, 3:153–54; Bishop Trelawny, 1:315; Joseph Trapp, 3:56; Tho. Hoy, 1:322.

p. 59) The lines on Wormius, 'To future ages may thy dulness last, / As thou preserv'st the dulness of the past!': Alexander Pope, *Dunciad*, book 3, 185–90. See James Sutherland, ed., *The Poems of Alexander Pope* (Methuen, 1968), 5:329. The wording of the anonymous couplet, 'Plague on't, quoth Time to Thomas Hearne, / *Whatever I forget*, you learn' is taken from W. Tuckwell, *Reminiscences of Oxford* (Cassell, 1901), 81. A slightly different version is given by Jan Morris in *The Oxford Book of Oxford* (Oxford University Press, 1978), 141: '"Pox on't!" said Time to Thomas Hearne, / "Whatever I forget you learn."'

p. 59) For Hearne's reference to 'King William and his Rascally Adherents', see Doble, *Hearne's Remarks and Collections*, 1:304.

p. 59) The wording of the verses by Joseph Trapp and William Browne is taken from Samuel F. Hulton, *The Clerk of Oxford in Fiction* (Methuen, 1909), 303.

p. 59) Amhurst's dismissal from the university is described in V.H.H. Green, 'Reformers and Reform in the University', in Catto, *History of the University*, 5:610. There appears to be some confusion about the spelling of Amhurst's name; J.B. Firth, *The Minstrelsy of Isis* (Chapman and Hall, 1908); Hulton, *Clerk of Oxford;* and Cecil Headlam, *Oxford and Its Story* (Dent and Sons, 1926), give 'Amherst', while the *DNB* and standard histories such as Mallet, *History of the Uni-*

versity, and V.H.H. Green, *A History of Oxford University* (Batsford, 1974), and 'Reformers and Reform', prefer 'Amhurst'. *The Encyclopaedia of Oxford,* ed. Christopher Hibbert (Macmillan, 1988), gives both variants, with 'Amherst' on p. 229 and 'Amhurst' on p. 450.

p. 60) 'With gen'rous Grief I mourn our *Oxford's* Fate, / Her fading Glories and declining State . . .': Nicolas Amhurst, *Strephon's Revenge* (1718), 6.

p. 60) Evelyn's description of *Terrae Filius* as 'a tedious, abusive, sarcastical rhapsodie . . .' is in his entry for July 10, 1669. See E.S. de Beer, ed., *The Diary of John Evelyn* (Oxford University Press, 1955), 3:532. (In 1974 the ceremony in which *Terrae Filius* used to appear named the Act was briefly revived at a ceremony to mark the installation of fibre-glass Muses on the Clarendon Building.)

p. 61) Steele balanced his portrait of Oxford in the *Spectator* with a more positive picture in the *Tatler* (no. 39, July 9, 1709), where he wrote of the splendour of the college buildings in which men were inspired by 'the magnificence of their palaces, the greatness of their revenues, the sweetness of their groves and retirements' to works commensurate with their surroundings.

p. 61) Information about Addison's Walk is taken from Peter Smithers, *The Life of Joseph Addison* (Oxford University Press, 1968), 16–17. The poem by Montgomery can be found in Firth, *The Minstrelsy of Isis,* 235, and that by Heath-Stubbs in Antonia Fraser, ed., *Oxford and Oxfordshire in Verse* (Secker and Warburg, 1982), 4.

p. 62) 'Only a few of these colleges are modern in construction and the other houses are contemptible . . .': Carl Philip Moritz, *Journeys of a German in England in 1782,* trans. and ed. Reginald Nettel (Jonathan Cape, 1965), 140.

p. 62) The quotations of eighteenth-century verse are taken from Firth, *The Minstrelsy of Isis,* as follows: Tickell, 38; Combe, 45; Warton, 40. Firth's statement, 'If only verses of high poetic excellence had been included . . .', is on p. vii.

p. 63) For the observation by Celia Fiennes that college fellows 'may live very Neatly and well if Sober', see Christopher Morris, ed., *The Journeys of Celia Fiennes* (Cresset Press, 1949), 37.

p. 63) Information about Jane Austen's Oxford connections is taken from John Halperin, *The Life of Jane Austen* (Harvester, 1984), 18–25. The remark by Ferrars, 'I was therefore entered at Oxford . . .': Jane Austen, *Sense and Sensibility* (Oxford University Press, 1933), 103. Thorpe's 'You would hardly meet with a man . . .': Jane Austen, *Northanger Abbey* (Oxford University Press, 1933), 64.

p. 63) For the remark by Steerforth, 'I am what they call an Oxford man', see Charles Dickens, *David Copperfield,* ed. Nina Burgis (Oxford University Press, 1981), 246.

p. 63) The passage from *Liberal Education* is taken from *The Works of Vicesimus Knox, D.D.* (1824), 4:255.

THE CLUB

p. 64) The suggestion by John Bayley that Terry Eagleton 'hates English literature for being English, as well as for being literature' was made in a letter to the
Times Literary Supplement, no. 4522, December 1–7, 1989.

p. 66) The wording of Johnson's lines about Warton's poetry is taken from the
Dictionary of National Biography, 30:893.

p. 66) The quotation about Johnson's room, 'the enthusiasts of learning will ever
contemplate it with veneration': James Boswell, *The Life of Samuel Johnson*
(Oxford University Press, 1953), 53. The quotation, 'the truth is he was
depressed by poverty . . .': ibid., 54.

p. 67) The comments made by Johnson can be found in Boswell, *Life of Samuel
Johnson,* as follows: about the excellency of the institution, 391; about the
improvement of the dons, 381; about dons' pay, 726; about lectures, 1136.

p. 67) The visit to Oxford of Johnson and Boswell is described in Boswell, *The Life
of Samuel Johnson* (Oxford University Press, 1953), 690–95.

p. 67) Information about the change in the time of dinner during the eighteenth century is taken from A.D. Godley, *Oxford in the Eighteenth Century*
(Methuen, 1908), 133.

p. 68) Moritz's anecdote can be found in *Journeys of a German,* 132–37. The quotation, 'Damme! I must read prayers . . .', is on p. 137. (The quotation from the
Bible is in Judges 4:13.)

p. 68) 'This Oxford expedition was, altogether, highly entertaining': Fanny Burney (Madame d'Arblay), *Diary and Letters of Madame d'Arblay,* ed. Charlotte Bar-
rett (Bell, 1891), 149.

p. 69) 'The Lounger' can be found in *The Oxford Sausage* (1772), 92–93. Tom's,
a coffee-house in the High, was known for being socially exclusive and expensive.
The Mitre still remains in High Street, and the Three Tuns, to give it its full title,
was the venue of the Poetical Club of which Warton's father had been a leading
member.

LISTLESS LANGUOR AND NATURE'S ODDITIES

p. 70) The quotations from Prideaux are taken from Humphrey Prideaux, *Letters
to John Ellis 1674–1722,* ed. Edward Maunde Thompson (Camden Society,
1875), 13, the DNB, and R.W. Ketton-Cremer, *Humphrey Prideaux* (published pri-
vately, 1955), 3.

p. 70) With regard too Woodforde, see W. N. Hargreaves-Mawdsley, ed., *Woodforde at Oxford 1759–1776* (Oxford Historical Society, 1969).

p. 71) 'The University over which the Duke of Wellington was installed as Chancellor in 1834 owned undissolved continuity with the Oxford of Addison,
Thomas Hearne, and the Wartons': Tuckwell, *Reminiscences of Oxford,* 2.

p. 71) Hogg's reference to 'the listless languor, the monstrous indifference, if not the absolute antipathy to learning . . .': Thomas Hogg, *Shelley at Oxford* (Methuen, 1904), 33–34.

p. 71) The anecdote about Shelley and 'sporting the oak' can be found in Hogg, *Shelley at Oxford*, 62–65. The description of Shelley's room is on pp. 31–32.

p. 72) For the incident of Shelley seizing the baby on Magdalen Bridge, see Hogg, *Shelley at Oxford*, 168.

p. 72) The quotation concerning 'the dominion of a singular and most unaccountable passion over the mind of an enthusiast': Hogg, *Shelley at Oxford*, 52.

p. 72) 'I have experienced tyranny and injustice before, and I well know what vulgar violence is . . .': Hogg, *Shelley at Oxford*, 22.

p. 73) 'A total neglect of all learning, an unseemly turbulence, the most monstrous irregularities . . .': Hogg, *Shelley at Oxford*, 218.

p. 73) 'With respect to its superiors, Oxford only exhibits waste of wigs and want of wisdom': Robert Southey, *Life and Correspondence* (Longman, Brown, Green, and Longmans, 1849), 1:177.

p. 73) Cobbett's charge that 'the great and prevalent characteristic is *folly*': William Cobbett, *Rural Rides* (Penguin, 1967), 34.

p. 73) The reference by Cox to the professor of Greek can be found in *Recollections of Oxford*, 167; the reference to the principal of hall: ibid., 180.

p. 74) 'The Oxford fellow of these years made Oxford his little world, viewing everything through the medium of a college and Common-room atmosphere': Cox, *Recollections of Oxford*, 8.

p. 74) 'The *blow* was indeed a heavy one to Lord C. Osborne's family': Cox, *Recollections of Oxford*, 245.

p. 74) 'Nature, after constructing an oddity, was wont to break the mould . . .': Tuckwell, *Reminiscences of Oxford* (Cassell, 1901), 11.

p. 74) Information about Routh is drawn from Tuckwell, *Reminiscences of Oxford*, 164–66, and Cox, *Recollections of Oxford*, 153.

p. 75) Information about Buckland is taken from Tuckwell, *Reminiscences of Oxford*, 35–40, and Hibbert, *The Encyclopaedia of Oxford*, 63.

p. 75) The anecdote concerning 'Presence of Mind' Smith is taken from Tuckwell, *Reminiscences of Oxford*, 128.

p. 75) The story involving Tom Davis comes from Tuckwell, *Reminiscences of Oxford*, 29–30.

p. 75) The anecdote involving Dr. Frowd is taken from Tuckwell, *Reminiscences of Oxford*, 27.

p. 76) Gladstone's description of Pattison's book as among 'the most tragic and the most memorable books of the nineteenth century' is taken from Mrs. Humphry Ward, *A Writer's Recollections* (Collins, 1919), 106.

p. 76) The description of Pattison as 'unsociable, ungenial, and morose . . .' is taken from Mark Pattison, *Memoirs* (Centaur, 1969), 263.

p. 76) For Pattison's account of the college election, see *Memoirs*, 273–92. The quotations about his reaction are taken from pp. 292–98. V.H.H. Green's account of the election can be found in his *Oxford Common Room*, 146–70.

p. 76) 'I am fairly entitled to say that, since the year 1851, I have lived wholly for study': Pattison, *Memoirs*, 331. The information about Pattison's final illness and calling for his books is taken from Thomas Wright, *The Life of Walter Pater* (Everett, 1907), 2:88.

p. 77) For the description of Lincoln as 'a small, unfashionable college . . .', see Green, *Oxford Common Room*, 16.

p. 77) The reference to Pattison's marriage as the 'sensation of the moment' is taken from Charles Oman, *Memories of Victorian Oxford* (Methuen, 1941), 210.

p. 77) The description of Casaubon as a 'dried-up pedant' is taken from George Eliot, *Middlemarch* (Penguin, 1985), 237.

p. 77) Mrs. Ward's impression of the Pattisons is given in *A Writer's Recollections*, 110.

p. 77) Pattison's reference to Newman's lack of German is in Pattison, *Memoirs*, 210, and runs as follows: 'A.P. Stanley once said to me, "How different the fortunes of the Church of England might have been if Newman had been able to read German."'

p. 78) Though Pattison was originally considered to be the original of Casaubon, the identification has since been belittled, and the fictional character is now thought to be a composite drawn from several real-life models, of whom Pattison may have been one. There was a discussion of the issue in the *Times Literary Supplement*, February 16, 1973. Gordon Haight in *George Eliot* (Oxford University Press, 1968) put forward a strong case in favour of R.H. Brabant, and reference books which cite Brabant as prototype include the *Oxford Companion to English Literature;* William Amos, *The Originals* (Jonathan Cape, 1985); Alan Bold and Robert Giddings, *Who Was Really Who in Fiction* (Longman, 1987). M.C. Rintoul, *Dictionary of Real People and Places in Fiction* (Routledge, 1993), 732, quotes Mrs. Humphry Ward as suggesting that the Pattison identification was improbable and the book cites five other possible models. It also suggests that Emilia's identification with Dorothea is unlikely, though the religious side of the character may have been suggested by the letters of Mrs. Pattison. Richard Ellmann's article can be found in *A Long the RiverRun* (Hamish Hamilton, 1988), 115–31. The historian V.H.H. Green claims that Pattison was not only a more sympathetic but a more vigorous character than Eliot's Casaubon, and interestingly he suggests that Pattison grew to be more like Casaubon in old age — a case as Wilde would have said of life imitating art. See Green, *Oxford Common Room*, 211–16.

p. 78) 'You want a secretary, housekeeper, nurse for your mother; I want a home of my own, and a "guide, philosopher and friend"': Rhoda Broughton, *Belinda* (Virago, 1984), 183. The anecdote concerning Pattison and the calling-card is taken from the introduction to Pattison, *Memoirs*, xii.

p. 78) Casaubon's blood is described as 'all semi-colons and parentheses' in Eliot, *Middlemarch*, 96.

OXFORD AWAKE!

p. 79) The description of Newman's *Apologia* as the Oxford Movement's 'abiding literary monument' comes from A.L. Rowse, *Oxford in the History of the Nation* (Weidenfeld and Nicolson, 1975), 178.

p. 79) 'Soon there will be no middle ground left and every man, and especially every clergyman, will be compelled to make his choice': from a contemporary notice quoted in John Newman, *Apologia pro Vita Sua*, ed. M.J. Svaglic (Oxford University Press, 1967), 93.

p. 80) The Oxford student who wonders 'how an Englishman, a gentleman, can so eat dirt' can be found in John Newman, *Loss and Gain* (Oxford University Press, 1968), 85.

p. 80) 'The scene of this new Movement was as like as it could be in our modern world to a Greek *polis* . . .': R.W. Church, *The Oxford Movement, Twelve Years, 1833–45* (Macmillan, 1892), 159–60.

p. 80) The quotations about the Oxford Movement are taken from Cox, *Recollections of Oxford*, 273; Tuckwell, *Reminiscences of Oxford*, 183; Pattison, *Memoirs*, 236, 182, 184, 185.

p. 81) 'The waters of the true Faith had dived underground at the Reformation, and they were waiting for the wand of Newman to strike the rock . . .': Lytton Strachey, *Eminent Victorians* (Penguin, 1948), 25.

p. 81) Pattison's description of Newman, 'The force of his dialectic, and the beauty of his rhetorical exposition . . .', can be found in *Memoirs*, 210.

p. 81) 'The name of Cardinal Newman is a great name to the imagination still; his genius and his style are still things of power . . .': Matthew Arnold, 'Emerson', from 'Discourses in America'. See R.H. Super, ed., *The Complete Prose Works of Matthew Arnold*, vol. 10, *Philistinism in England and America* (Ann Arbor: University of Michigan Press, 1965), 165.

p. 82) 'The magic of his personality, the rhetorical sweetness of his sermons . . .': Tuckwell, *Reminiscences of Oxford*, 184.

p. 82) Information about the manner in which Newman wrote the *Apologia* is taken from Ian Ker, *John Henry Newman* (Oxford University Press, 1990), 544–55.

p. 82) Joyce's reference to Newman's prose as 'cloistral, silver-veined . . ." is taken from Brian Martin, ed., *Macmillan Anthologies of English Literature*, vol. 4, *The Nineteenth Century* (Macmillan, 1989), 279.

p. 82) The charge that the arguments of Newman's *Apologia* were 'as meaningless as the inscriptions of Easter Island' can be found in Andrew Lang, *Oxford* (Seeley, Jackson and Halliday, 1885), 240.

p. 82) 'In him I took leave of my first College, Trinity . . .': Newman, *Apologia pro Vita Sua*, 213.

p. 83) 'If then a practical end must be assigned to a University course . . .': John Newman, *The Idea of a University*, ed. I.T. Ker (Oxford University Press, 1976), 154.

p. 83) Tuckwell's reference to Cox's poem as 'a satire of unusual force' is taken from *Reminiscences of Oxford*, 150.

p. 84) 'Oxford awake! the land hath borne too long / The senseless jingling of thy drowsy song . . .': George Cox, *Black Gowns and Red Coats* (Ridgeway and Sons, 1834), 2:28.

p. 84) 'The public opinion of the University . . . had come to regard a college as a club . . .': Pattison, *Memoirs*, 75. His observation that 'There were Tory majorities in all the colleges . . .' is on p. 244.

p. 85) Pusey's declaration that Oxford 'was lost to the Church of England' is taken from Mallet, *History of the University*, 2:332.

Chapter 4

Acknowledgment is made to the following two sources from which information was drawn for both this and the next chapter: Judy Batson, *Oxford in Fiction: An Annotated Bibliography* (New York: Garland, 1989), which lists all the fictional works set in Oxford with brief comments including quotations from contemporary reviews, and M.R. Proctor, *The English University Novel* (Berkeley and Los Angeles: University of California Press, 1957), which deals with the Oxford novel in some depth, though as its title indicates it has a wider concern.

p. 86) The opening quotation is taken from Gerard Hopkins, *A City in the Foreground* (Constable, 1921), 288.

p. 86) The estimate for the number of Victorian novels is taken from Michael Wheeler, *English Fiction of the Victorian Period* (Longman, 1985), 1.

p. 86) The estimate of 119 for the number of Oxford novels between 1945 and 1988 is taken from Ian Carter, *Ancient Cultures of Conceit: British University Fiction in the Post-War Years* (Routledge, 1990); though since the criteria for Carter's selection appear to exclude such works as John Fowles, *Daniel Martin* (1977), the figure may be even higher.

p. 86) The call for a moratorium on Oxford novels can be found in Julian Barnes, *Flaubert's Parrot* (Jonathan Cape, 1984), 98.

p. 87) The nominations for best Oxford novel have been as follows: (1) *The Adventures of Verdant Green*, by Oona H. Ball under the pseudonym of Barbara Burke, *Barbara Goes to Oxford* (Simpkin, Marshall, Hamilton and Kent, 1907), 18; (2) *Tom Brown at Oxford*, by W. Tuckwell, *Reminiscences of Oxford* (Cassell, 1901), 199; (3) *Robert Elsmere*, by A.M. Quinton, 'Oxford in Fiction', *Oxford Magazine* (1958) 76:214; (4) *Zuleika Dobson*, by Dacre Balsdon, *Oxford Now and Then* (Duckworth, 1970), 45; (5) *Sinister Street*, by Proctor, *The English University Novel*, 154; (6) *A City in the Foreground*, by John Betjeman, *An Oxford University Chest* (Oxford University Press, 1979), 185; (7) *Brideshead Revisited*, by Kingsley Amis, *Memoirs* (Hutchinson, 1991), 46.

p. 87) For the inspector who finds that Oxford 'looks like a back street of Birmingham', see G.D.H. Cole and M. Cole, *Off with Her Head* (Collins, 1938), 87.

p. 88) With regard to the college of Thackeray's *Pendennis,* this is usually presumed to be a fictional amalgam based on the author's memories of his student days at Trinity College, Cambridge, though Michael De-la-Noy in *Exploring Oxford* (Headline, 1991) identifies St. Boniface as the Oxford college of Pembroke, presumably because of the mention of Doctor Johnson and its location in the shadow of the grandest college of the university. Most authorities, however, accept the view of Sir George Saintsbury in 'Novels of University Life', *Macmillan's Magazine,* 77 (1898): 334–43, that though Thackeray's description could refer to both Oxford or Cambridge, there was 'no doubt just sufficient Cambridge flavour to identify the original'. Significantly, Judy Batson does not include the novel in her *Oxford in Fiction.*

p. 88) For the assertion that although Cambridge has the better poets Oxford has the better poems, see Evelyn Waugh, *A Little Learning* (Chapman and Hall, 1964), 167.

p. 89) Thomas Arnold's statement that 'rather than have science the principal thing in my son's mind, I would gladly have him think the sun went round the earth . . .' comes from T.W. Bamford, ed., *Thomas Arnold on Education* (Cambridge University Press, 1970), 116.

p. 89) Matthew Arnold's belief that Oxford came 'nearer perhaps than all the science of Tübingen' to full understanding is taken from the preface to *Essays in Criticism* (1865). See R.H. Super, ed., *The Complete Prose Works of Matthew Arnold,* vol. 3, *Lectures and Essays in Criticism* (Ann Arbor: University of Michigan Press, 1962), 290.

p. 89) 'Let him then who is fond of indulging in a dreamlike existence go to Oxford . . .': William Hazlitt, *Sketches of the Principal Picture Galleries,* in *The Complete Works of William Hazlitt,* ed. P.P. Howe, A.R. Waller, and Arnold Glover (Dent, 1930–34), 10:70.

p. 89) The quotations from Compton Mackenzie, 'dreaming became a duty' and 'Surely this whole city, with its happiness . . .' are taken respectively from *Sinister Street* (Penguin, 1960), 157, 490.

p. 90) 'What distinguishes Cambridge from Oxford, broadly speaking, is that nobody who has been to Cambridge feels impelled to write about it . . .': A.A. Milne, *Autobiography* (New York: E.P. Dutton, 1939), 159.

DISCOVERY AND SELF-DISCOVERY

p. 91) 'The reader who has made his way through the long list of English university novels cannot fail to note the remarkable sameness . . .': Proctor, *The English University Novel*, 1.

p. 91) Pater's description of the university as a 'dreamy or problematic preparation for life' is taken from 'Emerald Uthwart', in Walter Pater, *Miscellaneous Studies* (Macmillan, 1910), 226.

p. 92) The parson who claims 'Oxford is a place full of temptations . . .' can be found in Tom Hughes, *Tom Brown at Oxford* (Nelson, 1914), 336.

p. 92) For an account of the 'Hero's Journey', see Joseph Campbell, *The Hero with a Thousand Faces* (Princeton: Princeton University Press, 1973).

p. 92) The claim that *Reginald Dalton* was the first Oxford novel was made by George Saintsbury in 'Novels of University Life', 335–36. The assertion was supported by William S. Knickerbocker in *Creative Oxford* (New York: Syracuse University Press, 1925), 14, and, with reservations, by Proctor in *The English University Novel*, 207. Claims have also been made on behalf of Chaucer's 'The Miller's Tale' and Stephen Penton's *The Guardian's Instruction* (1688), though in the strict sense of the term neither of these can properly be considered a novel.

p. 93) 'I am ruined, undone, utterly undone . . .': John Gibson Lockhart, *Reginald Dalton* (Cadell, 1823), 2:91.

p. 93) The eponymous freshman who is so thrilled that he 'said to himself, a thousand and a thousand times over, that he had at length found the terrestrial Elysium' can be found in Lockhart, *Reginald Dalton*, 1:339.

p. 93) The quotation from Lockhart about 'the solemn antique scenery which had at first so much pleased his . . .' can be found in *Reginald Dalton*, 2:74–75.

p. 94) The description of student life as 'a great period of discovery—and of self-discovery too' is taken from Anthony Powell, *A Question of Upbringing* (Boston: Little, Brown, 1955), 180.

IN AN ENGLISH COUNTRY HOUSE

p. 94) The quotation about the gentlemen-commoners 'being better born, or wealthier than the commoners . . .' is taken from Mark Pattison, *Memoirs* (Centaur, 1969), 68.

p. 94) The advice of Charles Ryder's cousin to 'Dress as you do in a country house' is in Evelyn Waugh, *Brideshead Revisited* (Penguin, 1962), 35.

p. 94) The claim that most people in the late nineteenth century thought 'that life in the country was inherently better than life in the town . . .' is made by Mark Girouard in *Life in the English Country House* (Penguin, 1980), 303.

p. 95) 'Before the warr wee had scholars who made a thorough search in scholasticall and polemicall divinity . . .': Andrew Clark, ed., *The Life and Times of Anthony Wood* (Oxford Historical Society, 1891–1900), 1:423.

p. 95) Information about college and country house apartments is taken from Girouard, *English Country House,* 206, and H.M. Colvin, 'Architecture', in *The History of the University of Oxford,* ed. J. Catto (Oxford University Press, 1984–94), 5:843–45.

p. 95) 'I suppose your idea is to diversify games with a little rudimentary study?': Charles Edward Montague, *Rough Justice* (Chatto and Windus, 1928), 133.

p. 95) The cupboard in *Verdant Green* with 'wine above and whine below' can be found in Edward Bradley, *The Adventures of Mr. Verdant Green* (Blackwood, 1872–78), 83.

p. 96) The students in hunting gear at morning chapel can be found in Tom Hughes, *Tom Brown at Oxford,* 11. For the student cracking a whip, see Mackenzie, *Sinister Street,* 379.

p. 96) For the description of Michael Fane's arrival at college, see Mackenzie, *Sinister Street,* 374.

p. 96) The reference to 'English county families baying for broken glass' is in Evelyn Waugh, *Decline and Fall* (Penguin, 1937), 10.

p. 96) 'On the walls Michael's pictures had been collected to achieve through another medium the effect of his books': Mackenzie, *Sinister Street,* 472. The description of Charles Ryder's rooms can be found in Waugh, *Brideshead Revisited,* 36.

p. 96) 'Oxford May mornings! When the prunus bloomed / We'd drive to Sunday lunch at Sezincote': John Betjeman, *Summoned by Bells* (John Murray, 1976), 98.

p. 96) 'By the way, d'you go back to Oxford tomorrow?': Beverley Nichols, *Patchwork* (Chatto and Windus, 1921), 144.

p. 97) 'You seem to have found out a great deal about Christ Church . . .': Mackenzie, *Sinister Street,* 380.

p. 97) As regards the origin of the saying 'All rowed fast, but none so fast as stroke', the *Oxford Dictionary of Quotations* claims that it derives from the following passage in Desmond Coke's *Sandford of Merton:* 'His blade struck the water a full second before any other . . . until . . .as the boats began to near the winning-post, his own was dipping into the water *twice* as often as any other.' (The issue was discussed in *Oxford Today* 4, no.1, Michaelmas Issue, 1991, 62–63.)

p. 98) Waugh's response to the college toughs is described in *A Little Learning*, 164. Wilde's response is in Richard Ellmann, *Oscar Wilde* (Hamish Hamilton, 1988), 43.

p. 98) 'Keble like Mansfield and Ruskin Hall was in Oxford, but not in the least of Oxford': Mackenzie, *Sinister Street*, 508. The description of Queen's as 'that great terra incognita' is on p. 510. The Grid, restricted 'to those seven or eight colleges . . .', is referred to on p. 493.

p. 99) 'They learned finally that the colleges were merely a series of social differences . . .': Jean Fayard, *Oxford and Margaret* (Jarrolds, 1925), 17.

p. 99) 'Trinity has a very high percentage of men from the larger public schools': Betjeman, *An Oxford University Chest*, 35. The women's colleges too developed individual characteristics, and a saying of the 1920s ran as follows: 'LMH [Lady Margaret Hall] for Ladies, St. Hilda's for Games, St. Hugh's for Religion, and Somerville for Brains.'

p. 99) Jowett's 'If we had a little more money, we could absorb the University' is taken from Charles Edward Mallet, *A History of the University of Oxford* (Methuen, 1924–27), 3:346.

p. 100) 'The Age of Jowett'—Felix Markham's *Oxford* (Weidenfeld and Nicolson, 1967) provides one example of the reform period being characterised in such fashion.

p. 100) 'First come I. My name is Jowett' is taken from John Jones, *Balliol College: A History, 1263–1939* (Oxford University Press, 1988), 223.

p. 100) For J.A. Spender's description of Jowett, 'Sometimes he rewarded you with a brief "Good essay" . . .', see Jan Morris, *The Oxford Book of Oxford* (Oxford University Press, 1984), 272.

p. 101) The anecdote about Jowett, 'he scarcely ever spoke . . .', can be found in Augustus Hare, *The Story of My Life* (Allen, 1896), 1:420.

p. 101) The description of the Balliol manner as 'a tranquil consciousness of effortless superiority' is taken from Nichols, *Patchwork*, 34.

p. 101) 'I'm sure I could have got one [scholarship] anywhere else': Nichols, *Patchwork*, 28.

p. 101) The quip about the sun rising over Wadham and setting over Worcester was attributed by Evelyn Waugh to Ronald Knox.

p. 102) Information about Walter Pater's connections is taken from Thomas Wright, *The Life of Walter Pater* (Everett, 1907).

p. 102) 'You have come to Oxford, some of you to hunt foxes . . .': Mackenzie, *Sinister Street*, 395.

STUDENT HEROES AND MALE BONDS

p. 102) Forster's classification of characters into 'flat' and 'round' can be found in E.M. Forster, *Aspects of the Novel* (Edward Arnold, 1949), 65.

p. 103) The identification of Pendennis with Thackeray was acknowledged by the author in a quotation ('Pendennis is very like me') cited in M.C. Rintoul, *Dictionary of Real People and Places in Fiction* (Routledge, 1993), 889.

p. 103) The description of Nichols as 'a Post-Great-War-Super-Aesthete' is by George Alfred Kolkhorst in 'From Verdant Green to Oxford Marmalade; or, The Oxford Novel', paper given to St. John's College Essay Society, now in Oxford City Library, 1952, 10.

p. 103) The character of Charles Ryder was not intended by Waugh to be a self-portrait, but the similarity of situation is striking. In *The Brideshead Generation* (Weidenfeld and Nicolson, 1989), Humphrey Carpenter considers the similarities and the differences between the author's student career and that of his fictional character.

p. 103) 'It doesn't seem to me one gains the quintessence of the university unless one reads Greats': Mackenzie, *Sinister Street*, 590.

p. 104) The chemist who is 'treated like a Papuan dwarf' can be found in Fayard, *Oxford and Margaret*, 269.

p. 104) The assault on a scientist can be found in Mackenzie, *Sinister Street*, 514. The 'mouse of a man connected with the Natural Sciences' who lives above Charles Ryder can be found in Waugh, *Brideshead Revisited*, 30.

p. 105) 'Those are the golden sessions; when four or five of us after a hard day's walking . . .': C.S. Lewis, *The Four Loves* (Bles, 1960), 85.

p. 105) The remarks on women by Nicholas Amhurst can be found in *Terrae Filius*, no. 32 (1721).

p. 105) The quotation from Knox, 'Delightful retreat, where never female shewed her head . . .', comes from *Essays Moral and Literary* (1782) and is taken from Morris, *Oxford Book of Oxford*, 148.

p. 105) 'How a few flounces and bright girlish smiles can change the aspect of the sternest homes of knowledge!': Bradley, *Verdant Green*, 2:104.

p. 105) 'Yes, 'tis a serious-minded place. Not but there's wenches in the streets o'nights': Thomas Hardy, *Jude the Obscure* (New York: Norton, 1985), 20.

p. 106) For some startling language in *Loss and Gain* concerning male-female relationships, see John Newman, *Loss and Gain* (Oxford University Press, 1986), 134.

p. 106) For the duke of Dorset's comment on the 'sheer violation of sanctuary', see Max Beerbohm, *Zuleika Dobson* (Penguin, 1952), 24.

p. 106) 'The great point of Oxford, in fact the whole point of Oxford, is that there are no girls': Mackenzie, *Sinister Street,* 598.

p. 106) George Steiner's remarks about the centrality of male intimacy to English culture can be found in 'From Caxton to *Omeros*', *Times Literary Supplement,* no. 4717, August 27, 1993, 13.

p. 106) 'To the Balliol Men Still in Africa' can be found in Hilaire Belloc, *Complete Verse* (Pimlico, 1991), 43–44.

p. 107) 'It was as though he were leaving behind a part of his personality . . .:' Nichols, *Patchwork,* 157.

p. 108) 'I love watching you tub—you've such a glorious figure': 'An Oxford Scholar', in *The Massacre of the Innocents* (Billing, 1907), 186.

p. 108) 'The strange one-sexed education at public schools and universities . . .': A.J.P. Taylor, *English History, 1914–1945* (Oxford University Press, 1965), 260. Background information about homosexual affectation in the prewar university is drawn from Balsdon, *Oxford Now and Then,* 56. Information about the affair between Betjeman and Auden is drawn from Carpenter, *The Brideshead Generation,* 101, and Humphrey Carpenter, *W.H. Auden* (Allen and Unwin, 1981), 47–49.

p. 108) With reference to Housman's relationship with Moses Jackson, Norman Page writes: 'For Housman, it was the love affair of his life, and his unrequited devotion was still constant when Jackson died more than forty years later.' See Norman Page *A.E. Housman: A Critical Biography* (Macmillan, rev. ed 1996), 41.

p. 109) The reference to 'a naughtiness high in the catalogue of grave sins' is in Waugh, *Brideshead Revisited,* 56.

p. 109) Information about the antipathy between Betjeman and Lewis is drawn from Humphrey Carpenter, *The Inklings* (Allen and Unwin, 1978), and Bevis Hillier, *Young Betjeman* (John Murray, 1988). Walter Hooper suggests in *C.S. Lewis: A Companion and Guide* (HarperCollins, 1996) that Lewis mellowed in middle age and would not have minded Betjeman's youthful ways later in his career. To support the claim he refers to the friendly relations between the Magdalen tutor and one of his pupils at the end of World War II, Kenneth Tynan (1927–80), an even more flamboyant character than Betjeman.

p. 110) 'I'm dog-tired of driving and doing the High Street . . .' Hughes, *Tom Brown at Oxford,* 31.

p. 110) Information about *Peter Priggins* is taken from Proctor, *The English University Novel,* 74–75.

p. 111) For Mackenzie's claim to have invented the use of 'hearty', see Compton Mackenzie, *My Life and Times* (Chatto and Windus, 1964), 3:130.

p. 111) For the rowing set noticed by Charles Reding, see Newman, *Loss and Gain*, 161.

p. 111) 'Dear sweet clodhoppers, if you knew anything of sexual psychology you would know that nothing could give me keener pleasure . . .': Waugh, *Brideshead Revisited*, 61.

p. 112) The quotation about dons, 'they have lost not only time, but the elasticity of youth . . .', is taken from 'An Oxford Scholar', 231.

p. 112) 'He loved his college because it protected him . . .': Joanna Cannan, *High Table* (Oxford University Press, 1987), 84.

p. 112) 'Proctors and policemen were made by an all-wise Providence . . . .': 'An Oxford Scholar', 231.

p. 112) Information about Urquhart/Sligger is drawn from Carpenter, *The Brideshead Generation*, 89–89, and Cyril Bailey, *Francis Fortescue Urquhart: A Memoir* (Macmillan, 1936).

p. 112) The claim that Sligger was the model for Pater's 'Emerald Uthwart' was made in his obituary notice in *The Times*, September 19, 1934, and by his biographer, Cyril Bailey in *Francis Fortescue Urquhart*. The identification is endorsed by C.M. Bowra in *Memories, 1898–1939* (Weidenfeld and Nicolson, 1966), 119, and William Amos, *The Originals* (Jonathan Cape, 1985), 521. The similarity of last name would seem to support the assertion, though Thomas Wright claims in *Life of Walter Pater*, 2:166, that the portrait was in essence an idealised autobiography and that the physical prototype was a schoolfriend of Pater.

p. 113) Betjeman's description of Sligger surrounded by well-bred students is in *Summoned by Bells*, 104.

p. 113) 'He [Sligger] was not a wit; nor an Oxford "character" . . .': Evelyn Waugh, *Ronald Knox* (Cassell, 1988), 86.

p. 113) As regards the prototype for Waugh's Samgrass, Christopher Sykes is quoted in Rintoul, *Dictionary of Real People*, 219, as stating that the author himself identified Samgrass with Bowra. Carpenter in *The Brideshead Generation*, 362, claims that only the physical appearance is based on Bowra, though Christopher Hollis, *Oxford in the Twenties* (Heinemann, 1976), 32–33, and Alan Bold and Robert Giddings, *Who Was Really Who in Fiction* (Longman, 1987), 287, cite Bowra as sole model. A noted scholar, wit, and the dominating figure of his day, Bowra was himself a 'Sliggerite' in his youth, and the connection attests to the pervasive extent of Urquhart's influence.

p. 113) For Quinton's description of Sillery as 'perhaps the greatest bachelor don of fiction', see Quinton, 'Oxford in Fiction', 212.

p. 113) 'Urquhart (of some university fame, social rather than academic) has undoubtedly been portrayed in more than one novel . . .': Anthony Powell, *Infants of the Spring* (Heinemann, 1976), 150.

p. 114) Johnson's visit to Oxford in 1754 is described in James Boswell, *The Life of Samuel Johnson* (Oxford University Press, 1953), 191.

p. 114) 'Quarter to nine, sir! Breakfast getting cold, sir': 'An Oxford Scholar', 52.

p. 114) The description of Venner's as 'a treasure-house of wise counsel . . .': Mackenzie, *Sinister Street*, 475. Venner's buttery was based on the real-life Gunner's in Magdalen College, run for thirty-four years by Richard Gunstone. The portrait of Gunner's in Mackenzie's *My Life and Times*, 3:143, is similar to that of the novel, if less sentimentalised.

p. 114) The Balliol porter who 'could have taken a first class in any school . . .': Hopkins, *City in the Foreground*, 39.

p. 114) Oakleigh's 'gradually I found that something might be said even for men who had never been to a public school . . .': Stephen McKenna, *Sonia: Between Two Worlds* (Methuen, 1917), 65.

THE INITIATION OF BRADLEY'S FRESHMAN

p. 115) Information about the sales of *Verdant Green* is taken from Christopher Hibbert, ed., *The Encyclopaedia of Oxford* (Macmillan, 1988), 141.

p. 115) 'What do you expect undergraduates to be like?': Powell, *A Question of Upbringing*, 173.

p. 116) 'They were in good time for the coach . . .': Bradley, *Verdant Green*, 1:19.

p. 117) 'Keep your pecker up, old feller! and put your trust in old beans': Bradley, *Verdant Green*, 3:94.

p. 117) 'I can call spirits from the vasty deep . . .': Bradley, *Verdant Green*, 3:101.

p. 117) 'The chapel's the hopposite side . . .': Bradley, *Verdant Green*, 1:30.

p. 117) 'Ollidays, sir? Oh, I see sir! Vacation, you mean, sir': Bradley, *Verdant Green*, 1:55.

p. 117) Fosbrooke's demand of Filcher as to 'What the doose he meant by not waiting on his master?': Bradley, *Verdant Green*, 1:47.

p. 118) Fosbrooke's advice not to waste time on 'absolutions . . .': Bradley, *Verdant Green*, 1:51.

p. 118) The reference to Merton 'postmasters' can be found in Bradley, *Verdant Green*, 1:62.

p. 118) 'You see, Verdant, you are gradually being initiated into the Oxford mysteries': Bradley, *Verdant Green*, 1:64.

p. 118) 'Genelum anladies *(cheers)*,—I meangenelum . . .': Bradley, *Verdant Green*, 1:71.

p. 118) 'Time for chapel, sir! here is a chap ill, indeed!': Bradley, *Verdant Green*, 1:73.

p. 119) The reference to 'bill-ious fever': Bradley, *Verdant Green*, 1:110.

p. 119) Verdant's 'vaulting ambition': Bradley, *Verdant Green*, 2:49.

p. 119) 'The lettered Gown lorded it over the unlettered Town . . .': Bradley, *Verdant Green*, 2:15.

p. 119) The town and gown fight quotations are taken from Bradley, *Verdant Green*, 2:31.

p. 120) Verdant's offer to reveal 'some of the mysteries of College life' can be found in Bradley, *Verdant Green*, 3:101.

p. 120) The two years that pass in a single sentence occur in Bradley, *Verdant Green*, 3:100.

p. 121) Bouncer's claim that it is wrong to 'plough' a man from Harrow can be found in Bradley, *Verdant Green*, 3:89.

p. 121) The reference to Mr. Bouncer leaving with 'great credit' can be found in Bradley, *Verdant Green*, 3:101.

p. 121) 'I knew that the customs of Oxford must of course be very different . . .': Bradley, *Verdant Green*, 1:61.

p. 122) The proctors in 'their apparently insane promenade . . .' can be found in Bradley, *Verdant Green*, 3:110.

p. 122) For Auden's comment on the publication of *Alice's Adventures in Wonderland* 'as memorable a day in the history of literature . . .', see Martin Gardner, ed., *The Annotated Alice* (Penguin, 1970), 21.

FROM WARNINGS TO WONDERLAND

p. 122) 'Oxford is a place where men have lost their souls' is taken from Humphrey Neville Dickinson, *Keddy: A Story of Oxford* (Heinemann, 1907), 9.

p. 123) 'Ah, Ralph, could you but have seen to what depths of depravity you were soon to sink!': Desmond F.T. Coke, *Sandford of Merton* (Alden, 1903), 10. The examples of misinformation are as follows: the Sheldonian Theatre was not used for plays, but for university ceremonies; college staircases were not carpeted, but bare; male students did not drink cocoa, though the women did (the men prided themselves on pipe-smoking and their consumption of alcohol); and university bulldogs, who were often middle-aged and bowler-hatted, were not very fast and were often outrun by student miscreants.

p. 123) Tuckwell's claim that *Tom Brown at Oxford* contains 'Every phase of College life as it exuberated sixty years ago . . .' is *Reminiscences of Oxford*, 199.

p. 123) 'How in the world are youngsters with unlimited credit, plenty of ready money, and fast tastes, to be kept from making fools and blackguards of themselves up here?': Hughes, *Tom Brown at Oxford*, 37.

p. 124) Information about public schools is taken from John Honey, *Tom Brown's Universe* (Millington, 1977).

p. 124) The quotation about 'what Heads of houses, Fellows, and all of them put before them . . .': Newman, *Loss and Gain*, 179.

p. 124) 'A tutor's breakfast is always a difficult affair . . .': Newman, *Loss and Gain*, 55–56.

p. 125) 'I would gladly give away all I am, and all I ever may become . . .': J.A. Froude, *Nemesis of Faith* (Walter Scott, 1906), 30.

p. 125) Gladstone's article was entitled '*Robert Elsmere* and the Battle of Belief' and was published in *Nineteenth Century*, May 1888. It can be found in volume 23, no. 135, 766–88.

p. 126) The quotation about taking to Oxford 'as a fish into water' is taken from Mrs. Humphry Ward, *A Writer's Recollections* (Collins, 1919), 102.

p. 126) Langham's appearance as 'a skeleton at the feast' can be found in Mrs. Humphry Ward, *Robert Elsmere* (Oxford University Press, 1987), 217.

p. 127) 'The dreaming city seemed to be still brooding in the autumn calm over the long succession of her sons . . .': Ward, *Robert Elsmere*, 51.

p. 127) The quotation 'Life, what is it but a dream?', can be found in Lewis Carroll, *Alice in Wonderland*, ed. Donald J. Gray (New York: Norton, 1971), 209.

p. 127) The quotation from Desmond Morris, 'a typical Oxford book . . .', can be found in *Oxford Today* 2, no. 1 (1989), 37.

p. 129) 'Within Christ Church there are folds of puckered space . . .': Peter Conrad, *The Everyman History of English Literature* (Dent, 1990), 85.

p. 129) The assertion that Dodgson 'was stiffly conservative in political, theological, social theory' is in Tuckwell, *Reminiscences of Oxford*, 141.

p. 130) Charles Dodgson is described as the 'complete Oxonian' and the most donnish of dons' in A.L. Rowse, *Oxford in the History of the Nation* (Weidenfeld and Nicolson, 1975), 204.

p. 130) 'If Oxford dons in the nineteenth century had an essence, he [Dodgson] was that essence': Virginia Woolf, 'Lewis Carroll', in *Aspects of Alice*, ed. Robert Phillips (Penguin, 1974), 78.

p. 130) Information about Dodgson is drawn from Phyllis Greenacre, *Swift and Carroll* (New York: International Universities, 1955); Derek Hudson, *Lewis Carroll: An Illustrated Biography* (Constable, 1954); Anne Clark, *Lewis Carroll: A Biography* (Dent and Sons, 1979); Roger Green, *Lewis Carroll* (Bodley Head, 1960); Mavis Batey, *The Adventures of Alice* (Macmillan, 1991).

p. 130) 'That Dodgson was fascinated by little girls and that he fantasised playfully about turning into one . . .': Greenacre, *Swift and Carroll*, 211.

p. 130) The quotations by Alice, 'Who in the world am I?' and 'I'll stay down here till I'm someone else', can be found in Carroll, *Alice in Wonderland*, 15, 17.

p. 131) The Cheshire Cat's declaration that 'we're all mad down here' can be found in Carroll, *Alice in Wonderland*, 51.

p. 131) 'It's really dreadful . . . how all the creatures argue': Carroll, *Alice in Wonderland*, 46.

p. 131) 'How the creatures order one about, and make one repeat lessons!': Carroll, *Alice in Wonderland*, 82.

p. 131) The duck's questioning of 'it' in 'even Stigand, the patriotic archbishop of Canterbury, found it advisable' can be found in Carroll, *Alice in Wonderland*, 22.

p. 131) The paraphrase of 'Be what you would seem to be' can be found in Carroll, *Alice in Wonderland*, 72.

p. 132) The episode of Mrs. Liddell tearing up Carroll's letters is described in Hudson, *Lewis Carroll*, 168. In the *Times Literary Supplement*, no. 4857, May 3, 1996, p. 15, Karoline Leach reports on new evidence about Dodgson's rift with the Liddell family which suggests that Mrs. Liddell may have been worried that Dodgson was going to propose to Lorina, Alice's older sister (or even to their governess).

p. 133) The claim of the young Keddy to have passed 'through the looking-glass . . .' can be found in Dickinson, *Keddy*, 22.

p. 133) Acknowledgment is made to Humphrey Carpenter, *The Brideshead Generation*, for information concerning the connection between *Alice in Wonderland* and *Brideshead Revisited*.

p. 133) For Ryder's desire to find 'that low door in the wall . . .', see Waugh, *Brideshead Revisited*, 40.

p. 133) The reference to 'the loveliest garden you ever saw': Carroll, *Alice in Wonderland*, 10.

p. 133) Sebastian's 'I should like to bury something precious in every place where I've been happy . . .': Waugh, *Brideshead Revisited*, 33.

Chapter 5

p. 135) The opening quotation from 'A Passionate Pilgrim' can be found in *The Novels and Tales of Henry James* (Cambridge and New York: Harvard University Press/Scribners, 1907–9), 13:417.

p. 138) 'I'm so positive that the best of Oxford is the best of England . . .': Compton Mackenzie, *Sinister Street* (Penguin, 1960), 487.

p. 139) For the observation that 'the *Republic* lay open on every table . . .', see Jean Fayard, *Oxford and Margaret* (Jarrolds, 1925), 252.

p. 139) 'At least half of the undergraduates were sent to Oxford simply as a place to grow up in': Evelyn Waugh, *A Little Learning* (Chapman and Hall, 1964), 172.

p. 139) The remark by Gaveston ffoulkes that 'they, poor bats and moles, thought of Oxford as a place of learning!' can be found in Hamish Miles and Raymond Mortimer, *The Oxford Circus* (John Lane, 1922), 138.

p. 139) The impression of Auberon who 'found that the life of most men at St. Mary's was just about as strenuous as lying full length in the sun . . .' can be found in Charles Edward Montague, *Rough Justice* (Chatto and Windus, 1926), 137.

FROM ARTIFICE TO ROMANCE

p. 140) 'Reynolds, 'tis thine, from the broad window's height, / To add new lustre to religious light . . .': Thomas Warton, 'On Sir Joshua Reynolds's Painted Window in New College Chapel, Oxford' (1782). See *The Works of the British Poets,* vol. 39, *The Poems of Scott and Thomas Warton* (J. Sharpe, 1808), 28.

p. 140) The quotation by Walpole, 'as soon as it was dark I ventured out . . .', is taken from Jan Morris, *Oxford* (Faber and Faber, 1978), 146.

p. 141) The information about *Endymion* is taken from Charles Edward Mallet, *A History of the University of Oxford* (Methuen, 1924–27), 3:214. The verse parody by Keats, 'The Gothic looks solemn . . .', can be found in Miriam Allott, ed., *The Poems of John Keats* (Longman, 1970), 284–85.

p. 141) 'Rome has been called the 'Sacred City'—might not *our* Oxford be called so too? . . .': William Hazlitt, *Sketches of the Principal Picture Galleries,* in P.P. Hone, ed., *The Complete Works of William Hazlitt* (Dent, 1930), 10:69–70.

p. 142) Wordsworth's sonnet entitled 'Oxford, May 30, 1820' can be found in Nowell Charles Smith, ed., *The Poems of William Wordsworth* (Methuen, 1908), 1:461.

p. 143) Newman's reference to Walter Scott drawing attention to 'something deeper and more attractive' about the faith of the Middle Ages can be found in John Newman, *Apologia pro Vita Sua* (Sheed and Ward, 1976), 65.

p. 143) 'There used to be much snap-dragon growing on the walls opposite my freshman's rooms . . .': Newman, *Apologia pro Vita Sua,* 165.

p. 144) 'He had passed through Bagley Wood, and the spires and towers of the University came on his view . . .': John Newman, *Loss and Gain* (Oxford University Press, 1986), 243.

p. 144) Faber's series of Oxford poems can be found in J.B. Firth, ed., *The Minstrelsy of Isis* (Chapman and Hall, 1908). The passage from 'Aged Cities' is on p.

127; the quotation from 'College Library' beginning 'Of quiet ages men call dark and drear . . .' is on p. 133.

p. 145) John Ruskin's comments about Christ Church architecture, 'religion unbroken—the memory of loyalty . . .', can be found in *Praeterita* (Oxford University Press, 1978), 179.

p. 145) The quotation by Burne-Jones, 'Oxford is a glorious place; godlike! . . .', comes from a letter of his dated January 29, 1853, and is taken from Jan Morris, *The Oxford Book of Oxford* (Oxford University Press, 1984), 248.

ARNOLD'S DREAMING SPIRES

p. 146) The description of Arnold's poems as 'the two great Oxford poems' is by Firth in *The Minstrelsy of Isis*, x.

p. 146) The reference to 'each hallowed spot' of Arnold's poems is made in Barbara Burke, *Barbara Goes to Oxford* (Simpkin, Marshall, Hamilton and Kent, 1907), 177.

p. 146) The information about Arnold's *Essays in Criticism* being read out to Cecil Rhodes as he died is taken from André Maurois, *Cecil Rhodes* (Collins, 1953), 136.

p. 146) For Trilling's description of Arnold as 'everything of which his father would have disapproved . . .', see Lionel Trilling, *Matthew Arnold* (Allen and Unwin, 1939), 19.

p. 147) The critic who believes Arnold's poems to be 'second only to Keats . . .' is M. Thorpe in *Matthew Arnold* (Evans, 1969), 83.

p. 147) 'And near me on the grass lies Glanvil's book . . .': 'The Scholar-Gipsy', in *The Poems of Matthew Arnold*, ed. Kenneth Allott and Miriam Allott (Longman, 1979), 359. The quotations which follow can be found on pp. 361–62.

p. 148) The reference to 'this strange disease of modern life' can be found in *Poems of Matthew Arnold*, 366.

p. 149) 'We prized it [the signal-elm] dearly; while it stood, we said, / Our friend, the Gipsy-Scholar, was not dead . . .': 'Thyrsis', in *Poems of Matthew Arnold*, 540.

p. 149) 'I know nobody who ever saw, and recognised, Matthew Arnold's tree . . .': Edward Thomas, *Oxford* (Black, 1922), 230. William Tuckwell had in fact already identified the tree in *Reminiscences of Oxford* (Cassell, 1901), 97, in which he writes of a solitary hill-side tree 'which yet stands out clear against the flaming sunset sky', though as Oona Ball pointed out under her pen-name Barbara Burke (*Barbara Goes to Oxford*, 145), the tree in question was in fact an oak.

p. 149) 'Arnold's Tree is an Oak and not an Elm . . .': Henry Taunt, *The Oxford Poems of Matthew Arnold* (Taunt, 1910), 103. Sir Francis Wylie methodically retraces the topography of 'Thyrsis' in 'The Scholar-Gipsy Country' appendixed to C.B. Tinker and H.F. Lowry's *The Poetry of Matthew Arnold* (Oxford University Press, 1940). Starting from Lake Street, the route goes over the causeway known

as Jacob's Ladder to South Hinksey, where 'Sibylla's name' used to be on the
pub-sign of the Cross Keys, then up 'Happy valley' and past Chilswell Farm to the
hill-ridge. According to Maud Rosenthal in the *Boars Hill Newsletter,* Nov.–Dec.
1991, the tree was condemned some years ago by tree surgeons but continues for
the time being to stand defiantly.

p. 150) 'And that sweet city with her dreaming spires . . .': Arnold, 'Thyrsis', 539.

p. 151) 'Beautiful city! so venerable, so lovely, so unravaged by the fierce intellectual life of our century, so serene! . . .' comes from Matthew Arnold's preface
to *Essays in Criticism* (1865). See R.H. Super, ed., *The Complete Prose Works of
Matthew Arnold,* vol. 3, *Lectures and Essays in Criticism* (Ann Arbor: University of
Michigan Press, 1962), 290. (Byron's line '*There* were his young barbarians all at
play', can be found in *Childe Harold's Pilgrimage,* canto 4, stanza 141.)

p. 151) Arnold's letter to his brother, 'I find I am generally thought to have buttered her [Oxford] up . . .', is dated July 23, 1867. See George W.E. Russell, ed.,
The Works of Matthew Arnold, vol. 14, *The Letters of Matthew Arnold* (Macmillan,
1904), 140. Hilaire Belloc in *A Moral Alphabet* (1899) later made a humorous
rebuttal of the idealised image of Oxford (see *Complete Verse* [Pimlico, 1991],
254):

> O stands for Oxford. Hail! salubrious seat
> Of learning! Academical Retreat!
> Home of my Middle Age! Malarial Spot
> Which People call Medeeval (though it's not).

p. 152) Arnold's definition of culture as 'a pursuit of our total perfection . . .'
comes from *Culture and Anarchy.* See *Complete Prose Works,* vol. 5, *Culture and Anarchy* (Ann Arbor: University of Michigan Press, 1965), 233.

p. 152) The passage from Pindar is from the ode, Pythian 8, section 5. The translation is by C.M. Bowra. See Pindar, *The Odes* (Penguin, 1969), 237.

p. 152) 'More and more mankind will discover that we have to turn to poetry
. . .': Arnold, *Essays in Criticism,* 290.

p. 152) Arnold's claim that 'the cause in which I fight is, after all, hers
[Oxford's]' is taken from *Essays in Criticism,* 290.

p. 153) 'Yet we in Oxford, brought up amidst the beauty and sweetness of that
beautiful place . . .': Arnold, *Culture and Anarchy,* 106.

p. 153) 'Oxford, Oxford of the past, has many faults . . .': Arnold, *Culture and
Anarchy,* 105.

p. 153) The reference to a 'silver city of dream and shadow' can be found in Beverley Nichols, *Patchwork* (Chatto and Windus, 1921), 38.

p. 153) The description of Arnold as 'the truest representative of her [Oxford's]
culture' is by Firth in the introduction to *The Minstrelsy of Isis,* viii. The reference

to him as 'that prince among dons' is taken from J.I.M. Stewart, *The Madonna of the Astrolabe* (Gollancz, 1977), 132.

p. 154) Gladstone's 'To call a man a characteristically Oxford man is, in my opinion, to give him the highest compliment . . .' is taken from C. Day Lewis and Charles Fenby, *Anatomy of Oxford* (Jonathan Cape, 1938), 160.

p. 154) Arnold's assertion that culture 'is not satisfied till we *all* come to a perfect man . . .' is taken from *Culture and Anarchy*, 112.

NOTHING REMAINS BUT BEAUTY

p. 155) Butler's poem about looking down on Oxford mists from Shotover stile can be found in Firth, *The Minstrelsy of Isis*, 22.

p. 155) Information about the student days of G.M. Hopkins is taken from P. Kitchen, *G.M. Hopkins* (Hamilton, 1978). The quotation by Hopkins about the 'summit of human happiness' is on p. 44.

p. 155) The quotations from 'To Oxford'—'sweet-familiar', and 'my park, my pleasaunce'—are taken from Gerard Manley Hopkins, *Poems*, ed. W.H. Gardner and N.H. MacKenzie (Oxford University Press, 1970), 21.

p. 156) Information about 'Binsey Poplars' is taken from W.H. Gardner, *G.M. Hopkins* (Secker and Warburg, 1949), 275.

p. 156) The entry in Hopkins's journal containing the quotation, 'I heard the sound and looking out and seeing it [the tree] maimed . . .', is for April 8, 1873. See H. House and G. Storey, ed., *The Journals and Papers of Gerard Manley Hopkins* (Oxford University Press, 1959), 230.

p. 156) The text for 'Binsey Poplars' is taken from Hopkins, *Poems*, 78–79.

p. 157) The quotations by Wilde, 'There is no Pater but Pater . . .' and 'the holy writ of beauty', are taken from Thomas Wright, *The Life of Walter Pater* (Everett, 1907), 2:126.

p. 157) The passage from the conclusion of *Studies in the History of the Renaissance* is taken from Walter Pater, *Studies in the History of the Renaissance* (Macmillan, 1910), 236–39.

p. 158) Wilde's claim that 'Aesthetics are higher than ethics' can be found in 'The Critic as Artist'. See *Complete Works of Oscar Wilde* (Collins, 1966), 1058.

p. 158) 'In truth the memory of Oxford made almost everything he saw after it seem vulgar': Walter Pater, 'Emerald Uthwart', in *Miscellaneous Studies* (Macmillan, 1910), 228.

p. 159) 'Where at each coign of every antique street . . .': Lionel Johnson, 'Oxford', in *Ireland with Other Poems 1897* (Elkin Matthews, 1897), 32–33. Johnson's 'Oxford' and Quiller-Couch's 'Alma Mater' can also be found in Firth, *The Minstrelsy of Isis*, 91–93, 107–8.

p. 160) 'I was a man who stood in symbolic relations to the art and culture of my age': Rupert Hart-Davis, ed., *The Letters of Oscar Wilde* (Hart-Davis, 1962), 466.

THE INFAMOUS ST. OSCAR OF OXFORD

Acknowledgment is made to Richard Ellmann, *Oscar Wilde* (Hamish Hamilton, 1988) for much of the background information in this section.

p. 161) The information about the initials scratched on the pane is taken from Vyvyan Holland, *Son of Oscar Wilde* (Oxford University Press, 1988), 26.

p. 161) Wilde's involvement with Ruskin's Hinksey project is described in Ellmann, *Oscar Wilde*, 58. The quotation by Wilde, 'What became of the road?' comes from Sheridan Morley, *Oscar Wilde* (Weidenfeld and Nicolson, 1976), 24.

p. 162) 'I find it harder and harder each day to live up to my blue china': Ellmann, *Oscar Wilde*, 44.

p. 162) 'Greats is the only fine school at Oxford . . .': Rupert Hart-Davis, ed., *More Letters of Oscar Wilde* (John Murray, 1985), 33.

p. 162) Wilde's study habits are discussed in Ellmann, *Oscar Wilde*, 42.

p. 162) 'I don't see the use of going down backwards to Iffley every evening': Ellmann, *Oscar Wilde*, 38.

p. 162) For the story of Spooner and the quotation, 'Did you hear me tell you, Mr. Wilde . . .', see Ellmann, *Oscar Wilde*, 62.

p. 163) Wilde's performance in his final exam is described in Ellmann, *Oscar Wilde*, 91.

p. 163) Wilde's description of Oxford as 'The most beautiful thing in England . . .' is taken from Ellmann, *Oscar Wilde*, 36.

p. 163) For Wilde's claim that 'the dullness of tutors and professors matters very little . . .', see *Complete Works*, 1050.

p. 163) 'Our sweet city with its dreaming towers must not be given entirely over to the Philistines': Wilde, *More Letters*, 37.

p. 163) 'God knows. I won't be a dried-up Oxford don . . .': Ellmann, *Oscar Wilde*, 45.

p. 164) 'I envy you going to Oxford: it is the most flower-like time of one's life . . .': *Letters of Oscar Wilde*, 772.

p. 164) 'In spite of the roaring of the young lions at the Union, and the screaming of rabbits in the home of the vivisector . . .' comes from a review of '*Henry the Fourth* at Oxford' in the *Dramatic Review*, May 23, 1885.

p. 164) The quotation from the article attacking 'Pagan worship of bodily form . . .' is taken from Ellmann, *Oscar Wilde*, 85.

p. 164) For the quotation by Wilde, 'His left leg is a Greek poem', see Ellmann, *Oscar Wilde*, 38.

p. 164) 'Young Oxonians are very delightful, so Greek and graceful and uneducated': Ellmann, *Oscar Wilde*, 186.

p. 165) For Wilde's description of himself as 'the infamous St. Oscar of Oxford . . .', see *Letters of Oscar Wilde*, 720.

p. 165) Wilde's reference to 'the two great turning-points of my life . . .' can be found in *Letters of Oscar Wilde*, 469.

p. 165) 'Your conversation was brilliant, but it was simply a rechauffé of *The Importance of Being Earnest*': Nichols, *Patchwork*, 145.

p. 165) 'Whether one loved or hated him, Oscar Wilde was king': Fayard, *Oxford and Margaret*, 253.

p. 165) Sheed's 'every single bloke up here has a pose . . .': Wilfrid Sheed, *A Middle Class Education* (Cassell, 1961), 90.

p. 165) Balsdon's 'in Oxford acting was a large part of living': Dacre Balsdon, *The Day They Burned Miss Termag* (Eyre and Spottiswoode, 1961), 65.

p. 165) For the description of Oxford life as 'eternal dandyism', see John Fowles, *The Magus* (Triad/Granada, 1977), 17.

p. 165) The reference to 'the Oxford pretence of doing nothing . . .': Robertson Davies, *What's Bred in the Bone* (New York: Viking Press, 1985), 220.

p. 165) Wain's 'obligation to be amusing': John Wain, *Hungry Generations* (Hutchinson, 1994), 61.

ATHENIAN GROVES AND BEERBOHM'S GODDESS

p. 166) The description of the *polis* as 'small, isolated, self-contained . . .' can be found in Lewis Mumford, *The City in History* (New York: Harcourt, Brace and World, 1961), 179.

p. 166) 'College life is somewhat, as has often been said, like the old Greek city life . . .': Andrew Lang, *Oxford* (Seeley, Jackson and Halliday, 1909), 263–64.

p. 166) 'Oxford is one of the most democratic places . . .': Thomas, *Oxford*, 15.

p. 167) The description of *The Testament of Beauty* as 'a brilliant paper written on aesthetics for Greats' can be found in Stephen Spender, *World within World* (Faber, 1977), 33.

p. 167) For the quotation from 'All Souls' Night' beginning, 'Midnight has come, and the great Christ Church Bell . . .', see Norman Jeffares, ed., *Yeats's Poems* (Macmillan, 1989), 341.

p. 167) 'You came away from his [Auden's] presence always encouraged': Louis MacNeice, *The Strings Are False* (Faber and Faber, 1965), 114.

p. 168) The description by C.S. Lewis of his conversion can be found in *Surprised by Joy* (Harcourt, Brace and World, 1955), 149.

p. 168) For Beerbohm's reference to the 'peculiar race of artist-scholars . . .', see Max Beerbohm, *Zuleika Dobson* (Penguin, 1952), 138.

p. 168) The quotation about 'the starlit spires and Athenian groves . . .' comes from Miles and Mortimer, *The Oxford Circus*, 34.

p. 168) 'Zuleika speaker not hiker': Rupert Hart-Davis, ed., *Letters of Max Beerbohm, 1892–1956* (Hart-Davis, 1989), 213.

p. 168) The identification of the model for Zuleika is taken from M.C. Rintoul, *Dictionary of Real People and Places in Fiction* (Routledge, 1993), 312.

p. 169) 'I shouldn't be seen with you in that . . .': Nichols, *Patchwork*, 276.

p. 169) Information about Beerbohm's relationship with Wilde is taken from David Cecil, *Max* (Constable, 1983), 70, and Ellmann, *Oscar Wilde*, 291–92.

p. 169) Beerbohm's affected question, 'What river?' is taken from Cecil, *Max*, 38. The influence of *The Importance of Being Earnest* on Beerbohm's writing is discussed on p. 212.

p. 169) The reference to Zuleika as an 'adorable goddess' can be found in Beerbohm, *Zuleika Dobson*, 123.

p. 169) Zuleika's 'Oh, I never go in motors . . .': Beerbohm, *Zuleika Dobson*, 46.

p. 169) Ray Sheldon is described as filled with 'the desire to taste to the full the life of Oxford . . .' in Nichols, *Patchwork*, 108.

p. 169) 'My imagination was aglow with literary associations': Waugh, *A Little Learning*, 167.

p. 170) 'Well, yes, to be quite frank, it [Shangri-La] reminds me very slightly of Oxford . . .': James Hilton, *Lost Horizon* (Macmillan, 1949), 212.

p. 170) 'Sometimes dreaming in the sun, sometimes dappled by rain . . .': Nichols, *Patchwork*, 234.

p. 170) 'Somewhere in the silent college the thing unknown was waiting': Humphrey Neville Dickinson, *Keddy: A Story of Oxford* (Heinemann, 1907), 30.

p. 170) 'Oxford should be approached with a stainless curiosity . . .': Mackenzie, *Sinister Street*, 378.

p. 170) The reference to Oxford being 'imprisoned in a crystal globe' can be found in Mackenzie, *Sinister Street*, 429.

p. 170) The quotation about 'the peculiar air of Oxford . . .' is taken from James, *English Hours*, 123.

p. 170) The description of student life as a second childhood 'as blithe and untroubled as the first . . .' can be found in Thomas, *Oxford*, 103.

p. 170) 'It's just because Oxford teaches nothing in particular that she is such a priceless possession': Gerard Hopkins, *A City in the Foreground* (Constable, 1921), 182.

p. 171) The duke of Dorset is described as 'the most awful snob' in Beerbohm, *Zuleika Dobson*, 51.

p. 171) The Cockney Smithers of *Sinister Street*, who is picked on 'not from any overt act of contumely . . .', appears in Mackenzie, *Sinister Street*, 443.

p. 171) Mackenzie's two short paragraphs and the passage beginning 'February was that year a month of rains from silver skies . . .' can be found in Mackenzie, *Sinister Street*, 580.

p. 171) 'So each of his terms told off, in a delicious reverie of idle adoration . . .': Montague, *Rough Justice*, 157.

p. 172) 'Some clock clove with silver the stillness of the morning': Beerbohm, *Zuleika Dobson*, 27.

p. 172) 'Oxford, in those days, was still a city of aquatint': Evelyn Waugh, *Brideshead Revisited* (Penguin, 1962), 29.

WAUGH'S ENCHANTED GARDEN

Background information is drawn from Humphrey Carpenter, *The Brideshead Generation* (Weidenfeld and Nicolson, 1989).

p. 172) 'Proud and godly kings had built her, long ago . . .': James Elroy Flecker, 'The Dying Patriot', in *Collected Poems*, ed. J.C. Squire (Secker and Warburg, 1916), 210.

p. 173) The college is described as an 'ugly, subdued little College' in Evelyn Waugh, *Decline and Fall* (Penguin, 1937), 211.

p. 173) Information about the model of Sebastian Flyte is taken from Rintoul, *Dictionary of Real People*, 455. Christopher Sykes in *Evelyn Waugh* (Collins, 1975), 252, suggests that the model for Sebastian Flyte may have been the charming and aristocratic Hugh Lygon (1904–36) of Pembroke College, whose career after Oxford was plagued by illness, but states that the claim of Alastair Graham (b. 1904) of Brascnosc is stronger because in the original manuscript of *Brideshead Revisited* Sebastian's name is sometimes written as Alastair. From 1933 Graham became a recluse on the Welsh coast.

p. 173) The reference to Sebastian's 'nursery freshness' is taken from Waugh, *Brideshead Revisited*, 56.

p. 173) 'It seems to me that I grew younger daily with each adult habit that I acquired': Waugh, *Brideshead Revisited*, 56.

p. 174) The tone for Waugh's Arcadian motif is set by the title of the Oxford section, 'Et in Arcadia Ego'. The subject was first treated as a painting by Guernico, and Poussin painted two pictures on a similar theme named *The Arcadian Shep-*

herds. The second of these, the most famous, apparently provided the inspiration for Waugh's choice of title, though the inference he drew from the painting is unclear and the 'ego' of the title could be understood in two different ways. In the earlier version of the painting there is a tomb and skull with the implication that 'Even in Arcadia, there am I—Death'. In this case the suggestion is that the pleasure-seeking idyll of Charles and Sebastian is inevitably doomed and only enjoyed at the expense of their souls. In the second painting, however, Poussin omits the skull and the shepherds are shown reflecting in melancholy manner on the tomb of a forebear. This has been interpreted by the art historian Panofsky as a shift of focus, for the words 'Et in Arcadia Ego' would seem to be spoken by the dead forebear and to signify that he belongs to a golden age in the past from which the postlapsarian shepherds are excluded. In this case the suggestion would be that, following mankind's fall from grace, the happiness of Charles and Sebastian can only be temporary and illusionary. The nostalgic tone of the Oxford section alludes then not only to the lost happiness of student days, but to a lost golden age which can never be recovered.

p. 174) For Sebastian's championing of butterfly and flower over art and architecture, see Waugh, *Brideshead Revisited*, 37.

p. 174) 'Nature is so close . . .' is the opening line of Auden's poem 'Oxford': see Antonia Fraser, ed., *Oxford and Oxfordshire in Verse* (Secker and Warburg, 1982), 55. Another version exists in Auden's *Collected Poems*, ed. Edward Mendelson (Faber and Faber, 1991), 147, which begins, 'Nature invades: old rooks in each college garden / Still talk, like agile babies, the language of feeling'.

p. 174) The reference to the city's 'cloistral hush' is taken from Waugh, *Brideshead Revisited*, 30.

p. 174) The reference to Ryder moving 'through a world of piety' is taken from Evelyn Waugh, *Brideshead Revisited* (Penguin, 1962), 71.

p. 175) Bowra's view that 'he [Waugh] longed for some home . . .' can be found in C.M. Bowra, *Memories, 1898–1939* (Weidenfeld and Nicolson, 1966), 175.

p. 175) 'It is not given to all her sons either to seek or find this secret, but it was very near the surface in 1922': Waugh, *A Little Learning*, 167.

p. 175) Harold Acton's view of *Brideshead Revisited* is taken from Carpenter, *The Brideshead Generation*, 371.

p. 175) In Rintoul, *Dictionary of Real People*, 141, there is a quotation by Christopher Sykes to the effect that friends of Waugh identified Blanche with Acton because of the cosmopolitan background, Eton education, and larger-than-life character. Moreover, some genuine sayings of Acton were put into Blanche's mouth. Both Waugh and Acton denied the identification, however, and it seems that aspects of the character were drawn from another old Etonian aesthete, Brian Howard, particularly the affectation 'my dear' and the part-Jewish origins (Howard was also allegedly the model for Ambrose Silk in *Put Out More Flags*

[1942]). 'It is true that the characters in my novels often wrongly identified with Harold Acton were to a great extent drawn from [Brian Howard]', Waugh commented in *A Little Learning*, 204. See also Alan Bold and Robert Giddings, *Who Was Really Who in Fiction* (Longman, 1987), 33; and Carpenter, *The Brideshead Generation*, 356.

p. 175) 'It would be of course absurd to pretend that the story of Evelyn Waugh was the story of all Oxford in the 1920s': Christopher Hollis, *Oxford in the Twenties* (Heinemann, 1976), 92.

p. 176) 'Balkan Sobranies in a wooden box, / The college arms upon the lid . . .': John Betjeman, *Summoned by Bells* (John Murray, 1976), 93.

p. 176) 'Belbroughton Road is bonny . . . ': 'May-Day Song for North Oxford' in John Betjeman, *Collected Poems* (John Murray, 1988), 96.

p. 176) Arnold's claim of being 'stuffed with Greek and Aristotle' is from *Culture and Anarchy*, 126.

p. 177) Beerbohm's claim that 'he [Arnold], in small doses, pleases me and inspires me with a sort of affection . . .' can be found in Cecil, *Max*, 49.

p. 177) For Mackenzie's recognition of Arnold's influence, see M.R. Proctor, *The English University Novel* (Berkeley and Los Angeles: University of California Press, 1957), 193.

p. 177) The references to Pater can be found in Mackenzie, *Sinister Street*, 382, 491.

p. 177) The information about Waugh calling Beerbohm 'Master' is taken from Carpenter, *The Brideshead Generation*, 155.

p. 177) Wilde's manner of addressing Pater, 'Homage to the great master', is taken from Ellmann, *Oscar Wilde*, 820.

p. 177) The description of 1890s Oxford as feeling 'the outer world at its gates' is taken from John Buchan, *Memory-Hold-the-Door* (Dent, 1984), 51.

p. 177) For Beerbohm's observation about the city centre being connected to the outside world by its slums, see Beerbohm, *Zuleika Dobson*, 8.

p. 178) The reference to 'a life of beautiful uselessness' is taken from Stephen McKenna, *Sonia: Between Two Worlds* (Methuen, 1917), 91.

p. 178) The working-class students who 'wished not to fling wide the city gates . . .' can be found in Hopkins, *City in the Foreground*, 276.

p. 178) The lines by D.H. Lawrence are from a poem entitled 'The Oxford Voice' and can be found in V. de Sola Pinto and F. Warren Roberts, eds., *The Complete Poems of D.H. Lawrence* (Heinemann, 1964), 1:433.

p. 178) 'Let no man in future read the works of Cicero . . .': 'An Oxford Scholar', in *Massacre of the Innocents* (Billing, 1907), 305.

p. 178) 'We learned that a gentleman never misplaces his accents . . .': Louis MacNeice, *Collected Poems,* ed. E.R. Dodds (Faber and Faber, 1966), 126–27.

p. 179) 'The drunkenness of things being various' is taken from MacNeice's poem, 'Snow'. See *Collected Poems,* 126–27.

p. 179) 'So blow the bugles over the metaphysicians . . .': MacNeice, *Collected Poems,* 126–27.

p. 180) The information about Osbert Lancaster writing 'Alma Pater' on Kolkhorst's photo is taken from Bevis Hillier, *Young Betjeman* (John Murray, 1988), 144.

p. 180) Betjeman's lines on Kolkhorst, 'I see you pouring sherry . . .': Betjeman, *Summoned by Bells,* 97.

p. 180) Kolkhorst's paper is in the local section of the Oxford City Library. The quoted passage is on p. 30.

p. 180) Waugh's description of 1920s Oxford as 'submerged now and obliterated . . .' can be found in Waugh, *Brideshead Revisited,* 29.

p. 180) The quotation from Sheed about 'the famous Oxford culture, the English Athens and all that crap' comes from Wilfrid Sheed, *A Middle Class Education* (Cassell, 1961), 119.

p. 180) The reference to Oxford as a 'Malarial Spot' where 'with decent application, / One gets a good, sound, middle-class education' is taken from the section 'O stands for Oxford' in Belloc's *A Moral Alphabet,* 255.

Chapter 6

p. 182) The opening quotation is from John Galsworthy, *End of the Chapter* (Heinemann, 1948), 693.

p. 182) The 'charmed seclusion' is referred to by Henry James, 'A Passionate Pilgrim', in *The Novels and Tales of Henry James* (Cambridge and New York: Harvard University Press/Scribners, 1908), 13:417.

p. 182) The description by Saltonstall of 'A Townesman in Oxford' as 'one that hath liv'd long by the well of knowledge, but never sipt at it' can be found in Wye Saltonstall, *Picturae Loquentes* (Luttrell Society/Blackwell, 1946), 36.

p. 183) Nina Bawden's recollections of her student life can be found in *My Oxford,* ed. A. Thwaite (Robson, 1977).

p. 183) 'Oxford was not as I had imagined it would be . . .': Stephen Spender, *World within World* (Faber and Faber, 1977), 33.

p. 184) 'Survivors not Wanted' is the title of chapter 10 of Vera Brittain, *Testament of Youth* (Fontana, 1979).

p. 186) The statistics about public school numbers are taken from T.J.H. Bishop and Rupert Wilkinson, *Winchester and the Public School Elite: A Statistical Analysis* (Faber, 1967), 127.

p. 186) Numbers at the World War I university are taken from *The Encyclopaedia of Oxford,* ed. Christopher Hibbert (Macmillan, 1988), 473.

HARDY'S NEW JERUSALEM

p. 187) The poor 'elbowed off the pavement for the millionaire's sons': Thomas Hardy, *Jude the Obscure,* ed. Patricia Ingham (Oxford University Press, 1985), 156.

p. 187) The reference to parsons being raised 'like radishes in a bed' is in Hardy, *Jude the Obscure,* 20.

p. 187) 'It is a place much too good for you . . .' : Hardy, *Jude the Obscure,* 12.

p. 187) The reference to Jude being 'so romantically attached to Christminster . . .' is in Hardy, *Jude the Obscure,* 19.

p. 187) Jude hears 'the voice of the city' in Hardy, *Jude the Obscure,* 19.

p. 187) The university is described as 'the tree of knowledge' in Hardy, *Jude the Obscure,* 21.

p. 188) The description of the university as a 'paradise of the learned' is in Hardy, *Jude the Obscure,* 116.

p. 188) The list of Christminster figures 'among whom the most real to Jude Fawley were the founders of the religious school called Tractarian' is in Hardy, *Jude the Obscure,* 80.

p. 188) Jude 'awoke from his dream' in Hardy, *Jude the Obscure,* 119.

p. 188) 'You are one of the very men Christminster was intended for . . .': Hardy, *Jude the Obscure,* 156.

p. 189) 'But I don't revere all of them as I did then . . .': Hardy, *Jude the Obscure,* 414.

p. 190) The 'joyous throb of waltz entered from the ball-room at Cardinal': Hardy, *Jude the Obscure,* 430. The degree-giving ceremony is on the same page.

p. 190) 'Only a wall divided him from those happy contemporaries . . .': Hardy, *Jude the Obscure,* 86.

p. 190) For the 'freezing negative' of Biblioll on which the biblical quotation is written, see Hardy, *Jude the Obscure,* 351.

p. 191) 'Well—I'm an outsider to the end of my days!': Hardy, *Jude the Obscure,* 347.

p. 191) The reference to a 'city of light' can be found in Hardy, *Jude the Obscure,* 21.

p. 191) 'They started in quest of the lodging and at last found something that seemed to promise well, in Mildew Lane . . .': Hardy, *Jude the Obscure*, 347.

p. 191) The reference to 'an old intramural cottage' can be found in Hardy, *Jude the Obscure*, 351.

p. 191) The reference to the 'City of Colleges' can be found in Hardy, *Jude the Obscure*, 342.

p. 191) The reference to the 'obscure and low-ceiled tavern up a court' can be found in Hardy, *Jude the Obscure*, 97.

p. 191) 'It [Christminster] is an ignorant place, except as to the townspeople . . .': Hardy, *Jude the Obscure*, 156.

p. 191) Pity for 'the Dons, magistrates and other people in authority . . .' is referred to in Hardy, *Jude the Obscure*, 123.

p. 191) The 'shabby purlieu . . .' is referred to in Hardy, *Jude the Obscure*, 119.

p. 192) Jude's epiphany about the mason's stoneyard is described in Hardy, *Jude the Obscure*, 85.

p. 192) 'He began to see that the town life was a book of humanity infinitely more palpitating, varied, and compendious, than the gown life . . .': Hardy, *Jude the Obscure*, 121.

p. 192) Sue's description of the university as 'a nest of commonplace schoolmasters . . .' is in Hardy, *Jude the Obscure*, 329.

p. 193) Christminster is described as a 'unique centre of thought . . .' in Hardy, *Jude the Obscure*, 115.

p. 193) 'I love the place—although I know how it hates all men like me . . .': Hardy, *Jude the Obscure*, 337.

p. 193) The relationship of Jude to Hardy is discussed by C.J. Weber in the Norton edition of *Jude the Obscure*, ed. Norman Page (New York: Norton, 1978), 371–73 (hereafter cited as Norton edition).

p. 193) Hardy's letter to a friend in 1926 stating that Christminster 'is not meant to be exclusively Oxford, but any old-fashioned University . . .' is referred to in F.E. Hardy, *The Life of Thomas Hardy, 1840–1928* (Macmillan, 1972), 433. As regards the temporal setting of the novel, Robert Gittings in the Norton edition of *Jude the Obscure*, 448–50, demonstrates that Sue is a child of the 1860s, whereas Denys Kay-Robinson in *The Landscape of Thomas Hardy* (Webb and Bower, 1984), 173, points to physical features that belong to the 1880s, such as the building bearing the Latin inscription that Jude translates for the crowd waiting in front of the Christminster 'Sheldonian'. The motto *Ad fontes aquarum sicut cervus anhelat* ('As pants the hart for cooling streams') was part of a carved frieze on a Hertford College building not built until 1887.

p. 193) Jude's reference to reform, 'I hear that soon . . .': Hardy, *Jude the Obscure*, 421.

p. 193) The relationship of Hardy and Horace Moule is described in M. Millgate, *Thomas Hardy* (Oxford University Press, 1982), 68.

p. 194) There have been several topographical studies of *Jude the Obscure*, and there also exists a handwritten page in Hardy's hand in which the Christminster names are laid out alongside their Oxford equivalents (cf. the Norton edition of *Jude the Obscure*, 367). In addition to those mentioned in the text, other renamings include the low-ceilinged tavern up a court (the Lamb and Flag): Crozier College (Oriel); Crozier Hotel (the Mitre); Oldgate (New College); Rubric College (Brasenose); Mildew Lane (Magpie Lane); the octagonal chamber in the circular theatre (the cupola at the top of the Sheldonian); the church with the Italian porch (St. Mary's); and Lumsdon (Cumnor), where Phillotson lives and teaches. St. Silas, 'the Church of Ceremonies', is St. Barnabas in Jericho. The light-denying Sarcophagus College in whose shadow Sue lodges has been variously identified with All Souls and Corpus Christi, though the name and windowless wall suggest that it is simply a fictional caricature. Attempts have also been made to identify the houses where the deaths of the children and that of Jude take place, though it is usually assumed that these are purely imaginary.

p. 194) Hardy's comments on the proposal to name Ruskin College as the 'College of Jude the Obscure' can be found in *Jude the Obscure*, xxxviii.

DON'S DELIGHT: A GOLDEN AGE OF MURDER

Acknowledgment is made to Julian Symons, *Bloody Murder* (Faber and Faber, 1972) for the ideas underlying this section.

p. 196) 'Oh, detective stories! said the Dean . . .': Timothy Robinson, *When Scholars Fall* (New Authors, 1961), 13.

p. 196) Auden's claim to have served as model for Nigel Strangeways, the detective of Nicholas Blake (Cecil Day-Lewis) was made in the *Sunday Times,* June 4, 1972, and is quoted in M.C. Rintoul, *Dictionary of Real People and Places in Fiction* (Routledge, 1993), 166.

p. 196) 'This is a perfectly intelligible state of affairs. The classical detective story is, in an appropriately narrow sense of the word, pre-eminently intellectual . . .': A.M. Quinton, 'Oxford in Fiction', *Oxford Magazine* 76, no. 9 (Jan. 23, 1958): 216.

p. 197) 'Academics form by far the largest group of amateur detectives': T.J. Binyon, *'Murder Will Out': The Detective in Fiction* (Oxford University Press, 1989), 50. (T.J. Binyon is a fellow of Wadham and a specialist in Russian.)

p. 197) 'Oxford murders are literary murders . . .': Robinson, *When Scholars Fall,* 64–65.

p. 198) The quotations from Knox's *The Footsteps at the Lock* are as follows: 'Photography, he held, was the highest of all the arts . . .': Ronald Knox, *The Footsteps at the Lock* (Methuen, 1928), 19; Oxford 'breathing out from her gas-works . . .': ibid., 31; 'Who is this man next to you . . .': ibid., 79. The Rt. Revd. Monsignor Ronald Knox was a literary cleric who wrote light verse and a number of theological works in addition to his detective novels. His student career ranks alongside the likes of Wilde and Buchan as one of gilded brilliance. He won both the Greek and Latin verse prizes, was president of the Union, took a First in Greats, and had a widespread reputation for brilliance and wit.

p. 199) For the observation that the college 'offers such a capital frame for the quiddities and wilie-beguilies of the craft', see Michael Innes, *Death at the President's Lodging* (Gollancz, 1936), 5.

p. 199) The reference to murder 'in the only College in the University as no one can climb into' is in Robert Robinson, *Landscape with Dead Dons* (Gollancz, 1956), 33.

p. 200) 'The Master was finding it heavy going; for Jennings responded only in monosyllables to his conversational openings . . .': G.D.H. Cole and M. Cole, *Disgrace to the College* (Hodder and Stoughton, 1937), 198.

p. 200) 'Close confinement in colleges, sometimes for life . . .': Robinson, *When Scholars Fall*, 14.

p. 200) The reference to the porter as 'the uncrowned king of the college' is in Edmund Crispin, *The Case of the Gilded Fly* (Gollancz, 1944), 78.

p. 200) 'A good Porter is the centre of the whole nervous system . . .': Dacre Balsdon, *Oxford Now and Then* (Duckworth, 1970), 166.

p. 201) 'I see them come and I see them go . . .': Robinson, *Landscape with Dead Dons*, 34.

p. 201) 'The other thing I wanted to ask was, how free am I to go about asking questions . . .': G.D.H. Cole and M. Cole, *Off with Her Head* (Collins, 1938), 113.

p. 202) 'Your refusal to face facts reminds me of the two Christ Church men . . .': Robinson, *Landscape with Dead Dons*, 26.

p. 202) 'You aren't a scientist or anything like that, are you?': Robinson, *When Scholars Fall*, 64.

p. 202) 'It is true that the ancient and noble city of Oxford is, of all the towns of England, the likeliest progenitor of unlikely events . . .': Edmund Crispin, *The Moving Toyshop* (Gollancz, 1946), 58.

p. 203) For the passage beginning 'a collection of colleges and a row or two of shops . . .', see Michael Innes, *Operation Pax* (Gollancz, 1951), 94.

p. 203) 'You never know where you are with these college people': Cole and Cole, *Off with Her Head*, 86.

p. 203) 'Everything about the place is designed to encourage lunacy': Robinson, *When Scholars Fall*, 83.

p. 204) With reference to the autobiographical elements in Dexter's Inspector Morse, these also include the classical background, the love of real ale and Wagner, and the diabetes. Dexter graduated from Cambridge in 1953 and moved to Oxford in 1966 to work for the University Examination Board. His partial deafness and work experience are exploited for fictional purposes in *The Silent World of Nicholas Quinn* (Macmillan, 1977).

p. 204) Morse 'always enjoyed Agatha Christie . . .': Colin Dexter, *Death Is Now My Neighbour* (Macmillan, 1996), 208.

p. 204) Morse is described as 'arrogant, ungracious, vulnerable, lovable' in Dexter, *Death Is My Neighbour,* 212.

p. 204) The reference to Lewis being 'not unaccustomed to hearing Morse make some apposite quotation . . .' is in Colin Dexter, *The Daughters of Cain* (Macmillan, 1994), 181.

p. 205) Morse's denigration of the 'hideous structures they've put up in Oxford since the war' is in Colin Dexter, *The Secret of Annexe 3* (Macmillan, 1986), 174.

p. 205) The expression of contempt for 'the vandals who sit on the City's planning committees . . .' is in Colin Dexter, *The Dead of Jericho* (Macmillan, 1981), 20.

p. 205) The Chaucerian scholar who uses 'agrestal' can be found in Dexter, *The Daughters of Cain,* 184.

p. 205) Morse's distaste for 'the futility of academic preferment' is in Colin Dexter, *The Way through the Woods* (Macmillan, 1992), 210.

p. 206) The reference to 'the Oxford Disease . . .' is in Colin Dexter, *The Jewel That Was Ours* (Macmillan, 1992), 148.

p. 206) The tourists moving past 'a litter-strewn patch of ill-kempt grass . . .' are in Dexter, *Jewel That Was Ours,* 12.

Stewart's High Table

p. 206) 'I don't know why there has never been a serious study [of Innes] . . .': Philip Larkin, *Required Writing* (Faber and Faber, 1983), 53.

p. 207) 'It was a November evening in October and the air was stagnant . . .': Michael Innes, *Stop Press* (Gollancz, 1971), 19.

p. 208) The reference to the 'gluttonous, bibulous dining-clubs that dons love' is in J.I.M. Stewart, *The Guardians* (Gollancz, 1955), 122.

p. 208) 'The eminent Swede reached his peroration . . .': J.I.M. Stewart, *The Gaudy* (Gollancz, 1974), 108–9.

p. 209) The reference to 'the appearance of a medieval centre of learning sailing pristine through the centuries . . .' is in J.I.M. Stewart, *The Aylwins* (Gollancz, 1966), 13.

p. 210) 'I surveyed the quadrangle around me . . .': Stewart, *The Aylwins,* 78.

p. 211) 'It could be overpowering at times . . .': J.I.M. Stewart, *Vanderlyn's Kingdom* (Gollancz, 1967), 47.

p. 211) The 'tendency to regard oneself as impressively circumstanced . . .' is taken from Stewart, *The Aylwins,* 17.

p. 211) 'Anything characteristic of Oxford has faded away by the time you get to Linton Road': J.I.M. Stewart, *The Madonna of the Astrolabe* (Gollancz, 1977), 245.

p. 211) The reference to the 'learned and patrician paradise' is in Stewart, *The Aylwin,* 42.

SAYERS'S PARADISE, GAINED AND LOST

p. 211) Amhurst's comments about women eating the apple of knowledge out of the pockets of their brothers can be found in *Terrae Filius,* no. 38 (1721).

p. 211) Information about the early women's colleges and the account of A.M.A.H. Rogers is taken from Vera Brittain, *The Women at Oxford* (Harrap, 1960).

p. 212) Burgon's sermon, 'Inferior to us God made you, and inferior to the end of time you will remain . . .' is quoted in V.H.H. Green, *A History of Oxford University* (Batsford, 1974), 186.

p. 212) The reference to women students as 'virgincules' is in Max Beerbohm, *Zuleika Dobson* (Penguin, 1952), 72.

p. 212) 'It was a male community . . .': Evelyn Waugh, *A Little Learning* (Chapman and Hall, 1964), 168.

p. 212) 'The great point of Oxford, in fact the whole point of Oxford, is that there are no girls . . .': Compton Mackenzie, *Sinister Street* (Penguin, 1960), 598.

p. 212) 'There is no doubt that unless Oxford puts the women out while there is yet time, they will overrun the whole university . . .': Stephen Leacock, *My Discovery of Oxford* (Bodley Head, 1922), 89.

p. 212) The Somerville novelists are the subject of a critical study by Susan J. Leonardi, *Dangerous by Degrees* (New Brunswick: Rutgers University Press, 1989).

p. 213) Verney's reverence for 'the pile of books . . .' and her disappointment at her 'desolate looking' room can be found in Renée Haynes, *Neapolitan Ice* (Chatto and Windus, 1928), 17, 50, respectively.

p. 214) The reflections on 'the organ booming in the chapel . . .' can be found in Virginia Woolf, *A Room of One's Own* and *Three Guineas* (Penguin, 1993), 21–22.

p. 214) For the description of the three types in the postwar university, see Vera Brittain, *Testament of Friendship* (Virago, 1980), 82–83.

p. 215) The reference to 'dusty old dons and proctors . . .' is in Vera Brittain, *Testament of Youth* (Fontana, 1979), 149.

p. 215) 'You cannot take a hundred young women . . .': Vera Brittain, *Dark Tide* (Richards Press, 1941), 2.

p. 216) The reference to the 'promising scholars, distinguished in their studies and subsequently extinguished by matrimony . . .' is in Dorothy Sayers, *Gaudy Night* (Hodder and Stoughton, 1978), 65.

p. 216) 'The warped and repressed mind . . .': Sayers, *Gaudy Night,* 74.

p. 216) The quotation by Wimsey concerning 'the one thing which frustrated the whole attack . . ..' is taken from Sayers, *Gaudy Night,* 413.

p. 217) 'You needn't be afraid of losing your independence . . .': Sayers, *Gaudy Night,* 432.

p. 217) The quotation stating that 'words seemed to be badges of admission' is taken from Haynes, *Neapolitan Ice,* 44.

p. 217) 'One day she climbed up Shotover and sat looking over the spires of the city . . .': Sayers, *Gaudy Night,* 214.

p. 217) 'April was running out, chilly and fickle, but with the promise of good things . . .': Sayers, *Gaudy Night,* 213.

p. 218) 'With a gesture of submission he [Wimsey] bared his head and stood gravely . . .': Sayers, *Gaudy Night,* 440.

p. 218) The description of the college as a 'grey-walled paradise' can be found in Sayers, *Gaudy Night,* 22.

p. 219) 'To an American academic family, coming to Oxford was like coming to Olympus . . .': Muriel Beadle, *These Ruins Are Inhabited* (Hale, 1963), 2.

p. 220) Kate Fansler is 'besotted with the idea of Oxford' but repulsed by the 'hideously masculine quality . . .' in Amanda Cross, *No Word from Winifred* (New York: Knopf, 1976), 73, 130.

p. 220) 'Oxford's self-infatuated people . . .': Jennifer Dawson, *Judasland* (Virago, 1990), 91.

p. 220) The quotation about Clare, 'her life had more connections with banging pipes and toilet-roll invoices than with *Brideshead Revisited*', is taken from Jennifer Dawson, *Judasland* (Virago, 1990), 55.

p. 221) 'It's a pity Oxford's pursuit of excellence by its very definition . . .': Dawson, *Judasland*, 80.

p. 221) The quotation by Jeanette Winterson from *The Oxford Women's Handbook 1991*, 'as women we do not inherit the grandeur . . . .', is cited by Valentine Cunningham, 'Literary Culture', in *The History of the University of Oxford*, ed. J. Catto (Oxford University Press, 1984–94), 8:441.

The Less Deceived

p. 221) 'Would Oxford ever again be like that? Had it ever been like that . . .': Beverley Nichols, *Patchwork* (Chatto and Windus, 1921), 303.

p. 222) 'What he could see did not look very remarkable . . .': Philip Larkin, *Jill* (Faber and Faber, 1977), 24.

p. 222) Gaveston ffoulkes 'nodding kindly to the bewhiskered porter's obsequious welcome . . .' is in Hamish Miles and Raymond Mortimer, *The Oxford Circus* (John Lane, 1922), 16.

p. 222) 'John swallowed, and the two young men turned to look at him . . .': Larkin, *Jill*, 25–26.

p. 223) 'Come from Town?' 'Yes. From Huddlesford.': Larkin, *Jill*, 27.

p. 223) 'During the meal John hardly lifted his head . . .': Larkin, *Jill*, 37.

p. 224) 'What do we all do? We are kings in our nutshell . . .': Larkin, *Jill*, 129.

p. 224) The quotations from 'Poem about Oxford' are taken from Philip Larkin, *Collected Poems* (Faber and Faber, 1988), 179.

p. 224) Larkin gave voice to the desire to stuff Sebastian's teddy-bear down his throat in *Required Writing*, 132.

p. 225) 'Had people ever been as nasty, as self-indulgent, as dull . . .': Kingsley Amis, *Lucky Jim* (Penguin, 1961), 87.

p. 225) 'He had been equipped with an upbringing devised to meet the needs of a more fortunate age . . .': John Wain, *Hurry on Down* (New York: Viking Press, 1965), 18.

p. 225) The reference to 'the smug phrases, the pert half-truths . . .' can be found in Wain, *Hurry on Down*, 11.

p. 225) 'The formal beauty of the groves and flower-beds . . .': Wain, *Hurry on Down*, 119–20.

p. 225) The description of the university as 'a conventional sort of place' where 'The college scouts doubled as the Dean's Joes . . .' can be found in John Le Carré, *A Perfect Spy* (Hodder and Stoughton, 1986), 338. The passage beginning, 'With his first cheque Pym bought a dark blue blazer . . .' is ibid., 339.

p. 227) Tolkien's description of himself as 'a hobbit in all but size . . .' is taken from Humphrey Carpenter, *J.R.R. Tolkien: A Biography* (Allen and Unwin, 1978), 179.

p. 227) Stewart's description of Tolkien lecturing, 'He could turn a lecture room into a mead hall . . .', is taken from Carpenter, *J.R.R. Tolkien,* 138.

p. 227) Auden's letter to Tolkien, 'I don't think I have ever told you what an unforgettable experience it was for me as an undergraduate, hearing you recite *Beowulf* . . .', is taken from Carpenter, *J.R.R. Tolkien,* 138.

p. 227) Auden's reference to Tolkien as 'bard to Anglo-Saxon' is taken from 'A Short Ode to a Philologist', in *English and Mediaeval Studies Presented to J.R.R. Tolkien* (Allen and Unwin, 1962).

p. 227) 'The sage sat. And middle-earth / Rose around him like a rumour': U.A. Fanthorpe, 'Genesis', in *Standing To* (Harry Chambers/Peterloo Poets, 1986), 74.

p. 229) Carter's description of Oxford and Cambridge as 'Outdated, relics, living on the past . . .' can be found in Graham Greene, *Our Man in Havana* (Heinemann/Bodley Head, 1970), 179.

p. 230) 'Have you gotten something out of Oxford?': Wilfrid Sheed, *A Middle Class Education* (Cassell, 1961), 118–19.

p. 230) 'Small, undistinguished sort of place . . .': Sheed, *A Middle Class Education,* 372.

p. 230) 'I have recently come across a disgusting and loathsome habit . . .': Wilfrid Sheed, *A Middle Class Education,* 128.

p. 230) 'Chaps without the money to do it properly shouldn't come to Oxford . . .': Sheed, *A Middle Class Education,* 125.

p. 231) The claim that the university houses 'more virgins of both sexes than any comparable community in the British Isles' is made in Julian Mitchell, *Imaginary Toys* (Hutchinson, 1961), 17.

p. 231) The reference to the working-class student forced to 'fight every inch of the way to get past people . . .' is in Mitchell, *Imaginary Toys,* 29.

p. 232) The quotation concerning 'the floodgates of the 1960s and 1970s . . . .' is taken from John Wain, *Hungry Generations* (Hutchinson, 1994), 182.

p. 233) 'One wonders, in fact, how long the collegiate system will last . . .': Larkin, *Required Writing,* 25.

p. 233) 'The explanation was simple: I left the gas fire on when I was out . . .': Ved Mehta, *Up at Oxford* (John Murray, 1993), 137.

p. 234) 'My Oxford is likely to seem rather shapeless . . ..': Martin Amis in Ann Thwaite, ed., *My Oxford* (Robson, 1977), 203.

THE REWRITING OF OXFORD

p. 235) Wain's poem about Nuffield, 'Before he came . . .', can be found in Antonia Fraser, ed., *Oxford and Oxfordshire in Verse* (Secker and Warburg, 1982), 68.

p. 235) The comparison of Oxford to 'a cross-town street in Manhattan . . .' is in Beadle, *These Ruins Are Inhabited*, 21.

p. 235) The description of Oxford as 'a city blocked solid with juggernaut lorries . . .' is in Jeffrey Archer, *Not Penny More, Not a Penny Less* (Jonathan Cape, 1976), 65.

p. 236) The quotation, 'there is more of a sense that one is a student, much like a student from any other university . . .', is taken from Rachel Johnson, ed., *The Oxford Myth* (Weidenfeld and Nicolson, 1988), 23.

p. 236) 'Once you stop following the architectural lines upwards, it's just like anywhere else . . ..': Martin Amis, *The Rachel Papers* (Penguin, 1984), 211.

p. 236) 'Modern Oxford is grey . . .': Balsdon, *Oxford Now and Then,* 170.

p. 236) 'We are all becoming standardised . . .': Crispin, *Case of Gilded Fly,* 92.

p. 236) The fellows who 'know surprisingly little about their own subjects . . .' are referred to in A.N. Wilson, *Unguarded Hours* (Secker and Warburg, 1978), 27.

p. 237) 'Their Oxford' is in Kingsley Amis, *Collected Poems, 1944–79* (Hutchinson, 1979), 147.

p. 237) 'Oxford Canal' can be found in James Elroy Flecker, *Collected Poems,* ed. J.C. Squire (Secker and Warburg, 1916), 48.

p. 237) A reference to Auden walking by the gas-works can be found in C. Day Lewis, *The Buried Day* (Chatto and Windus, 1960), 177.

p. 237) 'It was not difficult, Miss Morrow thought, to imagine that heaven might be something like North Oxford': Barbara Pym, *Crampton Hodnet* (Macmillan, 1985), 117.

p. 238) 'A "Christminster novel" is always about the loves and hatreds and rivalries of the young . . .': Robert Liddell, *The Last Enchantments* (Jonathan Cape, 1948), 16.

p. 238) 'I should like to spend my eternity in Christminster . . .': Liddell, *The Last Enchantments,* 221.

p. 238) 'The great houses, behind their great trees . . . .': Brian Aldiss *Forgotten Life* (Gollancz, 1988), 192.

p. 238) 'That's the Oxford manner. Everything's effect . . .': Aldiss, *Forgotten Life,* 223.

p. 239) 'Show me one respect in which Episcopus College, as a human environment, is superior to the Bargeman's Arms . . .': John Wain, *Where the Rivers Meet* (Hutchinson, 1988), 440.

p. 239) The description of the scout as 'a man as worthy of respect as Canon Jenkins' can be found in John Wain, *Comedies* (Hutchinson, 1990), 112.

p. 240) 'Ultimately, I and my kind were the reason why Oxford University had come into existence . . .': Wain, *Comedies,* 25.

p. 240) 'In England, that kind of patriotism is something you do with other consenting adults . . .': Michael Dibdin, *Dirty Tricks* (Faber and Faber, 1991), 37.

p. 241) The description of Osney as 'this little water-girt place, these cottage streets . . .' is in Joanna Trollope, *The Men and the Girls* (Black Swan, 1993), 107.

p. 241) 'You will not teach the potato to grow in Ireland . . .': Ronald Knox, *Let Dons Delight* (Sheed and Ward, 1939), 20.

p. 241) 'You will find Elkanah Settle's name is still remembered when Dryden's is quite put out of men's minds': Knox, *Let Dons Delight,* 90.

p. 242) 'The Oxford dominance in this scene is all too obvious': Cunningham, 'Literary Culture', 8:430.

p. 242) The *Times Literary Supplement* is described as a 'welcoming home-from-home for very many Oxonians' in Cunningham, 'Literary Culture', 8:429.

p. 243) The description of the college as 'not quite a small Athenian state' is in Iris Murdoch, *An Accidental Man* (Chatto and Windus, 1971), 77.

p. 244) The quotation concerning the 'remorse, regret, the tarnished hope, the shattered dream . . .' is taken from Iris Murdoch, *The Book and the Brotherhood* (Chatto and Windus, 1987), 46.

p. 244) 'Oxford will strengthen whatever is bred in the bone': Robertson Davies, *What's Bred in the Bone* (New York: Viking Press, 1985), 207.

p. 244) 'Gunfire in Oxford is uncommon . . .': Davies, *What's Bred,* 250.

p. 244) The reference to 'the Oxford pretence of doing nothing . . .': Davies, *What's Bred,* 220.

p. 244) 'Do you notice they say he went to school in Canada but was educated at Oxford?': Davies, *What's Bred,* 10.

p. 245) The quotation concerning 'a magic circle of privacy and anonymity' is taken from Peter Levi, *Grave Witness* (Hogarth Press, 1985), 59.

p. 245) The reference to 'the magnetic hold on the imagination of a magical place, this formative Oxford matrix' is by Cunningham in 'Literary Culture', 8:432.

p. 245) The references to 'college beano' and 'Veuve du Vernay in the gutter' are in John Fuller, *The Beautiful Inventions* (Secker and Warburg, 1983), 59, 56.

p. 245) 'Here in this moist, stifling labyrinth between two rivers . . .': Peter Conrad, *Where I Fell to Earth* (Chatto and Windus, 1990), 31.

p. 245) The reiterations of 'static city preserved in syrup' can be found in Javier Marías, *All Souls* (HarperCollins, 1992), 8, 62–63, 96, 154, 210.

p. 246) 'Any university is a spiritual pyramid . . .': Jan Morris, 'Is Oxford Out of this World?' *Horizon,* January 1968, 85.

p. 246) 'There is an air of insubstantiality about it all . . .': Peter Ackroyd, 'The Myth that Failed', *Spectator,* Nov. 10, 1979, 15–16.

Conclusion

p. 247) 'Friends, we will let our final visit be . . .': John Betjeman, *Summoned by Bells* (John Murray, 1976), 105.

p. 247) 'O come then, Melancholy, queen of thought': Thomas Warton, 'The Pleasures of Melancholy', in *The Works of the British Poets,* vol. 39, *The Poems of Scott and Warton* (J. Sharpe, 1808), 38.

p. 248) 'It is as though the genius of the city dries up the sap in you': Jan Morris, *Oxford* (Oxford University Press, 1987), 124.

p. 248) The wording for the remark by Swinburne—'for they [Oxford people] never begin to live'—is taken from Morris, *Oxford,* 1987, 48.

p. 249) 'Is it from here the people come, / Who talk so loud, and roll their eyes . . .': see the Dedicatory Ode of Hilaire Belloc, *Lambkin's Remains* (Vincent, 1900).

p. 250) The description of 'the long front, and its windows with lifted eyebrows' that scoff at Jude is in Thomas Hardy, *Jude the Obscure* (New York: Norton, 1978), 312.

p. 251) 'Sir, it is a great thing to dine with the Canons of Christ-Church': James Boswell, *The Life of Samuel Johnson* (Oxford University Press, 1953), 693.

p. 252) Bertie Wooster's urge to dive into Mercury fountain is referred to in P.G. Wodehouse, *Thank You, Jeeves* (Barrie and Jenkins, 1934), 76.

p. 253) The reference to Christ Church as 'a theoretically impossible place' is in Falconer Madan, *Oxford Outside the Guide-books* (Blackwell, 1925), 129.

p. 253) 'Insanity is rooted in the air of Oxford': Dacre Balsdon, *Freshman's Folly: An Oxford Comedy* (Eyre and Spottiswoode, 1952), 64.

p. 253) The description of the cathedral as 'an epitome of English history' is in John Ruskin, *Praeterita* (Oxford University Press, 1978), 180.

p. 253) 'There remained in it the traditions of Saxon, Norman, Elizabethan, religion unbroken . . .': Ruskin, *Praeterita,* 179–80.

p. 254) 'I do not envy the disposition of a person who can stand at this Place of Pilgrimage and remain unmoved': Madan, *Outside the Guide-Books*, 84.

p. 255) 'It was a matter of architecture more than anything else': Wilfrid Sheed, *A Middle Class Education* (Cassell, 1961), 372.

p.255) 'If you came in from the street . . .': C.S. Lewis, *That Hideous Strength* (Bodley Head, 1945), 18–20.

p. 256) The passage from Donne, 'The University is a Paradise . . .', is taken from 'Sermon no. 11, Preached at Whitehall, March 4, 1624, on Matthew 19:17'. See Simpson and Potter, *The Sermons of John Donne* (Berkeley and Los Angeles: University of California Press, 1953), 6:227.

p. 256) The quotation about 'the necessity of hiding inner religious mysteries . . .' is taken from John Fowles, *Daniel Martin* (Triad/Granada, 1978), 291.

p. 257) The description of Oxford as 'the most English of all cities . . .' is in John Fowles, *Daniel Martin* (Triad/Granada, 1978), 162.

p. 257) 'Oxford is always a mirror of England . . .': Jan Morris, 'Is Oxford out of This World?' in *Horizon*, January 1968, 87.

p. 257) 'In Oxford there is no need to make a microcosm . . .': Peter Conrad, *Where I Fell to Earth* (Chatto and Windus, 1990), 83.

p. 257) 'Oxford colleges, like those of Cambridge, have always represented much more than material wealth . . .': Linda Colley, 'An Obsession with the State', *Times Literary Supplement*, March 13, 1987, 261–62.

p. 257) 'Yes/ You have come upon the fabled lands . . .': James Fenton, 'The Pitt-Rivers Museum', in *Children in Exile* (Salamander Press, 1983).

Appendix A

p. 262) The survey of clubs from which the quotations are taken can be found in Compton Mackenzie, *Sinister Street* (Penguin, 1960), 492–93.

p. 264) The references to a 'Remote and ineffectual Don' and 'Dons Admirable! Dons of Might!' are from 'Lines to a Don' in Hilaire Belloc, *Verses* (1910); see *Complete Verse* (Gerald Duckworth, 1970), 153.

p. 267) For the description of May morning in *Sinister Street*, see Mackenzie, *Sinister Street*, 429–31. The reference to Oxford being 'imprisoned in a crystal globe' is on p. 429, and the passage beginning 'Michael the moment of waiting for the first shaft of the sun . . .' is on p. 429–30.

p. 270) 'A yellow moon as large as a pumpkin shone overhead . . .', Aldous Huxley, *Those Barren Leaves* (Chatto and Windus, 1925), 128.

p. 270) The reference of the Rhodes scholars arriving in the 'home of the living causes' is in Mackenzie, *Sinister Street*, 510.

p. 270) The description of American Rhodes scholars with their 'splendid native gift of oratory, and their modest desire to please . . . and their constant delight in all that of Oxford their English brethren don't notice, and their constant fear that they are being corrupted' is in Max Beerbohm, *Zuleika Dobson* (Penguin, 1952), 91.

p. 272) 'That is the Master's window. And now, unless I am much mistaken, you will see the Master himself.' Calverley's words are taken from Christopher Hibbert, ed., *The Encyclopaedia of Oxford* (Macmillan 1988), 339.

Bibliography

All books are published in Britain unless otherwise stated and refer to the first publication of the title concerned.

Abbott, Claude Colleer, ed. *The Correspondence of Gerard Manley Hopkins and Richard Watson Dixon*. Oxford University Press, 1935.

Ackermann, Rudolph. *History of the University of Oxford*. 1814.

Acton, Harold. *Memoirs of an Aesthete*. Methuen, 1948.

Addison, Joseph. *Spectator,* no. 494, 1712.

Aldiss, Brian. *The Brightfount Papers*. Faber, 1955.

———. *Forgotten Life*. Gollancz, 1988.

Allot, Kenneth, and Miriam Allot, eds. *The Poems of Matthew Arnold*. Longman, 1979.

Allot, Miriam, ed. *The Poems of John Keats*. Longman, 1970.

Amhurst, Nicholas. *Strephon's Revenge*. 1718.

———. *Terrae Filius,* 1721.

Amis, Kingsley. *Jake's Thing*. Hutchinson, 1978.

———. *Lucky Jim*. Gollancz, 1954.

———. *Memoirs*. Hutchinson, 1991.

———. 'Their Oxford'. In *Collected Poems, 1944–79*. Hutchinson, 1979.

Amis, Martin. *The Rachel Papers*. Jonathan Cape, 1973.

Amos, William. *The Originals*. Jonathan Cape, 1985.

Ardener, S. 'Incorporation and Exclusion: Oxford Academic Wives'. In *The Incorporated Wife*, ed. H. Callan and S. Ardener. Croom Helm, 1984.

Armory, Mark, ed. *The Letters of Evelyn Waugh*. Weidenfeld and Nicolson, 1980.

Aubrey, John. *Brief Lives*. 1813.

Auden, W.H. 'Oxford'. In *Collected Poems,* ed. Edward Mendelson. Faber and Faber, 1971.

Austen, Jane. *Northanger Abbey*. 1818.

———. *Sense and Sensibility*. 1811.

Bailey, Cyril. *Francis Fortescue Urquhart: A Memoir*. Macmillan, 1936.

Baker, J.N.L. *Jesus College, Oxford, 1571–1971*. Oxford University Press, 1971.

Baker, Joseph Ellis. *The Novel and the Oxford Movement*. Princeton: Princeton University Press, 1932.

Ball, Oona H. *The Oxford Garland*. Sidgwick and Jackson, 1909.

Balsdon, Dacre. *The Day They Burned Miss Termag*. Eyre and Spottiswoode, 1961.

———. *Freshman's Folly: An Oxford Comedy*. Eyre and Spottiswoode, 1952.

———. *Oxford Life*. Eyre and Spottiswoode, 1957.

———. *Oxford Now and Then.* Duckworth, 1970.

Bamford, T.W., ed. *Thomas Arnold on Education.* Cambridge University Press, 1970.

Barnes, Julian. *Flaubert's Parrot.* Jonathan Cape, 1984.

Baskerville, Thomas. *Account of Oxford.* 1683–86.

Batson, Judy G. *Oxford in Fiction: An Annotated Bibliography.* New York: Garland, 1989.

Beadle, Muriel. *These Ruins Are Inhabited.* Hale, 1963.

Beddard, R.A., ed. *Restoration Oxford.* Oxford Historical Society, 1982–83.

Beerbohm, Max. 'Going Back to School'. In *More.* Lane, 1899.

———. *Zuleika Dobson.* Heinemann, 1911.

Bellingham, Leo. *Oxford: The Novel.* Nold Johnson, 1981.

Belloc, Hilaire. *Complete Verse.* Ed. W.N. Roughead. Duckworth, 1970.

———. *Lambkin's Remains.* Vincent, 1900.

Beloff, Max. 'Oxford: A Lost Cause?' In *Black Paper Two,* ed. C.B. Cox and A.E. Dyson. Critical Quarterly Society, 1969.

Bennett, J.A.W. *Chaucer at Oxford and at Cambridge.* Oxford University Press, 1974.

Betjeman, John. *Collected Poems.* John Murray, 1958.

———. *An Oxford University Chest.* Miles, 1938.

———. *Summoned by Bells.* John Murray, 1960.

Bill, E.G.W. *Education at Christ Church, Oxford, 1660–1800.* Oxford University Press, Christ Church, 1988.

———. *University Reform in Nineteenth-Century Oxford.* Oxford University Press, 1973.

Binyon, Laurence. *Collected Poems.* 2 vols. Macmillan, 1931.

Binyon T.J. *'Murder Will Out': The Detective in Fiction.* Oxford University Press, 1989.

Bishop, T.J.H., and Rupert Wilkinson. *Winchester and the Public School Elite: A Statistical Analysis.* Faber, 1967.

Blair, John. *Saint Frideswide: Patron of Oxford.* Perpetua, 1988.

Blakiston, H.E.D. *Trinity College.* Hutchinson, 1898.

Blish, James. *Doctor Mirabilis.* Faber, 1964.

Bliss, Philip, ed. *Wood's 'Athenae Oxonienses.'* Ecclesiastical History Society, 1848.

Bold, Alan, and Robert Giddings. *Who Was Really Who in Fiction.* Longman, 1987.

Boswell, James. *The Life of Samuel Johnson.* 1791.

Bowra, C.M. *Memories, 1898–1939.* Weidenfeld and Nicolson, 1966.

Bradley, Edward [Cuthbert Bede, pseud.]. *The Adventures of Mr. Verdant Green.* Blackwood, 1853–57.

Brandon, W.B. *Charley's Aunt.* Heinemann, 1892.

Brittain, Vera. *Dark Tide.* Grant Richards, 1923.

———. *Testament of Friendship.* Macmillan, 1940.

———. *Testament of Youth.* Gollancz, 1933.

———. *The Women at Oxford.* Harrap, 1960.

Brooke, Christopher, and Roger Highfield. *Oxford and Cambridge.* Cambridge University Press, 1988.

Broome, A. *The Oxford Murders*. Geoffrey Bles, 1929.

Broughton, Rhoda. *Belinda*. Virago, 1984.

Buchan, John. *Brasenose College*. Hutchinson, 1898.

———. *Memory-Hold-the-Door*. Hodder and Stoughton, 1940.

Burke, Barbara [Oona H. Ball]. *Barbara Goes to Oxford*. Simpkin, Marshall, Hamilton and Kent, 1907.

Burney, Fanny. *Diary and Letters of Madame d'Arblay*. 1842–46.

Burton, Robert. *The Anatomy of Melancholy*. 1621.

Buxton, J., and P. Williams, eds. *New College, Oxford, 1379–1979*. Oxford University Press, 1979.

Calderon, George Leslie. *The Adventures of Downy V. Green*. Smith and Elder, 1902.

Camden, William. *Britannia*. 1586.

Cannan, Joanna Maxwell. *High Table*. Ernest Benn, 1931.

Canziani, Estella. *Oxford in Brush and Pen*. Frederick Muller, 1949.

Carpenter, Humphrey. *The Brideshead Generation*. Weidenfeld and Nicolson, 1989.

———. *The Inklings*. Allen and Unwin, 1978.

———. *J.R.R. Tolkien: A Biography*. Allen and Unwin, 1977.

———. *W.H. Auden*. Allen and Unwin, 1981.

Carr, W. *University College*. Hutchinson, 1902.

Carroll, Lewis. *Alice's Adventures in Wonderland*. Macmillan, 1865.

———. *Sylvie and Bruno*. Macmillan, 1889.

——— *Through the Looking Glass, and What Alice Found There*. Macmillan, 1871.

Carter, Ian. *Ancient Cultures of Conceit: British University Fiction in the Post-War Years*. Routledge, 1990.

Catto, J., ed. *The History of the University of Oxford*. 8 vols. Oxford University Press, 1984–94.

Cecil, David. *Max*. Constable, 1964.

Chaucer, Geoffrey. *The Canterbury Tales*. c. 1387.

Cheetham, Hal. *Portrait of Oxford*. Hale, 1971.

Church, R.W. *The Oxford Movement, Twelve Years, 1833–45*. Macmillan, 1891.

Clarendon, Edward Hyde, Earl of. *The History of the Rebellion 1702–1704*.

———. *The Life of Edward, Earl of Clarendon*. 1759.

Clark, Andrew, ed. *The Life and Times of Anthony Wood*. 5 vols. Oxford Historical Society, 1891–1900.

———. *Lincoln College*. Hutchinson, 1898.

Clough, Arthur Hugh. 'Commemoration Sonnets, Oxford, 1844'. In *The Bothie of Tober-na-Vuolich*. 1848.

Cobban, Alan B. *The English Medieval Universities: Oxford and Cambridge to c.1500*. Scolar Press, 1989.

Cobbett, William. *Rural Rides*. 1830.

Coffin, Charles M. *John Donne and the New Philosophy*. Routledge and Kegan Paul, 1958.

Coke, Desmond F.T. [Belinda Blinders, pseud.]. *The Comedy of Age*. Chapman and Hall, 1906.

———. *Sandford of Merton*. Alden, 1903.

Cole, G.D.H., and M. Cole. *Disgrace to the College*. Hodder and Stoughton, 1937.

———. *Off with Her Head*. Collins, 1938.

———. *The Oxford Mystery*. Yodd, 1943.

Colley, Linda. 'An Obsession with the State'. *Times Literary Supplement*, March 13, 1987.

Collini, Stefan. *Arnold*. Oxford University Press, 1988.

Colvin, H.M. 'Architecture'. In *The History of the University of Oxford*, ed. J. Catto. Vol. 5, *The Eighteenth Century*. Oxford University Press, 1986.

Conrad, Peter. *The Everyman History of English Literature*. Dent, 1985.

———. *Where I Fell to Earth*. Chatto and Windus, 1990 .

Conradi, Peter. *John Fowles*. Methuen, 1982.

Cooper, William. *Memoirs of a New Man*. Macmillan, 1966.

———. *The Struggles of Albert Woods*. Jonathan Cape, 1952.

Coppard, A.E. *It's Me, O Lord*. Methuen, 1957.

Cordeaux, E.H., and D.H. Merry. *A Bibliography of Printed Works Relating to the City of Oxford*. Oxford University Press, 1976.

———. *A Bibliography of Printed Works Relating to the University of Oxford*. Oxford University Press, 1968.

Coulton, G.G. *Chaucer and His England*. Methuen, 1921.

Cox, C.B., and A.E. Dyson, eds. *Black Paper Two*. Critical Quarterly Society, 1969.

———. *Fight for Education: A Black Paper*. Critical Quarterly Society, 1968.

Cox, G.V. *Recollections of Oxford*. Macmillan, 1868.

Cox, George. *Black Gowns and Red Coats*. Ridgeway and Sons, 1834.

Crispin, Edmund. *The Case of the Gilded Fly*. Gollancz, 1944.

———. *The Moving Toyshop*. Gollancz, 1946.

———. *Swan Song*. Gollancz, 1947.

Cross, Amanda. *The Question of Max*. New York: Knopf, 1976.

Cross, Claire. 'Oxford and the Tudor State from the Accession of Henry VIII to the Death of Mary'. In *The History of the University of Oxford*, ed. J. Catto. Vol. 3, *The Collegiate University*. Oxford University Press, 1986.

Cunningham, Val. 'Literary Culture'. In *The History of the University of Oxford*, ed. J. Catto. Vol. 8, *The Twentieth Century*. Oxford University Press, 1994.

Daniel, C.H.O., and W.R. Barker. *Worcester College*. Hutchinson, 1900.

Danson, L. *Max Beerbohm and the Act of Writing*. Oxford University Press, 1989.

Davie, Michael, ed. *The Diaries of Evelyn Waugh*. Weidenfeld and Nicolson, 1976.

Davies, Robertson. *What's Bred in the Bone*. New York: Viking Press, 1985.

Davin, Dan. *Brides of Price*. Hale, 1972.

Dawson, Jennifer. *Judasland*. Virago, 1990.

Defoe, Daniel. *Augusta Triumphans*. 1728.

De-la-Noy, Michael. *Exploring Oxford*. Headline, 1991.

De Morgan, William. *Joseph Vance*. Heinemann, 1906.

De Quincey, Thomas. *Autobiography*. 1853.

———. *Confessions of an English Opium Eater*. Taylor and Hessey, 1822.

Dexter, Colin. *The Daughters of Cain*. Macmillan, 1994.

——. *The Dead of Jericho.* Macmillan, 1981.

——. *Death Is Now My Neighbour.* Macmillan, 1996.

——. *The Jewel That Was Ours.* Macmillan, 1992.

——. *Last Bus to Woodstock.* Macmillan, 1975.

——. *Last Seen Wearing.* Macmillan, 1976.

——. *Morse's Greatest Mystery and Other Stories.* Macmillan, 1993.

——. *The Riddle of the Third Mile.* Macmillan, 1983.

——. *The Secret of Annexe 3.* Macmillan, 1986.

——. *Service of All the Dead.* Macmillan, 1980.

——. *The Silent World of Nicholas Quinn.* Macmillan, 1977.

——. *The Way through the Woods.* Macmillan, 1992.

——. *The Wench Is Dead.* Macmillan, 1989.

Dibdin, Michael. *Dirty Tricks.* Faber and Faber, 1991.

Dickens, Charles. *David Copperfield.* 1849–50.

Dickinson, Humphrey Neville. *Keddy: A Story of Oxford.* Heinemann, 1907.

Disraeli, Benjamin. *Lothair.* Longmans and Green, 1870.

Doble, C.E. *Hearne's Remarks and Collections.* 11 vols. Oxford Historical Society, 1884–1918.

Doolittle, I.G. 'College Administration'. In *The History of the University of Oxford,* ed. J. Catto. Vol. 5, *The Eighteenth Century.* Oxford University Press, 1986.

Dowling, Linda. *Hellenism and Homosexuality in Victorian Oxford.* Ithaca: Cornell University Press, 1994.

Drabble, Margaret, ed. *The Oxford Companion to English Literature.* 5th ed. Oxford University Press, 1985.

Drayton, Michael. *Poly-Olbion.* 1622.

Earle, John. *Microcosmography.* 1628.

Eliot, George. *Middlemarch.* 1871–72.

Ellis, Walter. *The Oxbridge Conspiracy.* Michael Joseph, 1994.

Ellmann, Richard. *A Long the RiverRun.* Hamish Hamilton, 1988.

——. *Oscar Wilde.* Hamish Hamilton, 1987.

Emerson, Ralph Waldo. *English Traits.* Routledge, 1856.

Engel, A.J. *From Clergyman to Don.* Oxford University Press, 1983.

Erasmus, Desiderius. *Collected Works.* Vol. 1, *Letters 1–141.* Trans. R.A.B. Mynors and D.F.S. Thomson, ed. W.K. Ferguson. Toronto: University of Toronto Press, 1974.

Evelyn, John. *Diary.* Ed. William Bray. Henry Colburn, 1818.

Everett-Green, Evelyn. *A Clerk of Oxford.* Nelson, 1897.

Faber, Geoffrey. *Jowett.* Faber and Faber, 1957.

——. *Oxford Apostles: Character Study of the Oxford Movement.* Faber and Faber, 1933.

Fairer, David. 'Oxford and the Literary World'. In *The History of the University of Oxford,* ed. J. Catto. Vol. 5, *The Eighteenth Century.* Oxford University Press, 1986.

Falkner, John Meade. *The Lost Stradivarius.* Blackwood, 1895.

Fanthorpe, U.A. 'Genesis'. In *Standing To.* Harry Chambers/Peterloo Poets, 1982.

Farnell, L.R. *An Oxonian Looks Back.* Hopkinson, 1934.

Farrar, Frederic W. *Julian Home: A Tale of College Life.* Black, 1859.

Farrer, Katharine. *Gownsmen's Gallows.* Hodder and Stoughton, 1957.

Fayard, Jean. *Oxford and Margaret.* Jarrolds, 1925.

Fenton, James. 'Pitt-Rivers Museum'. In *Children in Exile.* Salamander Press, 1983.

Fielding, Henry. *The History of Tom Jones.* 1749.

Fiennes, Celia. *Through England on a Side-Saddle.* Field and Tuer, 1888.

Firth, J.B., ed. *The Minstrelsy of Isis.* Chapman and Hall, 1908.

Flecker, James Elroy. *Collected Poems.* Ed. J.C. Squire. Martin Secker, 1916.

Forster, E.M. *Aspects of the Novel.* Edward Arnold, 1927.

Fowler, Thomas. *Corpus Christi College.* Hutchinson, 1898.

Fowles, John. *Daniel Martin.* Jonathan Cape, 1977.

———. *The Magus.* Jonathan Cape, 1966.

Foxe, John. *Actes and Monuments.* 1563.

Fraser, Antonia, ed. *Oxford and Oxfordshire in Verse.* Secker and Warburg, 1982.

———. *Oxford Blood.* Weidenfeld and Nicolson, 1985.

Froude, J.A. *Nemesis of Faith.* J. Chapman, 1849.

———. [Zeta, pseud.]. *Shadows of the Clouds.* Ollivier, 1847.

Frye, Northrop. *Fables of Identity: Studies in Poetic Mythology.* New York: Harcourt Brace and World, 1963.

Galsworthy, John. *End of the Chapter.* Heinemann, 1934.

Gardner, W.H. *G.M. Hopkins.* Secker and Warburg, 1949.

Garland, A.P. *A Yank at Oxford.* Collins, 1938.

Gibbon, Edward. *Autobiography.* 1796.

Girouard, Mark. *Life in the English Country House.* New Haven: Yale University Press, 1978.

Gladstone, William. '*Robert Elsmere* and the Battle of Belief'. *Nineteenth Century,* 23, no. 135 (May 1888): 766–88.

Glanvill, Joseph. *The Vanity of Dogmatizing.* 1661.

Godley, A.D. *Oxford in the Eighteenth Century.* Methuen, 1908.

Goudge, Elizabeth. *Towers in the Mist.* Duckworth, 1938.

Graham, Desmond. *Keith Douglas, 1920–1944.* Oxford University Press, 1974.

Graves, Robert. *Goodbye to All That.* Jonathan Cape, 1929.

———. *Wife to Mr. Milton.* Cassell, 1943.

Green, Roger Lancelyn. 'Alice'. In *Aspects of Alice,* ed. Robert Phillips. Gollancz, 1972.

———. *Lewis Carroll.* Bodley Head, 1960.

Green, V.H.H. *A History of Oxford University.* Batsford, 1974.

———. *Oxford Common Room: A Study of Lincoln College and Mark Pattison.* Edward Arnold, 1957.

———. 'Reformers and Reform in the University'. In *The History of the University of Oxford*, ed. J. Catto. Vol. 5, *The Eighteenth Century*. Oxford University Press, 1986.

———. 'The University and Social Life'. In *The History of the University of Oxford*, ed. J. Catto. Vol. 5, *The Eighteenth Century*. Oxford University Press, 1986.

Greenacre, Phyllis. *Swift and Carroll*. New York: International Universities, 1955.

Greene, Graham. *Our Man in Havana*. Heinemann, 1958.

———. *A Sort of Life*. Bodley Head, 1971.

Greene, Robert. *Frier Bacon, and Frier Bungay*. 1594.

Halperin, John. *The Life of Jane Austen*. Harvester Press, 1984.

Hamilton, Sir William. 'Addenda ad Corpus Statutorum Universitatis Oxoniensis'. *Edinburgh Review* 53, (1831): 384–427.

Hardy, E.G. *Jesus College*. Hutchinson, 1899.

Hardy, Thomas. *Jude the Obscure*. Osgood and McIlvane, 1895.

Hare, Augustus. *The Story of My Life*. Allen, 1896.

Hargreaves-Mawdsley, W.N., ed. *Woodeforde at Oxford, 1759–76*. Oxford Historical Society, 1967–68.

Harrison, Paul. *Oxford Marmalade*. Peter Davies, 1946.

Hart-Davis, Rupert, ed. *Letters of Max Beerbohm, 1892–1956*. John Murray, 1988.

———, ed. *The Letters of Oscar Wilde*. Hart-Davis, 1962.

———, ed. *More Letters of Oscar Wilde*. John Murray, 1985.

Hartley, L.P. *The Sixth Heaven*. Putnam, 1946.

Hawthorne, Nathaniel. *Our Old Home*. 1863.

Haynes, Renée. *Neapolitan Ice*. Chatto and Windus, 1928.

Hazlitt, William. *Sketches of the Principal Picture Galleries*. 1824.

Headlam, Cecil. *Oxford and Its Story*. Dent and Sons, 1926.

Heald, Tim. *Masterstroke*. Hutchinson, 1982.

Henderson, B.W. *Merton College*. Hutchinson, 1899.

Henderson, Lesley, ed. *Twentieth-Century Crime and Mystery Writers*. St. James Press, 1980.

Hewlett, Joseph T.J. *Peter Priggins, the College Scout*. Colburn, 1841.

Heygate, William Edward. *Godfrey Davenant at College*. Joseph Masters, 1849.

———. *The Scholar and the Trooper*. Parker, 1858.

Heyworth, Peter. *The Oxford Guide to Oxford*. Oxford University Press, 1981.

Hibbert, Christopher, ed. *The Encyclopaedia of Oxford*. Macmillan, 1988.

Hillier, Bevis. *Young Betjeman*. John Murray, 1988.

Hilton, James. *Lost Horizon*. Macmillan, 1933.

Hiss, Tony. *The Experience of Place*. New York: Knopf, 1990.

Hogg, James. *The Private Memoirs and Confessions of a Justified Sinner*. 1824.

Hogg, Thomas. 'Shelley at Oxford'. *New Monthly Magazine*, 1832–33.

Holland, Vyvyan. *Son of Oscar Wilde*. Hart-Davis, 1954.

Hollis, Christopher. *Oxford in the Twenties*. Heinemann, 1976.

Honan, P. *Matthew Arnold: A Life*. Weidenfeld and Nicolson, 1981.

Honey, John. *Tom Brown's Universe*. Millington, 1977.

Hooper, Walter. *C.S. Lewis: A Companion and Guide*. HarperCollins, 1996.

Hopkins, Gerard. *A City in the Foreground*. Constable, 1921.

Hopkins, Gerard Manley. *Poems*. Ed. W.H. Gardner and N.H. MacKenzie. Oxford University Press, 1967.

Hudson, Derek. *Lewis Carroll: An Illustrated Biography*. Constable, 1954.

Hughes, Thomas. *Tom Brown at Oxford*. Macmillan, 1861.

———. *Tom Brown's Schooldays*. Macmillan, 1857.

Hulton, Samuel F. *The Clerk of Oxford in Fiction*. Methuen, 1909.

Hutton, W.H. *St. John's College*. Hutchinson, 1898.

Huxley, Aldous. *Crome Yellow*. Chatto and Windus, 1921.

———. *Eyeless in Gaza*. Chatto and Windus, 1936.

———. *Those Barren Leaves*. Chatto and Windus, 1925.

Innes, Michael [J.I.M. Stewart]. *Appleby's Answer*. Gollancz, 1973.

———. *Death at the President's Lodging*. Gollancz, 1936.

———. *A Family Affair*. Gollancz, 1969.

———. *Operation Pax*. Gollancz, 1951.

———. *Stop Press*. Gollancz, 1971.

James, Henry. *English Hours*. Heinemann, 1905.

———. *A Passionate Pilgrim and Other Tales*. Tribner, 1875.

———. *Portraits of Places*. Macmillan, 1883.

James, P.D. *The Children of Men*. Faber and Faber, 1992.

Jenkyns, Richard. *The Victorians and Ancient Greece*. Cambridge: Harvard University Press, 1980.

Johnson, Lionel. 'Oxford'. In *Ireland with Other Poems*. Elkin Matthews, 1897.

———. 'Oxford Nights'. In *Poems*. Elkin Matthews, 1895.

Johnson, Rachel, ed. *The Oxford Myth*. Weidenfeld and Nicolson, 1988.

Johnson, Samuel. 'Journal of a Fellow of a College'. *The Idler*, no. 33, 1758.

———. *The Vanity of Human Wishes*. 1749.

Jones, Jo Elwyn, and J. Francis Gladstone. *The Red King's Dream, or Lewis Carroll in Wonderland*. Jonathan Cape, 1995.

Jones, John. *Balliol College: A History 1263–1939*. Oxford University Press, 1988.

Kay-Robinson, Denys. *The Landscape of Thomas Hardy*. Webb and Bower, 1984.

Kelly, Regina Z. *Young Geoffrey Chaucer*. New York: Lothrop, Lee and Shepard, 1952.

Kenny, Anthony, ed. *The Oxford Diaries of Arthur Hugh Clough*. Oxford University Press, 1990.

———. *Wyclif*. Oxford University Press, 1985.

Kenyon, J.P. 'The Business of University Novels.' *Encounter*, 54, no. 6 (June 1980).

Ker, Ian. *John Henry Newman*. Oxford University Press, 1988.

Kilvert, Francis. *Diary*. Ed. William Plomer. 3 vols. Jonathan Cape, 1938–40.

Kingsley, Henry. *Ravenshoe*. Macmillan, 1862.

Kinsley, James, ed. *The Poems and Fables of John Dryden*. Oxford University Press, 1962.

Kitchen, Dean. *Ruskin in Oxford and Other Studies*. John Murray, 1904.

Kitchen, P. *G.M. Hopkins*. Hamilton, 1978.

Knickerbocker, William S. *Creative Oxford*. New York: Syracuse University Press, 1925.

Knight, W. *The Glamour of Oxford*. Oxford: Blackwell, 1911.

Knox, Ronald. *The Footsteps at the Lock*. Methuen, 1928.

———. *Let Dons Delight*. Sheed and Ward, 1939.

———. *Other Eyes Than Ours*. Methuen, 1926.

Knox, Vicesimus. *Essays Moral and Literary*. 1782.

———. *Liberal Education*. 1781.

Kolkhorst, George Alfred. 'From *Verdant Green* to *Oxford Marmalade;* or, The Oxford Novel'. Paper read to St. John's College Essay Society, May 11, 1952. Oxford City Library.

Kramer, John E., Jr., and John E. Kramer III. *College Mystery Novels*. New York: Garland, 1983.

Lamb, Charles. *Essays of Elia*. 1823.

———. *The Last Essays of Elia*. 1833.

Lancaster, Osbert. *With an Eye to the Future*. John Murray, 1967.

Lang, Andrew. *The Mark of Cain*. Arrowsmith, 1886.

———. *Oxford*. Seeley, Jackson and Halliday, 1885.

Larkin, Philip. *Collected Poems*. Ed. Anthony Thwaite. Faber and Faber, 1988.

———. *Jill*. Fortune Press, 1946.

———. *Required Writing*. Faber and Faber, 1983.

———. *Selected Letters*. Ed. Anthony Thwaite. Faber and Faber, 1992.

Lawrence, D.H. 'The Oxford Voice'. In *Pansies*. P.R. Stephensen, 1929.

———. 'Spirit of Place'. In *Studies in Classic American Literature*. Martin Secker, 1924.

———. *Women in Love*. Martin Secker, 1920.

Leacock, Stephen. *My Discovery of England*. Bodley Head, 1922.

Le Carré, John. *A Perfect Spy*. Hodder and Stoughton, 1986.

Leff, G. *Paris and Oxford Universities in the Thirteenth and Fourteenth Centuries*. Wiley, 1968.

Leonardi, Susan J. *Dangerous by Degrees*. New Brunswick: Rutgers University Press, 1989.

Levi, Peter. *Grave Witness*. Hogarth Press, 1985.

Lewis, C. Day. *The Buried Day*. Chatto and Windus, 1960.

Lewis, C. Day, and Charles Fenby. *Anatomy of Oxford*. Jonathan Cape, 1938.

Lewis, C.S. *The Four Loves*. Geoffrey Bles, 1960.

———. *Surprised by Joy: The Shape of My Early Life*. Geoffrey Bles, 1955.

———. *That Hideous Strength*. Bodley Head, 1945.

Liddell, Robert. *The Last Enchantments*. Jonathan Cape, 1948.

Lilly, William. *Christian Astrology*. 1647.

Lindop, Grevel. *The Opium-Eater*. Dent, 1981.

Lively, Penelope. *Treasures of Time*. Heinemann, 1979.

Loach, Jennifer. 'Reformation Controversies'. In *The History of the University of Oxford*, ed. J. Catto. Vol. 3, *The Collegiate University*. Oxford University Press, 1986.

Loades, D.M. *The Oxford Martyrs*. Batsford, 1970.

Lobel, M.D., ed. *The Victoria History of the County of Oxford*. Vol. 3, *The University of Oxford*. Oxford University Press, 1954.

Lockhart, John Gibson. *Reginald Dalton*. Cadell, 1823.

Lonsdale, R., ed. *The New Oxford Book of Eighteenth Century Verse*. Oxford University Press, 1987.

Lytle, Guy Fitch. 'Patronage Patterns and Oxford Colleges c.1300–c.1530'. In *The University in Society*, ed. L. Stone. Vol. 1, *Oxford and Cambridge from the 14th to the Early 19th Century*. Princeton: Princeton University Press, 1975.

Lyly, John. *Euphues, The Anatomy of Wit*. 1578.

MacInnes, Helen. *Friends and Lovers*. Harrap, 1948.

Mackenzie, Compton. *My Life and Times*. Chatto and Windus, 1964.

———. *Sinister Street*. Vol. 2. Martin Secker, 1914.

MacKenzie, Norman H. *A Reader's Guide to Gerard Manley Hopkins*. Thames and Hudson, 1981.

Macleane, Douglas. *History of Pembroke College, Oxford*. Hutchinson, 1898.

MacNeice, Louis. *Autumn Journal*. Faber and Faber, 1938.

———. *The Strings Are False*. Faber and Faber, 1965.

Madan, Falconer. *Oxford outside the Guide-Books*. Blackwell, 1923.

Magrath, J.R. *The Queen's College, Oxford*. Oxford University Press, 1921.

Mallet, Charles Edward. *A History of the University of Oxford*. 3 vols. Methuen, 1924–27.

Mallinson, Arnold. *Quinquagesimo Anno*. Dugdale, 1974.

Mallock, William Hurrell. *Memoirs of Life and Literature*. Chapman and Hall, 1920.

———. *The New Republic*. Chatto and Windus, 1877.

Marías, Javier. *All Souls*. Trans. Margaret Jull Costa. Harvill, 1992.

Markham, Felix. *Oxford*. Weidenfeld and Nicolson, 1967.

Marriott, John A. R. *Oxford: Its Place in National History*. Oxford University Press, 1933.

Martin, Brian, ed. *Macmillan Anthologies of English Literature*. Vol. 4, *The Nineteenth Century*. Macmillan, 1989.

Martin, L.C., ed. *The Works of Henry Vaughan*. Oxford University Press, 1957.

Masterman, John C. *An Oxford Tragedy*. Gollancz, 1933.

———. *To Teach the Senators Wisdom*. Hodder and Stoughton, 1952.

Maurois, André. *Cecil Rhodes*. Collins, 1953.

McConica, James. 'Elizabethan Oxford: The Collegiate Society'. In *The History of the University of Oxford*, ed. J. Catto. Vol. 3, *The Collegiate University*. Oxford University Press, 1986.

———. 'The Rise of the Undergraduate College'. In *The History of the University of Oxford*, ed. J. Catto. Vol. 3, *The Collegiate University*. Oxford University Press, 1986.

———. 'Scholars and Commoners in Renaissance Oxford'. In *The University in Society*. Vol. 1, *Oxford and Cambridge from the 14th to the Early 19th Century*. Ed. L. Stone. Princeton: Princeton University Press, 1975.

McGill, A.F. "From Dreaming Spires to Shattered Dreams." Ann Arbor: Dissertation Abstracts International, 1990.

McKenna, Stephen. *Sonia: Between Two Worlds*. Methuen, 1917.

McLeish, K., and V. McLeish. *Good Reading Guide to Murder, Crime Fiction, and Thrillers*. Bloomsbury, 1990.

Mehta, Ved. *Up at Oxford*. John Murray, 1993.

Melville, Herman. *Journal up the Straits*. New York: Colophon, 1935.

Merivale, Herman C. *Faucit of Balliol*. Chapman and Hall, 1882.

Miles, Hamish, and Raymond Mortimer. *The Oxford Circus*. John Lane, 1922.

Millgate, M. *Thomas Hardy*. Oxford University Press, 1982.

Milne, A.A. *Autobiography*. New York: E.P. Dutton, 1939.

Milton, John. *Of Education*. 1644.

Mitchell, Julian. *Imaginary Toys*. Hutchinson, 1961.

Mitford, Nancy. *Love in a Cold Climate*. Hamish Hamilton, 1949.

Monmouth, Geoffrey of. *The History of the Kings of Britain*. Penguin, 1966.

Montague, Charles Edward. *Rough Justice*. Chatto and Windus, 1926.

Moritz, Carl Philip. *Journeys of a German in England*. 1783.

Morley, Sheridan. *Oscar Wilde*. Weidenfeld, 1976.

Morris, Jan. *Oxford*. Faber and Faber, 1965.

———. *The Oxford Book of Oxford*. Oxford University Press, 1978.

Morris, William. *The Aims of Art*. In *Collected Works*, vol. 23. Routledge, 1910–15.

Mortimer, John. *Clinging to the Wreckage*. Weidenfeld and Nicolson, 1982.

Motion, Andrew. *Philip Larkin*. Methuen, 1982.

Mozley, Thomas. *Reminiscences*. Longmans, 1882.

Mumford, Lewis. *The City in History*. New York: Harcourt, Brace and World, 1961.

———. *The Culture of Cities*. New York: Harcourt, Brace, and Jovanovich, 1938.

Murdoch, Iris. *An Accidental Man*. Chatto and Windus, 1971.

———. *The Book and the Brotherhood*. Chatto and Windus, 1987.

Murray, D.L. *Folly Bridge*. Hodder and Stoughton, 1945.

Murry, J. Middleton. *Between Two Worlds*. Jonathan Cape, 1935.

Newman, John. *Apologia pro Vita Sua*. Longmans, Green, Reader, and Dyer, 1864.

———. *The Idea of a University*. Pickering, 1873.

———. *Loss and Gain*. Burns, 1848.

Newman, John. 'The Physical Setting: New Building and Adaptation'. In *The History of the University of Oxford*, ed. J. Catto. Vol. 3, *The Collegiate University*. Oxford University Press, 1986.

Nichols, Beverley. *Patchwork*. Chatto and Windus, 1921.

Nicholson, William. *Shadowlands*. Samuel French, 1990.

Oman, Charles. *Memories of Victorian Oxford*. Methuen, 1941.

Overbury, Sir Thomas. *Characters*. 1614.

'An Oxford Scholar'. *The Massacre of the Innocents*. Billing, 1907.

Pantin, W.A. *Oxford Life in Oxford Archives*. Oxford University Press, 1972.

Parker, James. *The Early History of Oxford (727–1100)*. Oxford Historical Society, 1884–85.

Pater, Walter. 'Emerald Uthwart'. *New Review,* 1892. In *Miscellaneous Studies.* Macmillan, 1895.

———. *Studies in the History of the Renaissance.* Macmillan, 1873.

Patterson, D. 'Hebrew Studies'. In *The History of the University of Oxford,* ed. J. Catto. Vol. 5, *The Eighteenth Century.* Oxford University Press, 1986.

Pattison, Mark. *Memoirs.* Macmillan, 1885.

Penton, Stephen. *The Guardian's Instruction.* 1688.

Pepys, Samuel. *Diary.* 1660–69 (first published 1825).

Phillips, Robert, ed. *Aspects of Alice.* Gollancz, 1972.

Pinion. F.B. *A Hardy Companion.* Macmillan, 1968.

Platt, Christopher. *The Most Obliging Man in Europe.* Allen and Unwin, 1986.

Plummer, Charles, ed. *Elizabethan Oxford.* Oxford Historical Society, 1887.

Potter, Dennis. *The Nigel Barton Plays.* Penguin, 1967.

Powell, Anthony. *Infants of the Spring.* Heinemann, 1976.

———. *John Aubrey and His Friends.* Heinemann, 1948.

———. *A Question of Upbringing.* Heinemann, 1951.

Price, Mary R. *A Portrait of Britain in the Middle Ages, 1066–1485.* Oxford University Press, 1951.

Prideaux, Humphrey. *Letters to John Ellis 1674–1722,* ed. Edward Maunde Thompson. Camden Society, 1875.

Proctor, M.R. *The English University Novel.* Berkeley and Los Angeles: University of California Press, 1957.

Pycroft, James. *Oxford Memories.* Bentley, 1886.

Pym, Barbara. *Crampton Hodnet.* Macmillan, 1985.

———. *Jane and Prudence.* Jonathan Cape, 1953.

Quarrell, W.H., and W.J.C. Quarrell, eds. *Travels of Zacharias Conrad von Uffenbach.* Blackwell, 1928.

Quennell, Peter. *The Marble Foot.* Collins, 1976.

Quiller-Couch, Lilian M., ed. *Reminiscences of Oxford by Oxford Men 1559–1850.* Oxford Historical Society, 1892.

Quinton, A.M. 'Oxford in Fiction'. *Oxford Magazine* 76, no. 9 (Jan. 23, 1958): 212–18.

Rannie, D.W. *Oriel College.* Hutchinson, 1900.

Rashdall, H.R.S., and R.S. Rait. *New College.* Hutchinson, 1901.

Rashdall, Hastings. *The Universities of Europe in the Middle Ages.* Oxford University Press, 1895.

Raven, Simon. *The Survivors.* Blond and Briggs, 1976.

Reade, Charles. *The Cloister and the Hearth.* Trübner, 1861.

Reade, William Winwood. *Liberty Hall, Oxon.* Skeet, 1860.

Richardson, Samuel. *Sir Charles Grandison.* 1753–45.

Rintoul, M.C. *Dictionary of Real People and Places in Fiction.* Routledge, 1993.

Robertson, G.R. *All Souls.* Hutchinson, 1899.

Robinson, Robert. *Landscape with Dead Dons.* Gollancz, 1956.

Robinson, Timothy. *When Scholars Fall.* New Authors, 1961.

Roston, Murray. *Sixteenth-Century English Literature.* Macmillan, 1982.

Rowse, A.L. *A Cornishman at Oxford.* Jonathan Cape, 1963.

———. *Oxford in the History of the Nation.* Weidenfeld and Nicolson, 1975.

Ruskin, John. *Praeterita.* G. Allen, 1885–89.

Saintsbury, George. 'Novels of University Life'. *Macmillan's Magazine* 77 (1898): 334–43.

Salter, H.E. *Medieval Oxford.* Oxford Historical Society, 1936.

Santayana, George. *The Last Puritan.* Constable, 1935.

———. *Soliloquies in England and Later Soliloquies.* Constable, 1922.

Sayers, Dorothy. *Busman's Holiday.* Gollancz, 1937.

———. *Gaudy Night.* Gollancz, 1935.

Schellenberger, John. 'University Fiction and the University Crisis'. *Critical Quarterly* 24, no. 3 (1982): 45–48.

Scheper, George L. *Michael Innes.* New York: Ungar, 1985.

Seccombe, Thomas, and H. Spencer Scott. *In Praise of Oxford.* 2 vols. Constable, 1910–11.

Seymour, Miranda. *Ottoline Morrell: Life on a Grand Scale.* Hodder and Stoughton, 1992.

Sheed, Wilfrid. *A Middle Class Education.* Cassell, 1961.

Shelley, Mary. *Frankenstein.* Lackington, Hughes, Hardy, etc., 1818.

Shorthouse, Joseph Henry. *John Inglesant.* Macmillan, 1881.

Smith, Nowell Charles, ed. *The Poems of William Wordsworth.* Methuen, 1908.

Smith, Philip E. II, and Michael S. Helfand, ed. *Oscar Wilde's Oxford Notebooks: A Portrait of Mind in the Making.* Oxford University Press, 1989.

Smithers, Peter. *The Life of Joseph Addison.* Oxford University Press, 1968.

Smollett, Tobias. *The Adventures of Peregrine Pickle.* R. Main, 1751.

Snow, C.P. *The Masters.* Macmillan, 1961.

Snow, Peter. *Oxford Observed.* John Murray, 1991.

Southern, Richard W. *Making of the Middle Ages.* Hutchinson, 1967.

———. 'Our Ends by Our Beginnings Know'. In *Oxford Today* 2, no. 1, (1989): 28–31.

Southey, Robert. *Life and Correspondence.* Longman, Brown, Green, and Longmans, 1849.

Spender, Stephen. *World within World.* Hamish Hamilton, 1951.

Spenser, Edmund. *The Faerie Queene.* 1590–96.

Stannard, Martin. *Evelyn Waugh: The Early Years, 1903–1939.* Paladin, 1988.

States, Bert. *Dreaming and Storytelling.* Ithaca: Cornell University Press, 1994.

Steele, Richard. *Spectator,* no. 43, 1711.

Stewart, J.I.M. *Andrew and Tobias.* Gollancz, 1981.

———. *The Aylwins.* Gollancz, 1966.

———. *The Bridge at Arta and Other Stories.* Gollancz, 1981.

———. *Full Term.* Gollancz, 1978.

———. *The Gaudy.* Gollancz, 1974.

———. *The Guardians.* Gollancz, 1955.

———. *The Last Tresilians.* Gollancz, 1963.

———. *The Madonna of the Astrolabe.* Gollancz, 1977.

———. *The Man Who Won the Pools.* Gollancz, 1961.

———. *Mark Lambert's Supper.* Gollancz, 1954.

———. *A Memorial Service.* Gollancz, 1976.

———. *Mungo's Dream.* Gollancz, 1973.

———. *Myself and Michael Innes.* Gollancz, 1987.

———. *The Naylors.* Gollancz, 1985.

———. *Parlour 4, and Other Stories.* Gollancz, 1986.

———. *Vanderlyn's Kingdom.* Gollancz, 1967.

———. *Young Patullo.* Gollancz, 1975.

Stewart, Michael. *Monkey-Shines.* Macmillan, 1983.

Stone, Lawrence. 'The Size and Composition of the Oxford Student Body 1580–1909'. In *The University in Society,* ed. L. Stone. Vol. 1, *Oxford and Cambridge from the 14th to the Early 19th Century.* Princeton: Princeton University Press, 1975.

———. 'Social Control and Intellectual Excellence: Oxbridge and Edinburgh 1560–1983'. In *Universities, Society, and the Future,* ed. Nicholas Phillipson. Edinburgh University Press, 1983.

Strachey, Lytton. *Eminent Victorians.* Chatto and Windus, 1918.

Stride, William Keatley. *Exeter College.* Hutchinson, 1900.

Stubbes, Philip. *The Anatomie of Abuses.* 1583.

Super, R.H., ed. *The Complete Prose Works of Matthew Arnold.* Ann Arbor: University of Michigan Press, 1962–77.

Sutherland, Dame Lucy. *The University of Oxford in the Eighteenth Century: A Reconsideration.* Oxford University Press, 1973.

Symons, Julian. *Bloody Murder.* Faber and Faber, 1972.

Taine, Hippolyte. *Notes on England.* Trans. Fraser Rae Hachette. 1872.

Taunt, Henry W. *The Oxford Poems of Matthew Arnold.* Taunt, 1910.

Taylor, A.J.P. *English History, 1914–1945.* Oxford University Press, 1965.

Thackeray, William. *Pendennis.* Bradbury and Evans, 1848–50.

Thomas, Edward. *Oxford.* Black, 1903.

Thompson, H.L. *Christ Church.* Hutchinson, 1900.

Thorpe, M. *Matthew Arnold.* Evans, 1969.

Thwaite, Ann, ed. *My Oxford.* Robson, 1977.

Tickell, Thomas. *Oxford, a Poem.* 1707.

Tindall, Gillian. *Countries of the Mind.* Hogarth, 1991.

Tinker, C.B., and H.F. Lowry. *The Poetry of Matthew Arnold.* Oxford University Press, 1940.

Trevor-Roper, H.R. *Christ Church Oxford.* Rev. ed. Oxford University Press, 1973.

Trickett, Rachel. *The Elders.* Constable, 1966.

Trilling, Lionel. *Matthew Arnold.* Allen and Unwin, 1939.

Tuckwell, W. *Pre-Tractarian Oxford.* Cassell, 1900.

———. *Reminiscences of Oxford.* Cassell, 1901.

Turbeville, A.S., ed. *Johnson's England.* 2 vols. Oxford University Press, 1933.

Tyrwhitt, Richard St. John. *Hugh Heron, Ch. Ch.* Strahan, 1880.

Utechin, Nicholas. *Sherlock Holmes at Oxford.* Dugdale, 1977.

Vance, Norman. *The Sinews of the Spirit*. Cambridge University Press, 1985.

Wain, John. *Comedies*. Hutchinson, 1990.

———. *Hungry Generations*. Hutchinson, 1994.

———. *Hurry on Down*. Secker and Warburg, 1953.

———. *Where the Rivers Meet*. Hutchinson, 1988.

Wallace, Doreen. *A Little Learning*. Benn, 1931.

Waller, A.R., ed. *Abraham Cowley: Poems*. Cambridge University Press, 1905.

Walpole, Horace. *Letters*. Ed. Peter Cunningham. 9 vols. 1857–59.

Ward, Mrs. Humphry. *Robert Elsmere*. Smith and Elder, 1888.

———. *A Writer's Recollections*. Collins, 1918.

Ward, Robert Plumer. *Tremaine*. Henry Colburn, 1825.

Ward, W.R. *Georgian Oxford*. Oxford University Press, 1958.

———. *Victorian Oxford*. Cass, 1965.

Warton, Thomas. *Companion to the Guide*. 1760.

———. 'On Sir Joshua Reynolds's Painted Window at New College, Oxford'. 1782.

———, ed. *The Oxford Sausage*. 1764.

———. 'The Pleasures of Melancholy'. 1747.

———. 'The Progress of Discontent'. 1746.

———. 'The Triumph of Isis'. 1749.

Watson, George. 'Fictions of Academe: Dons and Realities'. *Encounter* 51, no. 5 (1978): 42–46.

Waugh, Alec. *My Brother Evelyn and Other Profiles*. Cassell, 1967.

Waugh, Auberon. *The Path of Dalliance*. Chapman and Hall, 1963.

Waugh, Evelyn. *Brideshead Revisited*. Chapman and Hall, 1945.

———. *Decline and Fall*. Chapman and Hall, 1928.

———. *A Little Learning*. Chapman and Hall, 1964.

———. *Ronald Knox*. Chapman and Hall, 1959.

Wells, J. *Wadham College*. Hutchinson, 1898.

West, Paul. *The Modern Novel*. 2 vols. Hutchinson, 1963.

Westmacott, C.M. *The English Spy*. Blackmantle, 1907.

Wheeler, Michael. *English Fiction of the Victorian Period*. Longman, 1985.

White, H. J. *Merton College*. Dent, 1906.

White, Norman. *Hopkins: A Literary Biography*. Oxford University Press, 1992.

Wilde, Oscar. *Complete Works*. Collins, 1948.

Willey, Basil. *The Eighteenth Century Background*. Chatto and Windus, 1940.

———. *The Seventeenth-Century Background*. Chatto and Windus, 1934.

Williams, Emlyn. *George*. Hamish Hamilton, 1961.

Williams, Raymond. *Second Generation*. Chatto and Windus, 1964.

Wilson, A.N. *Gentlemen in England*. Hamish Hamilton, 1985.

———. *The Healing Art*. Secker and Warburg, 1980.

———. *Hilaire Belloc*. Hamish Hamilton, 1984.

———. *Unguarded Hours*. Secker and Warburg, 1978.

Wilson, Elaine, and Valerie Petts. *Oxford Words and Watercolours*. Shepheard-Walwyn, 1987.

Wilson, H.A. *Magdalen College*. Hutchinson, 1899.

Wither, George. *Poetry of George Wither*. Ed. F.D. Sidgwick. A.H. Bullen, 1902.

Wodehouse, P.G. *Thank You, Jeeves*. Barrie and Jenkins, 1934.

Wolfe, Thomas. *Of Time and the River*. Heinemann, 1935.

Wolff, Robert Lee. *Gains and Losses: Novels of Faith in Victorian England*. New York:
    Garland, 1977.

Wood, Anthony. *Athenae Oxonienses*. Ed. Philip Bliss. 5 vols. 1813.

———. *Survey of the Antiquities of the City of Oxford*. 1661–66.

Wordsworth, Christopher. *The Undergraduate (Eighteenth Century)*. Stanley Paul,
    1928.

Worth, George J. *Thomas Hughes*. Boston: G.K. Hall, 1984.

Wright, Thomas. *The Life of Walter Pater*. Everett, 1907.

Yurdan, Marilyn. *Oxford Town and Gown*. Hale, 1990.

Index

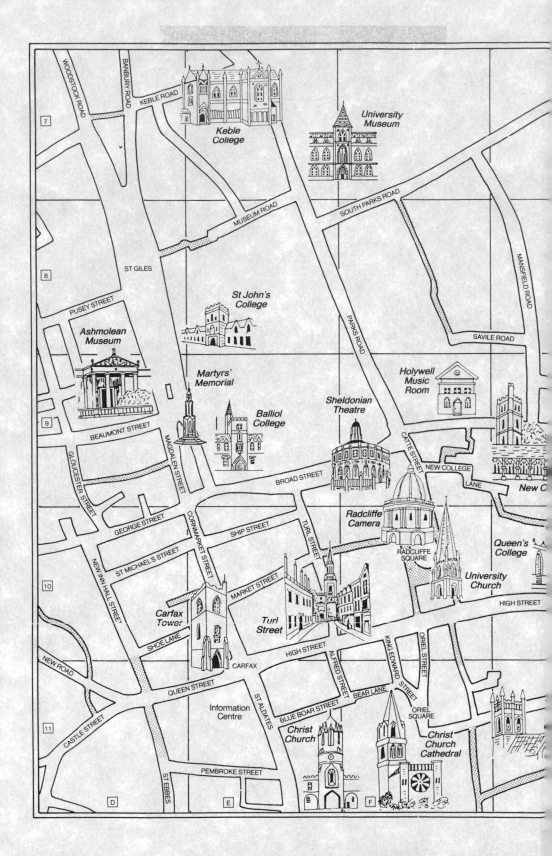